D0629526

In the Belgian Château

Detail from the Gothic façade of the town hall, Leuven

In the Belgian Château

THE SPIRIT AND CULTURE OF A EUROPEAN SOCIETY IN AN AGE OF CHANGE

Renée C. Fox

CHICAGO

Ivan R. Dee

1994

IN THE BELGIAN CHATEAU. Copyright © 1994 by Renée C. Fox. All rights reserved, including the right to reproduce this book or portions thereof in any form. For information, address: Ivan R. Dee, Inc., 1332 North Halsted Street, Chicago 60622. Manufactured in the United States of America and printed on acid-free paper.

Library of Congress Cataloging-in-Publication Data:
Fox, Renée C. (Renée Claire), 1928–
   In the Belgian château : the spirit and culture of a European society in an age of change / Renée C. Fox.
      p.   cm.
   Includes bibliographical references and index.
   ISBN 1-56663-057-6
   1. Belgium—Social conditions.   2. Belgium—Politics and government—1945–   3. Belgium—Civilization.   I. Title.
HN503.5.F69   1994
306'.09493—dc20   94-3810

For "Moeder Clara" and "Sabine,"
who welcomed me into their "houses"
in Belgium and Zaïre,
opened their lives and their lands to me,
and accompanied me, over many years,
in the writing of this book

Contents

Acknowledgments

THIS BOOK is based on my firsthand immersion (from 1959 to 1993) in Belgium, and (from 1962 to 1970) in Zaïre, the Central African country that was once its colony. It is impossible to thank every person individually who contributed to the making of the book. As readers move with me from one Belgian and Zaïrean context to another, they will meet a small cross section of the large and rich array of people I have come to know along the way. These persons not only represent themselves but also many significant others to whom I wish to express my gratitude for all the ways they have helped me with my research.

Everyone who appears in this book is "real," but in certain cases I have used pseudonyms for individuals who asked me to do so, or when I felt that divulging identities might have embarrassing, painful, or dangerous consequences for the persons or their families. I have retained the genuine names of those who gave me permission to use them (or even insisted on it in a few instances), and of those persons who are such well-known figures that inventing names for them would be pointless.

The women to whom this book is dedicated—"Moeder" Clara Van Marcke and Sabine Mosabu (pseudonyms)—played cardinal roles in its creation and occupy special places in my life. Through the medium of what "Moeder Clara," the matriarch of the Flemish working-class family who absorbed me into their "house on Izegemsestraat," taught me about the realities of her everyday world, I learned many important things about Belgian society and culture that extended far beyond the confines of her milieu. Her intelligent and wise observations on what has changed and what has not over the course of her eighty-eight years—in her family, community, and country—have also humanized my historical perspective.

Sabine Mosabu is known as "Mama Sabine" out of respect for her remarkable talents, leadership, and character. Through the sociological research we conducted together in Zaïre, and the dreams we exchanged, she and I became intimate friends. How we met in the midst of the 1964–1965 Congo Rebellion, the journey we later made to Lisala (her equatorial hometown on the banks of the Zaïre River), and what the Sabines of Zaïre have had to endure during the postcolonial phase of

i x

their country's development are chronicled in Part Three of the book.

With his characteristic modesty, André Molitor—one of Belgium's most esteemed civil servants, and Emeritus Professor of Public Administration at the University of Louvain—would say that he provided me with information pertinent to the writing of this book. That is true. But I have also been the beneficiary of the vast knowledge and culture, the devotion, and the scrupulousness with which he has served his country, and of all that it has meant to me to be welcomed by him and his wife Edith into their home and family.

Over the years of my work and life in Belgium, I have received intellectual help and human support from many Belgian academic physicians. Foremost among them was Henri Tagnon, Emeritus Professor of Medicine and Oncology at the University of Brussels, who established the medical service of that university's Institut Jules Bordet Cancer Center and was a founder of the European Organization for Treatment and Research of Cancer. His professional story and the convictions that underlie it are integral to the phenomena that I originally went to Belgium to study—how social, cultural, and historical factors affected medical research and research careers in a Continental European country.

I want to thank six other Belgian academic physicians who have patiently taught me over the years, offered me the gift of their friendship, and generously received me in their homes: Jan Blanpain (University of Leuven), Jean Crabbé (University of Louvain), Philippe Hoet (University of Louvain), Georges Lejeune (University of Liège), Serge Orloff (University of Brussels), and André De Schaepdryver (University of Ghent).

The wives of these physicians—Evelyn Tagnon, Dr. Hedewig Blanpain, Marie Crabbé, Roselyne Hoet, Simone Lejeune, and Monique Orloff—have all been colleagues and companions who helped to sustain me.

So has the Baroness Maddy Buysse, a *grande dame* of powerful intellect and a professional literary translator, with whom I spent many hours of discussion, overlooking a landscape that Flemish-Belgian artists have painted for centuries, framed by the windows of her house.

In Belgium I have also been edified and enriched by running conversations with paleontologist-theologian Edouard Boné, S.J., philosopher of science Jean Ladrière, physician Lucien Karhausen, and fellow sociologists Jan Kerkhofs, S.J., Yvo Nuyens, and Lydwine Verhaegen.

I have greatly benefited from Yves Winkin's talent and expertise in social science, from his generosity in providing me with a continual flow of data and documents about current events and developments in Belgian society, and from his insights into them.

In the United States there is one person above all others to whom I am indebted for this book's coming into being—my colleague, sociologist Willy De Craemer, S.J. He has been a constant source of social knowledge and cultural understanding of Belgium—his native land. He gave me the opportunity to conduct research in Zaïre and prepared me for my experiences in the heart of Africa. And he read each of the many drafts of the book. His candor and discernment have been as important as his belief in the book and its author.

Throughout all the years of our collaboration and friendship, historian of medicine and science Judith P. Swazey has always been there as well. She has been tirelessly interested in the unfolding of what we dubbed my "Belgian book," and has contributed to it in many intellectual and personal ways.

The African historian and anthropologist Jan Vansina is another friend who has constantly encouraged my research in Belgium and Zaïre. He brought his incomparable knowledge of Zaïre and Central Africa, and his Belgian origins to bear on a critical reading of a previous version of this book.

Paul Errera, a university-based psychiatrist in the United States, is also the son of the house and the *salon* on the Rue Royale in Brussels about which I have written in the first part of this book. He introduced me to the man who prevailed over that house, his father; entrusted me with documents from his family's archives; furthered my understanding of the haute bourgeoisie and power elite of Brussels to which the house of Errera belonged; and carefully read the "Salon on the Rue Royale" section of the book.

I am fortunate that John Brown, a former United States cultural attaché to Belgium, shared his comprehension and love of things Belgian with me, and that French anthropologist Eric de Dampierre gave me the opportunity to publish two essays—"Why Belgium?" and "Is Religion Important in Belgium?"—when he was editor-in-chief of the *Archives Européennes de Sociologie / European Journal of Sociology*.

Partly because this book is about such a tiny country, and combines autobiography with sociological observation and analysis, it has presented many literary and publishing challenges. Elizabeth Knoll's competence as an editor, and her literary gifts and taste have guided me in a major rewriting of the manuscript. I was heartened by the support I received from writers Peggy Anderson, Lee Gutkind, Robert Klitzman, and Jane Kramer, and from historian Natalie Zemon Davis, and helped by their experienced suggestions. It is because of sociologists Steven Grosby and

Edward A. Shils, and writer, editor, and man of letters Joseph Epstein—
what they stand for, and how they are linked to one another—that this
book found a publishing home.

Martha Rosso has typed and retyped and re-retyped every version of
this book, even coming out of retirement to do so. She belongs to the
company of editors, writers, and friends.

Over the thirty-four years of research that this book spans, I have been
the fortunate recipient of a number of research fellowships: from the
Council for Research in the Social Sciences of Columbia University for
my initial travel to Europe in the summer of 1959; from the Belgian
American Educational Foundation in the summers of 1960 and 1961; from
the John Simon Guggenheim Memorial Foundation in 1962; and from the
Social Science Research Council in 1963, for research in Zaïre. In
addition, the stipend I received from the Centre de Recherches Sociologiques in Zaïre during my years on its staff defrayed my travel and daily
living expenses there. Small grants from the University of Pennsylvania
and from the Fondation pour la Chimiothérapie Anticancereuse in Brussels, made it possible for me to return to Belgium several times to do more
focused research. Finally, a fellowship from the Woodrow Wilson International Center for Scholars of the Smithsonian Institution in Washington,
D.C., along with a small grant from Medicine in the Public Interest,
enabled me to spend an academic year in the center's West European
program, where I wrote most of the first draft of this book. During that
memorable year the accessibility and responsiveness of Prosser Gifford,
then deputy director of the Wilson Center, and of Ann C. Sheffield,
secretary of the center's Program on History, Culture, and Society, made a
crucial and appreciated difference.

THE COLLEAGUES, friends, and institutions cited in these Acknowledgments
are not responsible for my analyses and interpretations. But they *are*
responsible for the development and realization of the book and for the
personal meaning and the happiness that the process of creating it has
brought me.

                                                          R. C. F.
Philadelphia
May 1994

In the Belgian Château

Prelude:
Why Belgium?

Ⅰт wᴀs a sunny and rapid train ride today from Brussels to Leuven. The air was warm yet tinged with the coolness of mist and a touch of the sea. The light was golden, and the fragrance of summer made me think of certain days in Zaïre.

The sunny and familiar trip in this train in particular, my continuous voyaging over the Belgian landscape by railroad more generally, and the perpetual way that Belgians themselves travel back and forth on their trains, embarking and disembarking in a cycle as basic and precisely timed as the nightly scrubbing of Belgian railroad station floors—all this gives me an overwhelmingly happy and sad sense of busy journeying, of its curiously impersonal outwardness and its profoundly personal inwardness. On Belgian trains I ride back and forth, back and forth, inside myself, over a shiny maze of well-kept but unfathomable tracks. Inside the railroad cars the corpulent, earthy Belgian passengers ride with me, talking of houses and family, education and the children, work and vacation, finances and food, illnesses and deaths.

Outside the windows of the train is the disproportionately vast, ever-changing but ever-the-same, haunting Brabant landscape, speeding by yet somehow suspended in space. This time I feel as though I am looking down from a great height at a physical terrain and a human society that are the most real and unreal I have ever known. I am watching from somewhere in the Magritte-blue sky, with an acute sense that the passengers in the trains crisscrossing the Belgian tracks are not the same persons who filled them when I first came to this country many years ago. Some of those persons have died; others have grown too old or frail or sick to travel. Their children and grandchildren, immigrants and "new" Belgians have taken their place. But the coming and going, the everyday cycle of

existence, continue uninterruptedly—just as they will when I am
no longer here. . . .

IN JUNE 1959 I set sail on the ocean liner *Nieuw Amsterdam* to
explore how social, cultural, and historical factors affected clinical
medical research and research careers in a contemporary Western
European society. I did not know that my inquiry would become a
study; that the study would be located in Belgium; that I would
spend more than thirty years traversing this small country; and that
Belgium would become the land of my quest.

I was thirty-one then, and a neophyte sociologist. I had just
published my first book, *Experiment Perilous*,* based on my immersion as a participant observer, from 1951 to 1954, in the hospital
world of a research ward (Ward F-Second), its physician investiga-
tors, and its patients. It was in that ward, in ways I can now
identify but could not have foretold, that my journeying to Belgium
and this book began.

In the Harvard Medical School / Peter Bent Brigham Hospital
setting of Ward F-Second I met a number of talented young
European physicians. They had come to the United States during
this period just after World War II to prepare themselves for clinical
research careers in academic medicine. I not only became interested in why these physicians had selected the United States for
this postgraduate training, but also why most of them were apprehensively uncertain about whether they would be able to pursue
their research, or their careers, when they returned home. Much
more seemed to be involved than the material difficulties they
anticipated in obtaining the ample research funds and equipment to
which they had become accustomed in the United States. What
worried these physicians was how they, their professional outlook,
and their work would be received and viewed in the "old Europe"
milieux from which they came. They were not even sure that the
biomedical phenomena and questions in which they were absorbed,
or the scientific concepts, language, and techniques they employed,
would be understood or accepted by the powerful, gatekeeping

---

*Renée C. Fox, *Experiment Perilous: Physicians and Patients Facing the Unknown*
(Glencoe, Ill., Free Press, 1959; paperback edition, Philadelphia, University of Pennsylvania Press, 1974).

patrons of European academic medicine, under whose aegis their careers would obligatorily unfold. Their disquietude notwithstanding, almost all the physicians returned to their native countries, as they put it, "to try and see." I, in turn, followed some of them (originally to England, France, and Switzerland as well as to Belgium) to learn directly what sorts of conditions and problems they encountered in their home settings.

What began as a study of Belgian medical research, and its social and cultural framework, was rapidly transformed into a study of Belgium through the windows of its medical laboratories. The fact that I was trained as a social scientist to move back and forth between micro and macro levels of analysis, my personal as well as professional readiness to go where my work carried me, and, above all, the startling repercussions that my first publications on Belgian medical research evoked, swiftly projected me beyond the confines of my initial inquiry. Over time my exploration of Belgian medical research, and the angle of vision with which it provided me, became a study of Belgium—the gamut of social institutions and groups it encompasses, its characteristic social processes, and the values and beliefs, symbols and images out of which its distinctive culture, atmosphere, and worldview are fashioned. My persistent efforts to know and understand Belgium also transported me to Zaïre—the former Belgian Congo—where from 1962 to 1970 I did firsthand sociological research.

But "Why Belgium?" Why did you spend so much time studying this particular society, returning to it again and again to do so? Whether voiced by Belgians or non-Belgians, and however politely phrased, these questions have usually meant: What were you looking for, and what could you have possibly found that was so gripping in such a small, relatively insignificant, and conventionally "bourgeois" society?

At the beginning I had practical reasons for situating my research there, not the least of which was the greater receptivity I experienced in Belgium than in the other European countries where I considered conducting my inquiry. In addition, Belgium seemed to me to be a paradigmatically European society. Located geopolitically and culturally at the crossroads of Western Europe, it had been occupied consecutively throughout its history by a series of European nations that had left their marks upon it. Like numerous other European countries, it was a former colonial power in Africa to which it was still emotionally as well as economically connected. And it was a land of European paradoxes: very modern yet deeply traditional; highly international yet profoundly particularistic; diffusely Catholic, and strongly anti-Catholic and anticlerical at the same time. The fact that all these European attributes were concentrated in a country no larger than the state of New Jersey heightened them for me, as if they were magnified by Belgium's smallness.

Some of Belgium's more unique sociological characteristics captured my interest as well. Most notable among these was Belgian particularism and its centrality as an organizing principle throughout the society. I was struck by the extraordinary degree to which Belgians' family, community, region, the social class into which they were born, the ethnic-linguistic group to which they belonged, the religious-philosophical tradition out of which they came, and the political party with which they were affiliated enclosed them in enclaves that were not only insulated from one another but also rivalrous. As a result the society was enmeshed in its own cleavages. "Can one think of another country of the same size, economic and cultural weight," André Molitor, one of Belgium's foremost civil servants, has written, with two languages—one, a language of a large culture (French), the other of a small culture (Flemish); where the majority of the people speak the second language but 80 percent of the inhabitants of the capital (Brussels) speak the language of the minority; where the minority who dominated the country, linguistically, economically, and politically for one hundred years are now controlled by the majority; and where "the majority of the majority" are Christian (Catholic) in ideology, while the "majority of the minority" are "*laïciste*" (secular, Free Thought, and Free Mason)?

I was intrigued too by the society's repertoire of responses to the vying for power and for absolute equality in which its particularistic blocks engaged, and to the impasses this frequently created. Prominent among those that caught my attention were the so-called "*petits chemins*" of Belgium—adroit, semi-institutionalized, often subterranean, and marginally legitimate means for budging "the system" or getting around it; what Belgians ironically described as "the values of their faults"—their stabilizing "commonsense" and practical "spirit of compromise"; and the underlying aversion to violence and bloodshed that pervaded their land.

I was also sociologically fascinated by the peculiarly negative

national identity of the country—an identity that Belgians expressed with the uniformity and repetitiveness of a catechism.
Throughout my decades of involvement in the society I have
consistently heard Belgians declare that theirs is a country that
"barely exists"; that it is an "historical accident," an "artificial state,"
or a "nonstate," constructed in 1830 by diplomatic agreement
between other European powers (especially France, Germany, and
Great Britain); that it does not have the "chauvinism" of France,
the "nationalism" of Germany, or the "patriotism" of the United
States; and that it lacks both a distinct "culture of its own" and a
"common destiny." I have never encountered a society more prone
than Belgium inversely to articulate some of its most fundamental
values; more obsessively and doubtingly preoccupied with its "authenticity" and "reality"; more concerned about its progressive
"disappearance" and ultimate "survival"; and more constantly surprised by the discovery that "it still exists." The continual failure of
Belgians to recognize that this "Belgium-in-spite-of-itself" outlook
is part of the shared culture they deny possessing has never ceased
to amaze me.

It was not sheer sociological interest that drew me toward
Belgium. On more inward, personal levels I chose Belgium (or
perhaps Belgium chose me) because of what the Belgian playwright
Michel de Ghelderode would have called my "obsessions and cosmic
phantoms." Belgium's terrain somehow coincides with my inner
landscape, and its "buried strangeness"* with my own. From the
outset, the way the light suffused this foggy land stirred me—
especially at sunset, when it pierced the clouds, illumining the
sky and inflaming the red roofs of the houses. The music of Belgium's carillon bells reverberated inside me. And the statues on its
buildings—the Gothic galleries of sacred and profane, patrician and
plebeian "stone people" on the walls and turrets of some of its town
halls—spoke silently to me.

As I moved from one Belgian milieu to another, entering a
succession of private domiciles and public structures, I was increasingly impressed by the importance of these "houses"—by what they

---

*This phrase is taken from "A Hole in the Floor," a poem by Richard Wilbur.
Dedicated to the Belgian painter René Magritte, it turns around the image of looking
for a house's "very soul" and "the buried strangeness" within it, through a hole that a
carpenter has made in its parlor floor. The poem was first published in the July 4, 1961,
issue of the *New Yorker*.

represented as well as what they contained. It was inside the Belgian house, in its various incarnations, that I found Belgium and both the professional and personal meaning of my search.

But it was only after I had published an article in 1962 entitled "Medical Scientists in a Château,"* which for a time became something approaching a *cause célèbre* in Belgium, that I grasped the larger societal significance of the research I had undertaken. The purpose of this article was to describe and analyze the social structure within which clinical medical research was carried out in Belgium at that time, and to identify some of the problems this structure created for Belgian medical science and scientists. The passionate response it elicited from Belgian readers, on a national scale, made it evident that I had written about more than medical research.

The article began with a detailed description of a medical scientific colloquium held on November 15, 1959, in the royal palace at Laeken. This medical gathering in a château, I wrote, seemed a symbolic expression of the social structure and cultural tradition within which a good deal of medical research in Belgium functioned, and of the atmosphere surrounding it. The guests assembled for this occasion, I noted, represented virtually every major social institution, organization, and group in Belgium, even though this was supposedly a medical scientific event. Present, as might have been expected, were physicians, professors of medicine and science, officials of voluntary health organizations and relevant foundations, and the rectors of the four Belgian universities— Brussels, a then predominantly French-speaking "private" (nonstate) university, of Free Thought/Free Mason orientation; Ghent, a Flemish, state university, officially neither Catholic nor Free Thought but with many practicing Catholics in its student body and on its faculty; Liège, a French, state university whose faculty and student population leaned more toward a Free Thought than a Catholic outlook; and Louvain, a nonstate, Catholic university with both a French and a Flemish section. In addition, the invitees included a cross section of ministers and secretaries general of the national government and of officials of the local government, numerous members of the royal family and of the nobility, university profes-

---

*Renée C. Fox, "Medical Scientists in a Château," *Science*, Vol. 136, No. 3515 (May 11, 1962), 476–483.

sors from fields other than medical or biological science, directors
of various museums and libraries (some with no bearing on science
or scientific work), a number of bankers and businessmen, and five
bishops of the Belgian Catholic church. The array of guests, I
wrote, suggested that at the "summit" of the society these institutions and groups, and their "*messieurs les responsables*" (as Belgians
would say), came together and made joint decisions relevant to
many spheres of Belgian public life—medical research included.
And I implied that one of these *messieurs* (to use novelist Franz
Kafka's imagery) was the "count" in the "castle" of Belgian scientific
research, ruling over this domain.

In a metaphorical sense, I contended, Belgian medical researchers could be said to operate continuously in a "château"—in a
tenaciously traditional, "old European" structure that in many respects curtailed medical scientific creativity and the possibilities for
sustained research careers. In this connection I quoted what Raoul
Kourilsky had said in his inaugural lecture as professor of clinical
medicine at the University of Paris: "Like ruined *grands seigneurs* we
have preserved the old 'château' and its furnishings of another age,"
he proclaimed. "The great sacrifice has been research."

I am convinced that if I had published the same analysis of
medical research in Belgium without any allusion to the "château," it would have had far less impact. For, as the reactions to
my article dramatically taught me, Belgians are very sensitive to
symbols, and about them; and the château has metameaning in the
symbolic language of Belgium. It is the traditional and historical
Belgian house that rises up from and looms over the land. It is the
palace where the king of the Belgians and the queen officially reside
and carry out their royal functions. It is the central headquarters of
certain Belgian institutions and their governors, and of the political, economic, and emblematic power they command. It is also the
kind of Belgian castle in which so-called "conclaves" periodically
take place: extraordinary meetings of the power elite to negotiate
national conflicts concerning fundamental questions of values and
beliefs that Belgians define as crucial to the integrity and continu-
ance of their society. The "château" stands for all this in a way that
makes it a constitutive symbol, not only of the Belgian polity but of
Belgium as a nation and a society: its very existence, its core
identity, the structures and values and worldview within which
Belgians experience and order their individual and group existence.

André Molitor explained it best. "In writing about the 'château' the way that you did," he said, "you touched one of the *chasses sacrées* [the sacred reliquaries] of Belgium and of 'Belgian-ness' —the 'château' that is Belgium."

The Terrain
and the Time

O<small>N ONE</small> level this book is an account of an inquiry into a recent past. It spans the period from the close of the 1950s to the early 1990s. Within that time frame, it is especially concentrated on occurrences during the 1960s and 1970s.

A great deal has happened and changed in Belgium since my first journey to it. But the past of which I write is not totally past; and much in Belgium has not changed, in spite of all that has. This is visible in the dynamically constant social and cultural patterns that have had a shaping influence on the cardinal events and developments in Belgium during the decades that the book encompasses.

1959, THE YEAR of my first trip to Belgium, marked the culmination of the country's (and of Europe's) post–World War II reconstruction. It opened onto what came to be known as the "Golden Sixties," a time of unprecedented national prosperity that lasted until approximately 1973. In Belgium unemployment was negligible. Expanding public services and generous social insurance provided a comfortable protective umbrella for the population. Highways were built throughout the country. Automobiles became commonplace possessions for families of every social class. High-rise buildings were erected in the cities and their environs. Especially in the northern, Flemish part of the country, farmland was transformed into industrial plants and industrial parks. The landscape abounded with recently built family houses and second residences of the finest red Belgian bricks, fitted out with up-to-date kitchens, bathrooms, and central heating. Television (with French, Dutch, German, and English channels) appeared in every living room. People from all social backgrounds dressed well, ate well, and traveled abroad for their month-long, paid summer vacations. At the end of 1960, on

December 15, the marriage of King Baudouin I to Doña Fabiola de Mora y Aragon of Spain was experienced by royalist and nonroyalist Belgians alike as an event that symbolized the well-being and unity of their society.

But the early sixties were also a time of loss and turbulence in Belgium. At midnight on June 30, 1960, a joint proclamation was signed by the Belgian and Congolese governments that accorded the Belgian Congo its independence and national sovereignty. Although that document stated that this independence had come to pass "in full agreement and friendship with Belgium," the events surrounding and immediately following it were both bitter and violent. At the ceremonies that took place in Léopoldville on Independence Day, in the presence of King Baudouin, the first prime minister of the Congo, Patrice Lumumba, spoke passionately about how profoundly he and his "brothers" had suffered under eighty years of Belgian colonial rule, and about the "battle of tears, of fire and blood" that Congolese had had to wage in order to "end the humiliating slavery that was imposed on us by force." A week later, on July 7, 1960, a mutiny of the former Force Publique, newly renamed the National Congolese Army, erupted in Léopoldville and began to spread through the Lower Congo; and on July 11 the secession of the province of Katanga, and declaration of its independence by Moïse Tshombe took place. Belgians and Congolese panicked, and about three-fourths of the estimated 87,000 Belgians who were in the Congo at the time were evacuated to Belgium.

Only five days after the wedding of King Baudouin and Queen Fabiola, on December 20, 1960, Belgium came to a virtual standstill, as a twenty-four day national strike gripped the country. Ostensibly the strike was an acute reaction to the passage of an omnibus austerity bill which the governing Catholic and Liberal coalition contended had been made necessary by the loss of the Congo. But in fact it was not the economic but the psychological implications of the separation of Belgium from its former colony that were the most disheartening and costly. In losing the Congo, Belgium lost its horizon; as a consequence, its self-image changed. Turning its gaze inward, Belgium no longer saw itself as a peaceful, entrepreneurial little country whose flourishing industries ranked with the best of Europe, but as a society that had lost status and a grip on itself, and was succumbing to its ethnic-linguistic divisions.

What the dynamics of this generalized strike brought to the

surface was the growing discrepancy between the economic situation of the Walloon and Flemish sections of the country: the shift in the balance of political and cultural power and influence that was taking place between them; and the mounting pressure for greater autonomy that was being exerted by Flanders, and reactively reinforced by Wallony. Flanders's economy had previously been based on agriculture and textiles. The strongly Catholic Flemish, with their high birthrate, had become a demographic majority; but they had remained a sociological minority who lived and worked in what was essentially an underdeveloped region of the country. Wallony, with its flourishing coal mines, steel mills, and factories, had reaped most of the benefits of the first industrial revolution. It dominated Flanders economically, politically, and socially. The entire country, Flanders included, was ruled by a French-speaking bourgeoisie. Until a series of language laws was passed in the 1930s, the affairs of the national government and of most local governments were conducted in French. The army was commanded in French. The law courts judged in French. Education in Flemish was limited to primary school; secondary schools and universities taught exclusively in French. And it was only in French that one could have a professional or a civil service career.

At the beginning of the 1960s, however, a major reversal in the relationship between Flanders and Wallony was taking place. Flanders had entered a vigorous, post–World War II period of industrialization, and a significant percentage of the foreign capital (particularly from the United States) coming into Belgium to support new industries was being invested in Flanders. In contrast, Wallony's coal mines and time-worn steel plants and factories were in crisis. The region had lost thousands of jobs and much investment capital. A new, Flemish-speaking, upwardly mobile "populist bourgeoisie" was not only becoming visible and vocal in Flemish movements but also in both the local and national polity. As the strike unfolded, the opposition to the austerity law that had originally spurred it was replaced by a collective expression of the frustrations, anxieties, and grievances that Wallony was experiencing in response to its altered situation, and by the demands of the newly formed Mouvement Populaire Wallon for the kind of regional autonomy for Wallony that Flemish movements had long been proposing for Flanders.

Following the strike, in 1962–1963, under a Catholic-Socialist coalition government, linguistic and regional problems continued to dominate the national political scene. In 1962 the linguistic laws of 1932 were altered by new legislation that permanently established the so-called "linguistic frontier" and specified the official administrative and educational language of each of the nine Belgian provinces. Four provinces were designated as Flemish-speaking, four as French-speaking, and one—the Brabant province, in which the capital city of Brussels is located—as bilingual. These laws, which constituted a major first step toward federalism, unleashed strong protests from both ardent *Flamingants* and outraged *Wallingants* about the injustices done to their causes. Les Fourons, a group of Belgian communes made up of six villages, located on the linguistic border, with more French than Flemish speakers among its 4,500 inhabitants, became a national focus of these mutual recriminations when it was administratively "moved" from Wallony to the Flemish province of Limbourg.

Belgium's linguistic conflicts are deeply entwined with the country's history and culture, its economy and polity, its social class system, and with its religious and rationalist secular ideologies; and they are fundamentally related to the society's definition of itself as a nation-state. In this latter connection, since its foundation in 1830 Belgium had been both a unitary and decentralized state, combining a central administrative structure organized into ministries and governmental agencies, with a legacy of strong, local self-government by its nine provinces, and by its more than three thousand communes, whose significant role in the life of the country led someone to say that "Belgium is a republic of communes." What Belgians call the "Linguistic Problem" (written in capital letters) touched the distinctive structure, the ultimate values, and the core identity of Belgian society, and also its collective anxiety: the latent concern felt by the citizenry of this small, repeatedly occupied, conflict-prone land that their country might become so overwhelmed by centrifugal forces that it would no longer be able to function or, beyond that, might totally cease to exist.

In 1968 the far-reaching import of the Linguistic Problem (or the Community, Cultural, or Regional Problem, as it came to be alternatively called) was dramatized when the centuries-old Catholic University of Louvain officially split, geographically as well as administratively, into the French Université Catholique de Louvain

(UCL), and the Flemish Katholieke Universiteit te Leuven (KUL). The entire French section of the University was obliged to leave what had become the Flemish town of Leuven under the linguistic legislation of 1962. Supported by government funds, UCL rebuilt its medical school and academic center in the Woluwe–St. Lambert area of Brussels, and located all its other faculties in Ottignies, in the Brabant-Wallon countryside between Leuven and Brussels, where it also created an entire new city—Louvain-la-Neuve.

On a broader European plane, 1968 was a year when massive youth uprisings erupted in the universities of France, where students began by revolting against the unchanging traditional structures of institutions of higher learning, and went on from there to join workers in demonstrations that nearly unseated the Gaullist government. This movement—which coincided with significant increases in the number of students from less privileged social backgrounds now enrolled in universities—spread throughout Western Europe. In Belgium the most important student revolt occurred in the spring of 1968 at the Free University of Brussels, where it was centered in the medical school. Junior faculty and young medical researchers joined with students to effect changes in their school that ramified into other parts of the university. Over the course of the 1968–1969 academic year the University of Brussels, like its Catholic university counterpart, split into two universities—the French Université Libre de Bruxelles, and the Flemish Vrije Universiteit Brussel— once again with the legal mandate and financial support of the Belgian government.

Belgian Catholicism has changed significantly over the past thirty years; but as the dynamics of the splitting of Louvain University suggest, these changes are far from simple. The level of traditional Catholic observance has steeply declined. The younger generations are restive about ecclesiastical authority and defiant about the church's official position on sexuality, birth control, abortion, and the status and role of women. The incidence of divorce has significantly increased, and the cohabitation of unmarried couples has become more frequent and respectable. Anticlericalism is more vocal, and indifference about what the bishops and clergy think is more widespread than in the past. Nevertheless, a majority of Belgians still baptize their infants, send their children to Catholic schools, belong to Catholic sick funds and trade unions, and are both married and buried in the church. And relatively few inhabitants of Belgium are members of religions other than Catholicism. Out of a population of 9.9 million persons, there are only some 150,000 Muslims (mainly immigrant workers from Morocco and Turkey and their families), 100,000 Protestants, and 35,000 Jews.

Belgium has no state religion, and its constitution guarantees religious freedom and the noninterference of the government in religious matters. But it is the metaculture of Belgium—its ethos— that makes it a Catholic society, rather than its legal principles, religious demography, or its institutional religion. Many of the symbols and images, values and beliefs that pervade the economic and political, domestic and everyday life of the country, as well as its art and literature, have deep roots in the cultural tradition and cosmic outlook of Belgian Catholicism. In this sense its common culture is as Catholic as it is Belgian—not only visible in its paintings, its "living museums" of church objects, and its folkloric fêtes, but also present in the meaning of bricks, houses, and the family, the relationship to things, to nature, to light, and in some of the basic values of the society, such as courage, solidarity, harmony, nonviolence, compassion, and attunement to the human condition.

Even Belgian Free Thought and Free Masonry, the institutionalized opponent of the Catholic church and its supposed ideological antithesis, has been structured and shaped by Catholicism. In recent years, for example, a vigorous Free Thought–inspired "Laicity" movement has developed a youth feast, civil wedding and funeral ceremonies, and hospital, army, and prison chaplaincies that bear a marked resemblance to Catholic rituals and institutions. The movement has also asked for the same kind of national recognition and state funding that the Catholic church and the evangelical Protestant, Anglican, Jewish, Christian Orthodox, and Muslim communities all receive in Belgium.

Nowhere is the diffuse, latent influence of Belgium's Catholic ethos more present than in the supreme importance that Belgians attach to the family—perhaps more than any other Europeans. In spite of the considerable "values gap" that now exists between those over and under forty years of age, as a consequence of the worldwide social and cultural ferment of the 1960s and the conflicts between generations that it unleashed, the Belgian family remains an extraordinarily stable value.

Yet in spite of Belgian cultural patterns that Flemish and Walloons share (or perhaps because of them), the structural splits between the two linguistic communities have continued to multiply, bringing in their wake the doubling of many organizations and facilities as part of a fissionary process in the society that involves more than decentralization. Belgians sometimes refer to it as *morcellement* or *splinteren* (fragmentation). Since 1918, for example, with a brief exception from 1950 to 1954, it has not been possible to elect or form a politically homogeneous government based on the majority rule of one of the country's three major parties, or "families," as they are frequently called—Catholic (Social Christian), Liberal, and Socialist. Then, in the course of the 1970s, each of these parties separated into a Flemish and a Walloon party. This was further complicated by the rise of three militant linguistic-community parties—the Flemish Volksunie, the Walloon Rassemblement Wallon, and the Brussels Front des Francophones parties. By 1992 Belgium had as many as sixteen political parties, including a Flemish ecology party (Agalev) and a French one (Ecolo).

Some of the most astute observers and analysts of Belgium's evolution claim that partly because of the increased complexity and organization of these social divisions, and the changes of the past few decades, what has vanished from Belgian national life are the "permanent personalities" who were integrating forces in the society. These union officials, industrialists and financiers, churchmen, education and science administrators, and certain professionals had the charismatic authority and negotiating ability to foster agreement and concerted action from the major particularistic blocs (or so-called "pillars") in Belgian society on a wide range of nationally important, value-laden issues. Such national figures have been disappearing. They have been progressively replaced by persons of more specialized scope and delimited impersonal authority, more publicly identified with specific, particularistic groups than their predecessors, who function within the elaborate and constraining bureaucratic structures that now exist on all levels of the society.

1968–1970 marked the beginning of more than two decades of successive constitutional and institutional reforms through which Belgium moved progressively from a unitary to a federal state. The reforms of 1970 established the existence of three cultural communities—Flemish, French, and German*—each with its own legislature (council) and with jurisdiction over cultural matters, the use of language, and, subject to important restrictions by the national government, education. In principle three regions were also created—Flanders, Wallony, and Brussels—but at this juncture they existed only on paper. For the time being the importance that the Flemish movement placed on the autonomous expression of culture and language within a community predominated over the Walloons' emphasis on regionalism and having the political and financial means to move their area of the country out of the industrial doldrums. Whereas the French community wished to see Brussels created as a full region, the Flemish opted for its cogestion by both the Flemish and French cultural communities. Agreement on this question was not reached during the 1970s in spite of two national conclaves, held in the châteaux of Egmont and Stuyvenberg, at which it was vigorously discussed.

The OPEC decision of 1973 no longer to supply oil to Western European countries—"the oil shock"—ushered in a time of economic stagnation and serious unemployment that aggravated and laid bare other long-standing economic problems. The Belgian national budget and debt rose to unprecedented heights. A sizable proportion of it was associated with Belgium's enormous public bureaucracy; the generous social security system that it developed in the 1960s (including health insurance, sickness leaves, family allocations, unemployment benefits, and pensions); the government-supported expansion and proliferation of universities; and the reforms in response to the country's linguistic problems, that entailed creating and doubling many state-financed statuses, organizations, and structures. The economic crisis moved the public from a sense of abundance and open opportunities to a psychology of "blocked horizons," penury, and restrictions. Individualism and privatization seemed to gain momentum in Belgian life, while the cardinal Belgian value of "solidarity" (solidariteit/solidarité)—with its shared Catholic, socialist, and humanist conceptions of the common good, community, social welfare, and mutual aid—appeared to recede.

---

*The German-speaking cultural community of Belgium is located in a sparsely populated (sixty thousand inhabitants) area of the country (830 square kilometers) between Liège and the German border.

In 1980, in the midst of this economic time of troubles, a second set of state reforms was enacted. The institutional autonomy of the three cultural communities was reinforced. They were endowed with their own executive bodies, and their powers were enlarged to include matters pertaining to personal and social well-being in health policy and aid to families, immigrants, the handicapped, youth, the elderly, and prisoners. The national government maintained jurisdiction over health insurance and over legal aspects of the protection of youth. Authority over matters pertaining to scientific research was divided between the communities, regions, and the federal government. The regions were organized and given authority in the spheres of urbanism, the planning and management of territory, the protection of the environment, the production and distribution of water, rural conservation, agricultural policy, and housing. Although each of the communities and regions was accorded the same legislative and executive competences, it was at this point in the evolution of Belgian federalism that a so-called "asymmetry" developed between Flanders and Wallony. In Flanders the regional powers were absorbed by the community institutions, creating a unified ("fused") Flemish community that became the predominant entity. In contrast, Wallony maintained separate councils and governments for the Walloon region and the French community, thereby institutionalizing its preference for a regionally based federalism rather than the communitarian model adopted by the Flemish.

Between 1980 and 1988, while these new institutional structures were being broken in, the tension surrounding the country's linguistic disputes mounted and became more intricate. Les Fourons (the Voer), and José Happart, the apple grower–farmer who had been elected burgomaster of this cluster of six villages in 1982, came to embody these conflicts. Their stance led to the most prolonged national government crisis in Belgium's history. Happart absolutely refused to speak Flemish at communal council meetings and in the conduct of other official acts, even though the use of Flemish had been required by the Belgian constitution since Les Fourons had been attached to Flanders in 1962. As a consequence, Happart's decisions were regularly rescinded by the Flemish authorities in the Fourons jurisdiction, and in September 1986 Belgium's highest court ordered that he be stripped of office because of his intransigence. During 1987 he was dismissed repeatedly by Brussels, only to be reinstated each time by his local council who, along with two-thirds of the Fourons residents who were French speakers, had never accepted the transfer of their villages from Wallony to Flanders. Furthermore, Happart, who had been elected a deputy in the European Community in 1984 on the *Francophone* Socialist party list, defiantly insisted on defining Wallony as a "region of Europe" rather than of Belgium. What began as a local set of happenings, sparked by a folkloric figure, escalated into a national impasse that brought down what was known as the Martens VII government, and left Belgium without its successor for 147 days. After almost five months, in May 1988, a five-party coalition government—Martens VIII—was finally formed, made up of members of the French and Flemish Socialist and Social-Christian parties, and of the Flemish Volksunie, under the aegis of the same Flemish, Social-Christian prime minister, Wilfried Martens, who had headed the seven previous governments since 1979. For many Belgians the infinitesimal size of the Fourons issue (focused on a rural commune of less than five thousand inhabitants), and the immense symbolic significance it acquired, both epitomized and burlesqued the incalculable energy they had devoted over the years to linguistic conflicts. As one observer dryly and astutely commented, the Fourons drama vividly illustrated that Belgians who are "reputedly materialistic, quarrel more about ideas and symbols" than anything else.*

The Happart/Fourons events played a pivotal role in the constitutional reforms of 1988–1989. They strengthened the hand of the French community in the negotiations over the status of Brussels, and contributed to their success in pushing through the decision that Brussels-Capital become a full region. But Brussels was recognized as a bilingual region, some of whose cultural affairs would be managed by a Flemish commission, some by a French commission. In Belgian eyes these were special arrangements that constituted a second asymmetry in their federalism. The other major constitutional revision of 1988–1989 was the "communitarianization" of education—that is, the transfer of the entire Belgian system of education from nursery school through the university to the juris-

---

*André Molitor, "La Première Phase des Nouvelles Réformes," *Administration Publique*, September 1988 (reprint), p. 275.

diction of the communities, without any of the prior limitations. In addition, the reforms greatly expanded the economic jurisdiction of the regions.

The institutional labyrinth created by these three sets of constitutional reforms, and the complexity of the legal language in which they were phrased, made it difficult for Belgians to comprehend what Prime Minister Martens called the "federalism of union" that now existed. A public opinion poll conducted in the spring of 1990 revealed that only a tiny percentage of the persons questioned felt they had a good grasp of "the reform of the state"; close to half of the respondents said they "could not find their way in it"; and many persons confessed they did not even know whether or not they understood it. But the reform's most striking effect was the collective identity crisis it caused—acutely raising the question among Belgians, "Does the state exist any longer, or has Belgium become a 'nonstate,'" and bringing their indwelling anxieties about the "reality" of their society, culture, and history to the surface.

The country had already undergone another major shock to its sense of itself at the beginning of 1988, when the Italian businessman and financier, Carlo De Benedetti, had tried to take over the Société Générale de Belgique, Belgium's huge and venerable holding company. Although his attempt failed, it resulted in the passage of majority ownership of the company to the Groupe Suez of France. The fact that the Société Générale, a corporation with a revenue of 350 billion Belgian francs, that controlled 1,261 enterprises and was integrally associated with all of Belgium's history, had proven to be so vulnerable, so immobilized by its traditional "Old Europe" attitudes and structures, and so unprotected by the national government, made Belgians wonder whether it had "only appeared to be a giant in [their] social imagination."[*] This "fallen giant" image of Société Générale shook Belgium's self-conception as a land with the persistence and strength, the resourcefulness, and the manipulative ability to survive and prevail in the midst of larger, more aggressively nationalistic countries. The federalization of Belgium re-evoked and augmented self-doubts about the country's

---

[*] Trencavel, "Y-a-t-il un pilote dans l'avion?" *La Revue Nouvelle*, Vol. 87, No. 7–8 (July–August 1988), 10. Trencavel was the collective name of the political writers on the editorial staff of *La Revue Nouvelle* at the time this article was published.

national identity and continuing existence aroused by the "Affaire of the Société Générale."

"To federate is to unite," King Baudouin declared in a number of speeches on important ceremonial occasions. At the end of the 1980s and the beginning of the 1990s it was becoming urgently clear that Belgian unity would have to embrace more than Flemings, Walloons, *Bruxellois/Brusselaars*, and *Germanophones*. Belgium was facing the consequences of its failure to integrate its immigrant workers, their families, and their progeny into its local and national life.

Since World War II successive waves of foreigners had come to Belgium to work in the coal mines, the steel, construction, and textile industries, and in domestic service. Until the end of the "golden" 1960s Belgian industry, in concert with the government, had recruited such foreign workers for unskilled, dangerous, and low-paying jobs that were not filled by Belgians. The earliest group of foreign workers who migrated to Belgium were Italians, followed by East Europeans (Poles and Czechs), then Spaniards, Greeks, Portuguese, Yugoslavians, and, more recently, Moroccans and Turks. In 1974, at the height of the "oil shock," Belgium's open-door immigrant labor policy ended.

The hundreds of thousands of immigrant workers and their descendants living permanently in Belgium at that time made up 9 percent of the country's total population and 25 percent of the population of Brussels. The 269,000 Italians were the most numerous, followed by 123,000 Moroccans and 73,000 Turks. Legally the great majority of them remained "foreign," chiefly because the criteria for naturalization were so restrictive that even those of their children who were born in Belgium were not automatically defined as citizens. Only parents who were already Belgian could hand down Belgian nationality to their offspring.

Moroccan and Turkish immigrants, more than those from European countries, experienced prejudice and discrimination because they were foreign. The fact that many of them were Muslims contributed to the differentness with which they were viewed by Belgians, even though in 1974 Islam had been officially recognized as one of the country's religions. Belgian reactions to the decision made by the Islamic and Cultural Center in Brussels to open an Islamic school in September 1989 were revelatory in this regard. That decision not only triggered a heated national debate about

Islamic schools and courses in religion but also about whether young Muslim girls enrolled as students in secular public schools should be allowed to wear a head scarf (*hijab*) in class; about which *imam*, if any, was the legitimate head of Islam in Belgium; and about problems of integrating immigrants into the society. Some of these questions were addressed in the first biannual report of the Royal Commission on Immigrant Policy issued in November 1989, which stated that immigration policy was an important government concern. The commission's affirmation notwithstanding, the "less rights for immigrants" ideology and programs of radical right parties like the Vlaams Blok, on the one hand, and the Parti des Forces Nouvelles, on the other, were growing more strident. The Vlaams Blok party went so far as to recommend that non-European immigrants be discouraged from staying in Belgium through an arsenal of means that included progressively reducing their family allocations, expelling them after they were unemployed for three months, and imposing a special tax on employers who hired them.

In May 1991 confrontations took place between Moroccan youths and the local police that Belgians were prone to call "riots." These incidents lasted only a few days; they were confined to several streets in three Brussels communes—Forest, Molenbeek, and Schaarbeek—with large Moroccan populations; and they caused no deaths, serious injuries, or major property damage. What the Moroccan youths seemed to be expressing through street fighting was pent-up anger over their crowded living conditions, poor education, lowly jobs, unemployment, undignified treatment by police, and, above all, their sense of social exclusion.

Despite the fact that the Martens VIII government was making headway with the country's economic problems, it was voted out of office in the November 24, 1991, national elections. Persistent tension between the gamut of French and Flemish political parties over a wide range of issues contributed both to the Martens government's resignation and to the prolonged process of forming a new government. It was not until March 7, 1992, that another coalition government was constituted, this time one of the center-left, composed by the four French and Flemish Socialist and Social Christian parties, with Flemish, Social Christian Jean-Luc Dehaene as its prime minister.

1992–1993 was a momentous year for Belgium in a number of ways:

—It marked what was supposed to be the completion of the incremental process by which Belgium had evolved into a federal state. Through the "Saint Michael's agreements" of September 28 (named after the saint's day on which they were reached), the 1993 constitutional reforms were enacted. They modified the composition and the powers of the Parliament, particularly the Senate, to make it more compatible with federalism; introduced changes in the national government intended to give it greater independence and stability; and accorded the institutions of the Walloon region, the French community, and Flanders greater autonomy to shape their organization. In the final analysis, the idiosyncratically Belgian "asymmetrical" federal state that had come to pass was erected on an equally Belgian compromise of choosing by not choosing. It allowed the Flemish to maintain the primacy of a communitarian logic, and the French of a regional logic, by juxtaposing two regions (Wallony and Brussels-Capital) and two communities (the Flemish and the German-speaking), of which the strongest entities were the Walloon region and the Flemish community.*

—During 1992–1993 Belgium was centrally involved in the construction of the European Community and in efforts to unify it. Brussels became the established home of the European Community's Commission, its Council of Ministers' Secretariat, and its Economic and Social Council. In addition, although the European Parliament was located in Strasbourg, France, many of its meetings were held in Brussels. In the latter part of 1992 the Belgian Parliament ratified the Treaty of Maastricht on the creation of a European Union with a strong majority vote, opposed only by the French and Flemish ecology parties, Ecolo and Agalev, and by the Flemish nationalist parties, Volksunie and Vlaams Blok. From July to December 1993, when Belgium assumed the rotating presidency of the European Community, it piloted certain decisions that helped to deblock the Community's stalemate on the implementation of the Maastricht Treaty.

—In the course of 1992–1993 Belgium moved from a sense of expectancy about continuing economic recovery to a mood of

---

*Marc Uyttendaele, "Féderalisme Régional ou Féderalisme Communautaire," in, Francis Delpérée, ed., La Constitution Fédérale du 5 Mai 1993 (Brussels, Bruylant, 1993), pp. 119–123.

foreboding about a worsening recession that was engulfing all of
Europe. On November 17, 1993, the Dehaene government presented the Belgian public with its "Global Austerity Plan" for
reducing the national debt, creating employment, protecting the
social security system, and increasing the competitiveness of the
Belgian economy. Nine days later Belgium's major labor unions
called a national one-day strike in protest against some provisions of
the plan.

—On July 31, 1993, Baudouin I, King of the Belgians, died
unexpectedly at the age of sixty-three after a reign of forty-two
years. He was succeeded by his brother, Albert II. The intense
emotion elicited by King Baudouin's death was most dramatically
and poignantly expressed by the great crowds that congregated at
the Royal Palace in Brussels and placed masses of flowers in front of
the gates of the château. Belgians were astounded by their own
sentiments and behavior. At the end of 1993 they were still
pondering and debating its meaning.

Part One

PUBLIC HOUSES

Jacques Errera in the study of his mansion on the Rue Royale

Prologue:
Official Parlors

Y OU ENTER the public houses of Belgium through their official parlors, to which you are escorted by a gatekeeper/ usher of that establishment. These anterooms are furnished in various styles—more often pre-twentieth-century traditional rather than avant-garde modern, and ranging from crystal-chandeliered lavishness to monastic austerity.

I have sat in countless parlors like these over the years of my research, as I waited to see the occupants of the political, financial, educational, scientific, medical, and religious houses with whom I had scheduled appointments. Regardless of the institution and of the status of the person receiving me, in these public parlors I have always felt awed expectancy, the nostalgic presence of things past, and, above all, a sense of mystery about the inner sanctum of the house into which I was about to be admitted.

In a published excerpt from his personal journal, André Molitor has captured the atmosphere that pervades many of these "official premises" and their antechambers:

> I am going to see PW at the Ministry of Justice. When I return like this to one of the official premises where I worked several months or years, it is always a sort of *return to Brideshead*. . . . The worries and joys of the profession, pungent, profound, seize me again . . . from very concrete and very humble details: the anteroom of the Cabinet, the ushers and chauffeurs whom I find again and whose faces open up when they see me. . . . I seat myself in one of the armchairs of the waiting room where I recognize the carpeting or the linoleum, a little more worn, a little duller. In front of me, the same engraving that was there six or twelve years ago, and the same ashtray on a stand, model *État belge* [Belgian State], topped by an emptying-ashes push button, and sometimes attached to the wall to keep it from being stolen. . . .

Muffled atmosphere. A door suddenly slams, a secretary passes, chest high, heels also, a distant smile on her lips, and on her face all the importance conferred on her by proximity to Power and participation in Important Business.

The stroke of a bell: the chief usher introduces me into the sanctuary where—in times past or formerly—I spent so many hours by the side of the person who was then the master of this house. *

IN THIS culturally Catholic society I have spent a considerable amount of time in the parlors of religious residences and convents. The parlor of the Jesuit residence on Chaussée de Haacht/Haachtse Steenweg in Brussels—the "Gesu"—to which I repeatedly returned, became for me the quintessence of these anterooms.

Particularly during the early years of my research in Belgium, when the Catholic clergy still lived in more cloistered and strictly regulated pre–Vatican Council II communities, gaining entrée to the Gesu was an intimidating process. The great oak door of the residence, with its brass knocker and bell, resembled the doors of many other Belgian houses, both public and private. But for an American Jewish laywoman like myself, the solidly barricaded door of the Gesu seemed more mysterious and formidable than its secular counterparts. My feelings were reinforced by Gesu's *portier*, who was more a guardian of the house than a receptionist. Each time I passed through its doors, which he appeared to open with reluctance, he gave me the impression that I had already done something improper, if not illicit, by crossing over the threshold of this consecrated, celibate, all-male Society of Jesus community. From behind the pane of his glassed-in station, scowling at me suspiciously, he asked whom I had come to see, and rang the indicated Father X's room on his antiquated switchboard. Even though the priest in question legitimated my presence by indicating that he did indeed have an appointment with me, the *portier* was not mollified. He disapprovingly ushered me down the long, wide, cold stone corridor, filled with the indiscreet sound of my worldly feminine heel clicks, and ushered me into one of a series of visitors' parlors. Without uttering conventionally polite reassurances like "Make

---

*André Molitor, *Feuilles de Route: Extraits d'un Journal* (Paris-Gembloux, Editions Duculot, 1987), pp. 59–60.

yourself comfortable," or "Father So-and-So will be with you shortly," the *portier* swiftly left the parlor, firmly closing its door behind him, sealing me into the room.

In that bare, forbidding parlor I felt alone, impure, anxious, and guilty—as though I had committed some dimly remembered, grave sin which I ought to be spiritually preparing myself to confess to the priest who would soon be joining me. Hanging on one of the walls of the parlor was a big dark-wooden crucifix, to which an agonized Christ in a loin cloth was pinioned. A dried remnant of an Easter palm frond ornamented the cross. Straight, very hard chairs bordered the dusty room. On the small round table in the center of the room lay several old back issues of a Flemish missionary magazine (printed in Flemish, because the Gesu belonged to the Flemish Province of the Jesuit Order in Belgium). There was also a straggly snake plant on the table, and the one thing in the parlor that brought me to the edge of a smile: a bank shaped like a beehive, with a facsimile of a bee attached to it on a wire. A small sign invited one to drop alms for the missions into this bee bank. The parlor was filled with a gloomy, overcast, yellowish light that filtered feebly through the leaden stained-glass window. The shadowy silhouette of an otherwise invisible inner court and convent garden was discernible to the visitor who dared to walk up to that window and peer out of it.

Over the years I became more accustomed to such parlors in the array of religious community residences that I frequented in Belgium and in Zaïre. To some extent their ambience, if not their furnishing, was gradually altered by the "opening onto the modern world" of the Second Vatican Council. As these changes took place, even such a ferocious protector of The Faith, religious vows, the convent, and the Society of Jesus as the *portier* of Gesu began to see me as other than an intruder.

The "crisis of new vocations" for the priesthood has depopulated many religious houses in Belgium and led to the closing of some of them. Now there are fewer parlors, and they are less frequently used. But some remain, and to this day when I enter one of them I feel much as I did the first time the *portier* enclosed me in the Gesu parlor, where I sat in solitude, waiting apprehensively for the priest to appear.

La Maison de la Rue d'Egmont
and Its Director

J UNE 28, 1961, was a momentous day in my ongoing study. It turned round the interview I was granted by Jean Willems in his office at 11, rue d'Egmont in Brussels—the building of the club of the University Foundation. Willems was a director and first vice-president of the University Foundation and of what was then Belgium's most important agency involved in the conduct and support of scientific research—the National Fund of Scientific Research, known as FNRS. In addition, as director, vice-president, and/or treasurer, Jean Willems presided over the entire network of Belgian organizations that governed and funded scientific research at that time. A number of these organizations—FNRS, the University Foundation, the National Fund of Medical Scientific Research, the Francqui Foundation, and the Interuniversity Institute of Nuclear Sciences—were housed, along with Willems, at 11, rue d'Egmont. Willems's reign over the house of science was anchored in the convictions of the social class with which he fervently identified—the French-speaking Belgian bourgeoisie. He espoused and personified the view that a business and financial elite, with high culture and a patriotic sense of noblesse oblige, should govern the affairs of a royalist and unitarist Belgium. I had heard him referred to as the *patron*, the "big boss," the *Grand Manitou*, and the "dictator" of science and research in Belgium, and as its *éminence grise*, and its *Esprit-Directeur*. To me he was the count in the Belgian Château of scientific research.

Obtaining this interview with Willems was not a simple matter. The secretary in Belgium of the Belgian American Educational Foundation (BAEF), whose own office was located at 11, rue d'Egmont over which Willems reigned, made the appointment for me. Although the BAEF had awarded me two summer grants to support my research in Belgium, and though the secretary was personally as well as officially enthusiastic about my study, when I asked for his help in meeting Jean Willems he became visibly nervous. He went ahead and arranged the appointment for me, but he warned me to be careful, cautioning me that what I was undertaking was very risky, and that I should "move like a snake"! He seemed to be as worried about the unpleasantness to which I might be subject as he was about any trouble I might cause.

Behind Willems's extraordinary role in Belgium's scientific life and his aura lay a story of national import and of impressive personal achievement. The story was integrally associated with the establishment of FNRS in 1928, and the part that Emile Francqui, the man whom Jean Willems considered to be his *Maître* (master teacher), played in its creation, and in Belgian science policy more generally.

FNRS had its source in the famous speech delivered by King Albert I of the Belgians in Seraing on October 1, 1927, at an anniversary celebration of the John Cockerill Company, the metallurgy (ironworks) firm that was the starting point of Belgian industrialization in 1817. Scientific research, the king stated, was critically important for the political and economic standing and the progress of a modern society. Proclaiming "a veritable crisis of scientific institutions and laboratories in Belgium," he called for "substantial and sustained efforts, and multiple initiatives" to remedy this. "In our time, whoever does not move forward falls behind," he ringingly declared—an aphorism that is quoted by Belgians to this day. Emile Francqui was one of the key persons whom the king had consulted before delivering his speech. After the speech Albert I gave his approval to Francqui to form a small committee, equally divided between university academics and industrialists, whose task was to translate his appeal into a practical plan of action. Francqui was sixty-five years old when he organized this committee, and en route to becoming one of the most powerful personages in the history of Belgium.

Born in Brussels in 1862, he was orphaned at the age of twelve and joined the army as a "barracks boy" (*enfant de troupe*). At twenty-two, in the rank of a young officer, he left for the Congo, where he spent the next ten years as a topographical explorer and colonial administrator. He commanded the expedition to the Katanga region that enabled geologists to map its mineral richness and helped politically to integrate it into the Congo. King Léopold II sent him to the Upper-Uele region where he fought and vanquished the Mahdists and reorganized the area. The king then named him consul to China. His chief functions there were to watch over and develop Belgium's industrial and commercial activities, principally banking interests, the building of the Peking-Hanchow railroad, and coal-mining enterprises. In 1903 Francqui came back to Europe to stay and enter the field of finance, progressing from director, to vice-governor, to governor of the Société Générale de Belgique, Belgium's great holding company.

But it was the philanthropic relief work that Francqui undertook during World War I, the German occupation of Belgium, and the immediate postwar period that transformed him into one of the country's most important political figures and led to his involvement in higher education and scientific research. Francqui played a key role in creating the National Committee for Aid and Alimentation, which in collaboration with its American counterpart, the Commission for Relief in Belgium, and one of its founders Herbert Hoover, aided and fed more than 2.6 million Belgians throughout the First World War.

When the war ended, following a plan conceived by Francqui and Hoover and approved by the Belgian government, the National Committee and the Commission for Relief in Belgium were liquidated. In their stead two new "sister-foundations" were established— the University Foundation in Brussels, and the Committee for Relief in Belgium Educational Foundation in New York—which were funded with a portion of the money left over from the Belgian war-relief activities. The purpose of these foundations was to help young Belgians obtain undergraduate and graduate university training, and to promote the exchange of scientific and intellectual personnel and ideas between Belgium and the United States. Francqui was president of the University Foundation from the day it officially came into being on July 6, 1920, until he died in 1935, when Jean Willems succeeded him in that post.

On November 30, 1927, the committee that King Albert I asked Francqui to form as a follow-up to his 1927 Seraing speech on the "crisis of scientific institutions and laboratories in Belgium" held its first meeting under the chairmanship of Francqui, in his capacity as president of the University Foundation. Jean Willems, one of the two secretaries appointed to the committee, attended this meeting that prepared the way for the organization of the Fonds National de la Recherche Scientifique (National Fund of Scientific Research, FNRS). Francqui was the chairman and Willems the secretary of the commission that drafted its statutes. FNRS was founded on April 27, 1928, and recognized by royal decree on June 2, 1928, with Emile Francqui as its first president. Four years later Francqui was named governor of the Société Générale. At this juncture he set up the Francqui Foundation, which he viewed as a complement to FNRS and to the University Foundation (that he also headed).

In the midst of this milieu, under these historical circumstances, Jean Willems, a French-speaking man, born in the Flemish city of Ghent, came to professional maturity. He was not university-educated. The "classroom" that prepared him for his career in science administration was his participation, as a secretary and a protégé of Emile Francqui, in the genesis and early development of FNRS and the cluster of foundations that grew up around it. Francqui became Willems's role model as well as his mentor.

Willems was groomed by Francqui to succeed him in directing FNRS and the University and Francqui Foundations. Over time he also took charge of other science foundations, such as the National Funds of Medical Research and of Nuclear Research that were created by the Belgian government. Whether established through the initiative of the state, the monarchy, or private industry, this whole complex of foundations received subsidies from the national government. But they were managed by interuniversity committees, without direct intervention by the state; and their grants were always given in the form of individual awards to researchers and research teams. Jean Willems, who had progressively become the "boss" of all these foundations, was strongly in favor of confining the government's role in the sphere of science to that of a grant-giving agency. Like Emile Francqui, he was both ideologically and temperamentally wary about too much government interference. In addition he had a personal vested interest in protecting the lobby of science and scientific research over which he presided.

In June 1961, when my meeting with Jean Willems took place, he still dominated the traditional science "establishment" of Belgium from inside "the House of 11, rue d'Egmont." But major institutional changes were altering the premises and shaking the power base on which that "house" had functioned for more than thirty years.

In January 1957 a "National Commission for the Study of Problems that the Progress of the Sciences and their Economic and

Social Repercussions Pose for Belgium" had been created by royal decree. The task assigned to this commission was to advise the government on what could be done further to develop university education and both basic and applied research in the country. The most important idea the commission set forth was the concept of a national science policy, shaped by a "National Council of Scientific Research"—a permanent advisory body, made up of representatives from the economic world and the universities, which would continually provide the government with expert advice and proposals about the promotion of higher education and research in Belgium. Pierre Harmel, a distinguished former minister of public instruction and of justice, was appointed minister of cultural affairs by Prime Minister Gaston Eyskens, with the understanding that he would design an organizational structure and program of action that would enable the Belgian government to develop and implement a modern science policy.

At the time of my interview with Jean Willems, a National Council of Scientific Policy had been put into operation. Willems was one of the appointed members and directors of the council, but he was not at all pleased with what it represented. He was concerned about the encroachment of the state on freedom of research and threatened by the challenge to his power that the new science policy outlook and edifice posed.

JEAN WILLEMS received me in his office on the first floor of 11, rue d'Egmont, at 11:30 a.m. I pressed the bell outside his locked office door. It opened from the inside, apparently through some kind of push-button mechanism that Willems controlled behind his desk. I entered a spacious office that was immaculate and luxurious. Several gorgeous Persian carpets were laid on the handsome parquet floor. The polished wood surfaces of the furniture gleamed. The desk was swept clean of papers. The walls were lined with glassed-in bookshelves, filled with row upon row of leather-bound books embossed with gold lettering. The books, and every other object in the room, were perfectly placed. Framed photographs, lavishly dedicated to Willems with long, handwritten citations, were on every shelf, with the most important on the mantel of a fireplace. In places of special honor were the Queen Mother (of the Belgians) Elisabeth, in a silver frame with a crown at its top, and Emile Francqui. Standing in the corners of the office were two arrestingly lovely Ming vases and an interesting wood-carved African statue. The almost inevitable rubber plant, a fixture of every Belgian office, was particularly tall, well groomed, and shiny-leaved.

Willems beckoned me to one of the two large leather chairs arranged next to a round table near the fireplace. A beautiful old mortar and pestle and a silver cigarette box, inscribed to Willems in English, from the board of directors of the Belgian American Educational Foundation (BAEF), stood on the table.

Jean Willems (born in 1895) was sixty-six years old, but he looked like a man in his late fifties. His sparse hair was arranged as carefully as the furnishings in his office. His smooth face was impressively clean-shaven. His small eyes were pale blue and his gaze coldly imperious. He was dressed with meticulous, self-conscious taste in an expensive grey suit, an elegant white shirt with starched collar and cuffs and simple gold cuff links, a broad, striped silk tie, and stylish Italian shoes. Around him hung the clean, costly fragrance of a good *eau de cologne*. Several times in the course of my interview with him he rearranged his cuffs and his tie. Throughout the interview Willems used the pronoun "we" rather than "I," like a monarch, when he spoke of Belgian scientific research and science policy.

Things began badly. Willems took the initiative by brusquely stating that he was not at all sure why I wanted to talk with him, because I knew a great deal about scientific research in Belgium already—from people like Professor H., University Rector D., and Foundation Secretary V. His comment was sarcastic, and it was also intended to convey the message to me that he had detailed, inside information about whom I had seen in connection with my research, and what I had been told.

At first Willems forced me to do all the talking while he listened with truculent silence. When he finally began to talk, he took over completely. He did not converse but lectured to me about scientific research in Belgium, focusing on medical research "because that is what you want to talk about," he informed me. In his delivered remarks he boastingly emphasized the strengths and accomplishments of Belgian medical research, underscoring his key points through periodic summarizing statements.

The medical faculties of the Belgian universities are "very brilliant," he declared, "especially for a small country like ours." He cited the names of some of the professors of medicine in each of the four Belgian universities whom he considered distinguished scientists, dwelling upon the fact that these "persons of quality" included two Nobel Prize winners, Jules Bordet of the University of Brussels and Corneille Heymans of the University of Ghent. "Thus," he said, "it is uncontestable that we have very good schools of medicine, and great men within them."

Willems contended that since the creation of FNRS in 1928, the history of medical research in Belgium—in fact, of all scientific research in the country—had been one of continuous and "appreciable improvement" in funding and career opportunities. It was the foundation of FNRS by royal decree, stimulated by King Albert I, that had given impetus to the whole process, he said, implying by unsubtle innuendo that in this august company, under the tutelage of Emile Francqui, he himself had played a fundamental part in FNRS's establishment. "There has been an appreciable improvement," he repeated. Just the other day, he went on to say, "we" (FNRS) had distributed sixty million Belgian francs in grants to scientists in different fields affiliated with the whole gamut of Belgian universities. And a law had recently been passed that created two new categories of tenured positions in the universities—chargés de cours associés and professeurs associés—from which research as well as teaching could be conducted. Willems made it plain that as the long-standing director of FNRS and of "all the foundations that have their headquarters in this house," he had played a cardinal role for many years in the advancement of scientific research in the country.

Only two "specifically Belgian problems," Willems conceded, posed difficulties for research. The first were certain drawbacks caused by the fact that a number of university hospitals were owned and partly financed and administered by local Commissions of Public Assistance, established in the era of the French Revolution to organize hospital services, as part of their mission to care for the poor. In those hospitals run jointly by the university and Public Assistance, Willems said, the university did not have the "free hand" it ideally should to make certain staffing, administrative, and financial decisions affecting medical research. The second problem that Willems mentioned was a more general one: the "particularism" of Belgian universities that rendered it almost impossible ("almost, almost...") to be appointed to a faculty or research position in other than the university of which one is a graduate, or to make a career move from one university to another. This had led to "damaging inbreeding," Willems admitted. He quickly added, however, that some of the negative consequences of such inbreeding had been offset by the opportunity to spend time in the United States doing postgraduate study, an opportunity that BAEF and Fulbright fellowships had afforded many Belgian scientists, academics, and other professionals.

In the midst of Willems's rather propagandistic speechifying, the telephone rang. Pushing one of the buttons on the board next to his phone, Willems greeted the caller by his first name and used the familiar *tu* form of "you" in addressing him. As Willems spoke, I looked down at my notes and listened—as I suspect I was intended to. The reason for his previous call, Willems explained to the person on the other end of the wire, was that he wanted to propose "L." for the presidency of some organization whose name I did not catch, and therefore needed to know how old he was. After hearing from his interlocutor that "L." was sixty-seven, Willems said regretfully that this was too old for the formal requirements of the presidency. Before he hung up, Willems told the person to whom he was talking that he had seen Queen Elisabeth the other day. She was well, he said, and she talked brilliantly about the works of Oppenheimer, Heisenberg, and other physicists. But she had aged, of course, and she tired more easily. That was why, Willems said, her son Léopold discouraged the idea of inviting her for luncheon.

When this telephone conversation ended and he turned his attention back to me, Willems seemed more relaxed and somewhat more cordial. He told me that, if I wished, I might now question him further.

Did he think there were sufficient positions in the present university structure to enable the growing number of young Belgian physicians interested in academic medical research careers to pursue them? was my first question. Willems answered it primarily in terms of whether such physicians would be able to obtain financial support for their research. "*Pas de problème,*" he replied. There were various "grades" to which FNRS could name such "lads" (*garçons*): *aspirant, chargé de recherches, chercheur qualifié.* Each of these statuses was not only more advanced than the other but also carried more of a stipend. In addition FNRS gave supplements to young *assistants* with families. Of course, Willems continued, research physicians could combine their research with practice and earn extra income this way. He expressed his approval of this kind of research-and-practice combination which, he assured me, was characteristic even of men as high up in academia as Professors of Medicine B. and L. at the University of Brussels. In his opinion it was "antisocial" if physicians this expert did not see a certain number of patients.

"Can a young physician-researcher apply to FNRS on his own behalf, or must his chief apply for him?" I asked. *Les jeunes* could apply themselves, said Willems, though they had to be under the patronage of a professor. To my knowledge, a young researcher who applied to FNRS for a grant without both the formal and informal intervention of a sponsoring, very senior professor-patron stood virtually no chance of receiving one. But I thought it the better part of wisdom not to contradict Willems or to pursue this point further.

I ventured one more question. "You say that the opportunity to spend some time in the United States on Belgian American Educational Foundation and Fulbright fellowships has helped to 'combat inbreeding.' But do you think the experience abroad may also make it difficult for those who have been away—particularly the young—to adjust to certain traditional features of the Belgian university when they return?" "The net gains of these periods abroad far outweigh the losses," Willems retorted. "If they're not happy here, they can go back to the United States!" he added, in a vicious tone that startled me. And then, as if to compensate for being so undiplomatic to a young American like me, Willems gave his comments a benign rephrasing. "We have made great progress with the problems of inbreeding," he affirmed, "thanks to all these fellowship voyages to the United States, that are becoming more frequent and widespread, for senior people as well as for the young. On the whole, the *bilan* [balance sheet] is not bad. It's positive," he concluded.

I do not know what sort of connection he made here, but it was at this point in our meeting that Willems turned to the photograph of Queen Elisabeth displayed in his office. "She has been a great catalyst for medical research," he stated. Yes, I knew this was so, I replied. Willems informed me that he, accompanied by other members of the board of the Francqui Foundation, had gone to see Queen Elisabeth on Monday. I had read about that visit in the Belgian newspapers, I said.

I used Willems's comments on the queen mother as a spring-board for asking him more about his own historic role as the "master of the house of scientific research on rue d'Egmont." He warmed to this (as I thought he might), and proceeded to identify for me the organizations housed in 11, rue d'Egmont over which he had controlling direction: FNRS, the National Fund of Medical Scientific Research, the University Foundation and its Club, the Francqui Foundation, the Interuniversity Institute of Nuclear Sciences, and the Institute for the Encouragement of Scientific Research in Industry and Agriculture. The Belgian American Educational Foundation is also located in this building, he reminded me, without implying that he controlled it in the same sense that he did the other organizations he had named. "Everything under the roof of this house," he proudly stated, "is independent of the state." And I myself am "an independent agent," he declared. Although he acted as a liaison between the private foundations, funds, and institutes of rue d'Egmont and certain ministries of the government, he said, if these government bodies were not happy with his point of view, "*c'est ça*" ("that's that"): "I do not have to make concessions to them, because I am a free agent. It is our independence that has been the great factor that has contributed to our success" in science policy, he proclaimed.

I expressed genuine amazement and a certain amount of tactical admiration over the number of important positions that Willems held in the sphere of Belgian science policy. He became still more expansive, even autobiographical. "My situation, the place where I sit," he said, "is a very personal one. I grew up with all this. All these organizations were born here and yes, I am one of the fathers of all of them. I coordinate them, and I am the cashier for all these organizations, so everything returns to me. I am not a specialist, not even a university graduate. I occupy a policy position for which the only qualifications are certain human qualities. This is a position in which you are always on a tightrope, balancing. It takes intelligence, I won't deny that. But perhaps more important, it calls for alertness, knowledge of human nature, and diplomacy—these qualities harmoniously developed." I asked Willems how he had developed these traits. "I was formed by a great teacher," he replied, "Emile Francqui." Pointing to Francqui's picture, Willems described himself as the "spiritual son" of Francqui. He was with him all the time when Francqui dealt with industrialists, bankers, statesmen, and the like, Willems explained. He observed him and learned from him. "That was my tutelage."

Willems elaborated on his own style of direction. He did not see many people, he said. He did as much as possible by correspondence. By and large, he scheduled meetings with professors only if the questions involved were very difficult ones. He did, of course, receive people such as the prime minister and also personal friends. Willems compared himself with a great medical specialist whose expertise and services are sought by all but who agrees to act as a consultant for only a very limited number of selected cases. I remarked that his relative inaccessibility and invisibility must make it difficult for many people to know and appreciate the extraordinary role he played from inside this office and this house. Did that bother him? I asked. Not at all, he said. He noted, for example, that there was no painting of him in the building. Will you ever allow one to be made and hung? I queried. Perhaps, he answered noncommittally, if he ever found an excellent artist who was acceptable to him.

"I have been paid all of my life for doing the work I like best," Jean Willems affirmed toward the end of our interview. He worked every day in his office, he told me, including Sundays; and he lived in this building too. "There are those who say that the reason Jean Willems never married," he mused, "is because he married FNRS instead."

"In the future," Willems concluded, with a mixture of wistfulness and disdain, "things will necessarily be different."

MY INTERVIEW with Jean Willems on June 28, 1961, was the first and only time I had face-to-face contact with him. That same day the secretary of the Belgian American Educational Foundation, who had made this appointment for me, wrote a follow-up letter to me in which he said: "I saw *Monsieur* Willems who told me that he had much pleasure in conversing with you." On July 1, as he had promised, Willems sent me a copy of the law that had created the new statuses of *chargé de cours associé* and *professeur associé*, and, as he wrote, a copy of "a fine book 'LA BATAILLE DU RAIL', in which Monsieur Francqui is discussed." In addition he said he wished to "draw [my] attention to the interest that it could have for [me] to acquire another book by the same author, entitled 'KATANGA'."* At the end of 1961 I sent a holiday greeting to Willems and received in return a formally printed card with a standardly cordial message: "Jean Willems was very appreciative of your good wishes and addresses to you in turn his best wishes for the new year." Several months later, however, when my first article about Belgium, "Journal Intime Belge/Intiem Belgisch Dagboek," was published in the Winter 1962 issue of the *Columbia University Forum*,† Willems was sufficiently displeased by it to compose a venomously ironic letter to me on Fondation Universitaire stationery, and send it to my home in New York City.

21 March 1962

Chère Mademoiselle,

As French is familiar to you, I am writing in this language after having perused—belatedly—the article that you published in the "COLUMBIA UNIVERSITY FORUM", in relation to your stay in Belgium.

In it you give proof of your causticity, your thorough knowledge of the work of Michel de GHELDERODE [the Belgian playwright] and your general literary erudition.

Your article, which has the value of a caricature, might call for sharp rejoinders by all persons who are informed about academic activity in my country, if it were regarded by them as anything more than amusing banter.

Croyez, chère Mademoiselle, en mes sentiments distingués,

JEAN WILLEMS

LARGELY AS a consequence of the energy, vision, and the fierce intellectual and moral integrity of Jacques Spaey (the physician who became secretary general of the National Council of Science Policy in 1961), the new science policy program and structure launched by Pierre Harmel were strengthened, and their mission was clarified and enlarged. The secretariat of the National Council

---

*René J. Cornet, *La bataille du rail* (Bruxelles, Editions L. Cuypers, 1947); René J. Cornet, *Katanga* (Bruxelles, Editions L. Cuypers, 1952).

†Renée C. Fox. "Journal Intime Belge Intiem Belgisch Dagboek," *Columbia University Forum*, Vol. V, No. 1 (Winter 1962), 11–18.

was transformed into a real government administration: the Programming Services of Science Policy, dependent on the prime minister. In 1968 the first minister of science policy was nominated and a Science Policy Office was set up. And in 1969 a special science policy section was created within the budgets of different ministerial departments in order to establish a national budgetary program for science policy.

To accomplish this, Jacques Spaey had to deal with the tenacious opposition of Jean Willems and the "traditional bosses" of Belgian research at every step along the way. The fact that Spaey did not belong to the power elite that directed Belgian science and research—and many other sectors of Belgian political, economic, and social life—in the Willems era, and that he was unwilling to make any concessions to them, enhanced their dislike of him. Those who admired Spaey were convinced that he "paid with his life" for this—that his death at the age of sixty-three was precipitated by the great stress involved in battling the world of Willems.

Jean Willems continued to live and work inside the house on Egmont Street, and to resist the changes taking place in Belgian science that were incompatible with his worldview and his power base, until his death on July 31, 1970.

The Salon
on the Rue Royale

I T WAS one of the last *salons* of Belgium, located at 14, rue Royale—the Hôtel Errera*—in the midst of the Place Royale and the Park of Brussels, adjacent to the Royal Palace and the Palace of Beaux-Arts. I rode to the Rue Royale world of the Hôtel Errera for the first time on Tuesday, August 7, 1962, just before noon, in an orange taxi, along the balustrade wall that surrounds the house, past its ornamental stone vases, up to its main entrance, majestically and formidably guarded by two sculptured stone lions on pilasters mounted high above it. It was a ferociously stormy day. A cruel wind, blowing in from the North Sea, thrashed the trees in the park on which the hotel faces.

I had been invited—more exactly, summoned—to a noontime lunch by the master of the house, Jacques Errera, commissioner of atomic energy, because the two articles I had just published on medical research in Belgium, particularly the "Château" article had been brought to his attention. Although as a sixty-six-year-old widower he no longer held the biweekly *soirées* for which his parents and he and his wife had been famous, he maintained a *salon* tradition of daily lunches and three or four grand dinners per year.

I pulled the big brass bell by the Errera gate. It was opened by a maid who escorted me across a cobblestone courtyard to the front steps of the house where a butler in formal attire, with white gloves, greeted me, ushered me through the front door, and took my (perpetually-necessary-in-Belgium) raincoat. Preceded by him, I moved through one exquisite eighteenth century, Louis XVI room after another: over gleaming parquet floors and thick French and

---

*Here a hotel refers to a private mansion.

45

oriental carpets, past sumptuous white-and-gold, wood-panelled walls, extraordinarily carved mantelpieces, brilliant mirrors, gorgeously upholstered and brocaded chairs, opulent draperies, priceless *objets d'art* and collections—a superb Chinoiserie tureen, a rare Roman vase, museum-quality antique clocks, candelabra, and fans—all somberly lit by the muted crystal chandeliers overhead, the austere lamps *de style* on the many tables and consoles, and by the stormy sky outside the remarkably clear and simple window panes of the house.

WHAT BECAME the private mansion of the Errera family was built toward the end of the eighteenth century by the renowned French architect Guimard, as a *pied-à-terre* for the Premonstratensian (Norbertine) abbots of Grimberghen and the residence of their superior. Its architecture was determined by the Empress Marie-Thérèse and her requirement that the families and institutions permitted to reside around the park build their houses in a uniform style. During the French Revolution the abbey was abolished, and the domicile was sold as a national property. It was passed on from one owner to another until 1868 when it was purchased by Jacques Errera, founder of the Banque Errera, who gave it his family name.

The Erreras were descended from Italian Sephardic Jews who lived in the ancient ghetto of Venice until it was eliminated in the second half of the nineteenth century. Abramo, Jacques's grandfather, a banker, had been a member of the Group of 40 who were actively involved during the 1840s in the Risorgimento movement for the liberation and political unification of Italy. His grandson Jacques (Jacomo), who had been sent to Brussels to be trained at the Banque Oppenheim in the family business, settled permanently in Belgium. On September 3, 1857, he married Marie Oppenheim, daughter and sister of the owner-directors of the bank in Brussels where he had apprenticed.

Marie Oppenheim Errera was a *grande dame*. From the time she was a small child, chiefly through a series of Italian and French political refugees whom her Liberal banker-father befriended, she had close contact with many prominent political, literary, and artistic figures. She spoke and wrote French, German, English, and Italian fluently. She was an accomplished pianist with a strong, educated interest in the musical life of her times. She insisted that her two sons, Léo and Paul, study music.

The fields in which Marie and Jacques Errera's sons grew up to excel were far removed from music. Léo, the elder son, became a renowned botanist—a professor and founder of the Institute of Botany at the Free University of Brussels. He was also regarded as a philosopher in biology, a scholar of wide interests, and a speaker and writer of "aphoristic terseness" and poetic gift. Paul Errera, Marie and Jacques's younger son, was the jurist of the family, an expert on the historical evolution of property law in Belgium and professor of constitutional and administrative law at the University of Brussels. He served as rector of that university from 1908 to 1911 and was burgomaster of the Brussels commune of Uccle for many years. Along with his wife Isabelle, Paul transformed the Hôtel Errera into a celebrated and coveted meeting place for intellectuals, professionals, artists, writers, politicians, and diplomats of widely diverse backgrounds and outlooks.

The *salon* tradition was continued by one of Paul's sons, another Jacques Errera (a physical chemist and physicist, professor at the Free University of Brussels, commissioner of atomic energy from 1959 to 1970, and technical adviser and member of the board of directors of numerous industrial firms), and by his wife Jacqueline Baumann.

GUIDED BY the butler, I reached a small *salon*-anteroom where two men were listening to the twelve o'clock news on a Zenith transistor radio that had been placed on the marble-topped table. Around it stood several bottles of aperitifs, three glasses, and a mixture of cocktail crackers and nuts, all arranged on silver trays.

Jacques Errera turned off the radio and came forward with ponderous grace to shake my hand and welcome me. He was an imposing-looking, heavy-set man with a balding head, large face, brown complexion, dark, alert eyes behind big tortoise shell–framed glasses, a prominent chin, and a firm jaw. He was dressed impeccably in a hand-tailored dark suit, white shirt with starched high collar and cuffs, and a silk cravat secured by a hammered-gold stick pin set with a pearl and several diamonds. He moved precisely and deliberately, on surprisingly small, elegantly shod feet. His gestures, like his gait, were forceful yet mannered.

Jacques Errera introduced me to his companion, the other guest invited to lunch that day: Jean-Marie van G., a dapper young aristocrat and engineer in his mid-thirties, associated with the

Center of Nuclear Studies in Mol. Mr. van G.'s skillfully polite preluncheon conversation quickly revealed that his political opinions (Liberal party) and religious convictions (Catholic) were as patricianly conservative as his social origins.

It was only a matter of minutes before the butler appeared once more, this time to announce that luncheon was served. The dining room doors opened, and in formal procession we entered a gorgeous oval-shaped, wood-paneled room painted in French blue with gold-leaf moldings. The white linen cloth that covered the long dining room table, and huge matching napkins, were as starched as our host's white collar and cuffs. The gleaming white-and-gold wedding-band china, heavy silver place settings, serving utensils, salt and pepper shakers, and condiment containers, and the cut-crystal wine and water glasses were arranged and aligned with lavish perfection. The meal was served by the butler, still in spotless white gloves: a spinach, cheese, and mushroom entrée with wafer-thin toast, a chicken dish for the main course, garnished with *petits pois* and allumette potatoes; a choice of various French, Dutch, Swiss, and Belgian cheeses; a home-baked, fresh fruit tart with a dab of liqueur-perfumed whipped cream for dessert—red wine with the main course, white wine with the dessert.

The conversation was as artfully choreographed as the meal. Clever and playful, it was also manipulative and cruel. Jacques Errera was the stage manager, the master strategist, and the virtuoso performer in this verbal *salon* game. The tidbits of information, misinformation, and gossip he conveyed to us were selected as carefully as the food and wine we were served. The persons around whom his observations, insinuations, and questions pirouetted were chiefly politicians, diplomats, and civil servants, as well as several members of the royal family. Intimations of intrigue, mystery, and seduction, allusions to political power and sexual conquest, to masked and unmasked ambition and to outer and inner religious conflict permeated the patterned flow of his entertaining anecdotes and his brilliant, malicious commentary. His most sarcastic and malevolent remarks were aimed at the officials of the National Council of Science Policy, particularly its secretary general. (Jacques Errera "is not averse to making enemies," wrote an anonymous journalist for *Pan*, a Brussels-based, wickedly humorous, weekly newspaper, centered on inside information about political events and personages. "It is my luxury," Errera reportedly replied.)

My own comings and goings, appointments, and associations in Belgium, my research project and my "real" (i.e., covert) reason for pursuing it, my spoken French ("excellent"), and my manner of dress (approved), details of my private as well as my professional life (especially my family and my romantic attachments) also became foci of Jacques Errera's lunchtable talk. Through this ballet of words he flirted with me, entertained his two guests (and himself), challenged and tested us, gathered information, and planted messages that he hoped we would convey to others.

Coffee would be served upstairs, Mr. Errera announced, in the *petit salon* on the second floor that he used for a study. We rose from the table and were led by him to an elevator with wrought-iron doors that Mr. van G., a regular visitor to the house, said he had not known existed. It had been there for years, Errera replied gruffly.

When we emerged from the elevator, on the landing, sitting in front of a big picture window, looking out on the stone lions and the gate-enclosed park beyond, was a big parrot with beautiful red, blue, and green plumage. He was perched on a wooden stand that had once been the base of a tall, eighteenth-century wick lamp. The parquet floor under his stand was flecked with bits of feed he had dropped. Nearby, leaning against a white marble statue, was a generous supply of parrot food in a large cellophane bag. Unperturbed by our presence, the motionless, silent parrot continued to gaze out the window, basking in the few feeble rays of sun coming through the skittering storm clouds. "The parrot doesn't talk," said Jacques Errera, as he held out his hand and extended his arm to the bird who hopped onto it. At a signal from Errera, the parrot began to beat his outstretched, splendidly colored wings in the air, making the motions of flying while remaining perfectly stationary on his master's arm. "He enjoys doing that," said Errera, with the greatest degree of human warmth he had shown since I entered his house at noon. He gave the parrot another signal, and this time the bird spread its wings like a fan—the way a peacock does when it preens itself. "Can the parrot fly?" I asked. "Yes," said Errera, "if I toss him in the air." In this palace of a house, filled with breakable precious objects, menacing shadows, and an impenetrable layer of sadness left by his deceased wife, Jacqueline Errera, where would he fly? I wondered.

"AS FOR my mother [Paul Errera, the psychiatrist son of Jacqueline and Jacques wrote in a personal letter to me], she was the older of two children. Her brother Eddy is [seven years younger]. . . . She was born in Illkirsch, Alsace, in 1902. Her father was a very wealthy owner of flour mills—the Moulins d'Alsace. They moved to Paris. She sculpted. My father went to Paris to meet her. He was not indifferent to the fact that at the time he married her, Jacqueline was the daughter of a monied father. After their marriage, however, her father went broke.

"She liked being 'an Errera' and living and entertaining at '14, rue Royale.' Father loved it. Although she was cultivated, charming, and beautiful, she was very unsure of herself. In an article published about her after her death, she was described as a complex and tormented personality of tragic beauty. She and father led separate lives, but they stayed together."

Toward the end of her life, Paul told me, partly as a consequence of a complicated and psychologically damaging affair she had had with a prominent Belgian politician and statesman, his mother was converted to Catholicism. After consulting with a priest from whom she received a great deal of emotional and spiritual help, she called her son Paul to ask how he would feel if she became a Catholic. He supported her in this decision even though it belied his own religious history. Paul had been advised by his father, Jacques, to "shed" his Jewishness "like an overcoat that is heavy and burdensome to carry." But after a period of identification with the Protestant tradition of the prestigious American secondary school he had attended, Paul had "reconverted" to Judaism. In his own words, "that reconversion was a return to where I had come from—a discontinuation of a false façade."

IN THE second floor *salon*-study we were served coffee in white demitasse cups out of a silver pot, carried on a silver tray, by the discreetly omnipresent butler. Messrs. Errera and van G. and I all declined cordials and cigarettes, but our host lit a large, aromatic cigar and moved us into another phase of our midday conversation.

Now the talk centered on psychiatry: on Jacques Errera's son Paul, a psychiatrist in the United States, professor at Yale University, who "loves psychoanalysis so much that he is being analyzed for the second time"; on Jacques's own short-lived sessions with a psychiatrist, as a result of which hair had begun to grow back on his bald head (". . . but I enjoy my problems, and have no desire to be freed of them"); on his interest in hypnosis, and the hypnotic experiments he had conducted on many friends. Through the tones of mockery and self-mockery, a respect for the genius of Freud and paternal pride and affection for his son Paul were evident.

The allusions to psychiatry led to an Errera discourse on "the American way of life," delivered in English-punctuated French: on the excessive permissiveness—psychiatry-influenced—of child-rearing in the United States; on our high rate of alcoholism and other forms of "irresponsibility" legitimated by American psychiatry as illness; and on Americans' naive generosity.

"Do *you* have a psychiatrist?" he asked me provocatively. "And do you go to him to seek his advice?" (I said no.) "Are you sure you don't have your own psychiatrist?" he persisted, staring hard at my face and into my eyes as if he were about to use his skill in hypnosis to extract the "real" truth from me. I blushed, and said no again.

BEHIND Jacques Errera's comments on his son and on psychiatry and its relationship to the "American way of life" lay the story of his family in the United States. In August 1939, convinced that a major war was about to erupt, Jacques Errera sent his wife, son, and daughter to the United States for what he defined as a "vacation." Traveling with no more luggage than what one would take for a short holiday trip, they arrived in New York City. They stayed at the luxurious Hampshire House on Central Park South for a month. When war was declared in September, Mme. Errera and the two children moved to Princeton, New Jersey, where they were joined by Jacques Errera's sister, who had also arrived in the United States by this time. With the help of the English physical chemist Hugh Taylor, a friend of Jacques Errera and a professor at Princeton University, the Erreras settled in a large house which they shared with the family of an ex-minister of the Belgian government, who had also taken refuge in the United States.

Jacques Errera remained in Belgium where, as a major in the Belgian army, he was the commander in charge of chemical warfare (*Gaz de Combat*), a position he had also held in World War I. Although he later was decorated for his valor in action, he generally referred to his wartime role with characteristically depre-cating and self-deprecating humor as "leading the retreat."

His son Paul remembers his father telling him two war anecdotes. The first concerned an incident in which he was able to
rescue a mother superior and "her flock" from German soldiers. In
gratitude the religious sister said she would pray for him and his
family—to which, Jacques Errera told his son, with his usual brand
of mock heroics and doubles entendres, the Erreras ought to
attribute the fact that they were "saved." Second story: When, in
the course of their retreat from the German army, Jacques Errera
and his troops reached southern France, he contacted the Bank of
Brussels and asked them to send him a certain sum of money from
his account. The bank responded by dispatching far more money
than he had expected to receive. And so, with this windfall of
funds, in the midst of war and defeat, Jacques Errera went off to a
casino to gamble. He never revealed whether he had won or lost.

Eventually Jacques Errera arrived in Portugal. Here he began to
be anxious about the possibility that he would be identified as a Jew
as well as a Belgian, and picked up and sent back to Belgium where
he would be delivered into the hands of the Germans who now
occupied the country. He successfully arranged to migrate to the
United States, and in 1941 he joined his family there. Upon his
arrival they moved back to New York. In 1945, when the war
ended, Jacques Errera, his wife, and daughter returned to Belgium.

Paul stayed in the United States, went to Exeter and Harvard,
and became an American citizen. Every summer he went home to
visit his family and live at 14, rue Royale.

THE CONVERSATION moved on to Dante's *Divine Comedy*—which
Jacques Errera claimed to have just read for the first time—and to
Dante's conception of Hell. Errera was particularly pleased, he said,
to discover that Dante had nepotistically placed the members of his
own family in zones other than Hell, and that God had reclaimed
certain people that he had originally sent to Hell, giving them a
second chance. "There is hope for me!" he exclaimed.

Talk of Dante led to a consideration of genius. Genius, said
Jacques Errera, is partly endocrinologically based. Aiming his remarks at me, he alleged that no women had been geniuses in any
realm. I suggested, Madame Curie? Errera dismissed that: "She
derived her ideas from her husband and her lover." Albert Einstein,
whom Jacques Errera had known personally, was a genius, he

conceded. But even though he had been brilliant in his own field, he was naive in all others—in politics, for example.

I had engaged in verbal swordplay with Jacques Errera on many of the topics of conversation that had preceded this one, occasionally (to my surprise) scoring points. Errera seemed to enjoy my momentary successes in this jousting game that I found both intriguing and distasteful. I deliberately did not take up his challenge that authentic (albeit innocent) genius was exclusively male.

The clock on the mantel struck three. What were my plans for this afternoon? Errera asked me, a signal that it was time to go. Either he had surreptitiously rung for the butler, or else 3 p.m. was the ritually established time for luncheon guests to depart, because the butler was at the elevator on the ground floor of the house to meet us when we descended, and to help Mr. van G. and me back into our rain gear.

We thanked Jacques Errera for his hospitality, and he bade us a brusque farewell. Mr. van G. drove me out of the courtyard of 14, rue Royale, in his modest Volkswagen beetle, to Schaarbeek, the working-class district of Brussels where my next appointment, to visit playwright Michel de Ghelderode and his wife Jeanne, was scheduled.

THAT LUNCHEON was the first of several I attended at the Hôtel Errera during the summer of 1962. I was invited each time by a long telephone call from Jacques Errera—calls filled with the teasing, aggressive, seductive, innuendos of his *salon* talk and of gruffly disguised helpfulness too.

Lunch on Monday, August 20, was especially notable. The two other guests that afternoon were Jacques Errera's sister, Gabrielle (Madame Paul Oppenheim-Errera), and Claude de V., cultural attaché in the king's cabinet. Madame Oppenheim, the wife of an independently wealthy philosopher-intellectual, was a *grande dame* in the Errera tradition and style, with her own *salon* in Princeton, New Jersey. She was also strongly identified with her brother (even to wearing a parrot's feather in her hat) and devoted to him, as he was to her. She proved to be as adept as Jacques in extracting personal biographical information from me. And Mr. de V., an intelligent and gallant young diplomat, skillfully interviewed me about how I had become interested in Belgium and why I had made the medical scientific colloquium on cardiac surgery, held at the

Royal Palace in Laeken in November 1959, the symbolic center of my article on the "Medical Scientists in a Château."

Two critical events occurred at that lunch. The first began by my telling how I had been initiated into deep and hidden spheres of Belgian culture through my visits to the writer Michel de Ghelderode during the last year of his life, and through the extraordinary letters I had received from him. For reasons I do not remember now, I told Jacques Errera, Mme. Oppenheim, and Mr. de V. the story that Ghelderode had told me about his haunting relationship with Cardinal Mercier.

IT WAS at the time of his first Communion that Ghelderode had his initial encounter with the cardinal. Monsignor Mercier had come to his primary school to give Communion to Michel and his classmates. The very tall cardinal towered over the children, their teachers, and their families like the spire of a cathedral. After the religious ceremony was over, the cardinal moved through the gathering to meet the children and their parents. When his turn came to be introduced to Monsignor Mercier, it seemed to Michel that the cardinal stopped a particularly long time to gaze at him. Michel kissed the cardinal's glowing amethyst ring and said a few words to him. The cardinal looked deeply into his eyes; then, turning to Michel's parents, he told them that he felt their son would achieve remarkable things. "He was the first person to recognize me," Ghelderode said. The cardinal continued his round of greetings. Michel had the sense that over the heads of the crowd the cardinal's eyes returned again and again to seek out his face. And Michel could see and feel the amethyst light from the cardinal's ring following him. "That amethyst light followed me all of my life," Ghelderode declared.

Michel de Ghelderode never had another face-to-face meeting with the cardinal. Many years later, however, he happened to walk down the street where the cardinal's residence was located, at the precise moment when a priest came to an open window and made the sign of the cross to announce to the people assembled below that Cardinal Mercier was dead.

More than thirty years later, in April 1962, Michel de Ghelderode's own death occurred. Five months after his death his wife Jeanne found a small unsigned article in a current issue of a magazine called *Miroir de l'Histoire*. The article was entitled "*L'an-*

neau du cardinal Mercier" (*"Cardinal Mercier's Ring"*). It told the story of how just before Cardinal Mercier died in Brussels in January 1926, he received a visit in his hospital room from Lord Halifax of England. Under the aegis of Cardinal Mercier, along with a French priest (Father Portal), Lord Halifax had been a key participant in the famous "Conversations of Malines" effort to reunify the Anglican and Roman Catholic churches. Their hard work and ecumenical commitment notwithstanding, the three men encountered many difficulties that had impeded the accomplishment of their goal. Sensing that he was close to death, Cardinal Mercier wanted to leave some testimony of his hopes that the unification of the two churches would eventually come to pass. Taking his pastoral ring off his finger, he said to Lord Halifax: "You see this ring. Engraved on it are Saint Désiré and Saint Joseph, my patron saints, and Saint Rombaut, the patron saint of our cathedral. It was given to me by a family when I became a bishop. I have always worn it, even though I have other rings. When I am gone, I want you to have it." After the death of the cardinal, the ring was delivered to Lord Halifax. He wore it around his neck on a little gold chain until his death. Later it was set into a chalice that his heirs gave to the Cathedral of York.

Jeanne de Ghelderode typed a copy of this article and sent it to me in the United States with a note: "Could this be the ring that [Michel] told you about?" she asked.

THERE WAS a moment of silence in the small *salon* of the Errera house after I had told this Ghelderodean tale. And then, very quietly, Mr. de V. spoke up. "Thank you, mademoiselle," he said. "Cardinal Mercier was a cousin of mine. I will pass this story on to my aunt, Madame Mercier."

The second incident at this luncheon took place at its conclusion and was staged by Jacques Errera as a theatrical denouement. It was almost three o'clock. Errera was holding something in his hand that from a distance looked like a gold pocket watch. Mr. de V., Madame Oppenheim, and I interpreted this as a cue that it was time for us to go, and rose from our chairs to take leave of our host. Errera swiftly crossed the room and fastened something on my right arm. The gold pocket watch turned out to be a gold-filled bracelet that he had bought on a recent trip to Florence, and that he presented to me—or forced on me—as a gift, in full view of his sister and the king's cultural attaché. What did the gift and the publicly intimate way in which it was offered to me mean? How was I expected to respond? I composed myself sufficiently to express something resembling proper and poised gratitude. But I left 14, rue Royale that afternoon in a disguised state of shock—wearing a bracelet on my arm, clutching a small, blue Florentine leather box to contain it, and wondering what repercussions that gift and my several luncheon invitations would have in the "Old Europe" world of wealth and power, intellect and intrigue, that Jacques Errera inhabited.

Several weeks later I received a letter from a friend in New York City who wrote to tell me about "an uncomfortable exchange" she had had with Gabrielle Oppenheim-Errera. Because of a bout of illness, my friend had declined an invitation to lunch at Madame Oppenheim's house. She received a follow-up telephone call from Gabrielle Oppenheim who expressed concern about her health and regret that she would be unable to be present at the luncheon. But my friend had the impression that the major reason Gabrielle had called her was "to ask about you as she stepped off the boat. Many personal details she sought—which I did not know, and would not have provided had I known. . . ."

Some of the baroque consequences of these few contacts with Jacques Errera were soon apparent. They were epitomized by the obstacles I encountered in trying to make a follow-up appointment for a second interview with Dr. C., director of an important science museum in Belgium, in connection with my study of Belgian medical research. Elliptically in his telephone conversation with me, and more outrightly in the message he conveyed to me through his niece (who had befriended me), Dr. C. indicated that some of the contacts I wished to make had become problematic—because I had been "seeing too much of certain people." One of these complicating contacts was allegedly Jacques Errera who (according to Dr. C.) was "jealous" because I had been conferring with individuals other than himself, and who was also viewed as persona non grata by unnamed figures who occupied high places in the science and medicine milieux I was trying to enter. An even more serious deterrent, Dr. C. implied, was the rumor circulating that I had not only spent quite a bit of time with Count de L., patriarch of one of Belgium's most important industrial and banking families and empires, but that I had received the "inside information" I had used in my "Medical Scientists in a Château" article from him—an article, Dr. C. added, that was regarded by the entourage of Princess L. as a malicious attack on her involvement as a patron and donor in the field of cardiology research.

For a middle-class assistant professor at Barnard College, these allusions to jealous occupants of great houses, scheming counts, and maligned princesses were as mystifying as they were frightening. I had met Jacques Errera exactly twice. I had never laid eyes on the count and had no knowledge of the wealth, power, and culture he possessed, though I dimly remembered seeing his name on a plaque of donors in one of the Brussels hospitals I had visited. And if Princess L. had "court enemies," I certainly was not one of them; nor did I have more than a vague notion at that time what political issues and passions might be involved in the controversy surrounding her.

Even after more than thirty years of visits to Belgium, I cannot completely account for the web of circumstances, personalities, relationships, and issues in which my few visits to 14, rue Royale had helped to entangle me. But now I understand better what the Errera *salon* represented. It was a meeting place for what is sometimes called the "Establishment" of Brussels: a small, national elite made up of prominent personalities from diverse milieux. Their power was anchored in the important political, economic, and administrative positions they held and in the cross section of Belgian groups to which they belonged. Above all it derived from their collective ability to arbitrate, through a *salon*-like process, the perpetual crises and impasses among Belgium's particularistic enclaves.

The heterogeneity of the elite gathered at the Hôtel Errera notwithstanding, during the period of my visits to 14, rue Royale the *salon* was linguistically more French than Flemish; politically more allied with the Liberal party and its conservative, free-enterprise, capitalistic outlook than with the Social Christian and Socialist parties; more royalist than antiroyalist; and religio-philosophically more identified with a Free Thought/Free Mason perspective than with a Christian/Catholic view.

Certainly one member of the Brussels elite and of the Errera *salon* figured centrally in the reactions evoked by my several visits to 14, rue Royale. This was Jean Willems, director and first vice-president of the National Fund of Scientific Research, who was one of Jacques Errera's closest friends. If I had met any "count" in a "castle," it had not been Count de L., as had been suggested, but rather Jean Willems, the political, economic, and symbolic director of Belgian science policy.

In 1962 Willems was engaged in battle with the National Council of Science Policy, created two years earlier by the Belgian government, and especially with Dr. Jacques Spaey, the bluntly forthright secretary general of the National Council who was committed to reforming and modernizing science policy. For Willems, who was angered by my *Science* article, I was an ally of the National Council of Science Policy and of the Jacques Spaeys of Belgium, though not necessarily their agent. And though I had been received at 14, rue Royale, Willems certainly did not interpret this as meaning that his great friend Jacques Errera was plotting against him and the "house of science" at 11, rue d'Egmont over which he reigned. Quite to the contrary, as Errera had made patently clear during my first visit to his house, he was as viciously antagonistic to the National Council of Science Policy and its officials as Willems himself. And yet, in the complex and cruelly mischievous *salon* world to which both Willems and Errera belonged, it not only amused Errera to have me as a guest and to make this known; it probably also represented some kind of challenge to other members of the elite. In turn, they responded with rumors about my relationship to Errera, Count de L., Princess L., and so forth. As if that were not intricately plot-ridden enough, Jacques Errera also toyed with me by promising to invite Willems and me to lunch together some day so that we could have an informal, candid discussion under his roof. In addition, he suggested, he would do everything possible for me to meet the princess—a visit he was sure I would find professionally valuable and personally enjoyable. Predictably, neither the luncheon nor the meeting ever came to pass.

I DID not see Jacques Errera after 1962 for almost fourteen years, though I maintained a distant, sporadic contact with him through articles I sent to him and through occasional news about him that his son Paul supplied. But in October 1976, at the beginning of the sabbatical year I spent in Belgium teaching and doing research, I lunched once more at his house—for the last time.

We had arranged via telephone that I would arrive at 12:15

p.m. by taxi at his front gate, which Errera assured me would be open. And so it was, but my driver was too intimidated to drive through it. As I had done on past visits, I approached the house on foot: past the stone lions, over the cobblestones, up the worn marble steps. The butler (not the same one as in 1962—more loquacious, and with a pronounced Brussels accent) was waiting for me. As was customary, he took my raincoat and escorted me to the *salon* outside the dining room where the silver tray with nuts and crackers, aperitif glasses and bottles had been laid out on the round marble table, and as I approached it I could hear the noontime radio broadcast of the *Journal Parlé*.

The ground floor of the house looked as magnificent as ever, with its wonderful paneling, velvet and brocaded chairs, eighteenth century furniture in precious woods, draperies, mirrors, chandeliers, mantelpieces, and *objets d'art*. This time I noticed a Byzantine Madonna and Child over one of the mantels, a grouping of tiny, ancient Greek, Roman, and Egyptian statues, like those that Freud had in his office in Vienna, and a collection of geological specimens—fossils, petrified woods, minerals, rocks, and crystals.

Jacques Errera had already turned off the radio by the time I reached the *salon*. He greeted me with genuine warmth, and when he said, "Everyone in Belgium is glad to see you again, including me," I was tempted to believe him. This was scheduled to be a lunch *à deux*, just Errera and me. The next time you come to the house, he had said on the phone, I will invite whomever you want to meet to join us.

For an eighty-year-old man he looked remarkable. He was older, of course, and somewhat thinner. He walked more haltingly, and his hands were a bit less steady than in 1962. He also had some difficulty with his hearing and his vision, he told me. But he still carried himself like the true master of 14, rue Royale, with the same erect posture, and he was handsomely and impeccably dressed in a finely tailored suit, white shirt with starched collar and cuffs, silk cravat, and gold stickpin. His voice was firm and strong. His eyes behind his glasses were sparklingly alert. And his conversation was brilliant: wide ranging, stimulating, and pungent—both in French and English.

We conversed over glasses of sherry until Jacques Errera consulted a small gold pocket watch and rose to tell his butler it was time for lunch. The paneled doors between the downstairs *salon* and the dining room opened, and the meal was announced. Errera and I sat in solitary splendor across from one another, midway along the huge table, while the butler served one course after another of a meal worthy of a large and elegant dinner party.

When lunch was over we took the elevator to the second floor to have coffee in the *salon*-study. We emerged from the elevator and there, on the landing of the central staircase, as always, sat a big parrot on an antique bird stand, looking out of the picture window with the house's finest, most light-filled view of the park and the Royal Palace. But it was not the same parrot who perched there fourteen years earlier. He had fallen ill and died, Errera told me. His successor was a South American parrot, with royal blue and vivid gold plumage, who screeched a great deal and talked very little. Errera greeted him affectionately and put his hand out to caress him, cautioning me not to come too close to the bird. "He has never done anything, but . . ." Although I thought I knew what the answer to my question would be, I could not resist asking Jacques Errera why he did not consider getting a Congolese parrot— the species that is characteristically grey with touches of red in its tail feathers, and that is known for its repertoire of words and phrases, songs and whistles, and its mimicked sound effects. Errera's response was in a way admirably predictable: he was less interested in having the parrot talk, he said, than in having it be beautiful.

The upstairs *salon* showed the passage of time more than the downstairs one. The rugs were worn thin, and the upholstery and drapes were faded. Through the front windows of the room one could see a smaller version of the view of the park and the palace than the parrot possessed. The side windows faced toward the Rue Royale, directly onto the construction of the new headquarters building of the Société Générale de Belgique and, in the distance, the empty glass shell of a skyscraper that the Hotel Westbury formerly occupied. Errera seemed to be enjoying watching the building go up outside his windows, even though the pounding had made a crack in the ceiling of his downstairs *salon*. What delighted him was the traditional craftsmanship of the construction workers. Despite all the modern means at their disposal—particularly the giant steel crane that loomed over the structure, rhythmically depositing materials with engineering precision and mechanical grace on its various levels—the workers were constructing the frame of the building in the time-honored way of Belgian artisans, using more wood than prepoured cement, and sawing and hammering it by hand. With a touch of his old irony, Errera commented on how this very expensive way of constructing its headquarters mirrored the intermingling of traditional and modern elements in the Société Générale's structure and outlook, and how much more rational it would be for Belgium's most important bank to invest the money it was spending for a traditional wooden frame in the modernization of its organizational and management structure.

Jacques Errera was now an *honoraire* (emeritus) University of Brussels professor, commissioner of atomic energy, and adviser to the Belgian United Nations delegation, he told me. But he was still in active service as scientific adviser to the Programmation Services of Science Policy attached to the office of the prime minister. (This post, to which he had been appointed four years earlier, was associated with the organization that was the direct descendant of the National Council of Scientific Policy—against which he and his friend Jean Willems had led such a ferocious fight in the 1960s.)

Our talk roamed over many topics. Errera was in the midst of reading two books about Russia, he told me—one of them (*The Russians*), a "reasonably objective" contemporaneous account by the American journalist Harrison Salisbury; the others (*Lettres de la Russie*), written several centuries ago by the Marquis de Custine, when he traveled to tsarist Russia. Errera was intrigued by how many of the Marquis's observations were still true of Russia. He moved on to talk about various works of Belgian art, making appreciative comments about René Magritte's paintings but sarcastically expressing his distaste for those of Paul Delvaux. ("He paints too many women with pop eyes and nude breasts, too many men with derbies, and too many railroad trains." . . .) Errera also made sharp comments on the state of the Belgian economy, which he considered to be far less strong than those of Germany and Holland. Still, he observed, Belgians continued to "like the good life"—good things to eat and drink, good clothes and cars and houses—and they were spending more than ever on these things. ("They are very generous to themselves.") And the Belgian franc had remained stable, which was both "a miracle" and a matter of "bluff."

With greater seriousness and obvious involvement, Jacques Errera said that he had become increasingly concerned about "environmental problems," particularly overpopulation and pollution. In his view these were not only side effects of the unbridled development of modern science and technology, but of the egoistic and aggressive individual pursuit of material goods. The solution of these problems called for national and international action, he declared, and the active participation of an educated public. He expressed the cautious hope that out of this problem might come a "better quality of life," greater "human solidarity," and more identification with "collective well-being."

Errera verbalized equally strong, personally felt opinions about euthanasia and the "right to die with dignity." For him, prolonging human biological life through extraordinary medical means when an illness was fatal, consciousness was gone, or the quality of life of a person was drastically compromised was comparable to the unstinting use of science and technology that had done so much damage to the physical environment. With more serenity than a sense of conspiracy, he told me he had a stock of medications that he had collected for the purpose of ending his own life, when he deemed it necessary and desirable.

Jacques Errera had not lost his zest for talk about Belgian politics, its inner chambers, and its subterranean corridors of power. But this time a great deal of his commentary—largely approving and admiring—was focused on the young, Flemish, often Catholic, intellectuals and professionals who, under figures like the Flemish prime minister and statesman, Leo Tindemans, and the Flemish wing of the Christian Social party, had recently achieved national prominence in Belgian political life, and were now also predominant in the economy and in academia. Through his role as science policy adviser, Errera had personal contact with many members of this new, upwardly mobile elite. Errera was impressed with them: with their intelligence, competence, energy, ambition, achievement, and with the clever way they "played the political game while sticking to the rules." I had the impression they were among the persons most frequently invited to his house these days, and that Errera had assumed the role of a venerable *salon*-tutor for these young Flemish newcomers to the Brussels Establishment.

IN THE course of my conversation with Louis Beeckmans (the dynamic young Flemish director of research and development at the Katholieke Universiteit te Leuven), we discovered that we both knew Jacques Errera and the special experience it was to be received at 14, rue Royale. Beeckmans's relationship with Errera had developed in the context of the National Science Policy office, where he directed the program of social research and where Errera was an adviser.

Louis Beeckmans and his wife began to talk with animation about their friendship with Errera and his *salon* on the rue Royale. Jacques Errera was in good health, they said, although he was eighty years old and had a phlebitis condition in his legs that had slowed him somewhat. But he still entertained several times a week, more frequently at noon than in the evenings. And he still came regularly to the Science Policy office where he had more than an honorific role.

The Beeckmans had often been invited to luncheon and dinner parties at the Errera house. They enthusiastically described what those gatherings were like to their friend, Armand De Kuyper, a young professor of sociology at the University of Leuven, who had joined us. It was a "real *salon*," they said, with exquisite foods and wines and liqueurs and cigars and butlers, and sparkling, witty conversation. Jacques Errera was the host; he provided the meeting place; he introduced people to one another; and he played the role of manipulator with the highest, most elegant, and often cruel skill. It was a still vivid but now somewhat aged version of the powerful Old World "political *salon*" that Errera ran in his heyday, in an era when, according to Louis Beeckmans, ministers and governments as well as private individuals were made and broken around Errera's dinner table and in the upstairs *salon* where one went after the meal was over.

Armand De Kuyper tried to translate what the Beeckmans described into terms familiar to him. It was a "political lobby" then, he said. No, it was not a "lobby," Louis Beeckmans replied; it was a "*salon*." De Kuyper referred to the recent development of the "Thursday Night Club," created by influential Flemish, Catholic political figures, including Leo Tindemans, the country's prime minister. The Beeckmans did not consider this comparable to the Errera *salon*.

Mrs. Beeckmans was wearing a modern gold necklace that her husband had bought for her. It was made, she said, by the Lebanese goldsmith from whom Jacques Errera ordered a great deal of his own jewelry, including the many solid gold tie clips and stickpins he owned. "He loves gold!" Louis Beeckmans exclaimed with admiration.

TOWARD THE end of our time together, Jacques Errera told me he had attended the opening-day exercises of the Université Catholique de Louvain (Louvain-la-Neuve) on the occasion of the university's 550th anniversary, in the company of his son Paul, who had represented Yale University in the academic procession. It was the first "jazz mass" and one of the few Catholic masses he had ever attended, he said, and he described it in lyrical detail:

"The setting was perfect: a modern chapel with simple horizontal and vertical lines and plain chairs. The cardinal, bareheaded, was dressed in gold-colored vestments embroidered with a motif of wheat. There were lovely, autumnal arrangements of gold, orange, and brown fall flowers on each side of the altar. The other priests were dressed in simple, pure, highly starched white garments, embroidered with tiny gold crosses. The clothing was as beautifully designed as gowns made by the finest Paris *modiste*. The cardinal did not spoil the aesthetic effect by wearing his red hat. He placed it on the lectern where, throughout the mass, it gleamed like a gigantic ruby in that otherwise totally white-and-gold setting. I was stirred by the beat-beat-beat of the music that rose to crescendos of joy and contrition. And I thought it remarkable that when the mass was ended, the entire congregation burst into applause. I must confess that I was bewitched by it. . . ."

When he went to get a cigar to smoke with his after-dinner coffee, Errera showed me the box in which he kept his choice Dutch and Havana cigars. It was made out of slate that was thousands of years old, with ferrous markings that resembled a symmetrically abstract modern design. I told him that I thought it beautiful and fascinating, a synthesis between science and art. He responded quickly and silently by moving into the next room, where he opened a cabinet and took out a large fragment of the same slate, plus a little plastic stand to put it on, and gave it to me as a "souvenir." It was a paternally generous and affectionate gift, without any of the innuendos of the Florentine gold bracelet he had placed on my arm in this same *salon* in 1962, and I happily accepted it.

Jacques Errera had forewarned me that at 2 p.m. he would have to make a telephone call to his garage. He did this with his usual punctilliousness. After he hung up I suggested that this might be a good time for me to return to Leuven, where I was living and teaching. Errera offered to take me in a cab to the Gare Centrale railroad station, and then continue on to the ministry for his afternoon of work. Up went the phone again, this time to tell the butler over the house line to call a cab for us, and to be sure to open the gate so that the taxi could drive right up to the front door.

A few minutes later the front doorbell rang. The taxi had come. We descended in the elevator. In the cloakroom I retrieved my raincoat from the butler, who had Jacques Errera's tan raincoat, black fedora, and black umbrella waiting for him. We entered the waiting cab and drove the short distance to the station, where Errera helped me out of the cab before climbing back into it to go to his office. I kissed him three times on alternate cheeks in the Belgian fashion and thanked him for the meal, the visit, and the lovely gift. He said we would meet again soon, and drove away. That was the last time I saw Jacques Errera or passed through the portals of 14, rue Royale.

As I wrote out my notes that evening, I mulled over the curious and touching afternoon:

> Jacques Errera's enthusiasm about the new Flemish establishment and his appreciation of the mass celebrated at Louvain-la-Neuve were not easy to reconcile with the *Francophone*, Free Thought, anticlerical, Liberal party personage of the haute bourgeoisie that he appeared to be in the 1960s. To some extent Errera's seeming metamorphosis may be attributable to his political, social, and historical realism. It may also be a manifestation of the way the ostensibly divisive groups in Belgian society come together at the top of the political system. Errera's Old World sense of honor, however Machiavellian, may be involved too. If people play the political game according to certain rules, and play it with outstanding intelligence and skill, then it's hats off to them.
>
> As for his appreciation of the aesthetic beauty of the mass— whether it is the color of his parrot, the furnishings of his house, the dressing and embellishing of his own person, the food and drink on his table, art, women, or a religious ceremony, Errera likes to be surrounded by beauty. I also think there is a covert religious streak in him. Perhaps it has become more pronounced with advancing age; but it seems to me that it has always been there, masked by what he calls his "hobby"—his continuous inter-

est in hypnosis and telepathy, about which he talked to me today as he did in 1962, speculating this time on whether there was another life out of which we came and to which we will go after death. This, in turn, opened onto his discussion of euthanasia and the medical preparations he has made for his own death. Whether it does or does not have anything to do with a religious sense, Errera's curiosity about life and death are striking, and he spoke today like a man who, within the framework of his personal sentiments and principles, has proudly come to terms with his mortality. And then there is his concern about achieving an equilibrium between scientific and technical progress, and what he referred to as the "spiritual and moral" as well as the intellectual and cultural "elevation of humanity.". . . Was this just humanism?

The master of the Hôtel Errera at eighty is alone in his vast, opulent house except for his staff of servants, his parrot, and also his "phantoms," though those shadowy presences were less apparent today. His way of life is unaltered, ritualistically observed, and minutely regulated by his gold pocket watch. Regally and indomitably, he reigns over it from his canopied bed, his dining room table, and his downstairs and upstairs *salons*. Dressed in elegant, formal attire, he moves through his daily round as fluidly and erectly as he can, on painful legs, with diminished hearing and eyesight: reporting to work every day, keeping up his reading and hobbies, and receiving guests—though only three times a week now, mainly in the afternoon for lunch, because he tires more easily.

Jacques Errera died on March 30, 1977. He was accompanied to the Brussels cemetery by his son, his daughter, and one close woman friend, and buried on a typically grey and overcast Belgian day without any funeral service or ceremony. His passing, however, was both officially and personally noted by the king and queen of the Belgians and by the former king and his wife, who sent telegrams expressing their sorrow, condolences, and sympathy over the death of a man who was "a friend of our family" and a "devoted public servant of this country." The telegrams were sent to 14, rue Royale, Bruxelles.

Monday, July 6, 1987

At noon today I took a taxi to 14, rue Royale, which the Errera family has sold to the Belgian government's Koninklijk Muziekconservatorium [Royal Music Conservatory]. I told the driver that all I wanted was to stop in front of the house, get out of the taxi, look briefly, and then continue on to the Place Stephanie where he could leave me.

We drew up in front of the bolted entrance to the house. Standing on tiptoe, peering through the openings in its battered and rusted iron gate, I could see the remains of the Hôtel Errera. The house was intact, but it was blackened by soot and disrepair. The vestiges of gold filigree work on its façade were incongruously bright. From the outside there was no way of ascertaining how much damage had been done to the historic wood paneling in the *grand salon* by the break that is said to have recently occurred in the water pipes located behind the walls of that room. The parrot's window in the center of the second floor of the house was covered with a thick film of dust. The wing of the house where the upstairs *salon* was located was sheathed in wooden girding. The stone walls, which needed cleaning, had been covered with white paint. All the marks and seasoning of time had been removed from them. They looked blankly white in the summer noonday sun. Inside its wooden splints, this wing of the house made me think of a broken limb in a plaster cast. There was a sign affixed to the girding with the name of the firm in Ghent, specializing in restoration, that was responsible for whatever repairs the house was undergoing. No workmen, tools, or construction activity were visible or audible.

The dilapidated, lifeless old house seemed to have shriveled and grown smaller in size. The two stone lions on pilasters still watched over it, their eighteenth-century majesty undiminished. But urban grime had traced black mustaches on their lips and turned their mouths up in enigmatic smiles.

A Nobel Laureate,
His "Institute-Home"
and "Laboratory Family"

IN SEPTEMBER 1959, at the end of my first summer in Belgium, Jacques Houben, professor of medicine at Louvain University, invited me to be present at a work session that he and Corneel Heymans, a Nobel Prize–winning medical scientist, had arranged.* The meeting took place at Heymans's home in Le Zoute and concerned a research proposal that Heymans had asked Houben to draft on the studies of the interrelationship between diabetes, pregnancy, and the occurrence of various types of perinatal wastage and congenital malformation, studies in which Houben and his colleagues had been engaged for more than a decade. I was invited because I had translated Houben's grant proposal into English.

That first morning and afternoon I spent in Corneel Heymans's company gave me a double view of him. He impressed me as a highly serious, even severe man (with balding, red-blond hair, piercingly intelligent and observant eyes, heavy eyebrows, a thin mouth, and rather haughty, aquiline profile), who was also gregarious, warm and a zestful raconteur. Although he was enthusiastic about Jacques Houben's proposal and totally committed to presenting it in Geneva, as long as the discussion focused on scientific matters he displayed the "stern and penetrating look" that one of the his biographers has described: "as if one were not quite up to

---

*For a country as small as Belgium, it is remarkable that it has had five Nobel Prize winners in the twentieth century. Along with Corneel Heymans, they include three other laureates in Medicine or Physiology: Jules Bordet, in 1919, and Albert Claude and Christian de Duve in 1974 (who share the prize with Romanian George Palade). In addition, Belgian Ilya Prigogine was awarded a Nobel Prize in Chemistry in 1977.

talking about such matters of truth."* But once the working part of the meeting was over, particularly after his wife Berthe May had joined us and we went to a noontime dinner at the nearby Auberge du Vieux Zoute, he relaxed, became more social, and showed his softer feelings. With artistry and gusto he told stories about three cherished friends: Dr. Sidney Farber, professor of pathology and director of cancer research at Harvard Medical School's Children's Hospital; Sir Alexander Fleming the Nobel Laureate codiscoverer of penicillin; and Felix Timmermans, a renowned Flemish novelist and poet. Although his stories were sharply perceptive and fraught with human comedy, they were empathic, even loving.

WE MET again in Belgium the following summer (1960), when Heymans both literally and figuratively opened the doors of his institute, laboratory, and home to me. But before I returned to Belgium I made a special preparatory trip to Boston to see his old friend and colleague, Dr. Sidney Farber, and one of his young Belgian protégés, Dr. Omer Proost, who was doing postgraduate training on Farber's service at Children's Hospital. I learned a great deal more about Heymans from them.

Corneel Heymans was born in 1892 in Ghent. His father, J. F. (Jean-François/Jan-Frans) Heymans was the son of a farmer from the village of Gooik, in the Brabant area south of Brussels— "Breughel countryside," Proost said. At the time of his son's birth, J. F. Heymans had just been appointed professor and head of a new Department of Pharmacology at the Medical School of the University of Ghent. In 1899 the Medical School asked him to organize the first Department of Experimental Pharmacology in Belgium; and a few years later the school built a new Institute of Pharmacology for him, which was inaugurated by King Léopold II in 1902.

As Corneel's father and master-teacher (*Maître*, to use Corneel's phrase), J. F. Heymans had a powerful, direct, and lifelong influence on his oldest son. Following in his father's footsteps, Corneel began medical studies at the University of Ghent in 1911. But his

---

*A. F. De Schaepdryver, ed., *Corneel Heymans: A Collective Biography* (Ghent, Archives Internationales de Pharmacodynamie et de Thérapie, published for the Heymans Foundation). In the course of this chapter I quote a number of passages from this "collective biography" made up of firsthand reminiscences written by Heymans's former associates and friends and published after his death.

medical training was interrupted by the advent of World War I and the invasion of Belgium by the German army. Corneel served first in the infantry and then in the field artillery, and was involved in a number of major battles. When the war ended in 1918, after he was released from the army he resumed his medical studies. Upon graduation in 1921 he married his classmate, Berthe May, to whom he had been engaged for six years.

Corneel pursued the path his father traced out for him, following J. F. Heymans's pattern by initially doing postgraduate training in experimental physiology, and moving on from there to enter the field of pharmacology. Guided by his father, he studied successively in Paris, Lausanne, Vienna, London, and in Cleveland, Ohio. In 1922 Heymans was appointed assistant professor of pharmacology in his father's institute. In 1930, when his father officially retired, Corneel succeeded him as director of the J. F. Heymans Institute of Pharmacology and as professor of pharmacology and head of that department in the Medical School of the University of Ghent.

Corneel collaborated closely with his father on research concerned with the physiology of the respiratory and circulatory systems, conducting most of the experiments on dogs. The two Heymanses were pioneer developers of a physiological pharmacology. The work on the part played by the carotid sinus in regulating blood pressure and respiration, by response to pressure stimuli and to changes in the oxygen tension of the blood, for which Corneel was awarded a Nobel Prize in 1938, was the consummation of a line of joint research that his father and he had initiated in the late 1920s.

What should have been the period of greatest fulfillment and happiness in Corneel Heymans's life became instead a time of troubles and sorrow for him and his family. World War II began before the ceremony in Sweden took place at which Heymans would normally have received his Nobel Prize diploma. Belgium was invaded and occupied by the German army. Under these conditions of national defeat and occupation, it was not until January 1941 that the prize was conferred on him by the Swedish ambassador to Belgium, in the main auditorium of the University of Ghent.

In 1940 the Heymanses lost one of their five children, their eldest son, who at the age of eighteen contracted a fatal case of meningitis during the retreat of the Belgian army from the pursuing German invaders. It was this son who had shown the gift and the inclination to carry the Heymans medical scientific tradition into a third generation.

The conferring of the Nobel Prize on Heymans brought certain tensions to the surface in his laboratory, notably those emanating from the disappointment that Dr. J. J. Bouckaert felt over not having been named a corecipient of the prize. A longtime member of the institute, Bouckaert had worked especially closely with Corneel Heymans in the studies concerned with arterial baroreceptors and chemoreceptors that were integral to Heymans's discovery of the role played by the carotid sinus, and he also participated in the research that dealt with arterial hypertension. He was a coauthor of a great many of Heymans's publications from 1929 to 1939. Bouckaert and certain other members of the medical faculty of the University of Ghent believed that he should have been a joint recipient of the Nobel Prize with Heymans. Although there was never an overt falling out between the two men, in 1945 Bouckaert left the Heymans Institute to assume a vacant chair of physiopathology at the University of Ghent and direct the associated Laboratorium voor Fysiopathologie.

As World War II and the Occupation progressed, in some quarters Heymans began to be suspected of collaborating with the Germans. In 1944 he was formally accused of having aided and abetted the Germans and was publicly censured by the minister of public instruction. He was temporarily stripped of his teaching faculties, and he was shunned by a number of his University of Ghent colleagues, including some persons whom he had considered to be true and loyal friends. Both Sidney Farber and Omer Proost told me they were absolutely convinced of Heymans's innocence. In their view (and in that of many other persons with whom I later discussed this aspect of Heymans's history), the climate of humiliation, distrust, and fear that the Occupation had created in Belgium was conducive to the wave of accusations, and the acts of "repression" and "purification" (as they were called), that occurred just after the war.

In Heymans's case, several factors converged to make him the target of allegations of having collaborated with the Germans. His mother was German-born; his father had studied in Berlin; and his active involvement during the early 1930s in promoting the transformation of Ghent from a French-speaking university to one in which Flemish, a "Germanic" language, prevailed, was regarded by some who opposed it as pro-German "Flamigantism." Probably, above all, Heymans's receipt of the Nobel Prize aroused jealousy and rancor in certain of his colleagues in a small university and city of a small, war-wounded country.

Ironically, his Belgian Relief Committee work made him a target too. During the war Heymans was in charge of the Department of Medicine of the Belgian National Relief Committee, founded in September 1940. The committee worked with the Belgian and International Red Cross and with other Belgian charitable organizations to provide sufficient food to Belgian children, adolescents, pregnant women, and nursing mothers to prevent them from succumbing to malnutrition under the German occupation, as they had in World War I. In this connection Heymans engaged in a number of secret missions that required contact with German authorities in Belgium and, in 1941, travel to Berlin. Talk of these contacts, and their misinterpretation, helped trigger accusations of collaboration. Later he received some of the Belgian government's highest honors for these patriotic, risk-filled assignments he had undertaken.

In the midst of Heymans's greatest distress, when he was virtually a pariah in his own land, Farber invited him to give a major lecture at Harvard and told him he wanted to take the first steps toward having a chair in pharmacology established for him at Harvard. Moved as he was by this expression of friendship and trust, Heymans refused the offer. He told Farber he wanted to stick it out and fight it through in Belgium.

ON THIS same March 1960 day in Boston, after talking to Sidney Farber, I had a chance to speak to Omer Proost alone. He told me what it meant for a young Flemish man from a modest social background like his to be one of Corneel Heymans's students. His father was a secondary-school teacher, he explained to me—"*only* a schoolteacher." Because he wasn't the son of a physician, an engineer, a successful businessman, or a professor, Proost continued, he had many "social barriers" to overcome. "Who, *you?*" people said, when he expressed a desire to go to medical school. His response to this challenge, he said, was a "very Flemish one." It brought out his "desire for combat" and his "bulldog tenacity," he said, with illustrative scowls and thrusts of his jaw, and made him more determined than ever to try. "Pushed up against the wall" this way, he reasoned to himself, he had nothing to lose. If he didn't succeed, he would find another alternative; but he placed "a high value on daring." Professor Heymans did too, he affirmed. Heymans had impressed on Proost how important it was to have the resolve and the "courage to follow your idea."

Omer Proost graduated at the top of his medical school class. Despite the "jealous response" this elicited from some people, he contended, he was undeterred. He "had a plan to realize" that involved more than becoming a general practitioner. He knew that his desire to undertake specialized training, try his hand at research, and aim for an academic career would bring him face to face with more obstacles—"steel barriers," created by patrons of medicine who were not only socially prejudiced against a young physician with a humble background but who stood in the way of virtually any young person who wanted to get ahead. As he saw it, they were afraid of being surpassed by the new generation.

Professor Heymans, "one of the truly great men I have known," Proost declared, had been crucial to him in this struggle. He was not only a brilliant scientist but an outstanding teacher who had trained him, encouraged him, and made it possible for him to do postgraduate training under Sidney Farber's direction.

Proost described Corneel Heymans as "a man of absolute honesty" who "would not tolerate even the most innocuous form of social hypocrisy." But he was a demanding taskmaster in the way he introduced young research fellows to the investigation of the circulatory and respiratory systems. His major purpose was to teach critical thinking. He insisted that the scientists working in his laboratory base their work on null hypothesis reasoning* and try to prove that their own conclusions were wrong. When they discussed their methods and findings with Heymans, his most frequent response was, "No!"; and he made them repeat their experiments until the conclusions they reached were irrefutable. This was often a discouraging experience, Proost admitted, and Heymans could be very "stern" and even "rough" in his manner. But "underneath" he was "a wise, generous, and warmhearted man" who was "always accessible and willing to help young and old . . . without regard for origin or political or religious beliefs."

---

*A null hypothesis rests on the assumption that an observed difference (such as between two samples) is due to chance alone, not to a systematic cause.

IT WAS on June 15, 1960, that I spent my first day at the Institute of Pharmacology, named after Corneel Heymans's father. Located on a canal along the River Lys, it faced De Byloke on its south side—the ancient, university-affiliated hospital of Ghent with its thirteenth-century Cistercian convent and gardens. The institute was built in neo-Gothic style. It was a red-brick structure encircled by a wrought-iron fence, with turrets, cathedral-shaped windows, and elaborately carved doors decorated with fancy brasswork. The front door of the institute was locked when I arrived, and I had to ring to be admitted by the caretaker.

Once inside the institute I could see that it was built around two courtyards that contained a flower garden and a pond filled with goldfish, on which ducks serenely paddled. The institute's library, its chemistry laboratories, and the research assistants' offices were all on the main floor, and in a separate wing the laboratory animal kennels.

The caretaker led me up a winding stone staircase with an iron bannister to the first floor, where the secretariat, Corneel Heymans's office, an operating room, a darkroom and workshop, a series of experimental laboratories, a lecture room, and a guest room that overlooked the garden were located. The secretariat was an enormous light-filled room with high, vaulted ceilings, surrounded by glass windows that were lined with plants. In one corner some of the books, articles, letters, and autographs of renowned pioneers in medicine that Heymans collected were displayed in a glass case. I was particularly struck by a massive oil painting of a sallow, mustached and bearded young man in sixteenth-century dress that hung on one of the walls. It was a portrait of the Belgian anatomist Andreas Vesalius, for whom Heymans had great reverence and to whom he often referred as "one of the most illustrious medical scientists the world has ever known." All the walls of this vast room, along with the wood-framed plate glass that separated it from Heymans's office, were crammed with neatly hung photographs, many of which were signed: photographs of J. F. and Corneel Heymans; of the institute—its staff, student assistants, and foreign fellows; its animals, laboratories, and experiments in progress; and individual and group photographs of physicians and scientists who were part of the vast, international, interdisciplinary, and multi-generational medical network of which Corneel Heymans was a part. There were also countless framed diplomas conferred on Heymans in association with all the honorary degrees, prizes and medals, and civic and military honors he had been awarded. This gallerylike exhibition was made more down to earth by the humorous drawings, cartoons, and aphorisms with which they were interspersed.

The whole institute was hospitable, even domestic—a kind of home as well as a work setting, with its own folklore and its rituals, such as the daily four o'clock teatime of scientific discussion and sociability in which Heymans always enthusiastically participated when he was present. (A Japanese physician-scientist who did postgraduate training at the institute remembered that "like Sydenham in the seventeenth century, Professor Heymans loved to tell jokes which he gathered from all over the world, [and he] used to present the latest one at tea time. We all enjoyed watching him do so with sparkling eyes and with bended eyebrows.")

Heymans's office door was ajar when I approached it. It was a spacious room, almost like a glassed-in porch, with many windows and a large functional desk covered with neatly stacked piles of papers. Like his laboratory, it was a simple, basic place with little paraphernalia.

From the outset of my first visit to the Institute, Heymans gave me access to whatever I wished to observe or read and whomever I wished to interview. He provided me with work space in the institute—including a table, chair, and typewriter, to record my notes. I should feel perfectly free, he told me, to come and go at any time of the day or night.

At the time of my June 15, 1960 visit, Heymans had just returned from two international meetings, one in Prague, on hypertension, at which he had presided, and the other at the World Health Organization in Geneva, that had dealt with multinational medical research and the training of young medical scientists in both developed and developing countries. He had clearly become a teacher, consultant, and statesman of medical science and research all over the world.

Heymans welcomed me with smiling geniality, as if I were an old friend; and even though he was faced with a large backlog of correspondence and other work that had accumulated during his absence, he engaged me in a long discussion about my inquiry into what he called "the conditions of biomedical research in Belgium."

He showed particular interest in young researchers and the educational, financial, and occupational challenges they encountered. Scientific research was a "real vocation," he said. Young people who went down this path should be "irresistibly drawn to it— virtually infected by the virus of research." Their initiation into research should begin at a very early age and immerse young researchers in "the life of the laboratory," Heymans insisted. This was where they received their biological education, experienced the "arduous discipline" and "all the pleasures" of experimental research, and developed the "intellectual and moral qualities" of a scientist. What were some of those special qualities? I asked him. "There is no formula," he replied, but he did think that curiosity, imagination, and a highly developed sense of criticism and self-criticism were important, along with good powers of observation and reasoning, memory, judgment, and both tenacity and patience. "Daring to dare," was essential too, he added—including being willing to "risk yourself in doing some unplanned, foolish-looking experiments." But most important of all, Heymans emphasized, "the sine qua non condition of the young scientist's development is attaching and entrusting himself to a Teacher—a *Maître*," who would direct his first research steps, introduce him to methodology, "give him direction and hospitality," and proceed with his education. "In many cases the choice of this Teacher will determine the whole future of a scientific career."

As he described the material conditions surrounding medical research, Heymans seemed to be of two minds. On the one hand he saw a medical research career as a vocation that entailed willingness to "renounce the material advantages" of practicing clinical medicine. Financially speaking, he said, you earned enough in medical practice to eat "bread with butter"; in research "you live on dry bread." But the nonmaterial rewards of the "research life," he affirmed, above all the joy of being captivated by grippingly interesting questions, gave you another kind of compensation.

Like his outlook on the money that researchers made, Heymans's attitude toward the physical equipment used to conduct research was ascetic. He recognized the necessity and utility of equipment but, as he taught his students and associates, and said to me on this June day in his office, he considered the *brain* to be "the most important tool" for research. ("Use your brain first and then your instruments," was one of his favorite maxims.) He was inclined to believe that too much and too elaborate technology could divert attention away from that truth. Nevertheless, Heymans was concerned about the financial and other material difficulties that medical researchers faced, particularly young researchers in the early stage of their career; and he was especially attentive to the fact that persons from modest social backgrounds, with a real calling for research, might be deterred by concern over money from responding to that call. It was a waste for scientists to be so burdened and distracted by anxiety about their needed funds and equipment that they could not concentrate their thought and effort on the research, Heymans declared. In these respects, medical research and researchers in Belgium needed improvement.

Heymans told me that along with many other Belgian scientists, educators, and civil servants, he was working toward this end. Although he acknowledged that Belgium had many problems to solve in the domain of medical research, Heymans was strongly affirmative and optimistic about the overall Belgian situation. Fundamental and clinical research contributions made by Belgian scientists were "not bad at all for a country as small as Belgium," he said. He was also encouraged by how much better many things in Belgian society were now than they had been in his youth, both scientifically and with regard to the country's linguistic and religio-philosophical problems. When he first began teaching at the University of Ghent, he told me, professors from the different Belgian universities scarcely looked at or talked with one another; and there were frequent brawls in the streets of Ghent between French-speaking and Flemish-speaking university students, and between those of Catholic and Free Thought persuasions.

Heymans's identification with his country and its culture began to emerge. There was no question, he said, that Belgians were very "individualistic" and "particularistic," and that these attitudes could make scientific collaboration difficult. But it was all too easy to criticize the Belgian situation, he contended, and to say that the persistence of such strongly felt differences in a country as small as Belgium was ridiculous. These social and historical phenomena, he maintained, were facts that could not be changed simply by wishing them away. They not only existed, they were deeply rooted in tradition—"*our* tradition," he said. What was more, the particularism of Belgium was not only a negative fact. It was also a source of cultural richness and variety that was a "bulwark against standardi-zation, uniformity, and sameness."

Take the architectural style of the Heymans Institute, he said. Many visitors had commented on it because it was so different from the modern buildings in which scientific research was usually done. It had a long history, said Heymans, but in the era in which the institute was built it was essentially an attempt to construct some-thing in harmony with the milieu of Ghent. If he were building the institute now, he conceded, he would not necessarily make it neo-Gothic; but neither would he choose "standardized modern." He admitted that the high, vaulted ceilings of the institute made it expensive to heat: "You have to pay for this kind of ambience," he added half-jokingly. He clearly thought it was worth the price.

It was not Heymans's individual or traditional sentiments about Belgian particularism and the architecture of the institute that I found so striking. Rather it was his staunch attachment to his native country. What would have happened, I wondered, if during his time of troubles after World War II, when Heymans was formally accused by the Belgian government of having collaborated with the Germans and was denounced and ostracized by many of his local colleagues, he had accepted the Harvard chair in pharma-cology and migrated to the United States? Leaving the red-brick turrets of the institute behind him forever, and exiling himself physically from the history, culture, and landscape in which he was embedded, I thought, would have been personally and profession-ally devastating to him.

At the close of my conversation with Heymans that morning, he invited me to spend a weekend with him and his wife at their home in Le Zoute. We quickly settled on Saturday and Sunday, July 2 and 3, as the date for my stay at "La Renarde," the Heymanses' villa.

IT WAS close to noon when, along with a crowd of festive families migrating to the seashore for a summer weekend of elusive Belgian sun, I arrived at the Le Zoute station. Corneel Heymans was at the station to meet me and to drive me to his house in his 1960 black Opel.

In the social hierarchy of Belgian seaside communities, Le Zoute ranks at the top. Its splendid villas, with their exquisite gardens of geraniums, begonias, and roses and their manicured green lawns, are situated on the edge of the great dunes of the coastline. Le Zoute is known as "the garden of the North Sea." Every year the community offers a cash prize for the best garden. Le Zoute is also a haven for all sorts of birds—cormorants and peacocks as well as seagulls, swallows, and pigeons. As we drove through this opulently beautiful area of summertime peace, the occasional remnant of a cement blockhouse on its now-serene sands reminded me that such violent battles were fought here during World War II that virtually all the villas were destroyed and had to be rebuilt.

At La Renarde *Mevrouw* (Mrs.) Dr. Berthe May Heymans—a portly woman with very blue eyes and upswept dark hair touched with silver—greeted me warmly. She looked elegant in a blue-and-white silk print dress that made her remarkable blue eyes even bluer. I quickly learned that she had recently retired from her medical practice as an ophthalmologist in a clinic in Ghent and was now enjoying being a full-time wife, mother of four children, and grandmother of fifteen grandchildren.

La Renarde was a spaciously beautiful whitewashed villa with a peaked, red tile roof, built in bourgeoisified, Flemish rural style. It was set down in a parklike garden. Roses bloomed everywhere; there were many fruit trees; and a small fish pond, much like the one in the courtyard of the Heymans Institute, was bordered with late springtime flowers. Corneel Heymans was particularly proud of the roses.

La Renarde means female fox in French. A statue of a fox on the front lawn, and a fox weather vane on the roof, watched over the house. For Heymans they were more than decorative mascots. In choosing the name La Renarde for the villa, he said, he was also thinking of "foxholes"; and he proceeded to tell one of his "foxhole stories." It was about two British soldiers, entrenched on the front lines of a World War I battlefield, with enemy mortar shells exploding all around them. One of the soldiers suggests to the other that perhaps the wisest thing for them to do, under the circumstances, is to move to another foxhole. Smoking his pipe with English imperturbability, the second soldier replies, "Move to another hole, if you can find a better one!"

Mevrouw Heymans told me that she and her husband had settled in Le Zoute in 1951 after selling the big house in Ghent where they had raised their family. The Heymanses waited until their children were grown and married with homes of their own before they made this move, which was also impelled by Corneel Heymans's painful postwar experiences. Although living in Le Zoute entailed commuting between the Heymans Institute and La Renarde, Mrs. Heymans felt it gave her husband respite from the pressures and demands in Ghent, where they still kept a small apartment.

In certain basic respects the furnishings of the Heymanses' house, with its many comfortable, overstuffed armchairs, several couches, numerous oriental carpets, array of plants, gallery of family photographs, paintings by local artists, and souvenirs from trips, resembled the interiors of many Belgian homes, particularly those of Flemish families. The living room was filled with family photographs. The largest, most centrally placed of them was a picture of the Heymanses' eldest son who died early in World War II. In addition there were countless photos of the four other children, their spouses and children; a photograph of Berthe May and her fiancé, Lieutenant Colonel Corneel Heymans, taken in 1917 in front of the military hospital where the future *Mevrouw* Heymans worked as a nurse; one of her in later years being received in an audience with Pope Pius XII; and a picture of Marie-Henriette Heymans, Corneel's mother, taken on her eightieth birthday. The living room also contained a full-length painting of Heymans in his laboratory coat by the well-known Belgian artist Isidor Opsomer.

Crucifixes and madonnas were present in various rooms of the house. There were also photographic portraits of Pope Pius XII in the living room and in Heymans's study (the latter inscribed to *"notre cher fils, Corneille Heymans"* in the Pope's hand), and one of his sister Marie, who was both a nun and a physician. Judging from the memorabilia in Heymans's home, there were also two non-Catholic religious personalities who were especially important to him: Mahatma Gandhi, of whom he had a rare drawing, and Albert Schweitzer, from whom he had received a signed photograph as well as a handwritten postcard sent from his renowned hospital in Lambarene, Gabon.

As these artifacts suggested, Corneel Heymans was a religious Catholic who had been honored numerous times by the Vatican. Although he was a man of faith and piety, he was an unclerical Catholic. This was apparent in the rich stock of humorous stories about high-ranking Catholic clergyman that he had collected and greatly enjoyed telling.

Since 1953 the Belgian government, the International Union of Physiological Sciences, and the World Health Organization had been sending Heymans on special missions related to medical science and research. He had successively visited Iran and India, Egypt and the Congo, Latin America, and China and Japan. On Sunday he opened the cabinet reserved for the choice art objects he had received as gifts or purchased during these trips and showed me some of the pieces. One of his favorites was a statue of the Egyptian God of Science, the Ibis, depicted as a large bird with a tiny man kneeling in worship of him.

IN MID-AFTERNOON on Saturday, after we had lingered for a while over our coffee on the lawn, Heymans invited me to drive with him to Brugge to see some of the masterpieces of Flemish art at Sint-Janshospitaal and the museum associated with it. He did not talk much en route. Occasionally he remarked about the country-side, commenting on how close the farmland was to the sea, how all the trees on the prairies had been turned in one direction by the wind, how "poetic" the landscape was, or how much he liked Brugge in the winter when a hush fell on that medieval city along with the snow. Once in Brugge, as we viewed the Flemish paintings together, it was not Heymans's art expertise that impressed me as much as his love of these canvases, his familiar relationship to their every detail, and the continuing freshness with which he experienced them.

Upon our return to La Renarde Heymans took me into his study. He described it as "very disorderly," but in fact, though it was filled to overflowing with books and papers and photographs, everything in it was systematically arranged, including the piles of papers and books on his desk. The study was his true inner sanctum. It had no telephone, and it was here that he kept his most valued books along with his collection of letters, autographs, and manuscripts. This room also contained a striking photograph of his father—a surprisingly small and a rather severe-looking man, with brush-cut hair, thick eyebrows, a neatly clipped mustache and Vandyke beard, wearing a white laboratory coat over his dark suit, white shirt with high starched collar, and bow tie, who stood with folded arms in front of a window of the institute, through which one could see the gabled rooftops of Ghent.

Heymans was especially eager to show me his rare copies of Claude Bernard's and Laënnec's works, his historical volumes on Andreas Vesalius and William Harvey, the several letters written by Louis Pasteur that he had acquired, some of the correspondence he had received from distinguished medical scientists like Sir Alexander Fleming, Ernst Chain, Daniel Bovet, and Alexis Carrel (who had been a friend of his father), and the notebook of quotations about science, the scientific life, truth, struggle, friendship, and love that he had copied by hand from the writings of scientists, literary artists, philosophers, and statesmen. Flipping through the pages with the same delight in discovery and rediscovery that he had shown when viewing the paintings in Brugge, he read one quotation after another to me.

Heymans considered Claude Bernard to be a great philosopher of science as well as the founder of modern physiology and experimental pharmacology. He characterized Louis Pasteur as shy, even timid, but who nonetheless had the strength boldly to stand up for his scientific discoveries and his principles when his ideas and findings were attacked. But in the pantheon of Heymans's scientist heroes, it was Andreas Vesalius, "the Belgian anatomist," who occupied the highest place of all. Although Heymans was proud that Vesalius was a Belgian, he emphasized the fact that Vesalius's contribution transcended any and all nationalities. It "concerned all humanity," he said. Heymans explained that Vesalius had been the first to make a sharp break with the medical obscurantism of the Middle Ages and to dispute the Galenic theories of anatomy, physiology, and medicine that had been taught dogmatically since the third century. His immortal work, *De humani corporis fabrica* (*The Anatomy of the Human Body*), established the foundation of modern anatomy and opened the way to the discovery of the exact physiology of numerous organs. His "Fabrica," Heymans said, resonated with the innovative and revolutionary spirit of the Renaissance. Its every page was filled with modern ideas of free research and experimental medicine. What impressed Heymans almost as much as the world-shaking originality of Vesalius's scientific outlook and discoveries were the violent attacks that his work evoked from Galenists and other adversaries, and the way Vesalius stood up to these attacks and prevailed.

For Heymans, Vesalius's "struggle" was a titanic version of the difficulties that scientists often encountered in the process of trying to break through established ideas. When the criticism of the scientist and his research deteriorated into the personal attacks that Vesalius had to endure (for example, his former teacher, Sylvius of Paris, called him "a madman"), this was wastefully destructive. Under those circumstances, Heymans declared, the best thing to do was ignore the attack and go on with the work, as Vesalius did. "Keep silent," Heymans mused—"the silence of scorn." Science was a human endeavor, he continued, beset with very human failings, including jealousy and envy. But the knowledge and the kind of truth it yielded, he asserted, surpassed individual scientists, their qualities, and, in most instances, their identity. They were mortal and "return to the dust." The ideas and the work went on.

LATE ON Sunday the Heymanses and I drove to Damme and had dinner in a local restaurant. It was here, in the town chosen by author Charles De Coster as the birthplace of the legendary Till Eulenspiegel—the hearty and mischievous traveler and lover of freedom, who incarnates "the soul of Mother Flanders"—that the Heymanses told me what they had experienced after World War II when Corneel was accused of having collaborated with the Germans.

Prominent among those who denounced him, the Heymanses said, were some members of the medical faculty of the University of Ghent and a leading administrative officer of the university. During the Occupation this administrator had pleaded with Heymans to talk to the Germans on his behalf and ask that he be reinstated in the university position from which they had removed him. Heymans effectively performed this service for him, and when the war was over it was this same man who became one of his first, most public, and most bitter accusers. Heymans was formally charged with being a collaborator; legal papers were drawn up, and a kind of trial was held, after which he was suspended from his university professorship for a number of months and was confined to his home under house arrest. In *Mevrouw* Heymans's view, an opinion she stated with passion and considerable bitterness, the accusations were sparked by the jealous enmity of colleagues over the fact that Heymans had been awarded the Nobel Prize. They were small men, Heymans commented more mildly, with little ability or character, and so they used dishonest means. He went on to reminisce with pleasure over how "chic" his colleagues at the University of Brussels had been, and what splendid support he had received from University of Ghent students who drew up petitions on his behalf and held rallies in protest against Heymans's treatment.

Mevrouw Heymans expressed a certain amount of regret over their decision to remain in Belgium after Corneel had been offered a Harvard professorship. She liked the United States, she said, could have conceived of herself and her family in America, and had encouraged all her children to spend some time there. She admitted that to that day she found it hard to forgive the persons who had so unjustly and cruelly maltreated her husband. During the time he was under attack, she said, she had been "like a tigress." When the siege was over and Heymans was officially exonerated, it was very difficult for her—in some cases, impossible—to accept people's apologies, shake their extended hands, or even look at and speak to them. Corneel had been much more forgiving than she, Mrs. Heymans conceded. He is *"trop bon"* (too good), she said, with more admiration than rue. But despite the bad times to which they had been subject in their community and the problems and *"mesquinerie"* (petty meanness) that existed in their small country, both Heymanses agreed they were not at all sure they would be happy living elsewhere.

It was not by chance that our conversation moved from these troubling memories of Heymans's post–World War II experiences to his interest and pleasure in the *"jeunes"*—the new generation of young medical researchers training and working on the Belgian scene. There were many of real quality, Heymans said, remarking aphoristically, "Truth is always young." Heymans expressed optimism about what he hoped the newly formed Belgian Council of Biomedical Research, which he chaired, could do to improve opportunities and conditions for young medical scientists. He also spoke with respect and appreciation about the younger members of the Heymans Institute. As he did, the words of some of his young colleagues whom I had interviewed came back to me:

> Professor Heymans is very paternal. . . . He emphasizes discipline and clear thinking, . . . and he can be severe . . . but he never hurts or upsets you. When a piece of work that you do is good, he says so: *Experientia docet!* But he does not toss you bouquets or make flowery compliments to your face. Neither does he give orders. . . .

He has created a laboratory in which, on the whole, peace, tranquility, and friendship reign. . . . I think the laboratory family became more important to him because of the difficulties he experienced after the war. It was a bastion for him during that time of attack and adversity. . . .

Professor Heymans has his faults, like all men. But he is a good man, even a great man . . . a good father of his own family and of this laboratory family.

CORNEEL HEYMANS died on July 18, 1968. At the end of 1969 the Heymans Institute (it had been renamed the J. F. and C. Heymans Institute for Pharmacodynamics and Therapy upon Corneel's retirement in October 1962) moved to a new, modern, five-story building on the university hospital campus that it shares with the Department of Physiology. In an outer, architectural sense, it is the antithesis of the structure within which the institute was housed throughout Corneel Heymans's lifetime and that of his father. Nevertheless, when Heymans visited the new facilities in 1967, while they were still under construction, he responded positively to them. He would find it pleasing, he told his younger colleagues, to work in the office that had been reserved for him on the ground floor, near the library, and he commented appreciatively on how convenient it was to be located so close to the highway exit that led to Le Zoute and the seacoast.

The new J. F. and C. Heymans Institute of Pharmacology was officially inaugurated on March 24, 1972, almost four years after Corneel Heymans's death. At the ceremony that day, said the program printed for the occasion, "research work performed by . . . members of the Institute [was] presented as a tribute to C. Heymans, master researcher and founder of a research tradition, who inspired hundreds of friends and associates during a life of supreme accomplishment." With an expanded staff and greatly updated equipment, that tradition continues. The institute's main fields of research include clinical pharmacology, pharmacokinetics, receptor identification, and neurotransmission. A great deal of work is done in conjunction with clinics and other research centers inside and outside Belgium, and the institute is also a collaborative center for the World Health Organization in matters concerning essential drug policies.

The most personal living memorial to Corneel Heymans is the

Heymans Foundation. Established in 1969–1971 from donations given by alumni and friends of the institute, it supports research and finances guest professorships. It is located on the fifth floor of the institute in a room housing a collection of Heymans's memorabilia, dedicated to his memory. Here biannual Heymans Memorial Lectures are held and every day classes, seminars, and discussion groups on pharmacological topics take place in a setting where most of Heymans's library, correspondence, writings and publications, photographs, the diplomas and medals he received as awards, and other laboratory-associated mementos that he cherished (such as his favorite cartoons, caricatures, and adages) have been assembled. For André De Schaepdryver, Heymans's protégé and successor who created the room, this was not only an act of filial piety. It grew out of his conviction that young medical scientists and scientists-in-training at the Heymans Institute and the Medical School of the University of Ghent should know something about their lineage and how it fits into the "great chain" of scientific work to which the past, the present, and the future all belong.

A Meeting with the
Rector-Builder

I N 1959–1962, the initial period of my contact with
the Université de l'Etat de Liège and of my field research there, the
institution was undergoing a major transition. Marcel Dubuisson, a
biologist and professor at Liège, was still in the early phases of what
was to become his eighteen-year-long régime as rector of the
university. He had been chosen to fill this post by his academic
colleagues, and his nomination had been approved by King Baudouin in 1953, the same year legislation had been passed granting
the two state universities of Belgium—Ghent as well as Liège—
increased autonomy from the control of the national government.

At the time I met him in 1962, Dubuisson was known locally
and nationally as the "Last *Prince-Evêque* [Prince-Bishop] of Liège,"
the "Rector-Builder," and, along with Jean Willems, vice-president
and director of the National Fund for Scientific Research, as a *Caïd*
(Big Boss) of the country's research policy establishment. He was
one of the most striking figures in the Belgian scientific world,
renowned above all for his abilities as an administrator and organizer, with entrepreneurial and imperial qualities, it was said, that
would have admirably suited Dubuisson for "living in the era when
King Léopold II was carving out an empire, and for working side by
side with the king."

Dubuisson had quickly discovered that the new degree of
self-determination accorded the state universities was more nominal
than real. Attaining the level of subsidization, the size and quality
of teaching and research personnel, and the construction of the
kind of campus and buildings that he believed essential to the
florescence of the University of Liège entailed what he called
continuous "battling with the Public Powers."

At this juncture, too, the University of Liège had been engaged
since the mid-1950s in the promotion and study of community

development projects among urban and rural populations in the Katanga Province of Congo/Zaïre, and in teaching and research at the Université Officielle du Congo in Katanga's capital city, Elisabethville. In addition, through the intermediary of Dubuisson and of René Clemens, former dean of Liège's faculty of law and its senior professor of sociology, the university was embroiled in the Katanga secession.

During this same period Marcel Dubuisson was also deeply involved in the process by which the traditional structure of Belgian science and research was being transformed into a modern, national science policy framework. Dubuisson's role in this connection was dualistic. On the one hand he was a prominent member of the officially appointed commissions that were designing these changes; and he had even been considered a prime candidate for the presidency of the newly created National Council of Scientific Policy. On the other hand, along with Jean Willems and other members of the small inner circle of men who belonged to the power elite of Belgian science, he was outspokenly critical of the alterations that were occurring and how they were being executed, greatly threatened by them, and inclined to subvert them if he could through informal lobbying and subterranean "corridors-of-power" techniques.

It was within this historical context that in November 1962 I had my first—and what turned out to be my last—visit with Marcel Dubuisson. It took place on an exceptionally cold and snowy day for Belgium.

The rector's office was located in what was then the university's central administration building: a massive late-nineteenth-century edifice that dominated the Place du XX Août. I mounted one flight of marble stairs, passing a number of ornate marble statues as I climbed, and at the landing entered the suite of offices of the rectorate. A male receptionist promptly ushered me into the rector's office.

Marcel Dubuisson, who was standing at the door to greet me, shook my hand and beckoned me toward a grouping of armchairs around a coffee table at the far end of the office. This area was marked off from the rest of the room by a small Persian rug that formed a glowing isle in the midst of the somber wall-to-wall carpeting. The office was enormous, filled with light, and very beautiful. Its great dormer windows overlooked a panorama of Liège and its trinity of hills. The rector's large and handsome desk was covered with neatly arranged dossiers and surrounded by bookshelves through whose glass doors one could see an impressive array of both scientific and humanistic works. The phonograph equipment in that section of the office where the rector did his work suggested that on more private and solitary occasions it was filled with music. The art objects were also souvenirs: a big Zaïrean drum, for example, and a tiny Egyptian figurine. Most arresting of all, however, was Dubuisson's geological collection of minerals and stones. Its centerpiece was a massive slice of a gigantic African tree that Dubuisson told me was hundreds of years old. It shone like a gigantic jewel. He had polished this tree fossil himself, Dubuisson said proudly.

He was a tall, thin man in his late fifties with a very lean, browned face. For such a slender man, Dubuisson's hands were surprisingly thick. He had brown, slightly receding hair, a high forehead, light eyes behind tortoise shell–framed glasses, a rather bulbous nose, a thin, wide mouth from which a lighted cigarette constantly protruded, a small chin, and large ears. When he smiled he bared a mouthful of big yellow teeth. He was dressed in a smartly tailored, European-cut suit with a red ribbon boutonniere of honor in his jacket lapel. He gave the impression of a highly intelligent, piercingly alert, and self-confident man with a great deal of energy and a strong personality, who was not only accustomed to running things but enjoyed doing so. He was sophisticated and well schooled in diplomacy, without being conspicuously mannered. And yet, despite the courtesy and apparent forthrightness with which he received me, from the outset of our visit it was apparent that on more covert levels he was taking my measure and engaging me in a mischievous game of wits.

Dubuisson opened our conversation by saying he was acquainted with the article I had published in *Science*, "Medical Scientists in a Château." He did not recall the details of what I had written, he claimed, because it had been a number of months since he had read it, but he did remember how he had reacted to it at the time: "namely, 'it is not exact!'" I would be most interested in discussing what he considered inexact, I replied. No, said Dubuisson, dismissing either the article, the possibility of talking about it, or both with an imperiously sweeping gesture of his hand—that is past, read, and over and done with. The interview had not begun well, I thought, and so I changed the topic of conversation.

I asked Rector Dubuisson whether he could help me learn more about certain developments at the University of Liège, particularly in connection with its Medical School. I had heard, I said, that a decision had recently been taken to rebuild the entire faculty of medicine and to construct a new university medical center hospital, locating both of these in an area of forests and meadows in the environs of Liège known as Sart Tilman, to which he planned progressively to move the whole university. Many people in Liège and elsewhere, I said, had told me that he was not only the master-conceiver of this plan but that he had also been extraordinarily effective in persuading a chain of tradition- and bureaucracy-encrusted public authorities to grant the university the necessary permission and initial funding to undertake this construction project. (I did not mention that in certain Belgian circles these activities had earned him the title of "*Tsar Tilman*.") It was clearly a topic about which Dubuisson was enthusiastic. He began to speak animatedly, without further prodding, encouraging me to take notes on what he said.

The Hôpital de Bavière, Dubuisson explained, Liège's university hospital, was built in 1890. It contained three hundred beds at the outset. Over the years, in response to medical scientific developments and clinical needs, its pavilion-style buildings were enlarged, others were added, and the hospital grew to its current size of eight hundred beds. Dubuisson characterized the hospital's bed capacity, facilities, and space as "deplorably insufficient" to meet the needs of the university and the Liège area it served. He estimated an overall deficiency of some three thousand hospital beds in the region, and he described the patients, physicians, nurses, hospital personnel, and medical students involved in the activities of the Hôpital de Bavière as "suffocatingly crowded." The plan just approved, he continued, was to locate the entire faculty of medicine and a new hospital complex in Sart Tilman. The Bureau de programmation des structures médicales de Paris (Office of Programming of Medical Structures of Paris) had planned the hospital. Rather than being built like nineteenth-century pavilions, the hospital envisioned would consist of six square vertical towers, built around and integrated by an atriumlike central area. It would contain somewhere between 1,050 and 1,200 beds, numerous specialized outpatient services (*polycliniques*), classrooms and amphitheaters, and laboratories for both basic and clinical research as well as for routine clinical tests. Within the modern architectural frame and natural setting of this new medical center, as Dubuisson described it, the triple goals of advanced care, teaching, and investigation could be carried out in a way that combined the highest values of science and humanism, and served the needs of the city and the region in addition to the objectives of the university. With candor and a touch of irony, Dubuisson referred to the delays and "pitfalls" that the planning of the university hospital center had already encountered, politically, financially, and as a consequence of the "strong personalities" of some of the professors on the faculty of medicine, among others. Nevertheless, he exuberantly stated, he had every expectation that it would be completed and efficiently operating by 1969 at the latest.

Constructing this medical center, he explained, was an integral part of his plan to transfer the entire university, most of whose buildings were erected in the late 1800s, to two thousand hectares of wooded terrain in Sart Tilman, a relatively uninhabited forest area in the environs of Liège, on the hills between the valleys of the Meuse and Ourthe rivers. Here, Dubuisson declared, the university would be built in "sections," in a rhythm determined by and synchronized with the succession of grants received from the government. At Sart Tilman the university would have enough space to develop and expand in a setting where it could serve as a "bulwark against the industrial pollution" in the valleys and as the exemplification of "real communion between nature and man." The hospital would be located in the southern part of the land tract, Dubuisson said, on the sunny slope of the hill that descended toward the Ourthe River, where it would have a lovely, pollution-free view. Best of all, Dubuisson announced triumphantly, the University of Liège was "its own master" in this building endeavor. Thanks to legislation he had helped to shape, he contended, the board of directors of the two state universities—Ghent as well as Liège—now had the authority to plan their own construction projects rather than await the characteristically slow-moving and reluctant approval of the Ministry of Public Works, as in the past. Furthermore, a special construction fund for state universities and secondary schools (*athénées*) had been mandated by the government, from which Liège was then receiving 200 million Belgian francs per year.

Dubuisson was feeling so ebullient about the construction of a whole new University of Liège and about its vital "missions" that I thought he might now be willing to talk about the subject he had peremptorily avoided earlier. From his perspective as rector of a major Belgian university for close to a decade, who was also a distinguished biologist, I ventured to ask, how did he regard the current situation of scientific research and science policy in Belgium? Without hesitation and with considerable zest, he responded to my question in an expansively opinionated way.

He began somewhat didactically by telling me that the current state of scientific research and science policy in Belgium had to be understood against the backdrop of the report issued by the National Commission of Sciences in 1959. Dubuisson made it clear that he and his "good friend," Jean Willems, had been central figures in articulating the need for such a commission, in marshaling the political forces that brought it into being, and in promoting the idea that it would be concerned with matters of such societal importance that King Léopold of the Belgians should preside over it. Dubuisson informed me that when the commission was convoked in 1957 he was one of the twenty persons appointed to it. Throughout the two years of its existence, along with the other rectors of Belgium's universities and the secretary general of the Ministry of Public Instruction, he was involved in what he characterized as a particularly active subgroup of the commission—one responsible for dealing with the relationship between the country's system of higher education and its scientific research. With matter-of-fact immodesty, Dubuisson claimed he was the author of that group's final report and the originator of its proposal that the national commission be continued "in the form of a permanent organization of the same genre." It was this proposal, he contended, that was the basis for the entire commission's most important recommendation: that a National Council of Research and Higher Education be established—a central organization, advisory to the government, with a sufficiently competent, nonpartisan, and holistic perspective on the potentialities and problems of scientific research in Belgium to develop a dynamic science policy for the nation. The government responded with "extraordinary rapidity" to the commission's recommendation, Dubuisson said, by legislatively instituting the Conseil National de la Politique Scientifique (National Council of Science Policy) in September 1959. He called my attention to the fact that it was given this name rather than being called the National Council of Research and Higher Education as the commission had proposed—a decision, he declared, that was "unfortunate." It not only disconnected research from higher education, but because the word *politique* had several overlapping meanings—"polity" and "political" as well as "policy"—it left dangerously ambiguous how politically oriented the council was supposed to be.

And how well had the National Council of Science Policy functioned during these first years of its existence? I asked Dubuisson. "It was not created in the form I wished," he replied bluntly. "It has not yet found its way. And it is not functioning as it should." Particularistic interests, especially linguistic and political considerations, played too determining a role in the appointment of its current president and secretary general, he maintained. Its working atmosphere was fraught with "intrigue and distrust." It lacked coordination. It had tried to deal with so many questions simultaneously, and issued so many reports, that it had produced more confusion than clarification. Most insidious of all, Dubuisson stated vehemently, was the way the "independent status" of the council was being progressively compromised. Its secretary general had been drawn into acting as an adviser to the prime minister on matters of science policy. He was not keeping the members of the council informed of his actions or involving them in decision-making to the extent he should. They were becoming mere "tools" of an increasingly political process.

But now Dubuisson had begun to interview *me*: about why my *Science* article had focused on the medical scientific colloquium held at the Royal Palace in Laeken, and on the *château* as an image; about whether I had met Princess Liliane (he would be happy to write a note of introduction for me to this "very intelligent woman," he said); and about my contacts with the medical faculty of Liège. He winced when I told him how extensive and continuous my relationship with the faculty had been since my first visit to Liège in 1959. Just then, Dubuisson hastened to explain, the Department of Medicine was "not in a normal state. It is undergoing a crisis." What was the nature of the crisis? I asked. "It is very simple," Dubuisson replied. During the past year two of its members had become professors of medicine. Both of them were quite young. Working directly under them were several physicians who were contemporaries of these new professors, and who occupied the recently created tenured faculty position known as *chargé de cours associé*. Like the National Council of Science Policy, commented Dubuisson mischievously, the new professors, who "suffer from a malady associated with being young," were largely responsible for creating the crisis. What were the symptoms of their "malady"? I asked. They were treating their *chargés de cours associés* as if they were much more junior *chefs de travaux*, Dubuisson answered. Just this morning, he told me, he had seen two of the *chargés de cours* in his office, and at noon he had an appointment to see the third. What he then planned to do was call in the two professors of medicine, make it clear to them what the status of *chargé de cours associé* meant, and suggest that each of the persons occupying this position in medicine be accorded recognition and authority in a specialized area of the field. "No problem is really difficult, and this one is quite simple," Dubuisson declared. "Sometimes," he added jestingly, with calculated boastfulness, "a problem is so simple that one deliberately complicates it a little in order to make it more interesting, and to make the solution seem more dramatic and impressive."

I was not surprised to hear about this crisis, I told Dubuisson; in fact I had anticipated that such problems would occur. Dubuisson looked both interested and amused. Why had I expected these difficulties? he asked. Because, I said, when I first came to Liège in 1959 Professor Jacques Roskam was on the verge of retiring from his professorship of medicine, and that same summer the other professor of medicine, Lucien Brull, died, leaving his chair vacant as well. Then in 1960 and again in 1961 when I revisited the department, I found its faculty in an acute state of tension. Four young physicians in the same age group had been singled out as prospective candidates for the professorships. It was unclear if, in the end, one or two persons would be chosen to succeed Roskam and Brull. Rumors flew thick and fast; the process of decision-making about the professorships lasted for several years; and in the prolonged interim of competitive waiting, the candidates tried to carry on their work normally and to maintain their usual collegial relations with one another. Then, finally, two of the four eligible men were named to the professorships, leaving the other two to face the painful aftermath. How painful, I told Dubuisson, was brought home to me by an observation I made when I visited the Hôpital de Bavière this past summer. I noticed that the new professors of medicine now had special parking spaces in front of the hospital, designated by signs printed with their names and titles. It would be very hard to be the two physicians who did not become professors, I thought, and see those signs every working day for years to come. Dubuisson grinned and retorted, "But everyone can't be a professor!" That's true, I agreed, but, I continued, the competition for these professorships had been particularly intense and protracted, and in the Belgian academic system the two men passed over had not only forfeited any future possibility of becoming a professor in their own university but had virtually no chance to increase their status and advance their career by moving to another university.

"You are a terrible woman!" exclaimed Dubuisson, grinning more broadly than ever. "People should be afraid to say things to you, he said playfully, because you are a woman who can see right through them." It was obvious that he was greatly enjoying himself. He glanced at his watch. It was almost noon, he said. Would I be free to have lunch with him? I said I would be delighted to accept his invitation. Before we went to lunch, however, he said, he had an appointment to see one of the *chargés de cours associés* in medicine who had not been named a professor. This meeting should not take long, he assured me. I could wait for him in his secretary's office and peruse the copy of the National Commission of Sciences' 1959 report on Belgian scientific research that he had already told me I could borrow from him.

I waited no more than fifteen minutes before Dubuisson rang for his secretary to announce that he was ready to go to lunch with me. Dubuisson and I descended the ornately ugly, grand staircase and proceeded through the front door of the building where his car (a Mercedes-Benz) and chauffeur were awaiting us. In a commandeering tone of voice, Dubuisson ordered the chauffeur to drive us to a restaurant called Le Canadien, and when, in a matter of minutes, we arrived there he instructed the driver to come back to pick us up between 2:00 and 2:15 p.m., so that he would be in time to attend a scheduled meeting at 2:30.

No one was in the cloakroom to check our coats as we entered this small, comfortable-looking restaurant furnished in 1890s style.

Dubuisson impatiently called for someone to take our coats, to which the manager of the restaurant immediately and apologetically responded. Dubuisson asked if the corner table were free, and we were unhesitatingly escorted to it. There, near a large tank filled with big tropical fish, we ate our noonday meal. Several waiters hovered around our table. Without looking at a menu, Dubuisson began to order for both of us: oysters for two, with two glasses of vodka; and for the main course, venison *au poivre*, and the appropriate wine to go with it. Then he settled down to converse with me.

He began with remarks that I suspected were preplanned, about the young researchers of Belgium being really good scientists. They also had a collaborative outlook and a teamwork approach, he affirmed, that would help to remedy the "too individualistic" characteristics of their seniors. With the "maturation" of the *jeunes* over the next decade or two, he predicted, there would be a "natural evolution" in the Belgian system "in their direction."

Dubuisson deftly steered the conversation toward the nature of the contact I had had with Jean Willems, director of the National Foundation of Scientific Research. Had I seen *Monsieur* Willems? he asked me. Not on this visit, I replied, though I had visited him last year, in his office on the Rue d'Egmont, and upon my return to Belgium I had written to ask him if he would be willing to grant me another interview. In the note of reply I had received from Willems, I explained to Dubuisson, he had said he was too busy to receive me, and had nothing to add to what he had already told me; but if I had any specific questions to ask him, I should send them to him in written form and he would make an effort to answer them. Jean Willems and he were the closest of friends, said Dubuisson, smiling cryptically. If I wished, he continued, he could make arrangements for the two of us to meet. I told Dubuisson I would appreciate his help. It seemed to me impolite to be continually "turning around" Willems as I pursued my research; I would rather discuss things with him directly. I was also genuinely interested in talking in more detail about Belgian science policy with the man who had had such influence upon it for so long. But I was not very optimistic about Willems's willingness to see me.

Dubuisson agreed. What he would do, he proposed, was invite Jean Willems and me to his apartment in Brussels some evening for a cocktail, and then the three of us would go out to dinner together. By the end of the evening, he was certain, all would be forgiven and forgotten. And I would see for myself that Jean Willems was an unusual person, Dubuisson averred—an exceptionally intelligent man with many relationships in all Belgian milieux.

Willems and he usually saw eye-to-eye on most matters, Dubuisson contended, and they often constituted a "united front" in the many "combats they had waged to develop scientific research in Belgium." In fact, Dubuisson went as far as to say, "Jean Willems and I are the only men who are really making science policy in this country." Of course, he conceded, Willems was now in his sixties and was beginning to get more "irritated" with these problems and how they were currently being handled. Was Willems considering making way for a successor? I asked. That had not yet been decided, Dubuisson replied curtly.

Dubuisson moved on to another subject. This time it was Belgium's "linguistic problem," to which he claimed I had attached too much importance in my *Science* article. It was "not a real problem," Dubuisson declared provocatively; it was an "artificial" one, created more by the machinations and ineptitude of politicians than by the sentiments of ordinary Belgian citizens. Dubuisson was highly critical of what he considered the indecisive, unforceful way that Prime Minister Théo Lefèvre was handling the demands of the two linguistic communities. The only really strong, competent, and independent man in Belgian political life at this time, he contended, was Paul-Henri Spaak, the minister of foreign affairs. But even Spaak did not meet with Dubuisson's unmitigated approval. Spaak was *too* independent, Dubuisson added; fundamentally he was "always Spaak-ist."

No matter the issue, Dubuisson continued, Belgian politicians made so many concessions to particularistic groups, forging so many compromises to placate them, that they ended up being ineffective. That was why he preferred to be rector of the University of Liège, in his "own village," as he put it, rather than accept any of the several political positions that had been offered to him. He had much more influence on government officials, and much more chance of getting things done—of benefit to his country as well as to his university—as rector, he alleged, than as a politician. He assured me that Jean Willems felt the same way. That was why Willems never had and never would consider a political office.

Dubuisson cited his own professional history as a personal

example of the fact that the linguistic problem was "not a real one." Although he was the rector of a French-speaking university, he said, his origins were Flemish. He was born and brought up in Courtrai, in West Flanders. French was his primary language, but he also spoke Flemish. All his undergraduate and graduate education took place at the University of Ghent—in French—from which he received his doctorate in the natural sciences in 1924. After that he worked for several years in the anatomy section of the Medical School of Ghent University, first as a prosector in the anatomy laboratory and later as an assistant on Professor Georges Leboucq's human anatomy service. In 1931, by which time the University of Ghent had become completely Flemish, Jules Duesberg, holder of the chair in anatomy at the University of Liège, and rector of the university, arranged for him to become the first occupant of a new chair in general, plant, and animal biology attached to Liège's faculty of sciences. As a *Flamand*, albeit a French-speaking one, Dubuisson affirmed, he had had a very successful career in a French university. In 1936 he became a *professeur ordinaire* and in 1953, rector.

Listening to this synopsis of Dubuisson's professional history, I was impressed, and I said so. But rather than demonstrating how inconsequential the linguistic problem had been in his life, I thought to myself—the message that Dubuisson had tried to convey to me—his story did just the opposite. To be sure, though he had graduated from a university in Flanders, all but the first few years of his academic career had been situated in the major university of Wallony. But his "passage" from one to the other was an exceptional rather than a general pattern in Belgium, and what was more, it had been precipitated by the "flamandization" of the University of Ghent.

IT WAS on the subject of sociology that Dubuisson chose to spar with me next. Frankly, he said, although he saw the need for sociology as a humanizing discipline, he did not have much regard for it as a field, or for the people he knew who practiced it. Perhaps through me and my work, however, he coyly remarked, he would achieve greater rapport with sociology. The problem with "the sociologists in certain places" in his country, Dubuisson complained, was how deeply involved they were in the polity. Under those circumstances they could scarcely be expected to do sociological research that was objective and valid. He paternalistically advised me "not to be too influenced by such people." Dubuisson made his admonition more concrete. Quite frankly, he stated, he was referring especially to Arthur Doucy, professor of sociology at the Université Libre de Bruxelles and director of its Institut de Sociologie Solvay.

I knew that in the tangled history of secession of the Katanga Province from the newly independent former Belgian Congo, which had occurred in July 1960, Doucy had played a key role as an adviser to the so-called Katanga Cartel. This was an alliance of the *Balubakat*, *Atcar*, and *Fédéka* tribally based Congolese political associations that took a militant stance in favor of a unified Congo (with decentralization of power) and against separatism. But I was also aware of the fact that members of the University of Liège's social science faculty were just as politically engaged in the Congo as their University of Brussels counterparts, albeit on the opposite side of the Katanga question. These Liège sociologists were committed advocates of the autonomy of the Katanga within a federal Congolese state. Paramount among them was Professor René Clémens, who had not only taught at the State University of the Congo in Elisabethville, and directed action research in several Katangese communities, but was also the author of the constitution of Katanga and one of the chief advisers and supporters of Moïse Tshombe's presidency of the secessionist state of Katanga.

Dubuisson never mentioned Clémens's name and activities. I decided it would be self-defeating for me to do so, or to confront him in any way with my knowledge of the intensely politicized sociology practiced by faculty at his own university.

Dubuisson expanded on the dangers that Brussels and its university held for me if I were not on guard and spent too much time in that setting. Above and beyond its sociologists and Institut Solvay, he maintained, the "atmosphere" of Brussels was "very special." He could well understand why it was convenient and practical for me to be living in that city, he said, but it would end up "prejudicing" me in many ways if I did not get away from Brussels as much as possible and deepen my knowledge of other Belgian university milieux. In this connection, he suggested, if I were willing to spend a week or ten days in Liège, he would let me stay in a guest apartment he had at his disposal, provide me with a car, and help me set up a program that would enable me to become better acquainted with the University of Liège and its environs, including the beautiful Ardennes. In addition, Dubuisson offered to meet with me a number of times during my stay in Liège to discuss my observations and experiences. I thanked him warmly for his invitation, saying that I would like to make practical arrangements for this visit to Liège either before I returned to the United States at the end of January or when I came back to Belgium again in June.

Dubuisson's next conversational move was an aggressive one. Turning his attention to the fact that I was an American, he told me he had spent time as a young research fellow in the United States in the 1930s, both at the Marine Biological Laboratory in Woods Hole, Massachusetts, and at the Rockefeller Institute in New York. Frankly, he confided in me, he had not enjoyed his experiences in either of these institutions, nor had he liked the United States very much. To be sure, Woods Hole and Rockefeller were remarkably well equipped and filled with highly talented, even celebrated American and foreign scientists. But in both places, he contended, there was a minimum of interchange and collaboration between the assembled researchers: Woods Hole was overcrowded and inclined to favor the American scientists working there; Rockefeller was overly organized and centralized in what he characterized as typically American. Dubuisson's sharp criticisms of his youthful experiences in America served as a springboard for his bitter verbal attack on what he regarded as the essentially anti-Belgian way in which the United States was then exerting pressure on Belgium, directly and through the United Nations, to support the reintegration of Katanga into the Republic of the Congo, and on the "stupid innocence" with which America's handling of the Cuban missile crisis was playing into the hands of the Russians. He had to admit, proclaimed Dubuisson, that after the Soviet Union the country he disliked most was the United States!

By this time we had finished our *macédoine de fruits* dessert and were ready for our coffee, which we drank in the next room, where demitasse cups had been set out for us on a small table near a window. Dubuisson rapped on the table and ordered the coffee to be served.

Would I be free to dine with him in Brussels on some evening in the near future? Dubuisson asked. When I said I would be glad to do so, he referred once again to the possibility of asking Jean Willems to join us, so that by the end of the evening the animosity between us would be dispelled and we would "all be friends."

Consulting a small appointment book, he suggested that we dine together on Thursday evening, December 13, in Brussels, where he had a number of professional appointments that day. We would meet at his apartment, have a drink together, and then go to a restaurant for dinner. Did I like to watch dancing? he asked. Very much, I replied, assuming that he was thinking of taking me to the ballet after the meal, or perhaps to a modern dance performance. But no! What he had in mind was going to the Black and White Club in Brussels, where we could watch people dance the Twist and "make an informal sociological study of it." It was good to get out, enjoy oneself, and shed some of one's inhibitions, he suggested.

Dubuisson now signaled that it was time to be on our way. Since he was not presented with a bill, I assumed he had a running charge account with the restaurant. It was snowing when we left the place, and Dubuisson's chauffered car was not waiting for us in front as he had expected. He was both perplexed and annoyed. "This never happens," he commented. In a matter of minutes a different car, driven by another chauffeur, drew up to the curb. The driver explained to Dubuisson that his own chauffeur had become acutely ill with a high temperature while we were lunching. As we rode back to the university Dubuisson remarked on how "inconvenient" it was that the chauffeur was sick, because he had hoped to leave town tomorrow on a hunting trip and be driven to his destination by car. He needed to get away from this from time to time, he sighed, because his life as rector was "terrible"—"so full of tension." At least, I said, he had the satisfaction of knowing that what he was trying to achieve as rector was important. Dubuisson smiled pensively. "I don't know," he mused. "Whatever one does today is likely to look pretty ridiculous ten years from now."

We had arrived back at the central administration building of the university where the car stopped at a side entrance. Dubuisson said goodbye, shook my hand, exited from the car, and told the chauffeur to drive me to the train station. Inside the glass doors of the building, he turned around, grinned at me, and waved like a schoolboy.

TO SAY that this was a complex encounter is more than an understatement. On one level Marcel Dubuisson, a "national personality" of Belgium as well as the rector of one of its major universities, treated me with courtesy, generosity, and a certain gallantry. He spent more than three hours of his busy schedule with me. He not only received me in his office but squired me to an elegant lunch and invited me to dine with him at a future date. In addition he offered to help me with my research by giving me privileged access to his university, making himself available for future interviews, and acting as a personal emissary and negotiator with Jean Willems. But it was also true that throughout this visit he was constantly playing and jousting with me, teasing and testing me, patronizing and manipulating me, and also flirting with me. At a number of points in our conversation—especially when he was alluding to the country's science policy, the linguistic problem, and the politicization of Belgian sociology—he presented me with facts that were slanted in a calculatedly political and self-aggrandizing way. Beneath the surface of his graciousness and considerable charm were layers of sarcasm, hostility, and aggression which he displayed when it suited his purpose—for example, in expressing his disapproval of sociologists, in acerbically criticizing the secretary general of the National Council of Science Policy and some of Belgium's prominent statesmen, in belittling renowned American scientific institutes, and in denouncing American foreign policy. Yet there were still other respects in which he was candid, witty, and entertaining. He was intelligent, too, and shrewdly perceptive enough to recognize that I knew too much about a variety of Belgian milieux and personages to accept everything he tried to make me believe about them.

In many ways this meeting with Dubuisson reminded me of the atmosphere that prevailed and the scenarios that were played out in Jacques Errera's house on the Rue Royale, where he often received members of the country's Establishment—to which, in fact, Dubuisson belonged. Although I passed Dubuisson's challenges and tests, I did not enjoy the time I spent with him. I knew that the way he treated me was a stylized game, but it was a game that repelled and frightened me. I was not looking forward to dinner in Brussels with *Monsieur* Dubuisson.

In the end, that dinner never came to pass.

ON MONDAY morning, December 10, 1962, the following news items in Brussels's French-language newspaper, *Le Soir*, caught my special attention:

EMERGENCY MEETING OF COUNCIL
OF MINISTERS CONVENED

*Mr. Spaak Explains the Development
of the Situation in the Congo*

Summoned by telegram Saturday, the Ministers met in council on Monday morning, presided over by Mr. Théo Lefèvre.

No communiqué was issued at the close of the meeting, and the ministers were unusually reserved about what was discussed.

Nevertheless, we learned that Mr. Spaak, Minister of Foreign Affairs, gave a report to his colleagues on the development of the situation in the Congo, especially on the position taken with regard to Katanga.

MR. DUBUISSON ON MISSION
TO TSHOMBE?

*The Rector of the University
of Liège Has Left for E'ville*

According to Liège University circles, Mr. Dubuisson, Rector of the University of Liège, has left for Elisabethville.

These sources believe that, traveling outside his function as Rector, he was entrusted by the Belgian Government with a mission to Mr. Tshombe.

Early in the afternoon of December 10 I received a telephone call from Dubuisson's secretary. Perhaps I had read about it already in the newspapers, she said. Mr. Dubuisson was suddenly obliged to go abroad and would not be returning to Belgium until sometime the next week. So, regretfully, my dinner appointment with him on Thursday evening (December 13) in Brussels would have to be canceled. But Mr. Dubuisson would call me as soon as possible upon his return.

In the days that followed, the rumor that Dubuisson had been sent on an official mission to the Congo by Belgian authorities to confer with the president of Katanga, Moïse Tshombe, was confirmed. Dubuisson's task was to persuade Tshombe to accept the so-called Thant Plan of the United Nations (whose military troops were occupying Katanga). U Thant, secretary general of the UN, considered this plan to bring about a peaceful reintegration of

Katanga into the Congo as a final, nonnegotiable attempt at conciliation; it was supported by the Americans and the British as well as the Belgian government.

At first it appeared that Dubuisson's mission had been successful. According to news reports, when he returned to Belgium on December 17 he delivered a message of "cautious optimism" to Spaak concerning Tshombe's willingness to resolve the Katanga secession peacefully. But on December 24 battles broke out between United Nations troops and the Katangese gendarmery. Tshombe ordered a cease-fire which the gendarmery ignored. UN troops then attacked and cleared Katangese roadblocks around the capital city of Elisabethville, and captured the gendarmery headquarters. Tshombe retaliated by calling on the Katangan population to struggle against the UN forces, using all means at their disposal. He also threatened to practice a scorched-earth policy that would destroy the economic potential of the great Union Minière du Haut-Katanga mining company (the world's foremost producer of cobalt and third-largest producer of copper) and the entire economy of the region. UN forces moved on to occupy the mining center of Kipushi and marched from there toward Kolwezi, where the Katangan ministers and the last gendarmery unit were assembled. Not until January 14, when Tshombe arrived in Kolwezi from Elisabethville, did the Katangan ministers send a declaration to Spaak stating that they were ready to proclaim the end of secession, to allow UN troops freedom of movement throughout Katanga, and to return to Elisabethville to implement the U Thant plan.

On Saturday evening, December 29, in the midst of this turbulent finale to the Katanga secession, and one of the coldest, snowiest, and most prosperous Christmas seasons that Europe and Belgium had experienced for many years, I boarded a Sabena plane bound for Léopoldville and my first visit to the Congo. I had known I would be making this trip when I met with Dubuisson; but in light of the delicacy of the Katangese situation, Belgian sensitivity about it, the circles of influence of which Dubuisson was a part, his strong feelings about American involvement in the Congo, and the kind of public attention that my *Château* article was receiving, I thought it judicious not to mention to Dubuisson that I would soon be going to the Congo. When I opened my morning newspaper on December 10 and read about the Katanga mission on which he had been sent, I knew that maintaining silence about my forthcoming journey to the Congo had been a wise move.

ON NOVEMBER 6, 1967, the 150th anniversary of the University of Liège and the official inauguration of its new Sart Tilman campus were conjointly celebrated. Marcel Dubuisson played the role of master impresario for the occasion. In order to "pay homage" to the University of Liège, which he characterized as a *"grande dame* of culture and the mind," he mounted two days of ceremonies that began with an academic convocation at which *Doctors Honoris Causa* were presented to King Baudouin ("in gratitude for the vigilant interest he accords to higher education and research") and to thirty scholars from different disciplines, universities, and countries. The invited guest list, drawn up with the intent of assembling at Liège a broad spectrum of "noteworthy persons from the academic, political, religious, and military worlds," included three hundred university rectors representing forty-three countries, sixty ambassadors, and the highest Belgian authorities. At the inception of the proceedings Queen Fabiola was presented with a bouquet of "Sart Tilman" orchids: a variety that had been specially cultivated from seventeen crossings of nine species, by two generations of specialists, over sixty-five years. After a series of speeches, musical interludes, sumptuous meals, and symbolic acts, such as the signing of a special *Livre d'Or* (Visitor's Book) stamped with a new coat of arms granted by the state to the University of Liège for this occasion, the king cut the ribbon that was hung in front of a big white model (*maquette*) of Sart Tilman.

In the speech that Dubuisson delivered at the inauguration, he not only thanked all his collaborators who had helped him to realize what he called this "undertaking of faith" but also affirmed that "in participating in this faith" he had "experienced the most exalting moments of [his] career." Yet, only four years later, in September 1971, Marcel Dubuisson resigned as rector, in protest against the law passed by the government on July 27, 1971, that reformed the national system of funding and administering Belgian universities. The legislation was a response to the expansion and democratization of higher education, the linguistic splitting of the private universities (Brussels and Louvain), and the student uprisings associated with these changes that had taken place in the 1960s. The goal of the law was to achieve equality between the universities in the country, independently of their ideological orientation or their public or private status, by creating "analogous conditions of financing, management, and autonomy" for them all. As a means of insuring this equality, the law set forth a common set of norms for determining the amount of money that each university would receive annually from the government. The chief criteria for subsidization were the number of students enrolled in the university in different fields and faculties, in relationship to the proportion of university personnel and the average cost of a personnel member (estimated on the basis of two teachers for three researchers).

In addition, with the aim of establishing better budgetary and organizational control within the universities, the legislation created a structural division within their management between the rector, who was defined as responsible for academic affairs, and the administrator—a new role created by the law—who would deal with the university's financial situation and its nonacademic functions. In Dubuisson's view this new law placed the State University of Liège under a regime of budgetary stagnation in order to free extra funds for the private universities. It permitted the government to block all decisions made by the university's board of directors regarding the recruitment and promotion of personnel and the expenses of operation. And it dangerously restricted the rector's "mission." In adopting this law, Dubuisson declared, the state had deliberately ignored all advice, criticisms, and suggestions offered by those institutions and persons who were most involved and competent in these university matters, and to whom, under the law of April 28, 1953, very broad powers of self-government had previously been given that were now being usurped. On these grounds he refused to take responsibility for implementing the law. And so, as he said in a speech he made at the time of his departure from office, "this marked the end of my career as Rector." But "in taking leave of it," he continued, "it is towards the University that I turn":

> I owe it much. It has afforded me a scientific career full of enthusiasm, and a career as Rector that was no less than that. I have known the joy of action, the joy of struggle, and sometimes, the joy of victory. . . . Finally, and above all, I have lived to defend a great cause with all my being. I believe that nothing could be finer in the destiny of a man.

Marcel Dubuisson died in 1974 as the result of an accident. He had planned that the University of Liège would be gradually transferred to Sart Tilman, but he had not expected the process to take more than two decades. His determined optimism notwithstanding, it was not until December 13, 1985—twenty-three years and one month after Dubuisson and I met, and eleven years after his death—that a reduced (635 beds, five-towered) version of the Centre Hospitalier Universitaire du Sart Tilman ("C.H.U.") was officially inaugurated. On that occasion M. A. Bodson, rector of the University and president of its board of directors, looked back with historical pensiveness on the "golden" sixties in which the building of the center had begun, and on the time of troubles through which it had passed since then:

> Someday, inevitably, a scholar will write the history of this campus, of the architectural ensemble where we are now which is still in construction, and of this hospital which we are finally inaugurating today. If he is a good historian, he will link his explanatory story to the economic, social and political evolution of our country during the twenty to twenty-five years in the course of which this whole development has been built. . . . The university hospital of Sart Tilman, conceived and begun in a brief golden age, is . . . being completed after all . . . in an iron age, or [an age] of more base metal, whose end we do not yet perceive.
>
> Those with morose tendencies will perhaps think of the towers of unfinished cathedrals, not because faith had disappeared, but because the century and its vicissitudes were stronger than the faith. . . .

An Encounter with
La Société Générale de Banque

Paris, Jan. 18 [1988]—In what Belgians view as an assault on their nation, a Paris-based investment group headed by Carlo De Benedetti, the Italian financier, said today that it was starting a bid for control of Société Générale de Belgique, a holding company that is synonymous with Belgium.

It is not enough to say that Société Générale de Belgique is Belgium's largest and most prestigious holding company. La Générale, as this mysterious monolithic company is usually called, directly or indirectly controls 20 percent of Belgian industry. It holds interests in 1,261 concerns, including some involved with steel, diamonds, insurance, chemicals, and munitions, as well as controlling interests in Belgium's largest bank. The total value of Générale's common stock is about $1.67 billion. *

Brussels, Jan. 19 [1988]—Despite what must have been the company's most shattering news since it was founded in 1822, the marble halls of Société Générale de Belgique headquarters retained their usual hush today.

While much of Belgium was rocked back on its heels by the unexpected offer from the Italian financier Carlo De Benedetti for the holding company that is Belgium's largest commercial entity, messengers padded through Générale's corridors carrying trays of mineral water and dossiers tied with ribbon in what could have been a scene from the 19th century. It was as if no one had ever raised his voice or walked in haste down the echoing halls.

---

*Steven Greenhouse, "Belgian Giant Sought by Italian-Led Group," *New York Times*, January 19, 1988.

On the executive floor, where René Lamy has held the governor's reins since 1981, attendants in blue uniforms with brass buttons sat at tiny tables outside each leather-padded door.

Framed in the windows are the winter trees of the formal park shared with Belgium's Royal Palace and the Cercle Royal Gaulois, a private club favored by [those] who occupy posts in the upper reaches of Belgian business.

Mr. Lamy, a courtly 64-year-old executive, with silvery hair, ... has spent his life at Société Générale de Belgique, working his way up through the divisions that collectively have fingers in at least one-third of all the economic activity in Belgium.

While Mr. Lamy has the declared aim of modernizing Générale and guiding it into new areas like telecommunications and information technology, most analysts agree that the company remains tradition-bound. . . . *

No one can spend as much time in Belgium in all the ways, and for as long as I have, without encountering the Société Générale, the country's premier holding company. The economic and political presence of "La Générale" (or sometimes the "*vieille dame de la rue Montagne du Parc,*" as it is colloquially called) in so many sectors of Belgian life, and its symbolic association with the history of Belgian society, are too pervasive for that. Prime mover of Belgium's industrial revolution, founded when the country was still governed by King Willem I of the Netherlands, this "first development company in the world," whose existence antedates the political independence of Belgium, has become inextricably associated with its national identity and sovereignty—so much so that it is sometimes referred to as "Belgium, Inc." It is inescapable for Belgians and for their country's frequent visitors like me.

My research brought me into the orbit of some important shareholders in the company. From time to time I was given entrée to the kind of haute-bourgeois settings where both physically and socially I was next door to "the marble halls of Société Générale de Belgique headquarters," looking out on the same view of the Place

---

* Paul L. Montomery, "Hushed Belgian Halls Belie Takeover Crisis," *New York Times*, January 20, 1988.

Royale, the Park of Brussels, and the Royal Palace that the governor of the Société Générale could see from his executive-floor windows. When I was doing research and teaching in Zaïre between 1962 and 1967, I had considerable firsthand contact with the Belgian and African social worlds of Union Minière du Haut Katanga, the great mining company (of cobalt, copper, germanium, uranium, radium, and so forth) in the South Katanga region of Zaïre in which Société Générale had a major interest at the time.

But what gave me my deepest glimpse into Société Générale difficulties in transforming itself from an "old regime" to a modern enterprise was the banal experience of trying to open a personal checking account in a local branch of Belgium's largest bank, Société Générale de Banque, a subsidiary of La Générale.

ONE SEPTEMBER morning in 1976 I went to the Brussels-Louise branch of the Société Générale de Banque to open a checking account. It was a block and a half away from my apartment hotel—a huge white building with massive oak doors which occupied a whole corner of Avenue Louise, its clock tower overlooking the chic Galerie Louise shopping enclave across the boulevard. The building's former splendor was fading. Its whitewashed façade was peeling in places; the brass knobs on its big oak doors were not polished; and the surrounding pavement was stained with pigeon droppings.

The particularistic group to which one belongs in Belgium influences the bank one chooses, as it does so many other aspects of daily life. According to this criterion, as a visiting professor of sociology at the Katholieke Universiteit te Leuven, who would begin teaching there at the end of the next month, it might have been more appropriate for me to select the Kredietbank, which is the largest bank in Flanders, rather than La Générale. But I would also be teaching at the French-speaking State University of Liège; and I was living in Brussels until the academic year started. Besides, the Louise branch of the Société Générale de Banque was so conveniently close; and I knew there would be a local, Flemish "Generale Bank Maatschappij" branch of the Société Générale that I could use when I moved to Leuven.

The bank officer who did the paperwork required for opening a checking account was young, with dark blond hair and mustache, and spoke with a singsong Walloon village accent in a rather stiff, bureaucratic fashion. The number he assigned to my prospective account consisted of twelve digits—he proudly pointed out that the Société Générale had recently computerized its accounts.

FIVE DAYS later I returned to the bank to see whether my checkbook had arrived and to withdraw some cash from the sum I had deposited the week before. The bored-and-contemptuous-looking middle-aged man who presided over the old-fashioned hand-rotated files at the checking account station asked me for my account number. He was openly disdainful when I gave him the first five digits of my number (210-00): those did not identify my account, merely the Brussels-Louise branch of the bank.

Once past these elaborate preliminaries, he reported that my checkbook was not in. I asked him if I could withdraw some cash without a check. "Yes," he said. "How?" I asked. "Go to the window that handles your account number," he said. "Which one is that?" I queried. "You can tell by the numbers marked over the windows," he retorted. Well, I couldn't really. After the 210-00 prefix in my account number, the next digits were 30-672-72, and it was unclear to me whether I should approach the window whose numbers went up to 30-000, or the one whose numbers began with 30-000. After several tries I discovered that I could bank at both of these windows—*guichets* 7 and 8. There, at least, I had a helpful woman teller who took a while to locate my account. But once she found it in her files, she cheerfully gave me the slip I had to fill out to withdraw the five thousand francs I needed, and efficiently carried out the transaction without making acerbic comments on my lack of familiarity with La Générale's system. I was relieved.

ONE WEEK later I made another trip to the bank to inquire about the status of my checking account. At the correct window the man with the rotating file told me once again that my checkbook had not yet arrived. But it had now been two weeks since I ordered it, I said, and I was told at the outset that it would take no more than a week for it to come through. Was there a problem? To deal with that inquiry, I was predictably told, I would have to go to the window that handled an account with my number. So I went back to *guichets* 7 and 8 where I found the woman teller who had been gracious to me the last time. She looked my number up in the file and verified the fact that although the checkbook had been ordered, it had not come in. When I asked her if she could tell me what was causing the delay, she told me that normally with a new account it could take two or three *months* before the client received a checkbook. In addition, she informed me, at the present time this Brussels-Louise branch of the bank had a sizable backlog of orders for checkbooks.

I began to get nervous. I had only a few thousand Belgian francs left in the bank. My first salary check from the University of Leuven was due to be deposited in my account within a week; but if my checking account had not yet been activated, would the bank receive this check, process it, and make those funds available to me? I related my concerns to the teller, adding that this was the first time anyone had even intimated that the checkbook would not be coming along any day now. She suggested that I might find it helpful to talk to a *gérant* (bank manager). When I nodded eagerly, she made a discreet telephone call. A pleasant-looking, dark-haired man in his thirties, with trembling hands, emerged from the office behind the tellers' stations. He was dressed in a well-worn brown tweed suit, an ordinary white shirt, and an inconspicuous brown-toned tie. He greeted me politely and introduced himself as Monsieur Gilbert De Moulin. The business card that he later gave me indicated that his official title was *attaché commercial*.

"I'll be perfectly frank with you, mademoiselle," M. De Moulin began, once he had me comfortably seated in his office. "Your checkbook has not yet been ordered." The reason for this, he explained, was that with foreign accounts like mine it was customary for the bank to watch the account for a while and follow a number of its transactions before setting things like printing checkbooks into motion. Under these circumstances I asked M. De Moulin what would happen when the University of Leuven tried to deposit my first monthly salary check in my still nonexistent checking account, as they intended to do the next week? M. De Moulin interviewed me about what my monthly salary would be and where it was coming from. He took careful notes, saying that this might help him to speed the issuance of my checkbook. In the meantime, he tactfully suggested, perhaps it would be safer to have the University of Leuven pay me my first month's salary with a personal check rather than trying to deposit it directly into my account.

At this point he made a quick call to check on the code

numbers attached to my account. It turned out that there were two additional numbers that had never been communicated to me. The first was a 10 that referred to "conversion U.S.A.," allowing me to shift my money around in my account in a way that protected me against fluctuations in the value of foreign currency against Belgian currency. This was done for all depositors, Belgian and foreign. The second additional number was 30, M. De Moulin told me. "This gives you the possibility of speculating in currencies," he explained. "It is a number with which you do not have to concern yourself if you don't wish to." It was highly unlikely, I thought, that on a professor's salary, and particularly at a moment when I had no more than several thousand Belgian francs in my phantom account, I was going to engage in such sophisticated international currency maneuvers! What *was* essential, M. De Moulin emphasized, was the "10"—so essential, in fact, that I should convey it as soon as possible to Monsieur B., the administrator in the Leuven business office who was responsible for teaching and scientific personnel. For without that number, Monsieur B. would run into difficulties in trying to deposit my salary.

By this time I was well down the road to at least knowing what kinds of questions I had to ask. Would I be able to withdraw cash from a branch of the Société Générale bank in Leuven when I needed it, I inquired next, since this is where I would be living and working in the future. Terming my question "*très administrative*," M. De Moulin conferred with a colleague at an adjacent desk about it. The colleague replied that in Leuven, and "*dans les provinces*" in general, I would be allowed to withdraw up to five thousand Belgian francs (approximately one hundred dollars) at a time. That should be sufficient for whatever pocket money I might need, I decided.

Out of this meeting with Gilbert De Moulin, more than an ephemeral relationship was established. He became my agent-intermediary in the Générale system: the person who, when necessary, would act as my representative and buffer in my future dealings with its tellers, its microfilmed and computerized data, and its invisible higher management. Any time I had a problem, he told me, I should immediately contact him.

Because M. De Moulin was now *my* manager-intermediary, I was emboldened to discuss the difficulties I had encountered at Société Générale/Branch Louise with him in a more searching sociological way. "It's not the sheer existence of all the bank rules and procedures that have bewildered and frustrated me," I explained, "but the problems I've run into in trying to find out what they are so that I can comply with them. The impasse I had reached before you stepped in and deblocked the information I needed is an extreme version of difficulties I've had in obtaining information of many kinds in Belgium—in daily life and in my research here too. What's more, I've come to the conclusion that without the indispensable help of an intermediary, there's a good chance you'll be given misinformation (such as being told that my checkbook would be coming through in a few days), or that the critical piece of information will be left out (like the failure to tell me about the importance of '10' in my account number)."

M. De Moulin was not offended by my comments. On the contrary, he seemed to find them interesting. "The direction of Société Générale is aware of these problems with the bank personnel," he said. "Part of it is due to their hyperspecialization—to the fact that their knowledge is confined to the tasks for which they are responsible. Furthermore, some of the personnel are reluctant to tell clients anything that might displease them—such as the fact that it may take months rather than weeks to obtain a checkbook. The numbering of the *guichets* is coordinated with the recent microfilming of all information concerning the bank's accounts. The microfilmed records for 'x' number of accounts goes to each window. So, in principle, it should be more convenient and quicker, both for the bank and the client, if you go to the window where the microfilm of your account is kept. But there are clients who feel so identified with a certain teller who does not correspond to the number of their account, that they insist on doing all transactions with this teller, even if it takes longer. The bank hopes that with the new, numbered *guichets* system, a personal relationship will gradually develop between the tellers and the clients who always go to the same microfilm- and computer-indicated window."

The rationalization of Belgian particularism, I thought, but did not say so.

MY VISIT to the bank and with M. De Moulin had lasted an hour and a half. As I entered my studio apartment my phone was ringing. It was Jan Verachtert calling to tell me that he would pick me up at 6:45 that evening and drive me to our dinner appointment with Professor Debeer at the Leuven University Faculty Club. I was still so full of my Société Générale experience that I could not resist telling him about it.

"That is typical of Société Générale!" Jan declared after listening to my story, and he proceeded to describe similar difficulties he had had with the bank. "The Générale has rules behind rules behind rules; they lie; and their computer system is not properly coordinated." He went on to say that these traits were not characteristic of the Kredietbank, where he also had an account. "The Société Générale de Banque is sclerotic compared to the Kredietbank," was this Flemish physician's diagnostic opinion.

Jan's Flemish loyalties may have been speaking here. But my own "checkbook saga" certainly gave me the impression that, in spite of its apparent modernity, Société Générale de Banque, the richest, most important, and most impregnably French bank in the country, was deeply imprinted with "Old Europe," nineteenth-century attributes. Rationalization and computerization had been grafted onto the bank's traditional structure and patterns, it seemed, without fundamentally altering them. Those patterns lived on below its computerized surface, complicating what lay above it.

IN EARLY October Armand De Kuyper (head of the medical sociology section of Leuven University in which I was to teach) called to tell me that by the time he had contacted Monsieur B. in the university's business office about the difficulties with my Société Générale checking account, Monsieur B. had already sent my first month's salary plus the reimbursement for my New York-to-Brussels plane fare to my account at the bank, and could not recall the funds. He offered to pay me my second month's salary in advance by personal check if the complications with the Générale went on much longer. When Armand asked Monsieur B. if he would be willing to speak directly to M. De Moulin, my "agent" at the Louise branch of the bank, Monsieur B. was disinclined to do so, on the grounds that anything that had to do with Brussels fell outside his domain.

So Armand took the initiative and called M. De Moulin, speaking to him "in my best French," he told me. De Moulin was very cordial, Armand reported, and predicted that my checkbook and account would be straightened out by Monday or Tuesday at the latest. He promised that he would personally do everything possible to see that this was arranged "for such an important person as Professor Fox"!

WHEN I made what had become my daily visit to the Générale the next day, the man with the rotating checkbook files once again reported that there was no sign of mine. I asked for M. De Moulin and was told he would not be in till noon. One of his colleagues offered to help me handle whatever problem I was having, but I declined. I thought it best not to start explaining my difficulties to still another person.

When I arrived at the bank again, a bit after noon, M. De Moulin was in his office, looking more tremblingly harassed but as cordial as ever. He was genuinely surprised when I told him that my checkbook was nowhere in sight. I was becoming more convinced, I said, that the sensible thing for me to do was to withdraw whatever money I had in the Société Générale, Brussels-Louise, and use it to open an account in a Kredietbank branch in Leuven. I then asked him if he would check my account to see if the month's salary and the reimbursed airfare deposited by the University of Leuven had showed up in my balance. M. De Moulin accompanied me to one of the bank windows, where he gave my number to the teller who peered into a microfilm-reading machine and reported that I had a balance of only one thousand francs in my account. No sign of the Leuven deposit. M. De Moulin now confided that it might be some time before the deposit was cleared. "As you may have read in the papers, there is a strike of employees in the Société Générale system who work in the department that deals with the transfer of funds into accounts. At the moment there is no way of knowing when the strike will be settled, and there is an avalanche of backlogged business and of client complaints." Out of fastidiousness and a dauntless kind of optimism, he decided to inquire once more about the delivery of my checkbook, entering the *guichet* of the man with the rotating file in charge of this bank function to see for himself. Victory! M. De Moulin emerged triumphantly with my checkbook in hand: a small, dark blue plastic folder with a big gold "G" printed on its cover, containing fancily printed, multicolored (red, blue, black, and white), embossed checks.

Even though I now had my own checks, I was still faced with the problem that at this point, and for an indefinite period of time to follow, I had only a thousand francs in toto in my account. M. De Moulin kindly offered to advance me whatever sum I might need, but despite his helpfulness I was afraid that this would add more banking complications to those I already had. I decided that the best solution was to accept Monsieur B.'s offer to issue my second month's salary in advance, in the form of a personal check. That way I could pay my bills in Brussels and then deposit the remaining sum in a Leuven branch of the Kredietbank. After discovering there were only twenty-four checks in my new Société Générale checkbook, this seemed more sensible than ever. Knowing that as soon as I used up that small supply of checks I would once again be involved in petitioning the Générale for others was enough to speed me on to the Kredietbank.

TWO DAYS later I took an early train to Leuven, so that before Armand De Kuyper and I met with the rector of the university he could accompany me to the local Kredietbank where I had decided to open a checking account. He had alerted a member of the Kredietbank staff that I would be stopping by, and she was waiting for me when I arrived at the bank—an attractive, blonde-haired woman, well groomed and well spoken, who was both warm and professionally efficient. She asked for my passport, filled out the requisite forms with the information I supplied, and presented me with my banking card in a plastic jacket along with a brochure containing information about the bank and its procedures that was printed in English. She asked whether I preferred to receive my bank statements in Flemish or French, and assured me, in a way I found convincing, that I would have my checkbook the next week. From the bank I went to my 11:30 a.m. appointment with the rector of the university, and when that visit was over Armand and I proceeded to Monsieur B.'s office. There a young man was waiting for me with a personal check made out to me for the full amount of my second month's salary. I signed for it and was ushered into a big hall with counters where students were standing in line signing up for courses and paying university fees. A woman seated behind one of the counters accepted my check without raising any questions about it, and gave me cash in exchange for it. Armand and I then went directly to the Kredietbank where I deposited most of the cash.

After three weeks of continuous effort, with the help of two intermediaries, Gilbert De Moulin and Armand De Kuyper, I finally had a viable checking account—in the Kredietbank!

THE NEXT day I made my pilgrimage to the Brussels-Louise branch of the Société Générale de Banque to see M. De Moulin. This time I happily informed him that my emergency was over, thanks to the checking account I had opened at the Kredietbank in Leuven. I gave him my new Leuven address, since I had decided to keep the Générale checking account as well. It would be convenient to have a bank so close at hand when I lived in Brussels. Having M. De Moulin as my intermediary encouraged me. And I could not face the prospect of trying to close the account: that would surely be as baroque and consuming as trying to open one.

By this time the Générale was mistakenly sending statements to my home address in Philadelphia rather than to my address in Brussels. They had been posted via air mail, dispatched to me in the United States more often than monthly, and then forwarded to me in Belgium. Since the funds officially registered in my account at this point amounted to the grand sum of one thousand Belgian francs, or about twenty dollars, the bank would soon end up spending more money on my account than was in it. I brought the statements in their air mail envelopes to the bank that morning to show M. De Moulin.

We talked more about what he called the "bad luck" I had had with Société Générale. I told him that when I had related my difficulties to several Belgian colleagues, I had been regaled by what they regarded as comparable experiences in the Société Générale system. To be sure, more of the persons in my small sample belonged to the Flemish rather than to the French linguistic community; still, I said, the anecdotes I had collected suggested that my Société Générale troubles were not idiosyncratic or con-fined either to clients who were foreign or who belonged to one particular Belgian group.

At first M. De Moulin argued that my problems had been largely attributable to the "thoughtless" fashion in which the bank officer who had opened my account had gone about doing it. But he went on to admit that the Louise branch of the bank was then grappling with some of the repercussions of a recent fusion between the bank of the Société Générale and the Société Belge de Banque, controlled by the Solvay, Janssen, and Boël financial group. In fact, until the fusion took place the Louise branch had been a Société Belge de Banque rather than a Société Générale establishment. "The transition has been a difficult one," M. De Moulin confided. "At least fifteen of the sixty-five employees of this branch have worked most of their lives in the Société Belge de Banque. They are accustomed to an 'old regime, bourgeois' kind of private bank. For example, they are not used to handling flocks of clients whom they consider 'strangers' and who come to the bank for purposes like opening checking accounts. They feel more comfortable with the sorts of clients with whom they previously dealt: those who were known to them; who had solid references and impressive '*garanties*'; and whose business with the bank involved substantial deposits and the trading of securities and currency. Management is aware of this phenomenon, but it is difficult to know how to remedy it. The employees in question cannot be fired, but they will probably never be able to adapt to the new situation. It may be necessary to wait until retirements and deaths solve the problem." Meanwhile, M. De Moulin concluded, "these difficulties show up mainly in the area of '*renseignements*' [information], as they did in the case of your checking account."

SEVERAL WEEKS later I dropped into the Branch Louise of the Générale for a last visit before moving to Leuven. This time my reason for stopping by concerned the "disappearance" from my latest bank statements of the thousand francs left over from the American travelers checks with which I originally opened my account. M. De Moulin was out. For the first time in all my visits to the bank, a "hostess" was seated at the reception desk. She brought me to see a Monsieur F, one of M. De Moulin's colleagues, who was about his age and who, like him, was very helpful and had trembling hands. Monsieur F's phone rang constantly during the short time I spent with him. The calls seemed to involve persons who were giving orders to buy and sell securities while the stock market was in session. I assumed this was the real "backroom" business of the Société Générale, and that its depositors' *guichets* up front, though not façades, continued to represent more minor interests.

Monsieur F said he was not at all surprised that I did not understand what had happened to my thousand francs. He reminded me that I had two accounts under one number. One account was established through my travelers checks in American currency; the other account, established through the deposit of my first month's salary check from the University of Leuven, and the reimbursed plane fare, was in Belgian currency. The thousand francs were in the account that permitted me to speculate with currency rates, changing some of the Belgian francs from my Leuven salary into American dollars, then transferring them into the other account where they could be converted into Belgian francs, which was the stronger currency at the moment, thereby making several thousand additional francs on the spot. The "Leuven salary account," the nonconvertible one, gave me the same protection vis-à-vis the value of the Belgian franc against other currencies that Belgians have. I told Monsieur F. I thought I finally understood what the mysterious "10" and "30" digits were that M. De Moulin had added to my account number. Monsieur F. replied that the whole process was so technical that he and his colleagues had constantly to consult with one another about these money operations. He advised me, however, not to close out the convertible account when I begin using my Société Générale rather than Kredietbank money. I should ask M. De Moulin, he said, to advise me how much money to transfer to it so as to make a profit through the currency exchange option open to me.

I was set up, it would seem, systematically to speculate in currency, whether I wanted to or not.

I MAINTAINED a relationship with Gilbert De Moulin over the years, contacting him virtually every time I returned to Belgium. I even incorporated an allusion to an aspect of my Société Générale banking experiences in an article entitled "Why Belgium?" that I published in 1978, and I gave M. De Moulin a reprint of it. He was delighted with the vignette I had published, and he proudly showed the reprint to a number of Branch Louise colleagues. Each year when I paid him a visit, usually in the early summer after my university teaching duties in the United States were over, he seemed to be eagerly awaiting my latest observations on the sociology of his bank and of Belgium more generally.

In 1984 "my" Société Générale branch bank closed forever. The Société Générale de Banque, Agence Louise, Avenue Louise, 61, and the white building it occupied were shut down and boarded up. Tacked to the big oak doors of the building was a bilingual sign announcing that from April 9, 1984, on there would be a "*dédouble-*

ment et transfert/ontdubbeling en overplaatsing" of this *"agence/agents-chap"* of the bank. Half the branch was now located at Avenue Louise, 58, just across the avenue from the bank's former site, in a big new white building with Art Deco borders on its façade, which also housed Union Minière, Valentino, a Bruno Magli shoe shop, a swank jewelry store, Iberian Airlines, and Air Zaïre. The other "half" of the branch had moved around the corner to the Chaussée de Charleroi/Charleroise Steenweg. Why the Agence Louise of the bank had split in two, how these newly created subbranches differed from each other, and why two of them were needed within the radius of one block, I didn't know. Nor did I wish to inquire.

I cashed a $100 travelers check at the Avenue Louise, 58, branch. It was small and modern, quite stylish-looking, and equipped with IBM and Canon machines. The tellers behind the glass windows were very young. I asked the hostess at the reception desk if there was any way she could find out where my former *agent commercial*, M. Gilbert De Moulin, was now working, explaining that I would like to pay him a visit at his new location. Consulting a Société Générale directory, she made a phone call and informed me that M. De Moulin was now attached to the Heysel branch of the Société Générale de Banque, in the most northern section of Brussels.

Had M. De Moulin been promoted, as he anticipated? Had he merely moved laterally? And where were all the old Agence Louise employees, formed in private banks with privileged clientele, who had not yet adjusted to the democratization of banking, checking accounts, American Express travelers checks, Eurocheque charge cards, computers, and microfilms? Had they all retired or died? These were questions I was longing to ask.

THAT JULY I had a reunion with M. De Moulin in his small, simply furnished office with its computer terminal, at the small, modern-appearing bank that he directed, in a bleak commercial area on the northern outskirts of Brussels. The peripheral location of this branch bank and its modest style gave me the impression that M. De Moulin's advancement to manager was a routine promotion in the lower echelons of the Société Générale de Banque bureaucracy. This time we talked about the six weeks of medical sociological research that I had done in the People's Republic of China in 1981, as well as about things Belgian. And in the course of our conversation he rather shyly released the first personal information about himself and his family he had ever divulged to me. I knew that he was married, but only because he wore a gold wedding band on the third finger of his right hand. Now he told me that he had two children, both of whom were enrolled in Catholic schools, that he had built and owned his own house, and that his wife was a teacher, but she was not working while the children were growing up.

The taxi ride I had made from my studio on Avenue Louise to Heysel and M. De Moulin's bank was a long one. He offered to drive me to the Place Louise, assuring me that it would be no trouble because he had a luncheon appointment nearby. In his Japanese car, chatting amiably all the way, we drove back to the section of the city where we first met in 1976, at the Agence Louise of La Générale, inside a structure that was now scheduled to be demolished.

IN JANUARY 1988 the Italian financier Carlo De Benedetti staged a takeover raid on the Société Générale de Belgique. At several press conferences in Belgium De Benedetti was outspokenly critical of the Société Générale's "miserable growth, modest profits, and feudal organization"; and he declared that as a "pure capitalist builder" who sought "added value and growth," he was determined to do what he could to improve the performance of the company through processes of modernization, diversification, and internationalization, and through more effective management.

In the end De Benedetti's raid was repulsed, and a French holding company, Compagnie Financière de Suez (allied with Belgo-Luxembourg companies), gained a 78 percent control of the Société Générale de Belgique, thereby rendering its ownership more French than Belgian. The old Société Générale I had glimpsed through my experiences with one of its local banking houses and my conversations with one of its attachés had changed in spite of itself. It had reluctantly entered the forthcoming world of the European Community.

Farewell to
Sint-Janshospitaal

FROM JUNE to September 1976 the Public Assistance Commission of Brugge organized an exposition to commemorate the eight hundredth year of Sint-Janshospitaal (Saint John's Hospital) and to give testimony to its medical, religious, and artistic importance through the centuries.

This anniversary exhibit also marked the end of Sint-Janshospitaal's existence as a functioning hospital. The transfer of medical staff and facilities from the old buildings on Brugge's Mariastraat to a new, fifteen-story edifice in the commune of Sint-Pieters, on the outskirts of the city, had already begun. Once this exodus was completed, the historic structures of Sint-Jans, with their many small and charming rooms, narrow corridors and stairways, and monumental wards and attics, would become a hospital museum.

The need for a more modern hospital structure was indisputable. Sint-Jans was too small and too horizontal in layout for the specialization and technology of twentieth-century medicine. In addition to crowding and sanitation problems, certain high-tech diagnostic and therapeutic procedures could not be carried out within the antique walls of Sint-Jans or in the frail, temporary structures that had been put up to expand its space.

There had been overall agreement that a new hospital would have to be built, but whether to erect a modern hospital in Brugge, as close to Sint-Jans as possible, had been a matter of intense and prolonged debate. Dr. Louis De Winter, founder and first chief of the pulmonary service of Sint-Janshospitaal; the chief of the obstetrics and gynecology service; Canon Van Logghe, who was president of the hospital's governing tutors; the Communal Council of Brugge; and the local wing of the Flemish Christelijke Volks Partij (Christian People's party) were foremost among the individuals and groups who advocated building the new hospital inside Brugge. But the multistoried vertical hospital that seemed necessary made it increasingly unlikely that the hospital would be erected in the medieval center of historic Brugge.

The first architectural plan for the new hospital was drafted in 1960, but construction did not begin until 1964–1965. The work proceeded slowly, interrupted repeatedly because of insufficient funds. The national Ministry of Public Health (and Social Care), the chief source of subsidies for hospital construction in the country, was financially overextended by all the new hospitals that were being built in the 1960s. Furthermore, at that time the office of the minister of public health was considered a minor government position—one with a portfolio but without significant political influence or economic resources. The chief architect of the new Brugge–Sint-Peters hospital "went through" twelve consecutive ministers of public health before he finally received steady, adequate funding for the hospital's construction.

I WENT to say farewell to Sint-Janshospitaal two days before the exhibit ended. I arrived early, and for a while I was alone inside of Sint-Jans's enclosure, as I had hoped to be. The hot afternoon sun warmed and illumined the old bricks of the hospital. The bell tower of the Onze Lieve Vrouwkerk (Church of Our Lady) soared above them. Overhead, white doves and seagulls made silent, graceful circles in the pale Brugge sky.

I strolled through a small rose garden, past the famous eastern façade of the church with its thirteenth-century sculptured portal, beyond the door of the Augustinian Sisters' convent, into another courtyard. Inside this place of radiant stillness—underneath the belfry of the church and framed by a brick building with a large sundial on one of its walls—stood a gigantic statue, "Pax," by the pacifist Brugge sculptor Octave Rotsaert. The funds for this bronze statue of two barefooted and bareheaded monks—one of them young, the other old—in their tiered robes, leaning upon each other as they embrace and exchange the kiss of peace, were donated by the hospital's Dr. Louis De Winter, who was also a great patron of art and artists, and by the Friends of Brugge cultural society that he headed. It was Dr. De Winter who in 1947, two years after World War II ended, had the statue installed inside the cloister of the hospital.

As I stood there contemplating the statue, I remembered the

story that Michel de Ghelderode had told me about his friend Dr. De Winter's wish to be buried underneath what he called "my Pax," within the enclave of the hospital to which he had devoted his professional life. Dr. De Winter petitioned the city officials of Brugge to allow these arrangements to be made. Although they esteemed the doctor and were grateful to him for all the medical, artistic, and civic services he had rendered to the community, the city fathers did not see how they could authorize his request. When Dr. De Winter threatened to have "Pax" moved from the hospital grounds to the cemetery upon his death, and make it his tombstone there, the officials came up with a counteroffer. In exchange for Dr. De Winter's agreement to leave "Pax" where it was, they proposed, the city would donate a large enough plot in the cemetery for all forty-four members of his extended family to be buried in close proximity to one another. Dr. De Winter responded favorably to this proposal; the bargain was sealed, and he began to plan for what he referred to as his "house" in the cemetery where, in death as in life, the De Winter clan would share a common residence over which he would preside as its patriarch. Dr. De Winter's domestic image of death, I thought, when de Ghelderode told me this tale, was incarnated in the primitive Flemish paintings which had surrounded him all his life in Brugge. It was as if the burial conditions he shrewdly negotiated would enable him to step right into one of those paintings when death came.

Now, standing on the walk in front of "Pax," I realized for the first time that his unfulfilled dream of being buried in the courtyard of Sint-Janshospitaal also had a local historical and cultural precedent. For there, under my feet, was a flat marble tablet that marked the grave site of a long-ago Augustinian canoness who had been a mother superior of the hospital's nursing sisters.

By 2 p.m. a large crowd of visitors had assembled: busloads of Flemish schoolchildren with their teachers; many French- as well as Flemish-speaking adult Belgians; and numerous British, American, German, and Dutch tourists.

The doors of the exhibit opened promptly, directly onto one of the original wards of the hospital. It was an enormous hall, cathedrallike in its proportions, with Romanesque brick pillars and arches. At its far end was a big carved wooden fireplace that could not possibly have warmed the entire length of that cavernous room. The sculpture on the mantel depicted two patients in hospital beds, surrounded by hosts of angels. One of the patients was dead—wrapped in a winding sheet and burial shroud. Hanging above the mantelpiece was a sculptured wooden frieze that portrayed the life and death and the Assumption of the Virgin Mary.

The central area of this vast ward was filled with rows of enclosed wooden beds built around the pillars and under the arches. The beds were covered by wooden canopies and hung with curtains that could be opened and closed. Several human dummies lay side by side in each of the beds, demonstrating how in centuries past these beds were occupied by more than one patient.

A sedan chair stood nearby, used in the early nineteenth century to transport patients to and from the hospital. Not far from the beds and this chair, a frightening figure surveyed the scene. It was a male mannikin, dressed in a long black robe and gloves, wearing a black mask from which a large bird's beak protruded under a broad-brimmed, crimson velvet hat. This funereal figure loomed over a body wrapped in straw—an effigy of someone who had died in the plague and was about to be removed from the hospital and buried. During the years of the bubonic plague epidemics, it seems, the poor were buried in straw, not in coffins. The beaked mask of the medieval undertaker struck me as a terrifying ancestor of the carnival masks that are still worn at Belgian *kermesses* in Flanders.

Glass cases lining the walls of the ward contained displays of medical and surgical equipment and instruments. Intermingled with items like stethoscopes from the time of Laënnec, forceps from the eighteenth century, and a leather chloroform mask, were "clackers" that lepers in the sixteenth century were obliged to sound to warn persons of their approach, and a variety of prayer amulets that once hung over hospital beds.

In some of the other exhibit cases on the ward, and in various of the smaller rooms of the hospital, lay documents and manuscripts. Among them were the original January 1188 statutes of the hospital and the charter issued in 1230 by which Fernand of Portugal and Jeanne of Constantinople—counts of Flanders and of Hainaut—exempted part of the land situated in Zuinkerke from all feudal taxes and obligations, thus setting it aside for the hospital. Both these documents were written on parchment scrolls and festooned with ribbons and seals.

A corner of the ward was devoted to memorabilia associated

with the hospital's two most respected twentieth-century physicians. It was here that Octave Rotsaert's bronze busts of Dr. Louis De Winter and of Dr. J. Sebrechts, its renowned chief of surgery, were placed, along with a wooden hospital door in which generations of Sint-Jans's interns and residents had carved their names and gallows-humor symbols—like skulls and crossbones.

I climbed a narrow, winding staircase to the attic above the ward from which I could look down on the enormous hall below. I could almost touch the original wooden beams of the hospital. The trees out of which these beams were hewn were already centuries old at the time they were put into place eight hundred years before (without a single nail!). Standing in that ancient, vaulted room at the top of the hospital was like being inside a great wooden ship turned upside down.

I descended the stairs and moved quickly through the small room with its collection of illustrations of the hospital, and the chapel with the tile floor and carved wooden stalls that was still used by the hospital's sisters. I paused for a longer time in another room to admire the gorgeous array of church silver, and the silver- and gold-embroidered priestly vestments assembled there. Then, with a reverentially hushed crowd, I entered the painted splendor of the small Memling Museum, with Hans Memling's tryptichs of "The Adoration of the Magi" and "The Lamentation of Christ," his dyptich of "The Virgin and Maarten van Nieuwenhove," his altarpiece of "Saint John the Baptist and Saint John the Apostle," his "Portrait of a Woman, or the Sybil Sambetha," with her mysterious gossamer veil and, above all, his *châsse* (reliquary) of Saint Ursula (Het Ursulaschrijn).

But was this *châsse* the real one or the copy, I wondered? I knew that a legend involving Dr. Louis De Winter had grown up around this question. It seems that during World War II and the German occupation of Belgium, under Dr. De Winter's supervision a perfect reproduction of the *châsse* of Saint Ursula was made by local Brugge artists. Unbeknownst to the Germans, the real *châsse* was removed from Sint-Janshospitaal and hidden in Dr. De Winter's house, and the replica was substituted for it. The purpose of this deceptive exchange was to ensure that if the Germans decided to expropriate the *châsse*, they would be duped into taking the false one. When the war ended, the authentic *châsse* was supposedly returned to its rightful place in the hospital. But not everyone was sure. Some believed that the genuine Memling *châsse* was still kept in the De Winter house, under the doctor's protective custody.

My next stop was a visit to the hospital's famous pharmacy, in a small building adjacent to the one where the ward was located. On the shelves behind its wooden-and-brass shop counter were rows of blue-and-white Delft china and earthenware apothecary jars, and a series of round wooden boxes and small oak chests with the names of the medicinal herbs they contained inscribed on their sides. In a corner of the pharmacy stood an armoire where the most costly remedies were kept—plasters among them—and an array of copper and brass mortars and pestles dating from the sixteenth to the eighteenth centuries. The pharmacy also contained rare copies of an eighteenth-century *Winkelboek* (shop book) and an apothecary *hant-bouck* (manual) as well as early textbooks of medicinal herbs. From the walls a sunburst-haloed statue of the Virgin Mary and portraits of religious sister-apothecaries watched over this venerable pharmacy that still looked ready for use.

I climbed the staircase to the attic above the pharmacy and once again found myself in a universe of ancient beams. In this garret some of the raw materials from which the pharmacy sisters compounded medicine were stored, many in burlap sacks, along with books in which they had kept records of the herbs and drugs they dispensed and of patients' reactions to them. I passed through the cloistered section of the hospital, next to the pharmacy, where the community of Sint-Jans's religious brothers once lived, and then descended the stairs to the room in which the eccelesiastical and lay tutors of the hospital's corporation (the members of its board of directors) used to meet. A big oak table covered with green felt, and stern portraits of past tutors, dominated that very formal board room.

Leaving its juridical heaviness behind me, I exited through the back door of the hospital into a fragrant herb garden planted around shiny-leaved mulberry trees. At the outdoor café facing it I ordered a twentieth-century *tartine* and a cup of coffee to fortify myself, in the Belgian way, before starting for the railroad station.

Long after I arrived back in my apartment in Brussels, I was still under the spell of Sint-Janshospitaal. When I was finally able to sleep, I dreamed that I was inside a sailing ship constructed of enormous beams that were joined together like a gigantic human rib cage. The ship rocked dizzyingly back and forth as it carried me and unseen other passengers into oceanic depths.

Two Posters and
Two Speeches

Two posters hang side by side in my Philadelphia apartment. They are handsomely printed, bordered in Madonna blue, and the *Sedes Sapientiae* seal of the Katholieke Universiteit te Leuven (KUL), depicting the Virgin Mary seated in the Chair of Wisdom with the Infant Jesus in her lap, appears in their upper right-hand corner. The posters announce the fact that I will be awarded a *Doctor Honoris Causa* by the KUL Faculty of Social Sciences, in the Promotion Room of the University's Academic Hall at 5 p.m. on May 24, 1978; that my "promoter" is Professor (of Sociology) Armand De Kuyper; and that I will give a lecture on this occasion. The two posters are identical in all but one critical respect: the title of my lecture is listed as "Why Belgium? A Sociological View of Belgian Society Through the Windows of Its Medical Laboratories" on one poster, and on the other as "The Importance of Religion in Belgium: A Sociological View."

Armand De Kuyper gave me a copy of each of these posters. For personal and sociological reasons, he said, he knew that I would like to have them in my files. Besides, he added, he thought I would find them amusing. I do now; but at that time I certainly did not.

Having a *Doctor Honoris Causa* conferred on me by a Belgian university had great meaning for me. Finding myself back in Leuven, at the end of almost two decades of research in this society to which I was "called" as a sociologist, seemed to me symbolically fitting. For it was here, in an apartment facing University Hall, that I had lived during the summer of 1959 when my sociological inquiry into Belgian medical research began. The romantic young American sociologist I was then had been stirred by the carillons that rang out in Leuven, by the hoofbeats of the big grey muscular horses pulling rumbling wagonloads of beer kegs through the streets in the early morning, by the Gothic beauty, the stone lace, and the statuary of the town hall, by the lamplighter who came and went every dawn and dusk, and by the processions of seminarians, priests, and religious sisters and brothers, dressed in traditional robes, moving continually past my window over the cobblestones below. I could not have predicted at that time that my professional and personal life would become so enduringly entwined with Belgium, or imagined that one day I would cross the street to receive an honorary degree.

But there was a shadow on that otherwise happy day. I had originally planned to deliver a lecture on the importance of religion in Belgium; I had been politely but strongly pressured not to do so, and I had succumbed. As requested, I had sent the title of the lecture I was preparing for this occasion to my promoter, Armand De Kuyper, who headed the medical sociology division of the faculty of social sciences. Not long thereafter De Kuyper telephoned me in Philadelphia to report that "the scientific community" at Leuven was "perplexed" and "concerned" about the fact that I was planning to speak about religion. Why was I doing this? the unnamed "they" wanted to know. What relationship did this topic have to the sociology of medicine for which I was supposedly receiving my honorary degree? Could I at least change the title of my address so it would not be posted all over the university in its current form?

What did this imply? I asked De Kuyper. Was I merely being asked to modify the title of my lecture, or was this a veiled demand from unidentified others that I change its topic and content? De Kuyper admitted it was the latter. It would be highly inconvenient for me to do so, I told him, because I had already written a substantial part of my announced lecture, and there was not enough time left to draft another lecture on another subject. More important, I said, this matter violated the basic academic and intellectual principles of freedom of thought and speech, and also my personal integrity. I would have to think about how I was going to respond to the message he had conveyed to me.

In choosing the importance of religion in Belgium as the focus of my address, I was aware that it was a potentially controversial topic. In fact my decision to select it as the subject of my talk grew out of the discrepancy between the strongly felt statements that Belgians had recently been making to me about the diminishing significance of religion in their society, and my own quite different impression of the religious situation. "Religion is no longer important in Belgium!" friends, colleagues, and informants kept insisting during the 1976–1977 sabbatical year that I spent in the country. I was puzzled by their declaration because I had always considered Belgium to be a society deeply imprinted by religion—by its diffuse Catholicism and the complex reactions to it. Yet the picture that many Belgians now painted was of a society where religion had not merely waned but with great rapidity had virtually disappeared. I was intrigued by this allegation, though neither sociological theory nor my own firsthand observations in Belgium made it seem credible. Exactly how important *was* religion in Belgian society then? I found myself wondering; and what did Belgians mean when they said it was "no longer important" in their country? I considered the lecture I was preparing to be part of my ongoing exploration of these questions and of my continuing dialogue with Belgians about them. In my view it was not only a lively subject for the occasion of my honorary degree but also one with sufficient sociological breadth, because the concept of religion on which I planned to base my lecture was not confined to religious practice. Rather, I intended to delve deeply into Belgian culture: its key symbols and rituals, beliefs and values, its special ambience, and its distinctive worldview.

I was aware that I would be delivering this lecture exactly ten years after the splitting of Louvain University, and that resentment over the stand against the division of the university that the bishops had originally taken was still pervasively felt at KUL. I also knew that under the leadership of its distinguished Flemish scientist-rector, the first layman to hold this position in the many centuries of Louvain University's history, KUL was grappling with its definition and image of itself as a Catholic and a Flemish university. In this climate "the importance of religion" was a sensitive issue, but it was one I thought would be apt and stimulating as the subject of my lecture. I had not anticipated that it would be considered so charged that an attempt would be made to deter me from talking about it.

After Armand De Kuyper's phone call I spent the next day and a good deal of the night pondering what I should do. I felt I could not simply yield to the efforts at dissuasion. The most straightforward way of dealing with the situation would be to insist on my unconditional right to lecture on a subject of my choice, and to refuse to accept the honorary degree if the university did not accede to this. And yet I hoped to find a way to cleave to my principles without sacrificing the degree. Quite apart from the appeal of the honor, I was acutely aware of the fact that I was one of the only sociologists and women ever to receive such a degree from the university, and the first sociologist of medicine to be so recognized. I therefore felt I had some self-transcending responsibility to promote acknowledgment of the gender and the discipline I personified, through this ceremonial event. So I sought a compromise.

By the time I called De Kuyper back to give him my answer, I had decided I would drop my plan to give "The Importance of Religion in Belgium" address. I would replace it with a compressed version of the essay entitled "Why Belgium?" that I had written a year earlier while a visiting professor at Leuven, in response to the question that Belgians and Americans were always asking me about what I was discovering and learning in that small society that could possibly preoccupy me for so many years. But as part of the introduction to my presentation at the honorary degree ceremony, I would mention the talk I had originally planned to give—its title, its contents, and the reason why I had decided not to deliver it on this day. Furthermore, I would continue to work on the "religion in Belgium" manuscript with the goal of publishing it in the future.

All that I told De Kuyper in my return call was that I was willing to substitute "Why Belgium?" and the analysis of Belgian society that it contained for "The Importance of Religion in Belgium." He expressed great relief. The choice, he continued, had been between "freedom of thought and..." Here his voice trailed off. *That*, I replied, was the essence of the problem. Freedom of thought was crucial to me. It was a grave and ironic experience to have it tampered with in preparation for an event that was supposed to celebrate fundamental values of academic life. We will have to discuss this when I arrive in Belgium, I said.

THE SATURDAY before the conferring of the degree, after eating my noon meal at the De Kuypers' house, I had a serious discussion with Armand about what had occurred. It began when he presented me with the two sets of posters: the one announcing that I would give a lecture on "The Importance of Religion in Belgium," printed before his telephone call to me, and the "Why Belgium?" poster printed afterward. De Kuyper gave me an admirably frank and detailed account of the reactions that my original intention to talk about religion had elicited in several KUL groups. He insisted, however, that religion was "not a taboo subject at Leuven," and that there had been no intervention in the matter from the administration of the university, or from the rector's office. The major source of the problem, he emphasized, was located in the faculty of social sciences: its sociology department, the medical sociology and religious sociology subdivisions within it, and in the relationships between them. The faculty of theology was also involved in a more indirect and secondary way.

As the sociologists of religion in the department saw it, De Kuyper explained, I was treading on their intellectual territory and area of expertise by choosing religion as the subject of my address. In turn, they interpreted this as a precedent-setting encroachment by the medical sociology branch of the department upon their domain, with serious implications for the balance of power between them. But even if I had been a bona fide sociologist of religion, De Kuyper contended, serious questions would have been raised about a social scientist focusing a *Doctor Honoris Causa* address on matters pertaining to religion. For, as he put it, religion is "properly situated in the faculty of theology." In fact, he said, so much was this the case that the eligibility of a sociologist of religion to receive an honorary degree was problematic at best.

Before I left De Kuyper that afternoon I forewarned him that at the degree-granting ceremony on Wednesday I planned to mention the last-minute change in my talk and the reason for it, followed by a brief synopsis of what I would have said if I had given that lecture. Only after that would I proceed with my "Why Belgium?" text. De Kuyper did not appear to be disturbed by my strategy; rather, he gave me the impression I had his tacit support.

AFTER THIS meeting with Armand De Kuyper, for my own clarification I tried to identify the factors that had converged to create the minicrisis over my lecture topic. I still believed that an element of reaction against organized religion, the Catholic church, its clergy and hierarchy, and its historically tight grip on Flemish villages and cities (from which many students and professors of Leuven came) played an important role in the incident, along with the increasing declericalization and secularization of the Katholieke Universiteit te Leuven and of the new "populist Flemish bourgeoisie" and intelligentsia.

In addition, for centuries the University of Louvain had had a strong positivist tradition, occasionally bordering on scientism, even in the disciplines of philosophy and theology. At the same time science and religion at Louvain had always been sharply distinguished from one another, to the point of dichotomization. And the university had continuously felt the need to "prove" that being a believing, practicing Catholic was not incompatible with a scientific outlook and with being a scientist.

In my view the experience with my honorary degree speech revealed how these attitudes had been institutionalized at KUL. Sociology, on the one hand, and religion, on the other, were assigned to designated, airtight boxes. They were considered mutually exclusive, and to cross from one to the other bordered on an act of ritual impurity. "Religious sociology" did exist, but it was largely concerned with the demography, social organization, and formal practice of religion, in ways that lent themselves to "scientific" counting and quantification. It did not often delve into religious values, beliefs, symbols, and rituals. These touched too closely on the "religiousness" of religion.

In addition my experience seemed to illustrate how rigidly and jealously the different disciplines in the university defined and guarded their territory. These conceptions and boundaries were so deeply embedded in the university's structure and culture, it appeared to me, that there was no need for the administration of the university, or the rector's office, to intervene in the matter of what was an appropriate *Doctor Honoris Causa* topic. Powerful social control mechanisms would go into effect on the levels of faculties and departments if these institutionalized understandings were jeopardized. Thus in my case, for example, it could never be said that the university or its officials took a stand against a sociologist giving an honorary degree lecture on religion.

THE WEATHER on the day of the *Doctor Honoris Causa* presentation was characteristically Belgian—foggy, damp, and chilly. The centuries-old, sculptured stone façade of University Hall and its solid oak and hammered brass entrance doors were unchanged, but as I stepped over its high threshold and down into its interior, as if into a great vault, I realized that inside it had undergone extensive modernization. Usherettes, dressed in dark blue uniforms and hats that resembled those of airline attendants, were waiting to greet us. They escorted us to the second floor where, in a large, open area, faculty members were donning their academic caps and gowns, and guests were assembling.

The ceremonial procession began precisely on time, led by two *massiers* in black robes, carrying maces of heavy, ornamented silver atop long poles. The rector and I walked together behind the mace-bearers, followed by Armand De Kuyper, my promoter, the vice-rector of the university, the dean of the faculty of social sciences, and the chairman of sociology.

The *Promotiezaal* (Promotion Hall) in which the conferring of the degree took place, an impressive room with carved, pewlike seats of blond oak and big clear windows, was lined with full-length portraits of all the former *Rectores Magnifici* of the university in full academic-ecclesiastical attire. The raised platform in front of the hall, where a lectern stood, contained oak stalls like those in Belgian Catholic churches, monasteries, and courts of law. One stall was elevated above all the rest, from which the dean of social sciences presided on this occasion. I took my place in the front row of the audience, facing the platform. On my left was the rector, on my right the vice-rector.

The dean formally presented me to the rector and the assemblage as a candidate for a *Doctor Honoris Causa*. At this initial point in the program I was to deliver my "Why Belgium?" address. I rose to do so, prefacing it with the introduction I had described to Armand De Kuyper:

> Some of you who are assembled here today are already acquainted with the greater part of the talk that I am about to give. I hope that you will neither be disappointed nor bored by the fact that you are being asked to share these reflections with me again. I was willing, even eager, to prepare a completely new paper for this occasion. In fact, I had planned and written a substantial portion of another paper, with the provisional title, "The Importance of Religion in Belgian Society: A Sociological View." With your permission, I would like to read the introduction to the *other* paper, the paper I have decided not to present.

After reading these opening paragraphs I went on to say: "*If* I had delivered that paper today, . . ." and proceeded from there to present a brief resumé of "The Importance of Religion" manuscript. "My colleagues at the University of Leuven," I continued, "have persuaded me that partly because of the long-standing conceptions of religion, science, medicine, social science, and sociology, and of their proper parameters, that are profoundly rooted in Belgian universities and the society more broadly, my 'Importance of Religion' paper would be a less fitting and appreciated way to address you at this time and in this place than through the medium of the 'Why Belgium?' essay that I wrote last year when I was a visiting professor here. I have decided to follow their advice," I said, "not primarily out of polite compliance, but principally because . . . on this day above all, I want to do what I can, substantively as well as ceremonially, to help make sociology more intelligible and acceptable in Belgian milieux." I then proceeded with my *in extenso* presentation of "Why Belgium?"

Now it was Armand De Kuyper's turn to make the promoter's speech. "Health problems have always been linked with the social, cultural, and political conditions of particular groups of people," De Kuyper began, "but in earlier periods these relationships were not the subject of systematic investigation." He described the genesis and evolution of the still relatively new field of medical sociology. Then, with characteristically ironic and mischievous Belgian wit, De Kuyper asked the question, "Why Renée Fox?" and went on to answer it. "Therefore," he concluded, "the faculty of social sciences request the honorable rector to grant the degree of *Doctor Honoris Causa* to . . ."

A reception was held immediately following the ceremony in a room next to Promotion Hall. As I circulated among the diverse friends and colleagues whom I had invited for the occasion—Flemish and Walloon, Catholic and Free Thought, and from the working class, bourgeoisie, and nobility—I found them united in their approval of what they called my "double speech." One after another, they congratulated me not only for the honorary degree but also for the "very Belgian way" in which I had dealt with the equally Belgian attempt to change the topic of my lecture.

Meditations on the
Belgian Railroad and the
Belgian Postal System

THE RAILROAD...

Belgian trains...how many have I ridden during my more than thirty years of traveling from one Belgian house to another?

But trains are not just trains in Belgium. They are part of the history and sociology, the imagery and symbolic language of this small country that built the first and one of the finest railroads in all of Europe and became the railroad-builder for huge faraway lands like China and the Congo.

To "go to the railroad," to work for it, has always meant more than obtaining a secure and respectable job. It has been a way to progress socially in life—a source of honor and prestige. To become the chief of a local railroad station—its stationmaster—has been to achieve high status in the community. There was communal pride, too, in the way the station functioned and how it looked: in its workmanship and efficiency, its cleanliness and state of repair, and in its colorful array of flower boxes. Belgians have tended their stations with something like the care they lavish on their own red-brick houses.

Belgian railroad workers (*cheminots/spoorwegmannen*) have been heroic soldiers and intrepid saboteurs when their country has been beseiged by war or occupied by enemy invaders. A monument in the main hall of Brussels's Central Station commemorates "the 3,012 railroad workers who died for the Country" in World Wars I and II; and in the Second World War railway men banded together to form a special unit within "Group G," an underground movement that engaged in organized acts of sabotage against the Germans throughout their May 1940–September 1944 occupation of Belgium.

Belgian artists have been fascinated by trains, tracks, and railway stations. Paul Delvaux painted them again and again in a hauntingly surrealistic, dreamlike way—peopling his railroad stations with mysterious women and timid, petit-bourgeois men so preoccupied with what they are eternally awaiting that they are oblivious of one another. Delvaux received many national and international honors in the course of his artistic lifetime; but in his view none of them surpassed being named honorary stationmaster of Louvain-la-Neuve by the Belgian minister of communication, at the age of eighty-seven, complete with the mauve kepi, with its shiny black visor and gold trim, and the silver whistle that are the earmarks of the station chief's rank.

Because of all they connote, Belgian trains have been more than physical means of travel for me.

. . . OUR TRAIN began to move alongside the meadows under the most astonishing sky I have ever seen. The brilliant fields, newly washed by the rain; delicate lace patterns formed by the remaining leaves on the late October trees (strange, how much like the first leaves of spring these last leaves of fall look); the silhouettes of cows and sheep grazing; the horses pulling wagons; the red-roofed houses; our long, diesel-drawn train; we, the passengers within it—were no more than pinpoints before the enormity and expressiveness of that sky. There were great white mountains of clouds in some areas of the sky, huge black masses of clouds in others. From some of the clouds came ray after ray of light—golden paths that invited you to debark from your horizontally voyaging train and journey upward instead. In the sky spaces between the clouds were deep pools of pure, joyous blue, and on the edge of the horizon tiny pink clouds, dainty and shy, trimmed with faint tracings of gold. The train rode under a black cloud that began to rain on the fields, trees, animals, houses, and on us. When we emerged on the other side of the cloud, the rain marks left on the face of the train window began to roll down its surface like glistening tears—tears not so much of sorrow, as of wonder. . . .

SHE SAT by a window, serenely watching the landscape that Breughel had painted and that André Delvaux films.

She was a young woman, in her twenties, dressed in summer yellow—a simple blouse, jacket, and skirt, with no accessories. She wore a plain gold wristwatch and carried a small, black leather briefcase. Her hair was long and blonde, and gently wavy. It framed her oval but robust face with its Rubens complexion. Under her almond-shaped lids, her eyes were pensively focused on the landscape. They were very blue and clear, and filled with the light of the sky. There was a stillness all around her. She was untouched by the sharp gestures and the staccato sounds made by the passenger on her left as he turned the pages of his daily newspaper.

When I recognized her I was strangely moved. She was a reincarnated madonna from an ancient Flemish painting—a madonna with a gold wristwatch, red lipstick, and a black briefcase, riding in a twentieth-century Belgian train.

She left the train at Leuven and disappeared into the streets of that modern version of a medieval, Catholic university town.

HE WAS a technical education manager at IBM of Belgium, he told me, as we rode together in the same train compartment, en route from Verviers where he lived to Brussels where he worked. He reminisced about all the train trips he used to take when he was a boy, to tiny villages and small towns in Wallonie, over winding tracks that followed the curves of the countryside's hills and streams. He regretted that for reasons of economy and efficiency many local routes and station stops had been eliminated—more in Wallonie than in Flanders, he added with some pique. His dream, he confided, was to buy one of the small, abandoned railroad stations in a Walloon village and make it into a second home where he and his family could spend weekends and vacations.

TRAINS STILL arrive and depart continually and punctually in Brussels's Central Station on their customary, long-established tracks. They are clearly announced over the loudspeaker, in both Flemish and French, and by perfectly coordinated mechanical signs. The ticket-vending and multilingual information services function with speed and courtesy, but the station is no longer clean. When I arrived back in Brussels after ten o'clock this evening, an employee was washing its floors with a pail of soapy water and a torchon (a cloth mop). The water, the suds, and the cloth were so dirty, and the workman's motions so languid, that the mopping made no difference at all.

And each time I have taken a train from Central Station this summer, its waiting room—greatly reduced in size from the space it used to occupy—has been filled with vagrant men. Belgian passengers, waiting for their scheduled trains, seem reluctant to enter the room. They hover irresolutely outside its doors, as if they had just been expelled from it.

July 24, 1987

Passing through the Central Station in Brussels this morning, I noticed that two sets of signs have been posted on the double glass doors of the waiting room. Printed in white script on a black background in Flemish and French, they read:

> FOR REASONS OF HYGIENE AND SECURITY,
> THE WAITING ROOM IS CLOSED FROM
> 11:30 P.M. TO 6 A.M.

August 2, 1988

The homeless men, it would seem, have not been willing to relinquish the waiting room. Another set of bilingual signs has been added to those posted last summer:

> ACCESS IS AUTHORIZED ONLY TO PERSONS IN
> POSSESSION OF A VALID TRAIN OR
> PLATFORM TICKET. FAILURE TO
> RESPECT THIS MEASURE CAN LEAD TO
> A FINE OF 600 FRANCS

July 21, 1990

The signs on the door of the Central Station waiting room have been altered once more: FAILURE TO RESPECT THIS MEASURE [they now say] CAN LEAD TO A MINIMUM FINE OF 1000 FRANCS.

THE POSTAL SYSTEM . . .

Letters, as well as trains, have connected me with the Belgian houses I have entered over the years. Despite the importance the telephone had assumed in Belgium as a modern means of communication, an older, epistolary tradition was still alive in the country when I first arrived there. Writing a letter was not only viewed as a courteous way of communicating but as less invasive than a phone call. In this small, train-laced country, mail was delivered so quickly and reliably that corresponding was at least as practical as telephoning.

It did not take me long to notice the great volume and variety of transactions that Belgians carried out through the postal system. One had only to walk into a local post office and see the bewildering range of *guichets*: subscriptions to newspapers; fishing permits (license stamps, fiscal stamps, postage stamps); postage stamps (small quantities); business matters—bills (deposit, payment, liquidation); transactions of more than fifty thousand francs; savings accounts and insurance; proxies. . . .

I was also intrigued by the way the country's official bilingualism extended even to mailboxes. Attached to the wrought-iron gate on the small private street in Brussels where I lived in 1960 was a shiny red mailbox with two slots: the one on the left-hand side of the box with instructions for mailing letters printed in French, the one on the right-hand side of the box with the same instructions in Flemish. Should letters written in French be mailed in the French slot, I wondered as I contemplated it; those written in Flemish in the Flemish slot? And what ought one to do with a letter written in English?

I described this mailbox and my amused puzzlement in a published essay. Almost a year later a distinguished professor of medicine with whom I was trying to discuss the situation of Belgian medical research devoted a great deal of my interview with him to that double-slotted mailbox. At first he earnestly denied that such mailboxes even existed in Belgium; then, after conceding there might be "a few" of this type, he chastised me for failing to explain that, no matter which slot one used to mail a letter—the Flemish slot or the French slot—"everything ends up in the same mailbox!"

IN 1987 A.M. gave me a small Belgian bon voyage gift: a tiny, tablike stamp, beige and tan, that was used in the 1900–1910 era, when Léopold II was king of the Belgians. On the stamp, underneath Léopold II's bearded profile, is printed: *"Ne Pas Délivrer le Dimanche/Niet Bestellen op Zondag"*—i.e., "Not to Be Delivered on

Sunday." "Keep the stamp," A.M. wrote me, "as an example of *le compromis à la belge.*"

The "Belgian compromise" involved what was then considered to be a burning religio-philosophical question. In those days mail was delivered several times a day, seven days a week, Sundays included, by a postal service that was as historically noteworthy and as much a focus of national pride as the Belgian railway system. The homogeneously Catholic government then in power was intent on finding a way to exempt postal employees and mailmen from working on Sundays so they could attend mass and engage in other pious religious and family activities on this Sabbath day of rest. For reasons as integrally connected with the secular sacredness of Belgium's postal system as with the inevitable distrust that Catholic and non-Catholic Belgians alike felt (and still feel) about anything that threatens their constitutional separation between church and state, this proposed reform caused national controversy.

In the end the little Léopold II stamp was the compromise that all Belgian factions accepted. It was part of a larger stamp in such a way that it could easily be detached. The person using it had the freedom to decide whether to remove the "Not to Be Delivered" tab. If it was removed, then the letter was obligatorily delivered to its addressee through the Sunday work of whatever postal employees it took to handle this dominical mail.

THERE ARE no Sunday deliveries in Belgium anymore. But mailboxes continue to be bright red, with a gold horn, a gold crown, and a gold "B" emblazoned on them. Some of them have two slots, others a single slot. With the federalization of Belgium and its division into cultural communities and regions, the universe of Belgian mailboxes has grown more complex. There are Flemish mailboxes in Flanders, and French mailboxes in Wallony. Only in Brussels are the single-slotted mailboxes bilingual, labeled "*Hier, Post No. 1000*" on one side, and "*Ici, Poste No. 1000*" on the other.

Part Two

PRIVATE HOUSES

Michel de Ghelderode in his salon (photo: Charles Leirens)

The House and the Family
on Izegemsestraat

SEPTEMBER 12, 1962

"Willy *komt!*" proclaimed the grey Congolese parrot with the red tail feathers from his cage by the sunny window in the living room/dining room area of the Van Marcke house. "Willy *komt!*" Willy Van Marcke—the eldest son and first-born child of the family, a Jesuit priest, social scientist, and missionary in Zaïre—did come home today, after a two-year stint of graduate work in the United States. He brought me with him, and I spent most of the day in the West Flemish hamlet of Watermolen, close to the provincial city of Kortrijk (Courtrai)....

WHEN Cyriel and Clara Van Marcke, Willy's parents, initially settled in Watermolen in 1928, the population of the hamlet consisted of 1,235 persons. Its smallness notwithstanding, Watermolen had a complex social organization. Then, as now, different parts of the village were under the municipal jurisdiction of different surrounding communities—the towns of Heule and Kuurne, and the city of Kortrijk. At that time there were no less than twenty-five cafés in Watermolen, each with a different set of social, economic, and political functions and a different cross section of village clientele. By 1962, under the impact of growing industrialization and modernization, the population of Watermolen had doubled. The number of cafés had diminished.

Clara De Vlies and Cyriel Van Marcke were married in 1924. He was in his mid-twenties but she was only nineteen, and her parents thought she was still too young to be a wife and mother. The local parish priest, who knew Clara well, was impressed with her maturity and competence, and by the quality of her relationship with Cyriel. He reassured Clara's mother and father, supported the young couple's marriage, and presided over their wedding in the parish church.

Clara De Vlies, one of nine children, was born in the West Flemish village of Aarsele. Her family later moved to the nearby small city of Tielt. The De Vlieses had been tenant farmers, but once in Tielt their major source of livelihood came from running a hardware store. Sometime later they moved to a house on the outskirts of the city where they raised livestock, maintained a vegetable garden and an orchard of fruit trees, and grew wheat and potatoes. Some of Willy Van Marcke's earliest and happiest boyhood memories are of the time he spent at his maternal grandparents' house every summer—particularly the physical enjoyment he experienced working in their fields, and his silent communion with his grandfather who worked alongside him.

Like Clara De Vlies, Cyriel Van Marcke grew up in Tielt, a few houses away from the De Vlies family. He was one of seventeen children, mainly boys. Fifteen of these children survived infancy, but Cyriel's mother died very young, of what the family now considers to be "exhaustion from childbirth."

Cyriel's father sold woolen cloth in this area of the country known for its textiles (principally linen and wool). He was an itinerant merchant, a peddler, with regular clients whom he visited periodically on his bicycle. Willy still remembers the big brown cardboard sample case on the back of his grandfather's bicycle, and the monthly stops he made at their house for a noonday meal before continuing on his route.

Most of Cyriel Van Marcke's brothers became craftsmen and artisans: shoemakers, tailors, carpenters, and cabinetmakers. Cyriel himself became a printer. He was employed most of his adult life by a Christian Workers' Movement press, in which he was also an active trade union leader.

Cyriel's eagerness to marry Clara De Vlies was intensified by his yearning to establish a quiet and orderly life after his own youth in a motherless, predominantly male household of children. Clara and Cyriel Van Marcke spent the first years of their marriage living in a small apartment in Kortrijk, close to the printing press where Cyriel worked. Willy was born in 1926 in a hospital in Kortrijk. In order to rent the tiny house in Watermolen to which they moved in 1928, Clara had to borrow money from her mother. Within a year's time she had repaid the loan with earnings from dressmaking she had begun to do at home.

FROM THE Kortrijk station our taxi drove briskly through the streets of the city: past its *Grote Markt* (central marketplace and square); its Gothic and Renaissance *Stadhuis* (town hall), with the statues of the counts of Flanders sculpted on its stone façade; its belfry, and the gilded, folkloric figures that turn around the chiming clock in the bell tower; its seventeenth-century *Begijnhof*—the enclosed cluster of baroque houses within which a community of lay sisters (*béguines*) once lived; its busy tearooms and pastry shops; and its historic *Guldensporenslag* (The Battle of the Golden Spurs) monument. The monument, Willy explained dryly, was erected to commemorate "the only military battle the Flemish ever won against the French." In this battle of July 11, 1302, waged by an army of Flemish commoners against King Philip IV (The Fair) and his cavalry, seven hundred noblemen recognizable by their golden spurs were among the thousands of French soldiers killed. Although July 21 (1830) is the official date of independence of Belgium as a nation-state, every year Flemish-Belgians celebrate July 11 as *their* independence day.

Our taxi left the square and drove along the tree-arched avenue and public park bordering the River Lys that runs through the city, past the Broel Towers—the vestiges of the walls, the military defenses, and the castle that girded medieval Kortrijk—and then proceeded down a narrow, winding cobblestone road, lined on both sides with unbroken rows of small, shuttered houses, some with geranium-filled window boxes. This was the road that Willy walked four times a day when he was a boy, to and from the secondary school (*collège*) that he attended in Kortrijk—a half-hour by foot each way. On this weekday in mid-September the street was filled with many blond- and some black-haired schoolchildren, the boys in short pants, the girls in short, pleated skirts, with knee socks, sturdy shoes, warm hooded jackets, and big school bags. They were en route to their houses for the noontime meal—the same midday trek Willy used to make when he was their age.

Many of his classmates at his *collège*, Willy had told me, were the sons of French-speaking, middle-class merchant and professional families from Kortrijk and its environs. As a working-class, Flemish-speaking village boy he had never before had sustained

contact with people from their milieu, and at first he was somewhat
intimidated by them. Getting to know these young men and to feel
more at ease with them was a valuable experience, he said, but it
did not start him down the path of striving to be more like them.
Quite to the contrary, reflecting on his own background from this
new vantage point enhanced his appreciation of his own Flemish,
Christian, working-class heritage. This family heritage was epitomized for him by the work ethic of both his parents and by his
father's involvement in social movements.

Willy described his father as "a proud printer" who made books
and taught his son to revere them. Throughout Willy's boyhood
and youth, his father was a leader among his fellow printers in their
organized efforts to further the "social emancipation" of the Flemish
working class, improve their life conditions, and develop trade
unionism. In addition, as chairman of the local Christian Workers
Movement, a member of a number of other Social-Christian organizations in Watermolen, and head of the board of the parish
church, most of his father's time and energy were dedicated to these
goals. Because the meetings he led or participated in often took
place in their house, Willy had much opportunity to see him in this
role. Willy was deeply impressed and stirred by the generosity and
the "religious fervor" with which his father gave himself to this
mission.

The taxi slowed and stopped in front of the Van Marckes' home
on Izegemsestraat—a small brick house with a store window on its
ground floor. Two little blonde girls, the daughters of Willy's sister
Germaine, dashed excitedly through the front door. Seizing his
suitcase, they darted into the shop, announcing at the top of their
small voices that "Nonkel Pater Willy" (Uncle Father Willy) was
here.

We quickly followed the two girls (Lydie and Anne-Marie).
The bell on the shop door tinkled as we entered. Germaine and
Willy's mother—Moeder Clara—welcomed us with shy warmth.
However reticent their greeting, it was apparent that this home-
coming and visit had turned an ordinary Wednesday into a feast
day for the Van Marcke family.

Moeder Clara was a voluble, dynamic woman in her late fifties,
trim and agile, with sparklingly alert, intelligent brown eyes framed
by steel-rimmed glasses; a youthful, unlined, open face; and short,
greying brown hair, neatly arranged in the nondescript style of the

local beauty parlor. She wore a well-cut, blue-and-white silk print dress with a matching jacket that I later learned she had made. Germaine, heavyset, slow moving, pink-cheeked, and blonde like her daughters, in a freshly washed and ironed cotton house dress, hovered smilingly and deferentially in the background.

The small, dimly lit shop with its dark brown wood counters, shelves, and rows of supply drawers, and its curtained fitting room, was a well-stocked apparel store for women, men, and children. Its merchandise also included books, sewing supplies of all sorts, and linen tablecloths, place mats, and napkins. It was an economic and social hub of the village as well as a much appreciated family store. And it was the business, born out of Moeder Clara's imaginative and indomitable entrepreneurial spirit, that saved the Van Marcke family from the poverty they had faced when World War II ended. Over the years the revenue from Moeder Clara's store had made it possible for the Van Marckes to give a plot of land to each child upon marriage, funds toward building a home on that land, monies to help them open shops of their own, and a small (and equal) inheritance.

When the war ended in 1945 both Willy and his mother told me, as a consequence of the privation to which the German occupation had subjected West Flemish villagers, the whole Van Marcke family—Moeder Clara, Vader Cyriel, and their five children, Willy, Karel, Germaine, Mariette, and Marcel—had less than the Belgian equivalent of a hundred American dollars to feed, clothe, and house themselves. Moeder Clara took the situation in hand by beginning to sell the kinds of reasonably priced, practical, yet stylish articles of clothing that she knew, from her keen observation of the community, fit its inhabitants' needs, resources, and tastes. She produced some of the merchandise by working all day and deep into the night on her sewing machine. She also trained a number of village girls and young women in dressmaking. The dresses they cut from patterns and sewed by machine and hand were sold from her little shop; and the training the village women received from Moeder Clara gave them a skill they could use to their own financial advantage.

During the train ride from Brussels to Kortrijk, Willy not only gave me some background on his mother's store; he also explained why his sister Germaine and her two children were living with his parents. Germaine, he said, was born with a congenital heart condition of some sort and had been in fragile health all during her youth. In addition to her cardiac condition she was a slow learner. She was a basically good, hard-working, and obliging person who was an excellent housekeeper and helpful to her parents and siblings. When a couple whom Mr. and Mrs. Van Marcke had known for years suggested that one of their sons and Germaine might be encouraged to think of marriage, her parents agreed. Germaine's marriage prospects were not brilliant, and the Van Marckes felt secure in the knowledge that the young man who had been proposed as a husband for her came from a decent Flemish working-class family like their own. The marriage took place, and the two little girls were born of it. Although she did not complain, it became apparent that Germaine was being beaten by her husband, who was drinking too much and who also turned out to have a history of serious mental illness that his family had somehow managed to keep hidden. In effect, Mr. and Mrs. Van Marcke rescued their daughter from her husband and took her and their two granddaughters to live with them.

Germaine's separation from her husband created an acute crisis in the Van Marcke family. Clara and Cyriel felt responsible for their part in arranging her unfortunate marriage and for its breakup. From their perspective as pious Catholics, as the parents of a son about to be ordained a Jesuit priest, and as community leaders, they had brought disgrace on the family. For some months they retreated into what amounted to social isolation. Cyriel no longer went to the meetings of any of his local organizations.

Willy was in Belgium, studying theology in Leuven at the t.me. The family was so distressed that his religious superior permitted him to go home to do what he could to comfort and counsel them. They gradually became convinced that Germaine's separation from her husband was as right as it was necessary.

Willy was the first person in his family's history and entire kinship system to become a priest. No one, including himself, anticipated that the priesthood would be his vocation. From the time he was a boy he was recognized at school and in the village as exceptionally bright and studious. He was renowned in the village for reading his way through the collection of books in the local library. The citizens of Watermolen who knew him and his parents predicted an outstanding future for him. Why, someone with his ability and diligence, they said, could even become a *statiechef*—a stationmaster!

Like most of the boys and men of the village, Willy relished sports. He was particularly enthusiastic about soccer, the Belgian national sport, in which he excelled as a player. He had several close young male friends with whom he shared athletic activities, long bicycle rides in the countryside, books he read, and some of his thoughts and feelings. Although he was timid and taciturn in the company of girls his own age, he always took it for granted that boys and girls, and men and women, were equals. He respected women and appreciated their qualities. Moeder Clara was an important influence in this regard.

Willy was a highly sensitive and perceptive young man, thoughtful and serious, inwardly solitary, deeply moral, rather melancholy, covertly tender and romantic, privately humorous, gently ironic, capable of lacerating sarcasm; and he was filled with silence and dreams. He was attuned to nature and to the landscape within which his daily round took place. He had a painter's sense of beauty and imagery, a writer's sense of language, and a printer's sense of design and exactitude. His emphatic, down-to-earth relationship to the human condition, and his strong convictions about social justice and injustice, extended far beyond the parameters of his tiny village and small country. Though it was only through books and in his imagination that he had experienced anything larger, he yearned toward the spacious and the distant.

He was fourteen years old when World War II began and the Germans invaded and occupied Belgium. His most profound memory of the war concerned his father and himself, the principled responsibilities that Vader Cyriel expected his son to uphold, Willy's dutiful commitment to these expectations, and his ruefully comic sense of his inability to fulfill them. Because the Germans were rounding up and sending ablebodied Belgian men to work in Germany, Cyriel Van Marcke felt it important to prepare his eldest son for this eventuality. In a solemn conversation with Willy, he impressed upon him the fact that he would become the head of the family if his father were to be conscripted into the Nazi work force, or if any other wartime exigency were to remove him from the household. Under these circumstances, Vader Cyriel made clear, he not only expected Willy to take responsibility for the well-being of his mother and siblings in everyday ways, but to defend them against any danger that might arise, no matter what the peril for him. "If at any time you can save a human life," Vader Cyriel told Willy, "don't think about it, just do it—even if it means risking your own life." Willy gravely promised his father that he would do so. That same evening the Germans opened artillery fire in the area. Mortar shells exploded in the village. At the Van Marcke house pieces of shrapnel pierced the front door and shattered one of its windows. There was a great din, and the small house trembled. Acting on his first frightened impulse, Willy dived underneath the nearest available table. As soon as the commotion had subsided, his father grabbed him by the scruff of his neck, pulled him to his feet, and gave him several resounding blows, chastising him for his egotistically self-protective reaction. Willy's behavior, Vader Cyriel emphasized, was the antithesis of what he had pledged to do if called upon to assume the role of substitute head of the family.

As the war continued and the Occupation went on, the economic resources of the Van Marcke family dwindled. It was now 1944, the year Willy should have been graduating from secondary school. Because he was intrigued by technology in general and the electrification of the Belgian railroad in particular, the field of civil engineering attracted him as a profession. But his family could not afford to pay the tuition for university studies, and there were no scholarships available for a working-class village boy like himself in that era. Willy decided to help his family get back on their feet financially and also earn enough money to go to the university by seeking a term of employment in the Belgian Congo. For him, as for so many other young Belgians, the Congo held forth more than economic incentives. It was "the one open door and open window" in tiny, tradition-enclosed Belgium—a frontier and a dreaming space.

For the first time in his young life Willy traveled to Brussels—an hour's train ride from Kortrijk—where he had made an appointment to have a job interview with a big Belgian trading company that did a great deal of business in the Lower Congo. The idea of making contact with this company had been suggested to him by a Jesuit missionary priest who had preached the annual student retreat at Willy's school. The company was owned by a French-speaking Flemish family from Ghent who had a Jesuit missionary son in the Congo. The person who interviewed Willy was sufficiently impressed with his academic credentials and his motivation to offer him a three-year contract to work as a commercial agent in the Congo as soon as the war was over. Since Willy was only eighteen years old at the time, he was required to show the contract to his parents and obtain their signed accord. He left the office of the firm in a state of exhilaration; but for reasons that he still finds mysterious, after his return to Kortrijk and Watermolen he said nothing to his family or friends about the contract he had received. He walked around with it in his pocket for days, neither signing it himself nor asking his parents to endorse it. It was as if a curtain of silence and a restraining hand had descended upon him.

In the midst of his seeming reluctance to finalize the Congo arrangements, Willy became convinced that he was called to the priesthood, and to the Jesuit Order if the Society of Jesus would accept him. He was attracted to the Jesuits because of their traditions of self-discipline, intellectuality, and internationalism, and their relative autonomy of action within the Catholic church.

He has never described to family or friends what signs of a religious vocation he experienced, but he now felt certain that he had been called, and that it was as a priest, rather than as a commercial agent, that he would someday go to the Congo. He discussed this development with his parents, expressing great concern that if he did become a priest they would be losing a crucial family breadwinner. His parents insisted that this should not deter him. What did worry them, however, was that a young man of working-class origins like Willy aspired to enter the Society of Jesus—a religious order whose Belgian members came principally from upper-middle-class professional and business families. Wouldn't it be more appropriate and comfortable, his parents asked, for him to become a Scheut father in a Belgian missionary congregation whose priests were predominantly the children of farmers, craftsmen, and workers? All the same, Willy applied for admission to the Society of Jesus. Immediately following his graduation, in the final year of World War II, he began the novitiate phase of his Jesuit training. Seven years later he arrived in the Congo as a Jesuit missionary.

MOEDER CLARA and Germaine closed the shop and put a sign in the window to indicate that it would not resume business for several hours. We entered the family's living quarters behind the store through a door that opened directly into the main room of the house. It was a relatively small room, crowded and dwarfed by all that was in it: a coat rack virtually buried under the raincoats, topcoats, jackets, suits, dresses, hats, and mufflers that hung on its pegs; a big dining room table and many straight-backed chairs; several massive armchairs; an overstuffed couch; an oak breakfront crammed with dishes and glasses; a large radio; a grandfather clock; potted snake plants; ornate vases containing artificial flowers; mementos from a pilgrimage to Lourdes; a doll-like madonna under a glass bell-jar, dressed in amethyst velvet, brocade, and lace, wearing a gold crown; a crucifix; a colored portrait of Pope John XXIII; several paintings of the Flemish countryside by local artists; and a copper-colored, souvenir Statue of Liberty.

Large, elaborately framed wedding photographs of the married Van Marcke children and their spouses hung on the walls of this combined dining room, living room, and parlor, like pictures in an art gallery. A smiling photo portrait of Willy, wearing his Roman collar, occupied a place of honor in the midst of the nuptial display, elevated slightly above it. The same picture of *Pater* Willy was exhibited in the same way in his sister Mariette's and his brother Karel's houses, I discovered, when we visited them after our dinner at the Van Marckes. The family enjoyed teasing Willy about his embarrassment over the iconlike status his image had been accorded, and he enjoyed teasing back.

The dining room table was set with a beige linen cloth and plain white dishes. It stood near a window that looked out on the vegetable and flower garden in the rear of the house, and a small orchard of pear, apple, and plum trees. In this choice corner of the room the family's parrot Jacko (a gift to the Van Marckes from one of Willy's former Congolese students) had his domain. From the perch inside his cage he uttered a continuous stream of colorful phrases: "Willy is coming!" "Ger-maine!" "Down with Tshombe!" "You poor little fool!" he loudly declared in West Flemish dialect, interspersing his comments with a perfect imitation of Moeder Clara's high-pitched laugh. Jacko, I was told, was also notorious for his repertoire of profanity.

My thoughts turned momentarily to the nameless parrot in front of the upstairs window of the opulent Hôtel Errera on Brussels's Rue Royale—brilliantly colored, majestically isolated, and mute, overseeing a house of lonely splendor. Here, in contrast, was Jacko, drably grey except for his few red tail feathers, but vocal and gregarious—a spirited occupant of this modest house and a very audible participant in the busy, closely knit life of the family and the village.

At 1 p.m. Vader Cyriel came home from work to join us. Cyriel Van Marcke was a small-boned, slender, slightly stooped man with a beautifully chiseled face framed by a thick crop of snow-white hair. Like Willy, he was quiet, powerfully feeling, and self-controlled. On his return, Jacko the parrot became even more animated.

Dinner was a relatively simple but copious meal. Willy, seated at the head of the table, said grace. We then hungrily ate the food that Moeder Clara and Germaine put on the table. There were generous helpings of homemade soup and of the main course, a regional Flemish dish (one of Willy's favorites)—rabbit cooked in brown beer with stewed prunes—served with potatoes and string beans from the garden, and a choice of red table wine or Flemish beer. In a mixture of Flemish, French (of which the Van Marckes had a primary-school grasp), and English, with Willy acting as interpreter, we spoke of basic things: the family, the house, work, salaries and earnings, prices and the cost of living, local and national changes in Belgium. And everyone was eager to hear as much about *Amerika* as Willy and I were willing to tell.

When the meal was over Cyriel Van Marcke invited Willy and me to see his garden. But first he spent several minutes trying to coax Jacko into adding a French phrase to his vocabulary: "*Bonjour, Renée!*" Jacko cocked his head attentively when Vader Cyriel spoke, gazed at him through the bars of his cage, and showed no inclination whatsoever to greet me in this way.

In order to get to the garden we had to pass through the kitchen with its old-fashioned plumbing, its wood-burning and gas stoves, its framed collection of photographs of the Van Marcke sons and daughters when they were children, and its assorted religious objects. A curtain of multicolored plastic streamers hung at the back door. On warm summer days when the kitchen door was kept open, it acted as a screen to keep the flies out of the house.

Over the low whitewashed walls surrounding the garden we could see the neighboring red-brick row houses, the roof of the parish primary school, the spire of the local church, and the surrounding pasture land in which cows were grazing. Vader Cyriel stopped to examine the cabbages and the Brussels sprouts. It was his fruit trees, however, that he was especially eager to show us, particularly the pear trees, heavy with the fruit he most enjoyed eating as well as growing.

After our tour of the garden Vader Cyriel returned to work, riding his bicycle. Moeder Clara gave Willy and me a stack of family photograph albums to go through while she and Germaine washed the dinner dishes. The albums were filled with pictures of the Van Marcke children, their parents, relatives, and friends, at rites of passage and celebration times in the life of the family: photos of first communions, graduations, engagement parties, weddings, births, baptisms, holiday gatherings, and of certain village occasions like the *kermesse*. A sizable group of photos chronicled Willy's priestly career. There was one of him as a Jesuit novice, snapped through the openings of a wire fence that separated him from his family and the outside world at that stage in his training. And there were several pages of pictures of Willy taken on the occasion of his ordination in Leuven, and on the day he said his first mass in the village of Watermolen: Willy—genuflecting before the bishop while tiny choir boys sang Gregorian chants, standing on tiptoe to read the music on the tall wooden stand around which they were grouped; leaving the house on Izegemsestraat for the local parish church on a rainy morning, dressed in his black cassock, grinning sheepishly under the very feminine rose-colored umbrella held over his head by *Tante* Lisa; saying his first mass, hands outstretched in a blessing, a nimbus of incense floating around his head; passing under the arch of flowers over the front door of the Van Marcke house on his return from church; at the evening banquet given in his honor at the parish hall, to which village officials and *notables*, as well as family, friends, the local pastor, and two African priests came in recognition of the first "native" of Watermolen ever to become a Jesuit.

There were also snapshots of Willy the young missionary in a white cassock (and in some, a pith helmet), skeletally thin, with a long, full, black beard. *Fétiche* was the mischievous nickname his students gave him at that time, associating his beard with African magico-religious specialists and their fetishes. At the time Willy was teaching some of the 120 Congolese students at a Jesuit school in Kisantu in the Lower Congo. Young Congolese men of intellectual promise had been brought there from all over the country to be given the most advanced education the colonial regime would permit Africans to receive. Trained to be medical, agricultural, or administrative assistants, when independence came to the Congo in 1960 these men were among its most educated elite, and so they became important national leaders. They belonged to what Belgians called the *évolués*—that is, men who, in the eyes of the Belgian colonial administration, had "evolved" intellectually, socially, and morally beyond the "primitive" mentality, material conditions, and life-style of the Congolese "masses" toward the more "civilized" outlook, conduct, and standing of Europeans. Willy's emaciated appearance in the Kisantu photographs indicated how totally identified he had become with his students' aspirations and the problems they faced in realizing them. He was literally working himself to skin and bones helping them to obtain the best possible education and gain access to the professional fields they wished to enter. In several instances, with the support of his Jesuit superiors, Willy challenged Belgian colonial policy by enabling his students to surpass the educational and occupational limits that by fiat it imposed on the Congolese.

It was mid-afternoon now, and we still had visits to make to Willy's brother Karel and to his sister Mariette before taking the last train, the 8:13 p.m., back to Brussels. (I would not meet Willy's youngest brother, Marcel, today, I was told, because he was working a double shift at the steel plant where he was employed.) Germaine appeared with a rag and shoe polish in her hands. Kneeling before me, she wiped the day's dust and the mud from the garden off my shoes.

Karel—blond, handsome, resembling his father more than his brother, rather debonair in manner—arrived in his car to drive Willy and me to his shop and his home in the village of Marke. Over his street clothes he was wearing the starched white working-coat of his trade, that of a butcher. Twenty minutes later we drew up in front of Karel's shop where he immediately took us on a guided tour. It was the most immaculate butcher shop I have ever seen. It gleamed; and the prime cuts of meat in its show cases were arranged with artistry. The walk-in refrigerator was filled with sides of beef and other choice meats and equipped with the most up-to-date instruments. It was as spotless and as systematically organized as an operating room.

Karel and his wife Sylvie worked endless hours in this shop which they had opened earlier in the year. It was located within the orbit of a new housing development made up of prospering

Flemish, working-class residents. The customers who patronized the shop wanted no less than Grade A meat, for which they were both willing and able to pay; and so they appreciated the quality of the merchandise that Karel and Sylvie carried. The business was thriving, to an extent that emboldened Karel and Sylvie to take a weekend trip to Paris for the first time in their lives.

Adjacent to the store was the modern tan-brick house with a big picture window they had just finished building on a sizable corner lot. With Karel and Sylvie's permission, a statue of the Virgin Mary was being constructed in a section of their garden, where the local parish priest was planning to come regularly with members of the church to pray the rosary in the open air (weather permitting).

Inside the house Sylvie—a blonde, stocky, nervously smiling young woman with glasses and very red cheeks—and the four towheaded Van Marcke children, two girls and two boys, greeted us. There was high excitement over the return of Pater Willy and great curiosity about his guest and about America. The furnishing of the large living room/dining room area was still not complete, but the family photographs (Willy's picture included) and a crucifix were up on the walls, and there was a new record player in a bookcase that contained only a few books. Like his father, Karel was fond of opera (especially Wagnerian works, Viennese waltzes, and marching band [fanfare] music), and his small record collection reflected this.

The dining table was set with the best linen, dishes, glasses, and cutlery, as if we were about to eat another meal. Sylvie served us several platters of assorted, very rich Belgian pastries, washed down by glasses of Bordeaux wine and cups of strong brewed coffee, followed by chasers of brandy for those who wished them.

Once again the lively, news-filled conversation centered on the children and the family, the house and the store, and the village— plus a description of Karel and Sylvie's weekend in Paris. Out poured critical events that had taken place in their household since Willy's last visit. The overall tone was optimistic: with hard work, and the socioeconomic changes for the better that were taking place in Flanders, the family was moving forward.

Karel then drove us to Mariette's house in the nearby town of Kuurne. Mariette and her husband, Jan Declercq, had opened a grocery store only ten days ago in a community where another new project of working-class houses was just being developed. The Declercqs' store, and the house they had built behind it, were across the road from a Ford Motor Company center. Fanned by the wind from the North Sea, an American flag flew vigorously on a staff over its main building, looking very red, white, and blue in the intense Flemish light. Behind the center stretched the still undisturbed flax fields of West Flanders, and just beyond them, in the distance, the newly constructed superhighway to Brugge.

Mariette was a woman of quick intelligence, slender and black-haired, with an anxious version of Moeder Clara's energy; she was the mother of two sons—a four-year-old and a newborn baby. When she was younger, Mariette hoped to become a nurse. But she put these plans aside in order to help her brother Karel run his first butcher shop in Mouscron and to keep house for him. Mariette's sacrifice played a crucial role in whatever Karel was able to salvage from this initial business venture, when he belatedly discovered that the man who had sold him the store had cheated him by falsifying the account of its assets, profits, and losses.

Mariette was thrilled to see Willy, excited by my presence, and eager to show her grocery store and her home to both of us. If anything, her shop surpassed Karel's in its orderliness. All the groceries were perfectly aligned on their shelves, and every single item had been dusted. The interior of the house, like the store, was impeccable. The principal pieces of furniture in the living room/dining room area—the table and chairs and the breakfront—were made of heavy, blond, hand-carved oak. The same photograph of *Pater* Willy that was in his parents' and his brother's homes, flanked by Mariette and Jan's wedding portrait, smiled down from attractively papered walls on which a crucifix was also hung.

We were served liqueur-filled chocolates wrapped in an array of different-colored foils, arranged on a tray like an abstract painting. There were orange juice, wine, coffee, and water to go with the chocolates. The animated talk took the same form it had during our visits with Moeder Clara and Vader Cyriel, and with Karel and Sylvie: a synopsis of what had happened in the family, and of how they had progressed since the last time Willy was home.

Out came the Declercqs' photograph albums with their pictorial record of earlier family events. Mariette wanted me to see these. One album was devoted to her wedding, another to the births of her two sons. The latter was filled with pictures of Mariette in her hospital bed, a newborn child in her arms, Jan standing close beside them, mother, baby and father surrounded by two sets of grandparents and uncles and aunts.

The doorbell in the shop jingled. Moeder Clara and Vader Cyriel had arrived, accompanied by a large woman who spoke alternating Flemish and French at a breathless rate. This was *Mevrouw* Annick Nuyens, a close family friend and neighbor of the Van Marckes. Her husband, Albert Nuyens, a Watermolen *notable*, was the wealthy manager and sales representative of a branch of the food distribution chain from which Maria purchased all the merchandise in her grocery store. Like Vader Cyriel, *Mijnheer* Nuyens was very active in a number of village church groups. Along with Cyriel Van Marcke and other prominent village citizens—the bourgmaster, the notary, the lawyer, and the medical doctor among them—Mr. Nuyens belonged to the prestigious *kermesse* committee.

Moeder Clara, Vader Cyriel, Willy, and I were all whisked away by Annick Nuyens in her big car. She and her husband had insisted that we stop for supper at their house before boarding the train for Brussels. It was a whirlwind visit. Albert Nuyens, a stout, talkative, rather domineering man, was also an excellent raconteur. He regaled us with stories of his escapades at last year's *kermesse*. Somewhat the worse for wear after a whole night of carnival revelry and drinking, still wearing the *bolhoed* (derby) on his head that is obligatory for *kermesse* committee members (who were fined two hundred Belgian francs if they went without it on the day of the festival), Albert Nuyens got lost in a cornfield, he told us, and did not find his way home until sunrise.

The Nuyenses' house was a larger, more luxurious, and less cluttered version of the others I saw that day. Our meal—the fourth in six hours—consisted of a huge platter of cold cuts and cheeses of every sort, served with great stacks of bread, big bars of butter, a variety of condiments, and a choice of Belgian beers. In the midst of all the eating and the torrent of words that flowed from both the Nuyenses, Albert told Willy and me that if we were to make the evening train back to Brussels we had better start on our way to the Kortrijk station. He insisted on driving us there.

INSIDE THE Brussels-bound train, full of the day (not to mention all the food) and exhausted by it, Willy and I said very little to one another. The volatile Belgian weather had changed, streaking the train windows with heavily falling rain. I did not know it that September night, but this was only the first of many trips I would make over the course of the years to Kortrijk, Watermolen, and Izegemsestraat to see the Van Marcke family.

A Visit with a
Verviers Coiffeur
and His Family

O<small>N AUGUST 2,</small> 1988, I took a train from Brussels to
Verviers to visit Ivan and Georgette Demoulin. The last twenty
minutes of that trip—the interlude between Liège and Verviers—is
nostalgically scenic. The train follows the contours of the Vesdre
River, curving and bending with it as it wends its way past the
river's miniature falls and the gorges and green wooded hills that
line it. Victor Hugo wrote about the loveliness of this valley which
at the turn of the century was also an important site of the
country's first industrial revolution. The waters of the Vesdre were
known for their excellent dyeing properties; textile mills and stone
quarries were located here; and there was coal in the region. Now
all that remained of that era were the rusted remnants of factories
and the empty excavations around which the greenness of the hills
and valley had grown.

The Verviers railroad station was still a major terminal, located
on the main line from Liège to Aix-la-Chapelle/Aachen and
Cologne. But its size, the number of tracks it encompassed, and its
autre-siècle grandeur surpassed the current significance of Verviers—
a small Francophone city of some sixty thousand inhabitants.

Ivan and Georgette Demoulin had invited me to spend the day
at their house so that I could talk with them in detail about their
individual and entwined life stories. We had come to know each
other through the intermediary of their son Guy, whom I had first
met in the late 1970s when he was a graduate student in the United
States, working for his master's degree in communications and
social science. Quickened by the sociological interests we shared,
and above all by my involvement in Belgium, our initial teacher-
student relationship had rapidly developed into one of colleagues

and friends. It was primarily because of my link with their son and his professional world that the Demoulins had agreed to help with my research on Belgium by giving me entrée to their home and to their very private life within it. But "we are not very typical Belgian folks," they had forewarned me, with a mixture of shyness and pride, "so we hope that we don't bias your work."

Ivan and Georgette Demoulin lived on a dreary-looking street lined with nondescript row houses, many of which were shabby and some quite dilapidated. Although the street bore the name of a Verviers man from a noble family, its residents were largely members of the petite bourgeoisie, many of whom had reached the age of retirement. Ivan Demoulin used a Walloon term to characterize the people who lived on his street and in the surrounding neighborhood: *p'tits vieux* and *p'tites vieilles* (little old men and women) he called them, with familiar affection. The area in which the Demoulin house was situated was residential, but there was a merchandise warehouse in the vicinity, with associated customs and trucking services, and nearby was also a technical secondary school.

As soon as one entered the Demoulins' street, their house caught one's eye. It was conspicuously better kept than those around it, and until recently it had been distinguished from all the others by a red-and-white-striped barber pole on its ground-floor façade. (The glass tube of that pole was now an *objet d'art* in Guy's house.) Ivan Demoulin, sixty-seven years old, had been a *coiffeur* since he was a young man in his teens. He was semiretired, but he continued to work every weekday morning in the little barbershop attached to his house, cutting the hair of "old customers" (*vieux habitués*) who had been his clients since the 1950s.

On the August afternoon I came to interview them, Ivan and Georgette were waiting at their front door to greet me. Standing side by side in their doorway and dressed in their finest clothes for the occasion, they were a living domestic portrait—Georgette with her pretty, innocent face, and straight, girlishly bobbed hair, and Ivan, whose intelligent eyes behind steel-rimmed glasses were enlivened by his good-natured smile. The two of them gazed approvingly at the crew of workers across the way who were digging up the cobblestone street, and expressed satisfaction that, thanks to the petitions Ivan had circulated among their neighbors and delivered to the city government, the street's worn gas pipelines and stretches of pavement were finally being repaired.

Although the Demoulin house was clean and in good condition, it did not give an orderly or unified impression. Quite to the contrary, at first one was struck by what seemed to be the great and almost random differences in the way its various rooms were furnished. Only after becoming better acquainted with the house and its occupants did one begin to discern the organizing principles around which the Demoulins' house was structured and layered. The front rooms of the house, especially the *salon*/sitting room area on the second floor, were "bourgeois" in style, with staid, traditional furniture made of dark woods—tables, chairs, armoires, a breakfront, a sofa, and so forth—rather stiffly arranged. (Several of these pieces of furniture came from the château once owned and inhabited by the nobleman after whom the street on which the Demoulins live was named. Ivan and Georgette purchased this furniture from the persons in charge of demolishing the castle after it had been used as a technical school for a number of years.) What might be called the "middle rooms" of the house, the spacious dining alcove and the huge kitchen, located several steps below the *salon*, were more "popular" in feeling. As one moved deeper into this part of the house, where a bath, shower, and laundry were located—at the far end of the kitchen and on the threshold of the garden—the rooms took on the appearance and ambience of the residence of a small farmer. Here every conceivable kind of tool, apparatus, spare part, or object which might some day have practical value in the maintenance of the house and the garden were stored. The kitchen opened onto a spacious garden with a greenhouse that resembled a cultivated field. Under a patch of Verviers sky, encircled by the somber silhouettes of the ill-tended row houses nearby, Ivan grew an impressive array of fruits and vegetables as well as flowers. In a unique and rather curious way, Ivan and Georgette's farmer and petit-bourgeois social origins, along with the relatively modest amount of upward mobility they had achieved in the course of their lifetime, coexisted in the stratified layout of the house.

The socio-logic of the house notwithstanding, it had a number of what Ivan, Georgette, and their two sons, Guy and Emile, all considered "original" features which, they acknowledged with a certain pride, bordered on the "eccentric." The house was crammed with an odd collection and a pell-mell arrangement of things that were neither as predictable nor as conventionally placed as the family photographs, madonnas under bell jars, crucifixes, paintings by local artists, and souvenirs from trips that one finds in the homes of Flemish families of the same social class. The only comparable set of self-consciously arrayed possessions was Georgette's collection of dolls from different countries that were lined up on the mantel of the fireplace in the *salon*. But even these spread into other parts of the house, all the way up to the top of the big cupboard in Ivan and Georgette's bedroom on the third floor, where the dolls were displayed amidst an assortment of old hats, piles of books, souvenirs, and toys left behind by Guy and Emile who shared this room when they were boys and still living with their parents. The renowned Belgian artist René Magritte would have appreciated the unpremeditated but repeated ways in which the Demoulins put familiar objects in unfamiliar, even startling settings—as he himself did in his painting "*Les Valeurs personnelles*" ("Personal Values") that depicts a bedroom in which, leaning against a wall papered with a Magritte-blue, cloud-filled sky, a giant comb is propped up on a small, neatly made single bed, an oversized shaving brush lies on its side on the top of a very small armoire, and a huge matchstick, goblet, and bar of soap stand in the middle of tiny, overlapping Persian rugs.

MY AUGUST 1988 afternoon visit and interview with Ivan and Georgette began in the *salon*, moved outside to the back terrace overlooking the garden, and then, when it was time for a *goûter* (afternoon coffee), was transposed to the kitchen/dining area. Ivan and Georgette were no longer intimidated (as they had been the first time I called on them) by the fact that a university professor from America, who was affiliated with the institution where their son Guy had been a student, was a guest in their home. But it was apparent that they had not only spruced up the house for my visit but had also bought new porch furniture.

In their *salon*, where the first part of our visit took place, Georgette and Ivan described the sorts of families into which they were born, some of their childhood and growing-up experiences, and how they had met. Speaking in her slightly breathless, melodious voice, Georgette told me she was born in 1928, in Dison, a little city near Verviers that was formerly a commercial center where textiles and shoes were produced. She was the younger of two children; her sister was four years older. Her grandparents did leather work at home for shoe manufacturers; her father owned and ran a small gas station; and her mother, who was still alive and was then eighty-seven years old, was a housewife. Her parents' marriage was not a happy one, Georgette admitted, and she often acted as a messenger between them when they angrily refused to speak to each other.

Georgette's family was nominally Catholic. Her parents did not participate in church activities or even attend mass; but they saw to it that their two daughters went to church on Sundays and holy days. They had what Georgette described as a "strict" attitude toward religion, regarding it as "a kind of police force that kept you from doing wrong things."

After completing a middle-school education (six years of primary and three years of secondary education), Georgette did not go on to finish the *humanités* phase of her schooling. Nor did she and her parents even contemplate the possibility that a girl of her modest social class might undertake university studies. Instead she enrolled in courses in home economics, learned to type, and took piano lessons.

She was only seventeen, Georgette said with a radiant smile, when she met twenty-four-year-old Ivan at a local dance, just after World War II had ended. In those days it was not considered proper for an unmarried couple, even if they were engaged, to attend such a function unescorted, and so she had accompanied her sister and fiancé to the dance as a chaperone. Georgette's sister recognized Ivan as the neighbor's son who had spent most of the war in a German prison camp. She introduced Georgette to him, and they spent an enjoyable evening together. Despite the difficulties he had undergone as a prisoner, Georgette said, Ivan was a "gay-spirited" young man with engaging, *brave homme* (nice guy) qualities and real talent as a raconteur. That evening marked the beginning of a four-year courtship before Ivan and Georgette were married.

Here Ivan took up the tale. He was born in 1921 in Spa, some twenty kilometers from Verviers, the third-born of five children. When he was four years old his family moved to Dison, to a house no more than three kilometers from where Georgette and her family lived. His grandparents were small farmers. He had vividly happy memories of summers spent on his paternal grandparents' farm: the cows, the donkeys, the pungent smells, and especially his companionship with his grandfather. Ivan's father worked for the local tramway company, moving up through a progression of jobs until he became its chief supervisor (*contrôleur en chef*). His mother was a housewife.

Like Georgette, Ivan did not complete his secondary-school education. He left school at fourteen to take an apprenticeship as a *coiffeur*. He was strongly influenced in this decision by his conviction that his family could use his financial help, and he still remembered how proud he was the first time he brought home his seventeen-francs-per-week salary to his parents. His godfather, a man whom he greatly loved and admired, was a *coiffeur* and the role model for the occupation Ivan chose to enter. His choice was also shaped by what he called his family's "antiworker mentality." In their view, being employed as an industrial worker, in a factory or a mine, was unacceptable because of the oppressive and demeaning conditions it entailed, whereas work as an artisan, a craftsman, a tradesman, or a civil service employee had a certain dignity and autonomy. Ivan's brothers also entered "nonworker" occupations: his eldest brother became an accountant, the second a carpenter, and the third a *modeleur* (a maker of wooden models for a foundry). It was Ivan's sister who defied the family tradition. Although she was trained to do dressmaking, she insisted on going to work in a textile factory where her chief job became that of "cleaning up" the threads in fabrics with defects in them—very exacting work that had taken a toll on her eyes.

The practice of religion in his family, Ivan said, was "zero." Like their parents and grandparents, the children were baptized Catholics. They learned their catechism and had their first Communion, but as was the case in Georgette's family, no one attended mass or participated in church-affiliated organizations or activities. Nevertheless, Ivan conceded, the extraordinarily high value that his parents placed on upright behavior, and their severe condemnation of anything they considered vulgar, was loosely and distantly connected with their Catholicism.

By May 10, 1940, at the inception of World War II, when the Germans invaded and occupied Belgium, nineteen-year old Ivan Demoulin had finished his apprenticeship as a *coiffeur*, had decided to specialize in the work of a barber, and had already done eight months of obligatory military service. Along with many other Belgian soldiers he was taken prisoner by the Germans and shipped from Belgium to a work camp in Germany. There, because he was so young, was not considered robust enough for certain forms of heavy labor, and showed the ability to learn German quickly, he was assigned to work in the kitchen and was periodically called upon to act as a translator and interpreter. These were relatively privileged jobs which gave him a chance to form decent relations with some of the nonprisoner German women in charge of the kitchen (who surreptitiously gave him extra rations of food and did his laundry for him) and occasionally to catch a glimpse of such "civilized" things as a dining room table and chairs and buffet.

Within the camp a whole "little society" of prisoners developed, with its own "community life," division of labor, exchange system, bases of camaraderie, brand of humor, and even occasional theatrical performances. Ivan found it very useful to be a barber in this setting. His professional ability to shave men and cut their hair was not only appreciated by his fellow prisoners but was also a set of services he could trade for the basic necessities that others could supply. Although he believed then, as he did now, that a good education was a source of personal equilibrium and enrichment, he could not help but notice that many prisoners like himself, who had not had much formal education, were better able to maintain a sense of solidarity, humor, and balance in captivity than some of the educated people who were fellow prisoners. They appeared more isolated to Ivan, and more weighed down by grave thoughts about the meaning of the experience they were undergoing.

In 1941 the Germans established a policy that made it possible for male prisoners of Flemish origins to be released from the camps if they passed a quite superficial examination in spoken Flemish. This measure was part of a larger German strategy to try to mobilize support from Flemish-speaking Belgians, dividing them from those who were French-speaking by defining them as a Germanic people like themselves, and treating them preferentially. Ivan was impressed by the fact that there were numerous Flemish with whom he was imprisoned who did not take advantage of the option the Germans offered but chose to "stay with us" rather than be freed on those terms.

Toward the end of the war, after almost four years of captivity, Ivan was moved to Blechhammer, a prison camp near Auschwitz. He spent three months in this huge camp that was "as large as Liège," he said, and filled with many sorts of prisoners from different backgrounds. There were Jewish, Gypsy, Rumanian, and Yugoslavian prisoners, among others, who wore different kinds of insignia on their sleeves according to the category into which they fell. Ivan's insignia was a yellow triangle. The notorious concentra-tion camp of Auschwitz was very close at hand, and Ivan and his fellow prisoners were continuously aware of a strange odor coming from that direction. But it was not until the war was over and he was once again a free man that he fully realized that this smell must have come from the Auschwitz ovens in which the Germans were exterminating their prisoners. He later learned, too, that the disinfectant used to clean the living quarters of the prison camp where he was interned, which had been so irritating to everyone's eyes and nasal passages, was a diluted form of a gas used at Auschwitz to kill inmates.

Ivan's youth, his cheerful nature, and the support he derived from the prisoners' community all helped him to maintain buoyant spirits throughout his captivity. Nevertheless, for quite a few years after his release from the prison camp he had nightly dreams about his experiences there—bad dreams that still recurred from time to time. The painfully itchy chronic inflammation of the skin on his arms and legs (psoriasis) that he developed as a prisoner of war, from which he still suffered, was also a constant reminder of the darker side of his imprisonment. Still, at first Ivan did not find it easy to adjust to "life outside" the prison camp, and he even missed the camaraderie of the barracks. This led him to reenlist in the army for a year, where he worked as a barber and daydreamed about someday becoming a *coiffeur* on an ocean liner in order to "see the world."

Despite the positive, resilient way in which he handled his prison experiences, it was not until the 1970s, when he became an active leader of a group of former World War II prisoners like himself, that Ivan began to talk openly to his family about what those years in the camp had been like. He still did not take his freedom or everyday life for granted, he said.

In 1949 Ivan and Georgette (who were now twenty-eight and twenty-one years of age respectively) were finally married. Their first residence consisted of two rented rooms attached to the barbershop where Ivan was employed. He was deeply happy in his marriage and very content with their living arrangements. But, like virtually all young Belgian women and men, "I had dreamed of having a house of my own once we were married," Georgette said with feeling. She was surprised and frustrated to discover that her husband did not share this aspiration. After spending years in a prison camp where he had lived in one room with fifty men, Ivan explained, he "felt no need for a house. I thought it was wonderful that Georgette and I had a bedroom of our own, and another room in addition." It took years of discussion and many tears before Georgette was able to convince Ivan that they should purchase a house of their own. In 1957, on the day they moved into that house—where they had lived ever since—Ivan wept with joy. Utilizing all he had learned about carpentry, painting, and electrical work from the many craftsmen who were his barbershop clients, and continually seeking their advice, Ivan became enthusiastically engrossed in renovating the house. He applied his agricultural background to the creation of the large flower, vegetable, and fruit garden behind the house, which he devotedly tended. In addition he derived a great deal of satisfaction from cooking and baking for his wife and children, drawing on the storehouse of recipes and culinary techniques that his closest friend, a man in the hotel and restaurant business, who had also been a prisoner of war, shared with him.

From the outset Ivan and Georgette were united in their desire to have two children; in their conviction that the wife-mother of the family should not work outside the home; and in their determination to do everything necessary to ensure a good education for their children, including university studies if the children proved apt. The value of an advanced education, they felt, was not purely or even primarily financial. As Ivan put it, "A café waiter with a good 'terrace' can earn more than a university professor!" It was "the richness of an education for its own sake" that they especially wanted to impart to the children. It was their children, they agreed, and their family life together that were supremely important. Nothing should be allowed to encroach on that—not professional advancement, or economic progress, or even extensive socializing with relatives and friends. In their words, "The Costa Brava life was not for us!"

As they had planned, Georgette and Ivan had two children. Both of them were boys: Guy, born in 1953, and Emile, in 1957. True to their familial vision, Georgette became a full-time wife and mother who, by conviction, dismissed any possibility of outside employment, of demanding community activities, or of extensive involvement with her own or Ivan's siblings and their families in order to be totally accessible to her husband and children. She was always there "with a smile" when the children came home from school and when her husband returned from work, she said proudly, and both she and Ivan helped Guy and Emile with their lessons and school assignments. They also considered it important to know their sons' classmates and friends—including a good deal about their personal lives.

Georgette's one major extrafamilial involvement had been her participation in Présence, a Belgian *groupe féminin* (women's group) of which she had been an active member for more than twenty years. Présence was a national, French-speaking organization, recognized by the Belgian Ministry of French Culture, with thirteen chapters distributed among Brussels, Brabant Wallon, Charleroi, La Louvière, Liège, Mons, and Verviers. It was founded in the 1960s by women in their twenties and thirties, "from all social milieux, and all convictions," Georgette explained, who were either college educated or who, like herself, had superimposed on their high school training a considerable amount of self-education. Présence was neither a women's club nor a feminist group, according to Georgette. It was "in-between." It was not ideological, had no political platform, and steered a "middle-of-the-road" course between particularistic Belgian stances. Fundamentally, its founders and members were women deeply accepting of their lives as wives and mothers, whose affiliation with Présence kept them from being totally confined to a "home-husband-children-TV" perspective.

The Verviers chapter to which Georgette belonged consisted of middle-class, middle-aged women, forty to sixty years of age. They held monthly lectures and group discussions on topics ranging from the relations between grandparents and grandchildren, the wives of famous men, and how women who were housewives and those who were working outside the home should think about money, to the European Community, Nicaragua, Islam, and pollution. Once a year the Verviers Présence chapter had a two-day outing at some pleasant vacation spot. After her two sons were grown, Georgette felt she had the time to be treasurer of her chapter. But she was no more inclined now than she was when her sons were children to ask her Présence women friends to her house for coffee, a meal, or at-home socializing of any sort.

Even more than Georgette, the way Ivan had led his life reflected a single-minded commitment to home, marriage, and children. He had consistently accorded a higher priority to them than to his occupational activities. Ivan had always enjoyed his work as a *coiffeur*. He also excelled in it in ways that quickly began to earn him professional recognition. He won a prize in a national competition for *coiffeurs*. He was recruited into teaching others. In the mid-1960s he was awarded two medals for the essay that the Belgian Ministry of Work invited him to write on the history of hairdressing. Later he was asked to develop this essay into an illustrated book that could be used in schools of *coiffeur* in Belgium—a project that he and his son Guy talked about doing together someday, that in the end never materialized. It did not because Ivan felt that these concomitants of his growing professional success would take too much of his time and energy away from his immediate family—especially from raising and educating his sons. Without conflict or regret, he decided against a more cosmopolitan, high-fashion, and lucrative career and turned his back on the new opportunities opening up to him that were carrying him in that direction. Instead he contented himself with the career of a *petit patron-coiffeur*: that of the owner-barber of a small shop attached to his house, whose chief clients were middle-aged and older men of working class and petit-bourgeois origins, with little interest in *coiffeurs à la mode*. Most of these men were not just customers; they were friends, neighbors, and acquaintances with whom he enjoyed conversing. This was the main reason why he worked in his barbershop every weekday morning. And yet, however long Ivan had known the men who frequented his shop, however close he felt to them, he never invited them into his home. His contact with them was strictly confined to the barbershop on the ground floor of his house.

Since the 1970s Ivan had been the organizer and leader of a group of former prisoners of war made up of what he called "ordinary" men like himself, who were neither military officers nor members of the Belgian Underground, and were interned by the Germans during World War II. In Georgette, Guy, and Emile's opinion, his role as "animator" of this group had been good for their family as well as for Ivan personally. The comradeship with men who underwent and understood his wartime experiences, and the opportunity to engage in certain forms of social action on their behalf, had not only been gratifying to Ivan; they had also helped him psychologically to speak with his wife and sons in greater detail and with more emotion about what happened to him and his fellow prisoners during his years of incarceration.

Most of Ivan's activity as a representative of this group had been devoted to obtaining from the Belgian government the amount of compensation for hardship, illness, disability, and retirement to which he and his ex-prisoner associates felt they were entitled. For many years this was complicated by the reluctance of the government to open what it regarded as a possible Pandora's Box of discussion about some of the events that took place in such German prison camps. Most notably there was great concern that public allusions might be made to "fraternization" that may have occurred between some of the Belgian prisoners and the German women who worked in these camps. Ivan overcame this apprehension and organized negotiations that brought about significant improvements in the benefits accorded to ex-prisoners. In his own case the initial post–World War II disability compensation that he received for his psoriasis and other chronic medical problems that he developed while a prisoner, was sizably increased. Ivan did not intend to try to augment the compensation he now received. It was too much of a hassle, he said, and more important, he felt that he had obtained justice in this connection for himself and for the fellow ex-prisoners for whom he had been the chief spokesman and intermediary.

Although they had cordial relations with their siblings, their brothers- and sisters-in-law, and nephews and nieces, both Ivan and Georgette had kept a measured distance from them. Along with the intensity of their involvement in their own nuclear family unit, and the self-sufficient and protective atmosphere with which they had surrounded it, there were social class factors that entered into their insulation from their extended kin. Georgette and Ivan deliberately declined major advances in prestige and remuneration that were available to Ivan in his career. But the fact remained that they had achieved more upward mobility than their siblings, largely through their sons' university education and professional accomplishments. Tension existed in this area between Ivan and Georgette and their siblings, who they claimed were envious of what their sons had attained. Georgette felt hurt because her sister had told her she was not interested in hearing about Guy and Emile's studies and professional advancement.

In contrast to most of their siblings who, along with Georgette's father, believed that a secondary-school education was sufficient for children of their social background, Georgette and Ivan were intent on encouraging their boys to go further. Their ardor about such an advanced education was nonetheless tempered by realism. Guy remembered, for example, that when his parents first registered him in the local secondary school (*Athenée*), they asked its prefect whether he thought their son was qualified to undertake the school's most difficult course of studies, its "Latin Section" track. Basing his judgment on Guy's excellent primary-school grades, the prefect not only recommended that Guy register in *Latine* but insisted that he do so.

After completing secondary school Guy decided that before he began his university education he would spend a year abroad. "Reflecting back," Guy told me, "I can't quite explain how I came to feel that I 'needed' to do [this]. In a sense it was a very bourgeois move, because only families of the haute bourgeoisie used to train their children abroad." Ivan and Georgette did not influence his decision "either way," Guy said, but it was "very hard for them, both emotionally and financially." Guy spent 1971–1972 in the United States, in Lansdale, Pennsylvania, living with a professional family. Although being this far away from his family and country was not easy for him, he considered that year "extremely important": "I came back more self-assured; I knew English; and I knew I wanted to return for graduate work."

Ivan and Georgette were proud of their two sons' records and accomplishments as university students. Both Demoulin brothers graduated from the University of Liège with *la plus grande distinction*. Emile went on to take a master's degree in law at Columbia University in New York City. After completing a master's degree at the Annenberg School for Communication of the University of Pennsylvania, Guy returned to the University of Liège to study for his Ph.D. in the sociology of communication, which he was awarded with the "highest distinction." What is more, Georgette and Ivan pointed out, Guy and Emile received fellowships for their graduate training—an honor, they contended, more usually awarded to "sons of the bourgeoisie."

Despite their modesty about their own intelligence compared with their sons', and their resolute domesticity, Ivan and Georgette had been more than facilitators of Guy and Emile's education.

Within the confines of their house and tight family unit they were closet intellectuals. Both of them were voracious readers with a lively interest in ideas; and they took great enjoyment in mentally traveling to places and exploring subjects to which their sons' professional knowledge and experiences had given them access. On the August afternoon I visited them, Georgette was reading her way through Georges Duby and Philippe Ariès's five-volume *Histoire de la Vie Privée* (*History of Private Life*) that Guy had received from his publisher; and both she and Ivan engaged me in a well-informed discussion about the forthcoming American presidential election. They were particularly impressed by the fact that Michael Dukakis, the son of Greek immigrant parents, was eligible to run for the highest political office in the United States.

The Demoulins felt gratified by their sons' professional achievements and way of life. Emile was employed as a legal adviser to a company that manufactured agricultural and industrial chemicals. He had recently been put in charge of all the company's affiliated plants abroad, principally in England and in Spain. His wife grew up in a rather affluent suburb of Liège and was very close to her family. The daughter of a pharmacist, and a trained pharmacist herself, she worked for her father. Emile and his wife had purchased a plot of land in a village outside Liège, not far from his place of work, where they were building a house of their own.

Georgette and Ivan's pleasure in their new daughter-in-law and in the way that Emile had "settled down" was enhanced by the "time of troubles" through which they had passed a few years ago, when Guy was seriously dating a divorcée. Guy was surprised by how negatively his parents had reacted to the idea of divorce and the prospect of a divorced daughter-in-law in the family, and by how much anguish it had caused. All four Demoulins went through a rocky, strife-ridden period until Guy broke up with his girlfriend—at which point, in Guy's words, "the family was reunited" and things became peaceful again.

Unlike his parents, Guy felt considerable disappointment over the circumscribed and restricted mode of life to which he thought his "brilliant" younger brother was too happily succumbing. Emile was "not using all his capacities," Guy said. He had "turned down golden opportunities to move up" in his career, such as the position in the cabinet of a minister of justice that he was offered, and also a job in Luxembourg connected with the European Economic Community. Although Guy felt strongly attached to his brother, he had reluctantly concluded that Emile had "a very different vision" from his own.

Guy was the more ambitious, successful, and cosmopolitan of the two brothers. He was also more profoundly identified with his parents and in certain ways more rooted in Verviers, Liège, and Wallony than Emile.

Although he was not yet forty, he was already a tenured *chargé de cours* at the University of Liège, as well as a *chercheur qualifié* (qualified researcher) subsidized by the National Fund for Scientific Research. In addition to his teaching and scholarly work, he directed public relations for the university hospital and edited several in-house university magazines. Despite these accomplishments he was not content with his local situation. He was indignant about the way the chronically bleak financial situation of Liège University and the Walloon community had led to cutbacks and loss of staff in his department at a time when he believed that the communications field was "blooming all over Europe." He indicted "old guard" faculty members of the university for their stubborn traditionality and their lack of imagination, portraying them as more interested in "the transformation of a Germanic chair" and in the question of "whether we should maintain or expand Indo-European grammar" than in the fate of the communications department. Those same traditional attitudes, he felt, accounted for the "dwindling away" of the promise made to him by the university's rector that he would soon be named a *professeur ordinaire*. Older colleagues, he explained, who thought of promotions as "age-based"—"like for civil servants"—were against someone as young as he becoming a professor.

"If I crawl up too easily into my Liège nest, I shall be a dead scholar by the time I am in my forties," Guy worried. But his professional activities and reputation extended far beyond Liège, and he had had numerous offers from Belgian, European, and North American universities and research institutes to consider leaving Liège and joining them.

Guy said he was tempted to "pack up and leave" Liège, which he was "more and more convinced is losing ground." There were "no objective reasons" for him to stay there, he avowed. Yet, each time he considered the professional invitations he had received from other institutions, he hesitated and retreated. "Perhaps

Lausanne, Paris, or Bruxelles may not be as good as they seem," he mused. Still, he was pensive about the fact that he had ended up buying and living in a house in Verviers, less than five minutes from his parents' home. It was an *Art Nouveau*–style house that Guy and his father extensively renovated and on which Ivan worked every afternoon with great enthusiasm—and a notable improvement in his health—until the entire job was completed. When he was not abroad, Guy spent every weekend in Verviers in his house but took his main meals at his parents' home as they expected him to do.

They were "happy" and "relieved," Georgette and Ivan told me, that Guy had chosen to live in Verviers. It ensured that they would see him often; and they looked upon his house as a beautiful and chic extension of their own. They were also glad that Guy was not residing in Liège, a city they regarded as *trop mondaine*. In their opinion it was so replete with snobbish social life, expensive dinners, and fashionably promiscuous behavior, like consorting with divorced women, that it could have had a bad influence on Guy.

Though Guy's permanent residence was in Verviers, he had rented a studio in Liège where he stayed most weekdays. This was partly because he did not like continually to commute between Verviers and Liège. In addition the studio helped him to deal with the feelings of being lonely and trapped that he experienced when the tiny, family-framed world of Verviers seemed to be closing in on him, or when he was acutely aware that he was approaching forty and was still unmarried. Georgette and Ivan were convinced that his level of education and professional academic status qualified him to marry into a bourgeois family, or even one of the haute bourgeoisie. Guy thought otherwise. Even though in his professional life he moved with ease from one social group to another, in private, more intimate relations he did not feel he belonged with or would ever be accepted by persons of much higher social class origins than his own.

IVAN HAD baked three tarts in honor of my visit with him and Georgette—cherry, made with fruit from his garden, rhubarb, and cheese. Toward the end of the afternoon, when we had our *goûter* together in the kitchen, he insisted that I eat a slice of each tart, washing them down with several cups of the freshly ground and brewed coffee he had prepared for us.

Around 6 p.m., by prearrangement, Guy arrived at his parents' home to drive me to his house for a short visit before I took my scheduled train back to Brussels. Georgette and Ivan accompanied me down the stairs and out the front door to where Guy's car was parked. Standing there on that gloomy, shabby street with its dug-up cobblestones and sidewalk and exposed gas pipes, Ivan Demoulin took a deep breath and remarked with profound satisfaction how good the evening air smelled. It reminded him of the country air of his boyhood, he said, and of his grandfather's farm.

"Les Roses, Mademoiselle!"
The Universe of
Michel de Ghelderode

COME PREFERABLY at five o'clock," Michel de Ghelderode had written to me. "The light changes then." And so it was late in the afternoon when I left the Brussels apartment where I was living in July 1961 to make my first visit to the renowned Belgian playwright, poet, and storyteller.* My taxi moved swiftly down fashionable Avenue Louise, past the baroque Palace of Justice, and through the Place Royale of government ministries and the Société Générale, toward 71, rue Lefrancq, the house in Schaarbeek, a working-class district of Brussels, where Ghelderode and his wife Jeanne resided. As my cab proceeded along the Chaussée de Haecht, the domed basilica of the Eglise Sainte Marie loomed before me like a portal. Behind this church lay the address I was seeking.

The windows of their apartment were covered with green shutters when I arrived there, and the big, green front door felt massively shut. But as soon as I pushed the brass bell marked

---

*Michel de Ghelderode is best known as a playwright. The most complete published collection of his theatrical works can be found in the five volumes of his *Théâtre*, published by Librairie Gallimard, Paris, 1950–1957. Among his most renowned plays are: *La Mort du Docteur Faust, Barrabas, Pantagleize, Magie Rouge, Les Femmes du Tombeau, Un Soir de Pitié, La Balade du Grand Macabre, Mademoiselle Jaïre, Hop Signor!*, and *Fastes d'Enfer*. Ghelderode also wrote a number of plays for the marionette theatre, especially for the Toone Theatre of Brussels.

In addition, he was a writer of tales, many of them inspired by Belgian folklore, or with what he referred to as "confessional value." He was a poet as well. And he was an *épistolier*—a writer of letters that constituted a literary *oeuvre* in and of themselves. (I translated all of the passages from Ghelderode's letters to me that appear in this chapter from the original French. The entire collection of the letters I received from him were contributed to the Royal Library Albert I in Brussels.)

"Michel de Ghelderode," his wife opened the door and ushered me into—I can think of it no other way—"the Ghelderodean universe."

Michel de Ghelderode was at his worktable in the *salon*, seated in a carved, thronelike Spanish chair over which a crimson velvet cover, gold-embroidered with some kind of ecclesiastical or royal insignia, had been draped. He was a large-boned man, made lean by illness. His straight, brown, maestro-style hair was combed neatly behind his big ears, accentuating his high forehead, prominent cheekbones, and long, ample nose. Although his mouth was thin and drawn down by suffering, its sensual fullness in healthier, younger days was still discernable. His startlingly pale blue eyes, with their very dark pupils, dominated his hollowed-out and haunted face. His gaze came from some transfixing place inside of himself, and his eyes seemed to be hearing as well as seeing invisible things. His elegant artist's hands, of which he was not unaware, protruded gracefully from the sleeves of his velour jacket.

But Ghelderode's appearance was eclipsed by the "assault of images" that the furnishings of his *salon* and the spell of his words unleashed in me. "My little museum of inexpressible things, my collection of imponderables," was the way he referred to the *salon* and the objects in it. We talked surrounded by masks from Belgian carnivals and *kermesses*; marionettes from the traditional puppet theaters of Brussels and Liège; seashells from the beaches of Ostend in Flanders; swords and scabbards; ancient madonnas; crucifixes; church hangings; a Gothic stone frieze reputedly a fragment from the sculptured face of Brussels's Hôtel de Ville; mannequins in various states of dress and undress; two carousel horses; and whole walls of Belgian paintings.

The antiquely musical sound of his voice made me think of a harpsichord. It filled the room with his exquisite, lavishly poetic, and theatrical French—infused somehow with the enormous energy, sensual joy, and hallucinatory terror of Flanders. As he spoke, the objects in the *salon* took on life, as if animated by the enchantment of his words.

Before I left at sunset time, Madame de Ghelderode served me many large cups of coffee and a whole platter of delicious *pâtisserie*. "It must be she," I thought, "the good Belgian housewife, who keeps the Ghelderodean museum so exquisitely neat, systematically arranged—and perfectly dusted!"

Several days later I received a handwritten letter from Michel de Ghelderode in response to my thank-you note. He had been reluctant to have me come, he admitted, because he was only beginning to emerge from a long and grave state of illness, and he feared his appearance might cause me "some pain and disappointment!" Arriving at his doorstep and entering his house at this point in his life meant that I would have to accept seeing him in the same state "as that of the objects that surround me, wounded, worn by age, scratched. . . ." "But they have their poetic resonance," he added, "these humble things that were beautiful at the beginning. Would they be *pathétiques* and worthy of tenderness if they did not carry the trace of their former existence?" In any case he hoped that health was now "quickly returning" to him and that "it will not take many days before I lose this dilapidated style."

Whatever apprehension he may have had about my visit before I crossed "the threshold of [his] solitude," Ghelderode wanted me to know, had been dispelled by my somewhat "immaterial . . . presence" and the "moving memory" with which my visit left his "companion" and himself:

> But no, you are not a stranger to me, and without ever having seen you I recognized you but from where, when? My wife felt the same sentiment, without being able to explain it. . . . It is not necessary to search; one must accept Destiny and the souls that Destiny sends us. . . . Do we know very much in this world?

"Your gentleness [Ghelderode continued], your meditation, your sort of radiant wisdom express and reveal your rank in the poetic universe." He associated my aura, he said, with "the image of the rose, the most complete of flowers":

> quasi-carnal and with a perfume that evokes angels—the roses of Ronsard that express passion and tenderness, forged together! It is the royal flower, more so than the lily, and I will teach you that in my ancient country of Flanders and of Brabant, it was the flower of Coronations, of joyous entrances, of princely marriages, of the triumphs of rhetoricians and artists: a chapel of roses (meaning a hat or a crown) was accorded to the personage on whom one wished to confer honor on pageant days. The victors in combats also, like Saint George or Saint Michael, enemies of the oriental Dragons in whom Claudel saw the devil in his last metamorphosis!

Ghelderode invited me to come and see them often, whenever I wanted, at any time it suited me. "You need never feel lonely or exiled," he declared, "because my house and my heart are open to you. We are, my wife and I, your spiritual and emotional family." "I will try to make your stay easier in this country which is very beautiful and contains more than one would dare to imagine."

His letter ended with a "vision" that he wished to impart to me. Although he was ill and "in the twilight of my destiny," he wrote, "so tenacious still is my love of life, my faith in men and their becoming, that I cannot abandon myself to bitter thoughts, to nocturnal philosophies without signs of hope from better skies, where human beings end by finding their redemption, their transfiguration of what was their primitive condition, perhaps that of angels, from their tragedy, crumbling into the abysses fortified by the infinite":

> I leave you with this vision, *Mademoiselle*, who I already consider a friend, as does she who shares my days with such patience, and I rejoice at the prospect of seeing you again soon!
>
> With affectionate esteem, in happy anticipation. . . .

Because Ghelderode's letter and the visit with him and his wife had touched things deep inside me, I sent them twelve long-stemmed Baccarat roses.

One day later the postman brought me another message from Ghelderode—the most extraordinary letter I have ever received. It was written in his eighteenth-century script, with an old wooden pen dipped in an inkwell, on four long parchment pages. The cover page, imprinted with a royal stamp and the date "1720," was filled with a pen-and-ink drawing he had made of a huge, single rose in a vase, around which strange forms—some with wings—floated. "*Les Roses, Mademoiselle!*" the text of the letter began on its second parchment page, bordered with another Ghelderodean sketch of a gigantic rose—this one without a vase or phantasmagoric shapes:

> What a beautiful gesture of an artist yours was—and how you express the quality of my joy, I should say our joy—for are we not in my house but two souls in one . . . in a play of mirrors?
>
> You see me embarrassed before this gift from your hands, such as one finds painted on the shutters of ancient altar pieces.
>
> You will be happy when I state that you have been vested with Poetry, in a privileged way, as a second breath invigorating the world of learned truth with its corrective action—[Poetry] that precedes the Infinite and brings you revealed truth. . . .

... These carnivalesque flowers imposing the nostalgia of their imminent perishing! It is a law, is it not, ours and that of the pure, the poets, to give in the fashion of these roses of Holocaust, the best of their fervor, of their song, and of their vision even if this calls attention to how naked they are! Must we not very quickly return to ashes after having decreed to unknown persons, to possible hearts, our spiritual feast, our color, our perfume—it should be said, our virtues?

There is the speech about the noble rose: a single one of them is sufficient to put me in a state of grace!

[The roses] sumptuously light my hermetic room full of strange forms, impossible creatures, cosmic phantoms in a traveling theatre decor where the Old Temptation of Saint Anthony is playing, that all our satiric painters of the centuries have evoked as much out of love of the Carnal Saint of the Angels as for the surrealistic devils who inhabited their nights with mad music and violent spectacles! ... I forget my recent tribulations in [the roses], the physicians of Molière dancing their ballet, the *Danse Macabre* also that I must forget, and in which I failed to make my entrance, thank God!

Scarcely had they arrived when your flowers are scoured by a summer storm and open up with a violent and provocative suddenness, pearled with celestial water, like curiously budding creatures! ... Will they speak, in a sort of spasm, at the command of magicianly thunder? ...

Belles comme le péché! [Beautiful as sin!]

Michel de Ghelderode

At the bottom of the letter, alongside his description of the storm-seized roses, Ghelderode had drawn another sketch: a small vase filled with roses that had become eyes, over which an ambiguous entity, more angelic than demonic, hovered.

THIS IS the dramatic and mysterious way that one of the most profound and important relationships of my life began. Measured in calendar time it was brief. Michel de Ghelderode died less than a year after I met him—on April 1, 1962, two days before he turned sixty-four. But viewed in a Ghelderodean perspective, what he called "our great friendship" spanned two generations and two different stages in the life cycle—his and mine, four seasons, and almost an entire liturgical year. It was perpetuated by his wife Jeanne and me over the eighteen years that she survived him, through our correspondence and our long visits during my annual trips to Belgium. My emotional and spiritual encounter with Michel de Ghelderode transported me into the deepest regions of Belgium and the deepest recesses of my own psyche and soul—to that frightening but strangely beautiful innermost place where my unconscious and the cultural symbolism of Belgium met. In a sense he "took me to images" I already knew but had never before dared fully to acknowledge or contemplate. In his letters to me Ghelderode referred to Belgium as "this astonishing country of dream and action, of art and monuments, haunted by luminosity, by contrast, by meteroric spasms, which is ours and yours in sharing. Because you understand it. And people possess what they understand. You love it, too. . . ."

In part Ghelderode was my teacher. He wanted to help me learn as much as possible about the "familiar by-streets" and the "buried strangeness" of his home country—about the shapes and odors, the voices and silences of its past, and their incarnation in its present. Some of his teaching was explicitly didactic. He encouraged me to spend time in Belgian museums. "There are many secrets inside our museums in Gand, in Bruges, in Bruxelles!" In this "Country of Painting, so rich in hours of creative art," he said, he wanted me to "live a little of its hallucinatory past" through the works of historical and contemporary masters like Breughel and Bosch and Ensor—paintings that had led him "toward the art of theater" and inspired some of his plays. He also counseled me about how to derive the most value from these experiences. "Try to visit [the museum] in old Bruxelles before your departure. On your own. That is best. You are too much sovereign of your faculties to need a minister to help you prevail over this illusory world!" Occasionally his instruction took the form of giving me some of his less-known works to read:

> I inscribe this little "*acte mystique*" [he wrote on the title page of his "mystical farce," *Les Vieillards* (*The Old Men*)] which will tell you how much I am and continue to be close to the popular heart, in this Flanders of imagery. . . . You will see that the poet of this nation with such an intense past, metaphysically so rich, still produces realistic [works], close to the soil. . . .

Ghelderode also taught me about Belgium through the "reality" dimensions of his plays and stories. An astute social observer and critic, he transposed his perceptions of current Belgian life and his commentary on it to Flanders and Brabant in the fifteenth and sixteenth centuries. The characters in his play *Mademoiselle Jaïre*, for example, are "just as you might meet at random in the miniatures of the Burgundian period. Some wear turbans or preserve elements of orientalism in their dress," as they did in the port town of Bruges in a "bygone age." These characters "may seem to be invented," Ghelderode remarked, "but their voices betray inflections that could be caught nowadays by acute listening."* When he wrote for the Toone Marionette Theater of Brussels, Ghelderode made the puppets speak in the popular dialect and with the folk humor of the men and women who lived in the city's working-class Marolles district. Not only did he capture the distinctive language and comedic sense of such local milieux; he also ironically portrayed the particularism and the possessive love of things that he discerned in Belgians throughout the land:

> ... The philosopher [Kweibe-Kweibus] entered the city, which was like all other cities except that it was divided into one hundred very well delimited districts, each one having its belfry with its bell. Kweibus went from district to district, noting that the inhabitants of one district had no desire to know the inhabitants of the other. And in each public square the idlers, at the foot of the tower, exclaimed with admiration: "Isn't our bell unique; could there possibly exist another that even approaches it in accuracy, tone, size, form, the peal of its tongue! ... The marvelous bell! ..."
> "The marvelous bell, indeed!" Kweibus exclaimed to himself. And the idlers pursued him: "Having heard our bell, you would be very foolish if you went to hear those of our neighbors. What a pity! Just so much beating of cauldrons!" ... And Kweibus moved on into the adjacent district, where people pursued him with the same remarks. Having scoured the town in this way and heard one

---

*Michel de Ghelderode, "Mademoiselle Jaïre [Miss Jairus]," in *Seven Plays*, Vol. 2, translated and with an introduction by George Hauger (New York, Hill and Wang, 1964), 210. The original French text of this play was published in Michel de Ghelderode, *Théâtre*, Vol. 1. (Paris, Librairie Gallimard), 181–204. Editions Variées.

hundred different bells, Kweibus concluded that these connoisseurs of cowbells, by dint of hearing only one bell, heard only one sound. . . . *

. . . This book of yellow parchment contains the inventory of my possessions. . . . Hieronymus, healthy in mind and body, owns, by virtue of the just laws, a gabled house, with its garden, well, lawn, trees, the birds that live in the trees, and the air and wind that circulate around and within said property. There is the watchdog. . . . I own a wife and her clothing, and, furthermore, utensils and furniture. All of this, counting the wife and the dog, is worth a thousand royal florins. . . . I was forgetting that I owned a ghost which is domiciled here and which I bought with the house. . . . What would a ghost be worth? . . . The price of a night watchman. [*Lowering his voice*] And I own a bronze chest with cunning locks that contain four columns of ten florin pieces bearing the image of the emperor, and four of the same with the image of the empress, all arranged in battle order. . . .

I am the owner of my soul. . . . That is something I had forgotten in the inventory. [*He writes.*] Item, one immortal soul, ornamented with diverse virtues. . . . †

Ghelderode made it plain that he did not read the works of social scientists. In his view their analytic perspective was antithetic to the "instinct," "vision," and "divination" by which "the dramatic author must live."‡ Yet he supported my participant observation-based sociological research in Belgium, considering it analogous in some ways to his own observations of everyday life in Belgian

---

*Michel de Ghelderode, *Kweibe-Kweibus* (Bruxelles, Editions de la Renaissance d'Occident, 1926), pp. 14–15.

†Michel de Ghelderode, *Red Magic* [*Magie Rouge*], in *Seven Plays*, Vol. 2, 4–5. The original French text of this play, written in 1931, was published in Michel de Ghelderode, *Théâtre*, Vol. 1, 123–179. Editions Variées.

‡Michel de Ghelderode, *The Ostend Interviews* [*Entretiens d'Ostende*], in *Seven Plays*, Vol. 1, translated and with an introduction by George Hauger, (New York, Hill and Wang, 1960), 20. In the text that follows, a number of other short quotes have been taken from *The Ostend Interviews*, pp. 4, 6, 12, 21, 23.

society and his immersion in its culture that were vital to his art. He even suggested that when I wrote about Belgium it might be more effective—and safer too—if, like him, I transferred what I had noted and wished to say to a past century.

But it was primarily through the language of images and symbols that Ghelderode inducted me into the *ambiance* and the soul of the country that he inhabited and that inhabited him. He opened his *salon* to me, where the ancient and modern artifacts of Belgian culture that he had collected—what he called his *objets étranges* (strange objects)—were evocatively displayed. Under the spell of his theatrical genius and his magicianly qualities, the objects became live presences, sending messages that he helped me to perceive and decipher.

Ghelderode also gave me some of his "image-beings" as gifts—a wooden pen; a tiny, marionettelike doll; a watercolor portrait of him surrounded by objects and images from his salon and his plays; a photograph in which he was mounted like a chevalier on his favorite carousel horse, Borax. "For Renée Claire Fox—wounded angel with tender eyes. . . . A flame that the wind can curve, but extinguish, no. . . . In offering her this image of my obsessions and phantoms, I offer her my friendship, always," is the way he inscribed the watercolor.

With romantic tenderness, mischievous humor, and skill, Ghelderode gave me the best of his vision in ways that opened the inner chambers of Belgium to me—and of myself. He recognized the yearning writer in me, asserting from the outset that I had been "vested with Poetry." He brought that part of me to the surface by releasing the imagery in me and making me less fearful of it. He counted me among those who were "sensitive to the supernatural," he said—"to the secret signal from a mystic country." And he linked this spiritual perception with the capacity to make, as well as to hear poetry. I, in turn, responded to him both religiously and artistically.

Ghelderode was highly attuned to religious symbols, rituals, and signs: to old churches and chapels; to priestly vestments and liturgical chants; to religious offices, processions, and funerals (which he considered supreme, "stage-managed" performances); to statues of the Virgin Mary (the Notre Dame of Solitude and Sorrow, rather than "rosy" madonnas with self-satisfied expressions of "having so marvelously given birth");* and to the "everlasting language" which he said had accompanied him all his life—the "aerial music" of the bells and the carillons of Flanders, "both the tragic bells with bloody mouths and the triumphant with golden tongues." Prophets and saints, priests and bishops, angels and devils, Mary, Joseph, and Jesus, and the many visages of Death crowd the pages of Ghelderode's stories and plays. Like the Primitive Flemish painters, he placed them in the houses, the villages, the towns, the squares, the courtyards, the streets, and the fields of Belgium "in olden times," and gave them Belgian faces and garments. Ghelderode seemed to feel intimately acquainted with the members of the holy family and with certain saints like Saint Francis and Saint Anthony; his whole metabolism moved in the rhythm of the liturgical calendar:

> Jeanne and I send you our luminous thoughts across the cold air of this month of December [he wrote to me as Christmas approached], so somber, but in the heavens burns the admirable and symbolic star announcing the mystical *fêtes*, the arrival on our bloody planet of a prophet, a redeemer, who comes from one century to the next, and how dolorously, to announce peace to us, the advent of fraternal love and of all forms of love—Because there is only one way of loving, it is in forgetting one's self in sacrifice. One loves others, one can *only* love others. . . . This is the lesson of a god who died for this grandiose truth! The rest is lowly pride, impurity— it is sin! There is only one [sin]: it is to lack love, to be incapable of love. . . . This is the teaching of the Poor Son of that carpenter, of that humble Mary, mother of that child, whose gaze contained all the Mediterranean sky. He is already close to our West, this poor little one in his *crèche*. The Magi will come to initiate him! To what mysteries, with what words! And this miraculous newborn infant speaks and understands, listens and answers. Divinity! . . .
>
> Merry Christmas! The angels are going to cross the ocean and sing their carols of confidence under your window, great golden birds with adorable mouths! . . .

---

*See Michel de Ghelderode, "Nuestra Senora de la Soledad" and "La Vierge noire," in *Mes Statues* (Brussels, Editions du Carrefour, 1943), pp. 33–38, 45–50. A facsimile of this original, limited edition was published in 1978 by Louis Musin in Brussels.

Ghelderode was not a practicing Catholic in the conventional sense of the term. He did not attend mass. He was passionately critical of the "official church" because of its emphasis on obedience and dogma rather than "the eternal sob of prostrate man . . . at the foot of the incomprehensible cross." The priests in the cast of characters of his plays were often more "ugly" and less holy than the unordained populace to whom they supposedly ministered, and suffused with a decaying "clerical odor." He was no more a Catholic author, Ghelderode insisted, than he was a national Belgian one. Rather, what he tried to write were *"patriale"* works that were "ancestral and traditionally of my home" while expressing "the man of my time everywhere . . . and through him man eternal." But the imagery of Belgian Catholicism was in Ghelderode and all around him. It pervaded his *salon,* his letters to me, his theater, and his being. My friendship with him made me see and feel the Catholicism of Belgian culture and the Belgianness of its Catholicism. And in the process old churches, madonnas, carillons, and roses came to dwell in my Jewish-American soul.

I WAS at home in New York when I received Ghelderode's last letter. It was written on March 1, 1962, in the season when the "violet days" of Lent were approaching:

Great Friend, faraway princess!

There are silhouettes like yours, so intensely poetic that traverse the Theater of our friend Maeterlinck, the author of Pelléas and Melisande! Slender, purebred, far-reaching gaze, as far as the stars. . . . What is an ocean between our hearts? For Jeanne, for me, we stretch out our hand and we touch yours. In the fogs you are a phosphorescent statue. . . . I pity you in that hallucinatory, glacial city, where humanity is no longer more than a frightened herd, that watches the sky, not in the direction of the angels, but for a rocket that this time transports a madman, [and] tomorrow will transport Death in person! Oh Poetry! And the solemn silence of my dear old room, at twilight. . . . And the look . . . of my companion, who holds you in such tender friendship! Thanks to God! I ask nothing else, except the spring—and a few radiant friendships like the one you devote to me and that lights my last years. . . . I have written very little to you, you who have spoken so much to me, from afar, from near—because you have remained

close to us. . . . Sickness, yes. You knew it, no need to report it to
you. Since January 1. And the cold, the ice! I shivered near the
fire, poor little human being, contemplating the old black trees.
And then sleep. . . . I forgot all . . . except you, friend, . . . and a few
others—heralds of this Friendship as necessary as love. . . . I cannot
maintain this muteness much longer. Hope is reviving, the sun
mounts higher each day—our days are better—yes. . . . How much
gratitude I owe you for all the signs of your vigilant affection . . . of
very beautiful hours. . . .

Jeanne, very tired, because of me! What sacrifices. There are
days when I want to cry when I think of the poor lot I give her.
She never complains. If she were not near me, I would let myself slide into nothingness, I confess to you; I would sleep forever. Exhausted from suffering, physically also; because these last
months, I have undergone the anguish of being, of existing, and
also the desire to no longer be. . . . But there is this creature who
has fought so hard for me and my work: then there is my
unfinished work . . . this Theater, still two more volumes. Some
tales, Twilight Tales, you will like them I feel. It is very much me.
It is Ghelderode, it is your friend, your "human brother," as Maître
François Villon says to Louis XI in the ballads. . . . Condemned not
to go out, I who do not ask to leave the room where I have all, my
books, my paintings, my images, a vision of the garden, sometimes
a visit, and letters coming from everywhere. You will have better
news soon. Brussels-Capital gilds itself with sun—but what a
winter. . . . They are playing me in Paris, La Balade du Grand
Macabre, [put on] by the Free Theater of the University of
Brussels. . . . As for success, I scoff at it. Glory is a lie. Only the
heart counts. The only thing that matters is to be loved, love,
affection, outstretched hands. . . .

Great friend, au revoir! lassitude overtakes me; I am still very
weak! . . . The violet days of Christian liturgy are coming, the
desolation of the empty Tabernacle, God absent! The churches
are strange these holy days, Holy Thursday, Good Friday—and
then, the Pascal explosion, the carillons of Flanders, the bells
in the belfries that ring out: Alléluia! He is risen! Nature also!
And the harvesters of Breughel arrive with flasks on their hips!

Don't let me leave you without speaking of you, of your
work, of your projects. Jeanne embraces you. and I, your old
friend of the heart, rich with childhood, I send you my most

tender smile. . . . Come back to us, dear Renée Claire Fox; that will be festival and joy!

He did not live to hear the carillons of Flanders ring on Easter Sunday.

GHELDERODE CALLED me a friend, a younger sister, a wounded angel, a flame, a phosphorescent statue in the fog, and a faraway princess. He associated me with certain feminine "silhouettes" in the works of Edgar Allan Poe and Maurice Maeterlinck. My eyes, he said, were "not of this world, of a woman, a simple creature." He likened my hair, and the way I wore it—long, "loose," and "abundant"—to that of "The Women of the Tomb in our Primitives [paintings] of Flanders and Brabant." And in the letter he wrote to me on the eve of my departure for the United States, he addressed me as "the Skinny Angel, ready for flight."

Authenticity and ardor, imagination and whimsy were commingled in the ethereally romantic way in which Ghelderode saw and wrote about me. He responded to certain of my personal qualities, embroidered artistically upon them, and projected me into the final acts of his Theater and his life.

I came to his house bearing roses and crossed the threshold of his *salon* when he was mortally ill. I arrived there from the "faraway" land of New York City/America: a young, modern country that fascinated him but frightened him too because it was so different from the Old Europe in which he dwelled. I was an emissary from that foreign place where his plays were coming to be known, with whom he could communicate—a slender young woman with long, dark hair and dark eyes, whose appearance pleased him; and an intellectual, whose speech and gestures were literary.

I was young, from a young country, but I had what Ghelderode felt was an "old soul," partly because I was Jewish. He never discussed my Jewishness with me, but it was important to him. In his eyes it connected me with his favorite statue of "Our Lady," the "*Vierge noire*" [Black Virgin] in Saint Catherine's Church in Brussels, whom he regarded as a more genuine and pure representation of Mary than the blonde-haired, blue-eyed madonnas whom one usually saw in Belgian churches and paintings. Like her, I looked the way Ghelderode thought a "granddaughter of King David" should.

I was an old soul too because I was already intimately acquainted with illness and death. At the age of seventeen I had contracted a nearly fatal case of polio which had left visible marks on me. In Ghelderode's words I was "wounded" by illness, as he himself was. But "skinny" and "wounded angel" though I was, in Ghelderode's moral view I had demonstrated that I had tenacious hope and a supreme Belgian virtue—the "*courage*" to overcome adversity.

However serious and sincere Ghelderode was, if I had been so flattered by his romantic portrait of me that I failed to recognize its playfulness and humor, so awed by his dramatic self-presentation that I did not discern its staged aspects, or so out of touch with everyday reality that I could not participate in the down-to-earth dimensions of his life with Jeanne, our friendship would never have become what it was.

But from the beginning to the end I was, above all, the *mademoiselle* of the roses. In Ghelderode's emblematic universe, roses and death were associated. Death, he exclaimed, was as beautiful as "roses in the snow."* In a letter to a fellow poet, Garcia-Lorca, he declared that he was "now writing a kind of *opening-the-veins* poetry altogether averted from reality, with a feeling that reflects all my love for things and all my mocking of things. My love of death and poking fun at her." In his autobiographical *Ostend Interviews* he went on to say: "I laugh at death . . . and make fun of her, but she will return, be certain of that. Although you do not love her, she remains with you, and she is the only person of whose fidelity you can be certain. Crown her with roses!" . . . † To this day I wonder whether, along with the other ways he identified me, Michel de Ghelderode also thought I was a sign, if not a messenger, of his imminent death.

May 1962

This has been a spring of images for me. Preparing myself for this journey to Belgium has created a series of pictures in my mind.

---

*This phrase is cited by Samuel Draper in "Michel de Ghelderode: 1898–1962," *Commonweal*, May 11, 1962, p. 167. In Ghelderode's play, *Sire Halewijn* [*Lord Halewyn*], snow wrapping "the land of Flanders . . . in a white winding sheet," and a "sinful longing for heavy headed roses" are juxtaposed. *Seven Plays*, Vol. 1, 286–287.

†Cited by Samuel Draper in "Michel de Ghelderode: 1898–1962," p. 167.

Unframed and undeciphered, they float there, as if in a wall-less gallery.

A tree, lacing the frail April blue of the sky with its skeleton, all of its branches listening for leaves. A bush of forsythia, clamorously putting forth brazen yellow blossoms. Florist-perfect roses in a tall crystal vase, serene in the sunlight. The roses again, shaken by a spring storm, opening suddenly into huge crimson eyes. A bird, as red as roses, as blue as sky, singing from the highest and greenest branches of a tree in full leaf. Another bird trapped in a room as white as its body, flying again and again into an unyielding white wall. A red lamb, laying its gentle face on the white counterpane of somebody's hospital bed. A white-and-gilt carousel horse, detached from a merry-go-round, all sinew, nostrils, ears, and listening, wondering eyes. A puppet dressed as a *grand seigneur*, suspended in midair by its intricate strings, like a gorgeously plumaged bird, caught in a web of its own weaving. Numbers indelibly tattooed on the bare arm of a young woman, leaning on the railing of a ship, moving slowly, horns sobbing, out of some harbor. Red scratches and purple bruises on the hands of a young scholar, furiously beating his hands on the blank, white paper before him. A church altar on Good Friday, at the moment when the purple drapery on the cross is lifted like a theater curtain on invisible pulleys and strings, and a membrane of mourning is mystically shed by the soul. Carillon bells, ringing out—Hallelujah!—in the tallest, most solid belfry of Flanders, piercing the mist around the castle at the top of the only hill in that flat, foggy land. The windows of the castle lit up like opaque jewels by the great crystal chandeliers in every room. The silhouette of some person or presence who inhabits the castle, a lyric shadow against an amethyst-colored window. The face of Michel, who died in April: eyes that saw essences, ears that heard heartbeats, the flutter of wings, mysterious footfalls, muffled screams, stifled laughter, secret music; hands that moved like antennae, filling page after page with penstrokes, as beautiful, baroque, and haunted as the words they formed and as the strange, poetic world created out of those words.

If he were alive perhaps I would have written to him about all this—about the images and about the reasons other than my sociological research that I am returning to Belgium:

"I find myself haunted by images. Even here in New York, where the tall buildings are neither castles nor cathedrals and are

full of scrutable plate glass windows; where the only gardens are
florist shops and public parks, and the only bestiaries, public
zoos; where the streets, crowded with people and traffic, are so
frequently dug up, repaired, and dug up again that there are no
undisturbed spaces either above or below ground in which phantoms and apparitions can flourish—I see silhouettes moving behind
jewel-colored windows; gardens filled with yearning trees, violent
roses, clamorous forsythia; crimson lambs, bleached birds, carnival
horses. . . . And, everywhere, I hear bell music.

"There is a message in those images. They tell a story for which,
as yet, I have no words. But the bell music says that I will come to
know the story and find the words if I journey to Belgium once
more, and come home again."

JEANNE DE GHELDERODE, Michel's wife and "companion," was part of
every letter I received from him. Our friendship, he declared again
and again, was a "luminous trinity" that united Jeanne and him and
me, and made us a "spiritual and emotional family." Jeanne reaf-
firmed this in her letters to me after Michel's death. "Even if we
were never to see each other again," she wrote, "that marvelous
message, 'Les Roses, Mademoiselle,' . . . would remain a sign of union
between us, . . . and every rose encountered would make me dream
of you, of my faraway friend who is nevertheless so close to my
thought."

Jeanne was an intelligent, shrewdly perceptive woman who was
fiercely and lovingly protective of her husband and his work, and
acted as his gatekeeper. She considered herself to be (and undoubt-
edly was) less naively idealistic than Michel about the character
and motives of the procession of writers, painters, sculptors, pup-
peteers, actors, publishers, literary and theatrical agents, journal-
ists, public officials, students, professors, and the like, from different
parts of Belgium and Europe, and from many other countries in the
world, who wished to meet and interview the great author, see his
inner sanctum, and seek professional rights and favors from him.

It was Jeanne de Ghelderode, as much as Michel, who admitted
me into their universe. Out of a combination of intuition and
practical sense, she trusted me. Because I was a sociologist rather
than a literary, theater, or media person, she reasoned I was less
likely to have self-interested, careerist reasons for wanting to know
her husband. In addition, like Michel, she responded positively to

my "aura," and she shared his sense of mysterious familiarity with my "silhouette." She also knew that I saw her as far more than Michel's devoted spouse, helpmate, and housekeeper. It was apparent to me that she typed all his manuscripts. She was an important in-house critic of the various drafts of his plays and stories. She also influenced his decisions about whether a play was ready to be published or performed, and to whom the rights to produce it ought to go. I discovered too that she was not merely the guardian and duster of the Ghelderodean *salon* but that she had helped Michel to choose and arrange its *objets étranges*. My recognition of her role, and her awareness of the way I perceived her, reinforced our friendship.

It was with anxiety as well as expectancy, however, that we anticipated our first visit *à deux* since Michel's death. "Your great friend Michel will not be there, unhappily, to welcome you," Jeanne forewarned me. "Both of us...live with his memory, and...[our] friendship...is placed under [his] protection...."

July 31, 1962

My taxi pulled up in front of 71, rue Lefrancq, and departed. A note written in Jeanne's hand had been slipped into the Michel de Ghelderode nameplate on the big green front door. "Gone for five minutes," it read. Almost instantly Jeanne was standing beside me. We embraced, kissing each other three times on alternate cheeks, *à la Belge*. Jeanne wept silently.

Inside the house we entered the *salon* and seated ourselves in chairs near the small round table where Michel wrote, leaving the carved throne-chair, with its crimson-and-gold church hangings, empty, ready for his entrance. "I have left things just as they were," said Jeanne, weeping quietly again. Neatly laid out on his writing table, in their customary place, were Michel's green blotter, his old brown spectacles, his pipe in its stand, a small sword letter opener, an antique brass scale for weighing letters, and, in a special cup, all his *plumes*—wooden pen holders, fitted out with steel pen points, arranged like a painter's brushes. In one corner of the desk stood a tall crystal vase filled with garden roses. A book about Hieronymous Bosch and his paintings was propped on a nearby couch. A very large photographic portrait of Michel, which I had not seen before, had been placed in the center of the mantelpiece.

"I am not '*croyante*' or '*pratiquante*'," Jeanne said, referring to the fact that she was not a believing, practicing Catholic. "I was baptized and had my first Communion," she continued, "but though I tried I was never able to become '*croyante*.'" And yet, since Michel died, she confessed, she had the sense of being "doubly strong," as though Michel's spirit had entered into her.

Jeanne felt his continuing presence in the apartment, and so did I. She had opened the shutters on the front windows of the *salon* and drawn back the curtains on the glass doors that framed the apartment's small inner garden. An enchanted garden, Michel called it, and wove it into some of his tales and plays. On this exceptionally lovely summer day it was flooded with sunlight, very green, and filled with roses. The sun shone through the windows and panes of the French doors, illuminating the apartment as if an invisible stage director had turned a theatrical spotlight upon it. The light dispelled all the shadows in the house. It warmed the yellows, pinks, and reds of the roses in the crystal vase on the writing table. The bright-eyed carousel horses looked newly painted. The sequins on the red satin suit of the Gentleman-Devil puppet shimmered. The mantelpiece mirror gleamed. The crystal chandeliers sparkled. The amethyst necklace worn by one of the mannequins emitted a purple glow. And the paintings over the gold velvet settee were as radiant as a Flemish sky. Sunbeams fingered the green metal trunk filled with Michel's manuscripts and correspondence, and the old upright machine on which, for years, Jeanne had typed his manuscripts.

Jeanne smiled as she began to describe the visit she had received that morning from the notary. He admired the *salon*, Jeanne said, especially the religious objects in it, because he was a very pious Catholic. But for that same reason he did not understand why the crucifixes, the madonnas, the church candelabra, and the like were intermingled with masks, puppets, wooden horses, and semiclothed mannequins. With a perfectly straight face Jeanne had explained to the notary that when the windows and shutters were closed, the house started to smell like an old church, and so in order to offset this odor, the other objects in the *salon* were necessary. The notary listened respectfully to what he supposed was Jeanne's serious response, but he was clearly perplexed.

A visit that Jeanne thought would be comparable in its own way, and to which she was definitely not looking forward, she said, was the one she expected the assessors to make at the end of the year. They would come to estimate the value of all the furnishings and possessions in the house, in connection with the taxes that must be levied. How would the assessors appraise the objects in this *salon*? I wondered silently. What value would they affix to the long-legged mannequin whom Michel named "Hamlet," with her scarlet lips and nails, bare breasts, a crown atop her lavender-tinted wig, and a sword hanging from the satin poncho she wore? Or to Borax, the carousel horse, and Sire Mephistopheles, the *Grand Seigneur* Devil puppet?

Jeanne filled our afternoon and evening with anecdotes and stories about Michel. He was cared for by three physicians, she recounted: one from Brussels, one from Ghent, and one from Bruges. They were all Flemish and Catholic. One of these physicians felt it was important for Michel to see a priest during the last days of his illness. He asked a particular priest to visit Michel. But, Jeanne told me, this "wonderful priest" declined to do so. "Michel will find his way to Paradise by himself," the priest stated with conviction. Jeanne and Michel agreed that "the priest who never came to the house" was a "truly religious man."

Jeanne reminisced about her first meeting with Michel, their courtship, wedding, and honeymoon. They met when the two of them were working for the same stationer, she in the publicity department, he in school supplies. It was the beginning of the academic year, and the store was filled with children and their mothers coming to buy supplies for classes. All the employees of the firm were asked to help with the long line of customers. Jeanne and Michel were seated at the same table, dispensing merchandise and collecting cash. He was Adhémar Martens then, and in the course of the remarks they exchanged in the midst of the sales, Michel/Adhémar discovered that Jeanne had gone to school with his sister, Germaine Martens. Later he asked Jeanne to type a tale for him, telling her he was the literary executor for the works of a young author-friend who had recently died. The story was signed, "Michel de Ghelderode." Jeanne typed the manuscript, knowing full well it was written by Adhémar Martens because its style was so similar to the way he spoke. "What do you think of it?" he asked her when she returned the typed story to him. "Not bad," she replied. "Not bad?" he responded with some indignation. "The boy has talent!"

Vowing to each other that they would never marry, Jeanne and

Michel began going out together. Jeanne continued to type his manuscripts. She was also invited to his Saturday *soirées*. At the first of these evenings she attended, she was greeted at the front door of the house by Michel who was wearing a robe of some kind and whose hair, she said, was longer than mine. Michel was holding a candlestick in his hand. He led her up the staircase to the attic of the house where he had a bedroom-studio. There, by candlelight, with huge shadows flickering on the walls, Michel received his friends on Saturday nights. Jeanne was startled when she noticed that the pile of coats thrown on the bed by the guests had begun to move with a strange, rocking motion. And then, from under the pile, a tiny dog with a red face emerged. It was Michel's dog!—one of the only "possessions" with which he entered marriage, she added.

Jeanne and Michel were married in a civil ceremony that lasted only a few minutes. She wore a very pretty black dress for the occasion, she said, and they went to Paris for their honeymoon, using the money that Michel had received from his first literary prize.

With a burst of candor Jeanne told me she knew her husband's faults well. He was "very influenceable," she said, and during a certain period of his life he drank too much in local cafés with writer, artist, and actor friends. At a critical point in their marriage she had a very serious, "severe" discussion with Michel about the problem, particularly about the adverse way it was affecting his writing. After that conversation, Jeanne alleged, Michel stopped drinking, and the problem never occurred again.

As Jeanne recalled past events I learned more about Michel's parents. His mother, she told me, like her own father, was a "child of love," born out of wedlock. Michel's father, the son of a "good family" from Louvain, was the principal clerk at the General Archives of Belgium. It was he who introduced Michel to "parchments...faded writings...great wax [and] metal seals," and antique objects; and like his father, Michel was employed for many years as an archivist (in the Communal Hall [*Hôtel Communal*] in the Brussels commune of Schaarbeek). Despite what they had in common in this regard, father and son "did not have a good understanding," Jeanne said. A major source of conflict between them was that Michel's father expected him to choose a "respectable" and "safe" occupation—preferably one in the civil service.

It was Michel's mother, Jeanne continued, from whom he received the "secret life" out of which he became a writer. She "grew up in a convent in Louvain [Michel wrote about his mother], and there she was taught the life of the saints. . . . She knew liturgical chant, spoke ecclesiastical Latin, and believed in the devil whom, she said, she had seen many a time. . . . She was rich in proverbs, in forgotten songs, . . . in ancient legends, . . . and in haunted stories," which she told "wonderfully well." Michel claimed that he was her one and only listener. Neither his siblings nor his father were interested in her tales. There was always something "celestial" about her face, Jeanne mused, her eyes filling with tears as she spoke of her mother-in-law.

Just before Jeanne and I had lunch together, the Ghelderodes' *femme de journée*, Madame Lambert, dropped by for a short visit. She had worked for Jeanne and Michel for more than thirty years, helping with the cleaning, laundry, and other chores around the house. They first met when she was the concierge in the house where they lived before moving to 71, rue Lefrancq. In her earlier years she was a singer and a dancer in the Flemish Art Theater.

I had never been impressed with Madame Lambert's housekeeping abilities. When I had watched her at work on previous visits, it seemed to me there was no particular order in which she did things, and that she spent quite a bit of time leaning dreamily on her mop, staring into space with a dustcloth clutched in her hand, or chatting animatedly with Jeanne and Michel—who always respectfully addressed her as "*Madame* Lambert." Jeanne told me that Madame Lambert was Michel's confidante during the last days of his illness. He knew he was dying, he said to Madame Lambert, and he asked her to look out for Jeanne. Artistically as well as humanly, Madame Lambert fit into the decor and atmosphere of the Ghelderode house. With her tousled blonde hair drawn into a knot at the top of her head, her expressive light blue eyes, her long, upturned nose like those you see on carved wooden folk dolls, in the rumpled, shapeless dress, and huge carpet slippers that she donned for cleaning, she had always given me the impression of a comedienne, playacting the role of a servant or of a living, giant-sized marionette!

Jeanne had prepared a special lunch for me of Belgian dishes: small fresh tomatoes stuffed with tiny shrimp (*crevettes*), stewed rabbit, new potatoes, *petits pois*, a choice of cheeses, and for dessert a mixture of fresh strawberries, raspberries, and red currants (*groseilles*), accompanied by a glass of red wine and a cup of her good strong coffee. Over the meal she discussed the problems she was encountering in obtaining permission for Michel to be buried in the Laeken cemetery. It was his ardent wish to join the renowned artists, war heroes, and noblemen who were interred in what he called this "necropolis" near the Royal Palace, the cathedral of Laeken, and the bronze cast of one of his favorite statues, Auguste Rodin's *"Le Penseur"* (*"The Thinker"*). Technical, bureaucratic, and political considerations were delaying the decision about whether the honor of being buried on the "Avenue of Artists" of this national cemetery would be accorded Ghelderode and his literary works. Meanwhile his coffin remained on the Laeken cemetery grounds, in what Jeanne referred to as a *cave d'attente* (waiting vault), and the Belgian association of "The Friends of Michel de Ghelderode" was launching a public drive to collect funds to erect a special tombstone for him. [*]

After lunch, at about four o'clock in the afternoon, Jeanne's brother Gérard and his wife Josette came for the kind of long visit they had been making at least once a week (usually Sunday) to Jeanne and Michel for many years. In appearance and manner Gérard was a classical, almost vaudevillean *Bruxellois/Brusselaar*. He was a huge, rotund man with a protruding stomach. His tremendous trousers were pulled all the way up to his chest and held there with suspenders; and he wore a very large, floridly printed tie. He was a jolly, fun-loving man who enjoyed good stories and jokes, food and drink, and the ladies: a bon vivant, raconteur, and *rigoleur* rolled into one. He held a minor civil service position in Brussels from which he was now retired. He was a gifted amateur photographer who had taken many outstanding artistic photos of Michel and the objects of his theater and *salon*. He was also an adroit practitioner of some of the more underground activities in Belgian community life. During World War II and the German occupation, for example, he used both his photographic and forgery skills to produce false identity cards for endangered citizens, among

---

[*]Michel de Ghelderode was finally buried in the Laeken cemetery on December 6, 1964. Jeanne had her name as well as Michel's inscribed on the tombstone and when she died in November 1980 she was buried alongside him.

them many Brussels Jews. He was not an educated man, but both Jeanne and Michel always considered him to be highly intelligent, with a great deal of unused and to some extent misdirected talent. When I had heard them talk about Gérard in the past, they implied that what they regarded as the narrow, rather vacuous way in which he lived was largely attributable to Josette.

Josette was a "very proper woman," to use Jeanne's phrase, with perfectly set, greying hair, a rather doll-like pretty face, and an ample, tightly corseted, Rubensian body. She spoke in a singsong voice with a thick Brussels accent like her husband's. Jeanne said she was a compulsive housekeeper who spent hours every day dusting and mopping. She doted on Poupée, the little white fluff of a dog she and Gérard owned, whom she "dressed up" each day with a different colored ribbon.

Gérard and Josette's visit took place in the framework of an established routine. Josette unfolded a special cover she had brought with her, spread it out on Jeanne's bed, and placed Poupée on it. The dog curled up comfortably and promptly went to sleep. Gérard and Josette chatted with Jeanne and me, watched some television, and at an appointed time unwrapped the cold cuts and sandwich supper they had brought along. They ate it on the kitchen table while Poupée lapped up milk from a dish and nibbled on bits of chocolate. At about 10 p.m. they packed up their belongings and their little dog and bid an affectionate farewell to Jeanne and me.

My visit with Jeanne did not end until very late in the evening. She was not accustomed to sleeping much during the night, because that was when Michel did most of his writing. We continued to converse, and I moved about the house with her as she made her rounds to put things back in their proper places and to touch some of the objects. For the first time I touched them too, patting Borax's head and daring to shake the hand of the Gentleman-Devil puppet as if he were an old friend.

We called for a taxi. As Jeanne and I stood together in the doorway of 71, rue Lefrancq, waiting for the cab to come down the empty, silent street, both of us smelled roses.

Return to Rue Lefrancq: July 30, 1987

I am leaving Belgium the day after tomorrow. During the brief interlude of sunshine that appeared this afternoon I made my first trip to 71, rue Lefrancq in years, to the house in the Brussels commune of Schaarbeek where Michel and Jeanne de Ghelderode lived in 1961 when I met them.

Riding in the taxi into the Schaarbeek world that exists behind the peeling and battered basilica of the Eglise Sainte Marie, I felt the same stirrings I experienced when Michel and Jeanne were alive and I was approaching their house for a visit. Since that time Schaarbeek has become a district inhabited by many North Africans. I have been told they tried, but did not succeed, in having the domed Eglise Sainte Marie converted into a mosque.

The streets were quiet at three o'clock in the afternoon. An occasional North African woman passed by, dressed in an ankle-length robe, her head covered in the Islamic way. A few children were playing summer games on the sidewalks. When I reached Rue Lefrancq it was totally devoid of people, and very still.

The windows of the Ghelderodes' ground-floor apartment were covered with green shutters, as they always were. And on the left side of the big green entrance door, attached to the faded brick wall, was a white stone memorial plaque. "On April 1, 1962, Michel de Ghelderode died here," the plaque said, in both French and Flemish. At the bottom it read, *"Les Amis de Michel de Ghelderode"* (The Friends of Michel de Ghelderode), exclusively in French. There was no mention of Jeanne.

On that momentarily sunny street, filled with the kind of light that Michel used to arrange for my visits, I sensed his presence. The carousel horses, the madonnas, the mannequins, the marionettes, the masks, the swords, the seashells, the walls of eloquent paintings, and the strange, secret garden might still be there, I felt, behind the green shutters. The enigmatic roses, too.

The Meaning of the
Belgian House

I HAVE ALWAYS felt that the countless red bricks Belgians make, and all the houses they build for themselves with the bricks, have more than tangible meaning. But Belgians do not readily admit this is so. Quite to the contrary, they are more inclined to associate their brick-making and house-building with their domestic materialism. They self-mockingly refer to themselves as a people "with a brick in their belly," whose respectability and very being depend on having a house of their own—preferably one they have constructed themselves—filled with personal and family possessions. Occasionally, however, a Belgian expression is coined that suggests there is more to it than that—for example, when the national government is accused of "eating its bricks," because it is consuming far more revenue than it is investing. Here bricks are metaphorically associated with the most fundamental values and basic resources of Belgian society. And then there are all the paintings of houses and of the objects inside them by Belgian artists like Magritte, with titles like, "The Human Condition," "The Unexpected Answer," "The Secret Life," and "Time Transfixed." What is one to make of them if a Belgian house is only a house?

Hilde and Luc Timmermans helped me to understand the deepest spiritual significance of the Belgian house through what they shared with me about their lives and Hilde's death. "One thing that helps us to escape a little bit that overwhelming threatening feeling and allows us to make and realize some plans for the future," they wrote, "is the construction of our new home." For them, as for most Belgians, I believe, their house was not just a dwelling place or a mortar-and-brick expression of how much social and economic progress they had made. It was also a physical and symbolic bulwark—a structure that gave them protection and security in the face of the vicissitudes, the dangers, and the sorrows of life. And it was a haven too—a sanctuary of their love and of the courageous hope that there would be a future.

I was thinking of all this when I arrived at Izegemsestraat to spend the day with the Van Marcke family. I had not seen them for a year, and, as always, they were eager to share with me what they termed the "slice of life" they had experienced since my last visit.

At Moeder Clara's house I was shown the continuing changes, improvements, and repairs she had made in various rooms since Vader Cyriel's death five years earlier. We also toured her flower and vegetable garden and stopped to see the brood of chickens and the litters of rabbits she was raising. At Karel and Sylvie's house we pored over photographs of their youngest daughter Hedwig's marriage to Roel. The whole family crowded around to look at the pictures with me, as if they had never seen them before. At Mariette and Jan's house I inspected the new wall-to-wall carpeting, the small oriental throw rug, the vinyl flowered wallpaper, and the dark green draperies hung over sheer white embroidered curtains in the living room; the big oak breakfront in the dining room; the marble slabs soon to be laid down as flagstones on the front lawn; and the recently purchased Toyota car. With lively interest and satisfaction, Mariette told me how much each of these acquisitions had cost; and she expressed pride in the work that Jan had done, such as papering the living room walls and doors, and even the walls and doors of the tool shed in the garden. At the home of Germaine and her (second) husband Marnix, I was shown the ways in which they had enlarged and transformed what they called their *fermette* [little farm]. Marnix was eager for me to enter his home workshop where he kept the tools and materials he had used to make these alterations, and framed pictures of himself as a young man, playing amateur soccer on a local team, and in his World War II soldier's uniform.

Since my last visit, I was told, not only had Hedwig married, but Karel and Sylvie's oldest child, Marie-Hélène, and her fiancé, Guy, had set their wedding date for the month of July; Germaine's eldest daughter, Lydie, had given birth to a baby boy; and her younger daughter, Anne-Marie, had had her Solemn Communion.

IN 1977, following his visit to the concentration camp in Auschwitz, King Baudouin initiated the construction of a Belgian memorial there. It was designed by the Belgian artist Serge Creuz and dedicated in 1984.

The soul of the memorial consists of an enormous pair of eyes fixed on a bourgeois "interior" of the 1930s—the inside of a house, inhabited by a family, dressed for their daily life in the clothing of the time, and surrounded by the usual objects with which a home is furnished. Alongside this interior, the physical things and traces left behind by those who perished at Auschwitz are displayed: shoes, slippers, valises, eyeglasses, dental bridgework, locks of hair. These relics of everyday life are enshrined here—in their commonplace humanity and their silent condemnation of human evil.

Nothing could be more movingly and profoundly Belgian than this exhibit of domesticity, and things, and huge eyes watching.

Hilde's Death

$\mathbf{M}$ECHELEN, the 5th of February 1977

Dear Renée:

It's not so easy to tell you in such few words all that happened in the last months. Let me begin with Tim, the youngest and most uncomplicated in our family. Since you saw him last time he became a "big boy" and a real tot. He's a very enthusiastic fan of his "school juffrouw" [unmarried woman schoolteacher]. He enjoys very much going to school (since September, only half-time: before noon) and has learned already a lot of new things, becoming a "socialized" human being. From time to time he remembers "Mevrouw Fox" as the lady who came to Mechelen by train, brought him an airplane and some T-shirts, speaks English, and called him one time "Timmy!"

Unfortunately the news I have to tell you about Hilde is not so good. Two weeks ago x-rays showed new complications of her disease. Before, most of the symptoms (in the lungs) had disappeared; now some are increasing again. Next week doctors will make a decision about intensifying or changing the therapy. For her and for us all, this is a new fact, hard to get through after the relative success during the past year of therapy. . . . Fortunately there are no acute physical complaints of pain. Between the therapy sessions she feels relatively well and tries to live the life of a normal mother and housewife (with success).

One thing that helps us to escape a little bit from this overwhelming threatening feeling and allows us to make and realize some plans for the future is the construction of our new home. It is now at a stage that we hope to move in during the month of April. So when you come back to Belgium, . . . we'll be able to receive you in our new home. . . .

Dear Renée, I guess Belgium and Belgians are so close to your heart that we may expect you "back home" in the near future. I hope we'll find enough time at that moment to discuss quietly all that has happened. You know you are always welcome!

Kind greetings from us all,

Luc

P.S. During the time I had to wait at his office, I rewrote Luc's letter. So long, Renée.

Hilde

+ HILDE TIMMERMANS
Spouse of Luc and
mama of Tim VERWILGEN
Born in Mechelen [Malines] on 20 July 1952 and
died there on 24 May 1978.

Each one of us knew her in a different
way, but she was always simply
herself: full of love and devoted,
faithful and constant, quiet and courageous.

At the end of '75 the life that she had
dreamed of for herself and for her family
was disrupted for the first time by her illness.
But each time she found the strength to begin
again and to adjust her plans to the new situation.
She believed in and fought for her life.

In the end she sought and found eternal life.

Her example can help each of us.
Continue to think of her.

For your expressions of sympathy thank you from the families

TIMMERMANS AND VERWILGEN.

HILDE VERWILGEN TIMMERMANS died on Thursday afternoon, May 24, 1978, while I was receiving a *Doctor Honoris Causa* at the Katholieke Universiteit te Leuven, where I first met her and Luc, her husband, a graduate student and teaching assistant in the sociology department. She died of cancer of the bone with metastases to her lungs. She had managed to meet most of her responsibilities as a wife and mother until the very end, despite the amputation of one leg, metastases, massive chemotherapy treatments, their side effects, and the progression of her disease. Luc and she took great pride in this. But once the new house was built and the Timmermans moved into it in the spring, she became very weak and began to decline rapidly—almost as if the house had been a prayer-in-bricks that she had offered up and waited to see fulfilled. On Thursday, May 24, ten minutes after Luc came home to see how she was doing, she died wordlessly, without struggle, in his arms.

The funeral mass took place at 11 a.m. in the parish church of Sint Jozef in Battel, Hilde's village right outside Mechelen. Battel had been lacerated by the superhighway built around and through it. Sint Jozef's church was nondescript, more ugly than lovely. On this chill, foggy morning it was filled to capacity by the whole village, the Leuven University sociology department, family, friends, children from the school where Hilde taught physical education—virtually everyone who knew them. Throughout the whole mass, though there were probably several hundred people assembled, there was deep silence broken only by occasional quiet sobbing, the litany, the music, and the bells.

"Hilde was a very simple person," Luc said later. He knew she would not have wanted elaborate flowers, artfully arranged with ribbons and the names of the senders displayed. So he asked that no flowers be sent, and in the church, on the altar, there was only a single, clear glass vase filled with several sprays of white lilacs that were in bloom all over the countryside (what Luc called an "anonymous" bouquet). To the right of the altar, on a little ledge in front of the tabernacle where the Communion wafers were kept, there was an even smaller glass vase with one twig of white lilacs and two twigs of deep dusky purple lilacs. Purple and white: the colors of the blossoms, of the priest's vestments, and of death, royalty, purity, life, and resurrection. Next to the blossoms, the eternal light burned in its red glass container.

Silence—and then the bells in the church tower rang and rang and rang, vibrating inside us and announcing their tragic message for miles around. They continued to toll for what seemed an unbearably long time. Finally they stopped. Several men in black livery wheeled Hilde's coffin to the front of the church. It was covered with a black cloth embroidered in silver threads. They were followed by the mourners, led by Luc, and Hilde's closest male relatives. Luc carried the only other flowers in the church—a bouquet of mixed flowers, mainly roses, that he placed on Hilde's coffin.

The mass unfolded in Latin and Flemish, in words and music and song, and in sacred gestures, purified and made aromatic by incense. At a certain point in the mass we all filed to the front of the church to offer a gift of money, to kiss a small, round metal plate with a cross engraved on it, held by the younger of the two priests presiding at the mass, and to receive a printed memento of Hilde's death.

I drove to the cemetery with the chairman of Leuven University's medical sociology unit and his wife. The hearse and the family had preceded us. We joined the line of mourners following the hearse to the far end of the cemetery where Hilde was to be buried. The cemetery seemed relatively new. Its rows of poplar trees were still very young. The avenue down the middle of the cemetery was perfectly paved. Luc had told me that after her leg was amputated, Hilde liked to walk here because it was quiet and peaceful, and because it was easy for her to learn to walk again on such an unproblematic path. As we neared the open, raw grave site where Hilde's name was printed on a temporary wooden cross, a train passed rapidly and silently by on the tracks just beyond and elevated above the cemetery grounds. Then, for the first time in almost a week, the sun pierced through the cold fog. Suddenly it was very warm, and I was aware of how many flowering trees were in bloom in the cemetery and all over the countryside: white and pink and lavender and gold. They had been enveloped in mist all May.

The black-and-silver cloth was removed from Hilde's coffin by the men in black livery, folded like a flag, and put back in the hearse. The coffin, made of the same heavy golden oak that Flemish families consider the choicest wood for furniture, was carried to the grave. A few prayers were said beside it by the priest, and then the coffin was lowered into the grave on ropes. Now, beginning with Luc, we all filed past the grave, each of us dropping a flower onto the coffin. Luc's was a fully opened lily. He kissed it before he gently released it. Many people made a sign of the cross with their blossom.

The family was waiting on the other side of the grave in a reception line to greet us with dignity, handshakes, embraces, and quiet tears.

We moved back down the path toward the entrance of the cemetery, leaving Hilde alone in the blossom-filled sunlight. Another train sped noiselessly by. Luc drove back with us to the parish hall where coffee and a light lunch were to be served. He seemed to need to talk about Hilde's last days and her death in descriptive detail. He was dry-eyed and even smiled from time to time.

As we approached the church the brass band of the village (its *fanfare*), playing a funeral march in honor of Hilde, was receding mournfully down the street. At the parish hall several long wooden tables were laid out simply with platters of meat and cheese sandwiches on crisp Belgian rolls (*pistolets*) and buttered sandwiches of white raisin bread—the holiday bread of Flanders. Women came and went continually with steaming pots of strong coffee, filling and refilling our cups. All of us, including Luc, were surprisingly hungry.

A bit before 2 p.m. I was driven to the Mechelen station where I caught the first of three successive trains en route to Watermolen, the world of Izegemsestraat, and the busy, untragic lives of the Van Marcke family.

As I rode through the fields of Flanders, flowering under a hot spring sun, and a pale blue sky, my heart ached for the valiant young woman with the shiny blonde hair who died at the age of twenty-six; for her husband; and for her little son. I shall never forget the lilacs, or the bells, or the silent train speeding past the open grave.

A Gala Dinner at the
Royal Palace of Brussels

ON MAY 24, 1977, I received a formal invitation to a "Gala Dinner" to be held by Their Majesties, the King and Queen of the Belgians, the next Tuesday, May 31, at 8 p.m. at the Royal Palace of Brussels, in honor of His Excellency, President Kenneth Kaunda of the Republic of Zambia, and his wife, Madame Kaunda. The envelope in which it was sent bore the postmark of the palace but no stamp, and a mauve-colored engraving of the Belgian national crest in its center—two lions facing each other, holding a crowned heraldic shield of a single lion between their paws, with the motto, "*L'Union Fait La Force*" ("Union Makes for Strength") emblazoned on an undulating banner beneath their feet. Herman Libaers, grand marshal of the court and former head of the Belgian National Library, had placed my name on the guest list.

On the evening of the dinner I was not transported to the palace in a glass coach but in a Brussels taxi. The floodlit white palace, under a full moon, was visible from a distance. The cab moved rapidly through quiet streets, passed 14, rue Royale, the Errera house, turned the corner, and stopped in front of the palace gate, guarded by soldiers in sentry boxes. There I produced the big green pass that was included in my invitation envelope. One of the guards glanced at it, clicked his heels, saluted, and beckoned my taxi on, down a long, cobblestone path to the carriage entrance of the palace.

Dazed by my anxiety about how a guest should behave at a palace dinner, I emerged from the taxi as gracefully as I could, aided by several footmen who then ushered me through the entrance of the palace. Feeling very small and solitary, I passed through a series of rooms with burnished wooden floors that were quite bare of furniture. Uniformed personnel of various kinds, whose costumes, statuses, and functions were difficult for me to sort out, were posted all along the way. I finally arrived at the foot of a huge white marble staircase where a gracious young woman, dressed in simple, tailored street clothes, asked for my name and gave me a small card with my name typed on it: "Mademoiselle Renée Fox, Professeur à l'Université de Pennsylvanie." There was a minidiagram of the dinner table on the back of the card, with a red dot to indicate where my place was located.

I took a deep breath, gathered the folds of my long skirt in my hand, and started up the *grand escalier*. Overhead was an elaborate, painted wooden ceiling, garnished with gold leaf. Palace guards lined both sides of the entire staircase, standing at attention on its steps. They were dressed rather Napoleonically, with high black boots, white breeches, crimson vests, white frock coats, cummerbunds, and tall, black, furry hats with black chin straps, and they carried silver swords in their scabbards.

After the first landing there were no more guards; but on the second landing photographers with flashbulb cameras were standing in wait. I was rescued from them by a comfortable-looking middle-aged woman in street clothes, with a pile of papers in her hands, who greeted me and deftly guided me toward a palace man in black and white livery. He admitted me to a long *salon* with casement windows that looked out on the palace square and the park beyond it. The chairs and benches that lined the walls of the *salon* were upholstered in gold-bordered royal mauve, and each of them was embroidered with a gold crest. The matching mauve drapes at the windows were pulled back to allow the painterly evening light to illumine the *salon* along with the chandelier overhead. The room was filled with men in tuxedos, a few military officers in dress uniform, women in every conceivable kind of long gown, from chiffon to Mexican cotton, and a cadre of male palace staff, their somber black and white attire softened by the lace jabots that cascaded down their shirt fronts.

The first familiar face I saw was that of Nobel Laureate biochemist Christian de Duve, professor at the Université Catholique de Louvain and the Rockefeller University in New York City. He caught my eye, and I scurried over to greet him and his wife with relief, as if they were old friends. He kindly introduced me to several other people. When the Dean of Louvain's Medical School, Dr. Meulders, and his wife arrived and joined us, I began to feel more relaxed in the presence of four people whom I already knew.

We chatted and waited while in the next room the king and queen and the Kaundas were receiving members of the government and of the diplomatic corps. Then the smiling, soft-voiced men in black and white and lace jabots came to tell us that it would soon be our turn to enter the next room. They lined us up in a protocol-determined order: the Meulders first, the de Duves second, and "Mademoiselle Fox" just behind them.

The door to the next room opened, and through it I could see King Baudouin, Queen Fabiola, Prince Albert, and President and Madame Kaunda standing in their appointed places in the receiving line, waiting to greet the procession of guests. It was startling to be this close to such an array of political personages. Because of their frequent appearance on television and in newspapers and, in the case of King Baudouin, his image on Belgian stamps and coins, they looked familiar. And yet, in this ceremonially theatrical setting there was an illusory quality about their appearance, as if the men and women I saw were actors and actresses, brilliantly made up and costumed to play the parts of king and queen, prince and president. A page began to announce us. "Professor and Madame Christian de Duve!" called the page. I studied them intently as they crossed the threshold and moved down the reception line, noting whose hand Professor de Duve did and did not shake, the small curtsy that Madame de Duve made to the king and the queen, and the subtly respectful way in which both de Duves lowered their heads. "Mademoiselle Renée Fox, Professeur de l'Université de Pennsyl-vanie!" the page's voice announced, and as he turned smilingly toward me, I stepped forward into the reality and unreality of the receiving line. Kenneth Kaunda was a venerable chief whose majestic blackness was accentuated by his white hair and his white *abacos*-style suit. His wife was a figure of regal grace in her *pagne** and turban. The slender, earnest, still youthful-looking king, in a full-dress military uniform, smiled shyly behind his spectacles. The fine-boned queen, with her narrow, Goyaesque face, dark, intelli-

---

*A *pagne* is a long sheathlike skirt worn by African women in countries south of the Sahara. It is usually made of printed cotton cloth that is wrapped around the waist and draped over the hips. The finest *pagne* material is considered to be batik, treated in the Javanese/Indonesian way, so that the parts of the cloth not intended to be dyed are covered with removable wax. In Zaïre the best *pagne* material has been imported from Holland and is commonly referred to as "wax."

gent eyes, pale skin, and bouffant hairdo, wore a classic white dress with a gorgeous purple cowl, a single strand of pearls, and long pearl and diamond earrings.

But what impressed me up close was (to my surprise) not these elegant details. Rather it was how life-size and human the king and queen looked—gracious, conscientious, and hard-working.

I followed the moving line of people out of the reception hall into another long room where drinks and canapés were being served by waiters carrying large silver trays. André Molitor, the king's *chef de cabinet*, noticed me in the crowd and came over to greet me. "It's good to see you again," he said, shaking my hand. "Herman Libaers told me that you would be attending the dinner. But why haven't you come back to see me in my office, to go on with our interesting discussion about your research and about Belgian science policy?" From his tone of voice and manner it was clear that he was not just being polite. I was astounded. "The answer is quite simple," I replied. "I consider you and your responsibilities far too important to bother you with requests for further interviews." Without coyly denying what I had said, Molitor urged me to call him, telling me I could simply look him up in the Brussels phone book and call him either at home or at his office to make an appointment. "But not this week," he hastily added. "Any time *after* this week," he said, with a knowing smile.

What Molitor was alluding to when he asked me to wait a week before calling was the state of crisis in which the Belgian national government then found itself. The king had asked Prime Minister Leo Tindemans to form a new government. (This would be Tindemans's third). Forty-five days had passed since then, and Tindemans still had not been able to put together a governing coalition of parties and a distribution of the twenty-three ministerial and twenty-three secretary-of-state positions that would break through the political impasse created by the linguistic problem. In fact the day's newspapers had reported that representatives of six Belgian parties—the French and Flemish Christian Democrat and Socialist parties, and the Volksunie and Front des Francophones parties—had spent until 2:24 a.m. that very morning meeting with Tindemans in his house on Rue Lambermont, had gone home to sleep for a few hours, and had resumed their negotiations that afternoon. Tindemans had returned to the meeting a little before 8 p.m., after a conference with the king, to announce that he was ready to continue negotiations after attending the gala dinner for the president of Zambia at the palace.

The palace staff began gently to shepherd the guests toward the Throne Room. It was in that mirrored room, with its beautiful wooden floor, sumptuously painted ceiling, and brilliant crystal chandeliers that the dinner was held. Long tables were covered with thick, white, starched linen tablecloths, with big napkins to match. Each place was set with a silver dinner plate, several Val St. Lambert white crystal glasses of different sizes, and an array of heavy, ornate silver flatware. At every guest's place was a printed dinner program embossed with the royal crest—a golden "B" in a circle, with a crimson-and-gold crown at the top. It announced, first in French, then in Flemish, that this was a Gala Dinner at the Palace of Brussels on May 31, 1977, in honor of His Excellency, the President of the Republic of Zambia, and of Madame Kaunda. The courses of the austerely elegant dinner, and the wines we would be served, were listed in French. In Flemish, and then in French, the program indicated that music during the dinner would be performed by the Chamber Orchestra of the Band of the Guides, under the baton of Captain-Commander Conductor of Music Yvon Duecène. On two different sets of white cards that had been slipped into the cream-colored program were French and Flemish texts of the dinner speech that the king would deliver in English, out of linguistic respect for President Kaunda.

The guests found their assigned places and stood waiting behind their chairs. To the strains of a processional march played by the orchestra, the royal party, their guests of honor, and entourage filed into the Throne Room. The cortège included Herman Libaers, André Molitor, the papal nuncio, and the Zambian ambassador to Belgium, as well as the king and queen, Prince Albert, and the Kaundas. As they moved toward the head table they nodded greetings to various of the guests.

With the quiet Flemish-Belgian ambassador to Zambia on my left, I talked about my research in Zaïre and Belgium, and about his daughter who was a student at the Medical School of the University of Rochester in the United States. The more loquacious Mr. Godeaux, on my right (president of the Belgian Banking Commission and of the board of trustees of the Université Catholique de Louvain), told me he was born in Wallony. He and I talked about the major social and economic changes that had occurred in

Belgium since World War II, the remarkable degree to which the great fortunes in Belgium were nonetheless still intact, and mostly about how culturally exciting he found New York City, where his pianist son was receiving extraordinary training at the Julliard School of Music.

As we spoke, phalanxes of waiters came and went, bearing the courses of the meal and the wines on silver trays. They were all dressed in black and white livery, and some of them were very young men who wore their long hair in the traditional style of court pages. The chamber orchestra played quietly in the background, and the king and queen talked animatedly with the Kaundas.

When the waiters came to pour the champagne into our glasses, King Baudouin rose from his chair, adjusted the microphone on the podium before him, and began to deliver his prepared speech to President Kaunda. He welcomed Kaunda and his wife to Belgium, recalling with gratitude the official visit he and Queen Fabiola had made to Zambia in 1975, where they had been warmly received. That journey, he said, had given them a chance to see for themselves how admirably President Kaunda was shaping the development of his country, tapping into the innate qualities of his people, trying to maintain an equilibrium between industry and agriculture, progress and tradition, and, in contrast to a number of other countries in Central Africa, doing this in a way that respected human rights. He praised Kaunda for the patient and courageous role he had consistently played as a mediator who sought peaceful means to end white rule and racial discrimination in Rhodesia and South Africa, and for his nonaligned foreign policy that had enabled Zambia to maintain excellent relations with the societies of Western Europe.

But the king also raised several delicate issues. He implicitly responded to public statements that Kaunda had recently made about reaching the limits of effective nonviolent measures to eliminate racial discrimination in Southern Africa, and to the fact that along with four other African nation-states, Zambia had just agreed to accept military assistance from the Soviet Union to aid African liberation movements intent on waging guerrilla warfare against Rhodesia and South Africa. "Armed struggle of any kind would mean innocent victims and would again delay indispensable progress in Africa," the king said. "We want to believe that reason will prevail and that there is a place everywhere in Africa for a peaceful and multiracial society." Europe's role in Africa, the king affirmed, was to "contribute to development through economic and technical assistance to African autonomy, without a spirit of neocolonialism." Then, with soft-spoken frankness, he told President Kaunda, "It is painful to note that this same Europe that puts so many people and financial means at the disposal of cooperation and development is accused of imperialism by those from whom a contribution is practically nonexistent."

More soothingly, the king declared his pleasure with the growing collaboration between Zambia and Belgium, and said that since his visit to Zambia, specific agreements had been reached between the two countries in the spheres of agriculture and public health. "Ladies and gentlemen," then king then proclaimed, "I invite you to lift your glasses to the health of His Excellency the President and Madame Kaunda, to the well-being of their people, to the friendship between our two countries, and to peace in Africa." We all stood and raised our glasses while the orchestra played the National Anthem of Zambia.

Still standing behind his chair, President Kaunda announced that before he responded formally to the king's address he would break protocol for a few minutes. He summoned the Belgian ambassador to Zambia and all the Zambians at the dinner to his side so they could "sing a song together." Suddenly the Throne Room of the Belgian palace was transported to Africa, as Kaunda, in a strong, exuberant voice, led his "choral group" in the singing of the Zambian Hymn of Freedom, accompanied by rhythmic clapping. It was Kaunda who sang the solo parts of the lively chant— Kaunda, the venerable African *Tata*, chief, and Protestant pastor, as well as president of the Republic of Zambia. When the song ended the whole room resounded with the applause of the delighted and liberated guests.

Kaunda donned a pair of old-fashioned spectacles and took a white handkerchief from his pocket in preparation for his speech. It was delivered in English and was very African in style, with stirring eloquence and rhythmic repetition. It was also morally exhortative and militant. After greeting the king and queen and the Belgian people, and thanking them for the warm welcome he had received, Kaunda paid homage to the "profound impression" that the Belgian sovereigns had made during their visit to Zambia. Kaunda thanked the king for the "encouragement" he had received from his "appreciation of our limited efforts" to further peace in Africa. He affirmed that peace was a "moral imperative." But "unless the great part of Africa recovers its human rights," he warned, "there will not be peace in South Africa." He denounced the way that "Europe has tried to ignore the disastrous events that are unfolding in South Africa. . . . Europe cannot have two faces with regard to human rights," he sermonized, "one turned toward Africa, and the other toward other regions of the world."

Kaunda brought his speech to a close with a ringing personal testimony. "I have never abandoned the principles of nonviolence," he declared, "but I have always made it clear that wherever there exists a choice between slavery and violence, I would choose violence to defend human dignity." Kaunda called upon Belgians and other Europeans to join Zambia in dedicating themselves to the "mission" of "peace and freedom, entirely founded on justice for all humanity." Lifting his glass high, he proposed a toast to the king, the queen, and Belgium, and to Belgian-Zambian relations. Once again we rose from our seats and raised our champagne glasses, this time to the orchestral strains of the Belgian national anthem, the "Brabançonne."

The dessert was quickly served on beautiful old hand-painted, gold-bordered china, and just as quickly eaten. We stood at our places while the royal party and guests of honor exited from the Throne Room and wended their way into an adjacent drawing room. There we all gathered for coffee served on big silver trays by palace personnel, and chatted over our after-dinner demitasses.

It was past eleven by this time, and the crowd had begun to thin out. Herman Libaers, who until now had been a figure of perpetual motion, stopped to talk with me. With a twinkle in his eye he made a gesture toward the other end of the room where Leo Tindemans and King Baudouin were just leaving the dinner gathering, en route to another meeting over the crisis concerning the formation of the new government. "You are really in the 'Château,'" he gleefully exclaimed. Then he asked me if I had a way of getting back to Leuven, and offered to put a palace car and chauffeur at my disposal to drive me home. As I had already accepted a ride, I had to decline—reluctantly—the opportunity to be a passenger in a royal vehicle. I thanked Mr. Libaers for having made possible my inclusion at the dinner, and bid him good night. Considerably more relaxed than I had been upon my arrival at the palace, I moved back through its various anterooms, down the grand staircase on which the uniformed guards no longer stood, through the front door, and along the paved path to the gate. The palace was still illumined, and the full moon had not waned. But the sentries were no longer visible, and the surrounding streets were bare. In the distance I could hear the Belgian ambassador to Zambia being called to his car over a loudspeaker.

ON JUNE 1, and again on June 2, 1977, Belgian newspapers carried headline stories about President Kenneth Kaunda's state visit, the gala dinner at the palace, the speeches delivered by Kaunda and by the king on that occasion, and about the formation of a new, six-party coalition government under Prime Minister Tindemans. I spent the entire morning of June 1 writing up these events in my field notes. The palace chandeliers still gleamed in my mind, and the affairs of state that had taken place under them unfolded like a pageant before me. But as I wrote I realized that the most enduring message I had carried away from the palace was the antithesis of the ritual splendor, the dramaturgic exercise of diplomacy, and the suspense-filled government negotiations I had glimpsed.

> The Royal Palace—the "Château"—is a Belgian house. Despite its opulence and ceremony, it is not that much different from all the others I have visited. The people inside it are very familiar to me. On this particular evening there were many whom I knew personally. Those whom I did not know were mostly just like the variety of Belgians whom I have met, and with whom my life has become entwined since I first journeyed to this land. Even the king and queen looked like a couple of my own age whom I might have enjoyed knowing, if only they weren't monarchs. . . .
>
> The commonplaceness of this discovery is deeply satisfying. After so many years of searching and researching in Belgium, a very human, ordinary truth is one of my most significant findings.

Part Three

BELGIUM AND ZAÏRE

Entrance to Hôpital Mama Yemo, Kinshasa, Zaïre

Arrival in
Léopoldville/Kinshasa,
Congo/Zaïre

Ⓘ N MANY of the Belgian houses I visited over the years, Belgium's former colony, Congo-Zaïre,* was lovingly present. The numerous rubber plants in private houses and on public premises, the African sculpture and masks on display, the parrots who dwelt in the houses on Izegemsestraat and the Rue Royale, the appeals for contributions to the African missions that were regularly made in parish churches—all reminded me of the strong human connections that existed between Belgium and the Belgian Congo. For seventy-five years, from 1885 to 1960, the tiny European country of Belgium ruled over an African land that was eight times larger. More than political, economic, and social domination was involved in this colonial relationship. The vast African territory that stretched far beyond the restricting boundaries of Belgium, and yet "belonged" to it, provided Belgians with an horizon, and with an existential as well as a geographical frontier.

Both literally and figuratively, Belgium built many houses in the Congo. Belgian society and culture were exported to the Congo along with the thousands of Belgians who came to live and work there. Belgian attitudes and values, customs and beliefs, structures and conflicts were implanted in this region of Africa. But it was also true that through the long and encompassing association of

---

*Throughout this section of the book I have used the place names that existed in the Congo, now Zaïre, in the early 1960s, when the events I recount occurred. Since then many of these place names, along with personal names, have been Africanized.

In addition to its direct rule over the Belgian Congo, Belgium was the trustee of the territory of Ruanda-Urundi, now the independent countries of Burundi and Rwanda.

these two countries, the landscape of Central Africa, its sights and sounds and smells, its cadences, its peoples, and its cosmic view, entered deeply into the Belgian psyche.

Witnessing the way that Belgians responded to the first weeks of the Congo's independence heightened my awareness of what the Congo meant to them. On June 30, 1960, the day the Congo officially ceased to be a Belgian colony and became an independent nation-state, and during the July days that followed, the sky over Brussels was filled with Sabena planes bringing Belgians out of the turbulence that had erupted in Léopoldville, the Lower Congo, and Katanga. Virtually every Belgian family I knew made at least one trip to the Brussels/Zavantem airport to meet a relative or close friend who was part of the wave of Belgians returning from the Congo. Mingled with the shock and indignation that many Belgians were feeling was their anguished sense of exile and loss.

I became progressively convinced that Belgium could not be fully understood without firsthand knowledge of its relationship with ex-Belgian Africa (and vice versa). So when I was invited by the Centre de Recherches Sociologiques (CRS) in Léopoldville to spend several weeks late in 1962 as their guest, I accepted enthusiastically. *

ON THE cold and snowy post-Christmas night of December 29, 1962, I boarded the 8:25 p.m. Sabena flight from Brussels to Léopoldville with many Congolese and some Belgian passengers. At the Madrid airport where we were delayed for two hours with engine trouble, I was incorporated into the friendly, animated visiting patterns of the Congolese passengers. Most of them seemed to be members of the country's new political elite.

Once we were airborne again, the plane flew uninterruptedly through the night, across the Mediterranean Sea, over the vastness of the Sahara Desert and through the intricate air currents that its cooling sands emitted, past the equator, deep into the heart of Central Africa. All night long a big red star and the radiant white star of Epiphany shone outside the windows of the plane. A little before 6 a.m. a faint pink glow appeared on the eastern rim of the

---

*The CRS was founded by the secretary general of the episcopate of the Catholic church in the Congo.

sky as the light slowly began to dawn. The sky turned from pale green to pale blue, and then the sun rose crimson and gold. The landscape of Africa was beneath us—sunlit, tropical green hills, rolling plains, and the shimmering power of the mighty Congo River. Our plane was rapidly descending as we passed Brazzaville, capital of the former French Congo, and crossed the river to land in Léopoldville.

Although it was still early morning, the terminal was filled with crowds of people who had spilled out onto the balconies overlooking the airfield to watch the passengers disembarking from the plane. Belgian and African colleagues were waiting for me and helped me to navigate through the steamy, swarming, cacophonous bedlam of customs and the retrieval of baggage. As we drove from the airport to the city, all the sights and sounds and odors were burned into my mind by the heat, the humanity, and the rhythmical throbbing of the Congolese universe that enveloped me. Whizzing by us on the road, with a great honking of horns, ringing of bells, and chorale of talking, shouting, and singing voices, were trucks and buses and taxis crammed with passengers, jeeps of Congolese and United Nations soldiers, Volkswagens and Land Rovers of missionaries, and throngs of bicycles pedaled by African men in shorts and sandals. The air was thick with dust, humidity, the pungent smell of wood smoke and the African earth, and a haunting fragrance, almost like incense, that seemed to come from the cascades of golden blossoms hanging from certain flowering trees. Through the blur of my first impressions I caught glimpses of African palms and conifers, purple bougainvillea, and huge orange flowers. Hundreds of African men and women were walking along the sides of the road, traveling on foot to work as they did every day over a distance of many kilometers. Draped in their colorful cotton *pagnes*, wearing kerchiefs and turbans, carrying infants on their backs and bundles of wood and produce on their heads, the women moved with upright dignity and fluid grace.

We drove through the *Cité*—the densely populated, urban village area of Léopoldville where the majority of Congolese lived in tight clusters and jagged lanes of small, tin-roofed, cinder block houses. The unpaved sandy streets surrounding the houses throbbed with the vibrant voices and energetic play of masses of children, the outdoor cooking and sweeping of the women, the busy transactions of small and large markets, the crowing of roosters, and with the catchy beat of modern African dance music and popular songs blaring from loudly playing transistor radios and phonographs.

The commercial and administrative center of Léopoldville was more European-looking, with broad avenues and majestic boulevards, historic statues and monuments, massive white government and office buildings, foreign embassies, white-and-pastel-colored stucco mansions, churches and a red-brick cathedral, stores, restaurants, and hotels. But the life on the street was teemingly African: filled with noisy, erratically driven vehicles and men, women, and children on the move, talking, singing, waving, and calling to one another. Office workers on the ground floor of some buildings leaned out of the open windows, conversing with friends on the street; and all the shady spots on the sun-drenched sidewalks were occupied by groups of people who sat with their backs against a wall or the trunk of a palm tree.

We finally reached our destination, the Hotel Memling, where I would be staying. It was surrounded by Congolese soldiers, big, shiny American cars, and a crowd of spectators who had gathered to catch a glimpse of the political leaders entering and leaving from the hotel on this last day of a meeting of the Pan-African Congress in Léopoldville. I made my way through the maelstrom of the lobby, checked in at the front desk, and was escorted to my room by a hotel "boy": a barefooted male African servant dressed in a yellow sweatshirt with "Englebert Tires" printed on it, who carried my luggage and told me that his name was Fidèle. The sensual heat, the city dust, the sound of zooming car motors, African voices and music from the streets, the songs of the tropical birds and whistles of the parrots in the hotel's courtyard, and the distant crowing of a rooster permeated that room, with its shabby furniture and broken *Appel Boy* (Call Boy) button on the wall that, in colonial days, could be pushed to summon a servant.

I had traveled far, far away from the Belgian, Brugge, Sint-Janshospitaal universe of the painter Hans Memling after whom this hotel was named. And yet the Belgian world to which he belonged, and the African world to which I had come, were part of each other.

AS A result of this first, brief trip to the Congo I became a scientific adviser and active member of the Centre de Recherches Sociologiques. I spent a great deal of time from the end of 1962 through

1967 doing firsthand fieldwork in Congo/Zaïre that carried me into many geographical regions, social contexts, and cultural spheres of the country.

Out of all these experiences, none meant more to me than what happened in 1964–1965, the year of the Congo Rebellion, when a group of young African women initiated me into their world, and one of them—Sabine Mosabu—became my colleague, friend, and, in the African way, my "younger sister." Together she and I then traveled to Lisala, her home in the interior of the country where, in full view of the red-brick Belgian Catholic mission that loomed over the town, I was the first white person ever to be a house guest of a local Congolese family.

Inside the Pension
on Avenue Tombeur de Tabora

SEPTEMBER 6, 1964

It is eight o'clock on this my first Sunday morning in Léopold-ville. The sun rose two hours ago, but the light is somber. This is the end of the dry season, and the sky is so heavy with clouds every morning that you would think rain was imminent. Flying into Léopoldville on Tuesday, over "*Le Fleuve*" (the Congo River), we could see the clouds and mist hanging low at dawn. The earth below us was parched, with occasional patches of phosphorescent green. There are some trees, even some flowers, that persist throughout this waterless season; and new fronds are appearing on palm trees in anticipation of the rains that will begin in a few weeks. Church bells are ringing all over the city, accompanied by the medleys of song birds and the crowing of roosters. The voluptu-ous scent of African earth is in the air, as well as the lingering fragrance of the fires that the Congolese who inhabit the Cité used to cook yesterday evening's meal and to keep themselves warm during the chill night.

I have been here for five days, living temporarily in a sort of *pension* [boarding house] for young Congolese women in their late teens. It is located on Avenue Tombeur de Tabora, a few steps from the mission of the Scheut fathers on one side, and from the huge municipal hospital, the Hôpital des Congolais, on the other. My room is sparsely furnished and badly lit. What redeems it is the balcony onto which it opens, fringed by palms, and over which hang the topmost leaves and the first fruits of a young papaya tree.

Eventually I hope to find an apartment of my own. But at present living here is not only a convenient arrangement, it is also full of human richness, largely because of the Congolese women boarders. Alternating between their brightly colored *pagnes* and European-style clothing, their heads coiffed with the crowns of tiny braids that they plait for one another and tie with strings, they are physically lovely and beautifully groomed. They are also youthfully energetic and high spirited—and something more. They have the special grace and perceptive wisdom that I associate with African women.

Four of them are leaders of the "JOC/F": the feminine wing of the Jeunesse Ouvrière Chrétienne, an international movement of young Catholics founded by the Belgian Cardinal Joseph Cardijn. The JOC is premised on a vision of workers as sons and daughters of God, belief in their dignity, and the conviction that unjust conditions in their lives and work can and should be transformed. What Cardijn termed its "appropriately lay apostolic mission of the laity" is grounded in the "See, Judge, Act," participant-observation methodology it has developed for gathering facts and generating insights about the situations one wishes to change, so that the social action undertaken will be more effective. The four JOC/F leaders were attending the annual national convention of the organization in Léopoldville when the series of rebellions that have swept through the Congo this year moved into their home areas of Bunia, Lisala, and Stanleyville. Under the circumstances they cannot travel back to these regions, and there has been no news from their families for weeks.

Yesterday, at the supper table, Sabine Mosabu—whom all the Congolese women call *Mama* Sabine, out of respect for the office she holds as national president of JOC/F and in recognition of her extraordinary personal qualities—talked at length about the mixture of news and rumors she has heard concerning the happenings in her home community of Lisala. With the approach of the rebels, she said, most of the population has evacuated the town and taken refuge in the surrounding forest. Some report that Lisala's Catholic cathedral and its town hall have been bombed and that at least one religious sister has been killed. A sack of Chinese communist propaganda was supposedly found in the area, and some people reported seeing soldiers with "skin like ours, but with strange, slanted eyes" among the rebels. Sabine recounted all of this in Lingala; but then, despite her personal anxiety and sadness, and without any prompting on my part, she proceeded to translate what she had said into French for my benefit.

In the course of this first week the group of Congolese women who are staying in this house have decided to make a Congolese outfit for me. They are planning to go to the market on a shopping expedition to pick out just the right quality and color of printed cotton fabric—material that will be in harmony with my skin tones, they say—out of which they will fashion a *pagne* and matching blouse for me.

But other aspects of living in this *pension* pain me. Most of them have to do with the Belgian *"mesdemoiselles"*—sincere, dedicated, pious Belgian women, trained as *assistantes sociales* [social workers], who manage and watch over this house and its occupants. They run it more like a convent than a residence, and despite, or because of, their real concern for the welfare of the Congolese women who are boarding with them, they have cordoned them off in certain colonialistlike ways. Most notably, the Belgian *mesdemoiselles* eat together in their own dining room while the Congolese women are served their meals in a separate room. One of the fortunate things that has happened to me is that I have been assigned to eat my meals in the Congolese rather than the Belgian dining room. Still, Georges, the Congolese "boy" of the house, who does all the cooking and cleaning, insists on giving me preferential treatment. He has put me at the head of the table and set my place with the one available napkin, the one intact cup and saucer, and the one nonplastic drinking glass.

October 3, 1964

News of the fate of my companions' families who are caught in the throes of the rebellion is beginning to filter back to us. Sabine now knows that the groups of rebels who invaded Lisala came to her parents' house looking for her older brother, Aimé, whom they defined as an enemy—a member of the exploiting elite of the country—because he is a teacher and director of a Catholic primary school in the community. Fortunately, Aimé is in Léopoldville. At the time the rebellion spread to Lisala he was attending a meeting here on education and community development, and like his sister Sabine, he has been waiting it out in Léopoldville until it is possible and safe to return home. But, from what Sabine has heard, the rebels pillaged his house and her parents' as well. Sabine's father took Aimé's wife and children with him into the surrounding forest to protect them from harm. Sabine's three sisters and her two younger brothers fled into another part of the forest with a group of townspeople. Only Mama Elisabeth, Sabine's mother, remained in the family dwelling, defending what remained after the rebels had plundered it. Until Sabine succeeded in getting a message to her this week, Mama Elisabeth was cut off from all communication, did not know where the members of her family were, and was convinced that the rebels now had all the Congo under their control. I sat with Sabine in her room as she told me this story, wrapped like an African queen in the folds of her *pagne*, with tears coursing down her cheeks.

October 11, 1964

It is cool, windy, and overcast—almost autumnal. There are now twelve fruits on the papaya tree overhanging my balcony, and many more are in bud. The fan-shaped leaves that form a green canopy over the papaya move like the fingers on gigantic green hands, in response to the currents of wind.

Since I first arrived here more than a month ago the financial difficulties facing the Belgian *mesdemoiselles* who run this house have been increasing. To begin with, as *assistantes sociales* who work during the day for Catholic agencies and provide living quarters for young women in Léopoldville largely as an extra social service, they earn very small salaries, receive minimal support from their agencies or other missionary sources to help defray the house expenses, and charge the lowest possible fees for those who board here. Their economic problems have been enhanced by the steeply rising price of food in Léopoldville, mainly due to the fact that produce from villages in areas invaded by the rebels is no longer being shipped from the interior of the country to the city. In addition, the young women currently living here who are refugees from rebel-occupied regions are penniless; so the good ladies of the house are letting them stay here free of charge.

One of the serious consequences of these straitened conditions is that the meals served to my Congolese housemates are meager, insufficiently nourishing, and often consist of European foods, such as cheese, that they do not like and will not eat even if they are hungry. This has greatly concerned me. I decided that perhaps I could help to improve the situation by contributing a fixed sum of money each week to my Congolese companions. This would enable them to go directly to the big outdoor market in the *Cité* and buy indigenous foods of their choice to supplement what they are being served at table—bargaining for the prices they pay for their purchases in the traditional African manner. I conferred with some colleagues and with Sabine about the appropriateness and practicality of my idea—chiefly about whether I could offer to subsidize the food in a way that would neither offend the Belgian nor the Congolese women of the household. After receiving their encouragement I informed everyone in the house of my plan and, following Sabine's advice, I asked the Congolese women to set up whatever arrangements they thought best. They chose Marie-Christine Bangala, a JOC/F leader from rebel-beseiged Stanleyville who is living here, to be in charge of buying and distributing the food.

This week the system they organized has been set in motion. Friday evening there was a gentle tap on my door. I opened it to find Marie-Christine standing there, holding four bananas and two oranges in her hands. She had come to give me my share of this week's food distribution—exactly the portion of extra things to eat that every one of the Congolese girls was receiving. I was surprised and moved. By virtue of the interpretation that my Congolese friends have collectively made of my gift, I have become a recipient on equal terms and in union with them.

Down in the kitchen, from which I have just returned, Sabine is cooking a Congolese Sunday dinner for us, using more of the food that the group purchased this week. Rice was bubbling in one of the pots on the stove, and a native fish of some sort, prepared in palm oil and the juice of fresh tomatoes, was simmering in another pot. Sabine was grinding up the fire-hot red peppers that Congolese use to season everything—*pili-pili*—using a wooden mortar and pestle to pound it into a powder. A little before noon, she told me, she will begin to make the *foufou*, the local Lingala term used in this part of the Congo to refer to a dish made of cassava, the root that is as basic to the Congolese diet as bread and potatoes are to ours. By the time the *foufou* appears on the table it will be a big, elastic ball of white doughy paste, served in a bowl. Each of us will cut a section from it with our knife and eat it with the fish, and with the palm oil and tomato juice sauce in which the fish was cooked, poured over it.

October 18, 1964

The main avenues and boulevards of Léopoldville are decorated with the blue, gold, and red flags of this country, which has recently been renamed the République Démocratique du Congo, to distinguish it from the former French Congo, Congo-Brazzaville, across the river, whose official name is simply the République du Congo.

This has been a week of festivity in Léopoldville. Thursday, October 15, was a national holiday. In colonial times it was celebrated as the birthday of King Albert of the Belgians. Now, through the alchemy of independence, it has become a holiday that honors the birthday of Joseph KasaVubu, a founding father of this independent nation-state and its first president.

But an even bigger day of public rejoicing preceded KasaVubu's birthday. On Tuesday, October 13, Prime Minister Moïse Tshombe arrived back in the Congo from a state visit to Cairo where he was received by the president of the United Arab Republic, Gamal Abdel Nasser. Léopoldville newspapers and radio broadcasts reported that more than 25,000 people were at the airport to greet him, and that a quarter of a million persons lined the streets of this capital city to hail him with cries of "Long Live Tshombe," and even "Hosannah." Tshombe's assumption of the top position in the national government on July 9, only eighteen months after he was forced by military and political pressure of the United Nations to put an end to the secession of Katanga of which he was president, and go into exile, was a real *coup de théâtre.* Many factors, including his national and international machinations to return to power, and the failure of outgoing Prime Minister Cyrille Adoula to stem the tide of the Congo Rebellion, contributed to his remarkable return. Since assuming office he has opened negotiations with the leaders of the rebellion, made moves to hire white mercenaries to fight with the National Congolese Army against the rebel partisans, and integrated the organized units of the Katanga Gendarmerie that were previously stationed in Angola into the Congolese army and sent them to the front. As his reception in Léopoldville this week demonstrated, in record time he has become very popular throughout the country, especially in the cities.

October 21, 1964

At 4:15 this morning I and all the young Congolese women in the house where I live piled into two little Volkswagen cars and drove to the N'djili/Léopoldville airport to see Sabine off. She is returning to Lisala and her family now that the rebels have evacuated the area. A fragment of moon was setting, and it was still dark as we sped along the highway. Long rows of fast-pedaling Congolese men on bicycles were moving along both sides of the road, already en route to work from their homes many kilometers away from the center of the city where they are employed.

At the airport we said very little to each other. Our feelings of sadness about Sabine's departure underlay our silence. Although we were glad she was about to be reunited with her family, we were concerned about the state in which she would find them and her home town; and in this time of troubles the Congo is facing, we tacitly wondered if we would ever see her again. After saying our farewells we pensively watched her board an Air Congo DC-3 with a small group of Lisala-bound passengers who consisted of several Congolese families, two military policemen, several Belgian religious sisters, and a number of Portuguese and Sudanese merchants and shopkeepers. As Sabine flew northeast toward the equatorial region of the country, we rode back to our *pension*. It was a little after 6 a.m. when we arrived home. By this time the sky was full of color and light, and the entire population of the city seemed to be on foot, on bicycle, or in a bus, truck, or car.

This has been a week of events full of personal meaning. On Monday night we had our first rain. It was a gentle storm compared with the great deluges that have yet to come before the earth turns moist again and the foliage and flowers burst into brilliantly colored bloom. On that same evening François Nkayi, who has been acting as my chauffeur, became a father for the first time. (Because I do not drive, and because the distances are so vast in Léopoldville and the public transportation so erratic and overcrowded, the CRS has hired François to drive me where I need to go, in a small car they have put at my disposal.) François has still not decided, he told me, whether his baby daughter will be named Françoise or Renée!

On Tuesday morning, at 6:45 a.m., someone knocked softly on the door of my room. Still in my nightgown, I opened it to find

Adéline Bolamba standing there. She had come at dawn to bring me two coconuts from the palm tree in front of her father's house. It was her way of thanking me for the friendship I had shown to her and her husband, Albert, and for the fact that I went to the airport last Saturday to wish him a *bon voyage* as he flew off to Italy to do postgraduate training there in economics, on a Common Market fellowship.

October 30, 1964

I went out on the balcony of my room to greet the day and my papaya tree. The tree is bigger and more gawky now. Its upper branches and leaves have grown higher than my porch. The fruits on it are still very green, but somehow they look smaller, as if their growth has been arrested. Or is this because the whole rest of the tree has grown so much larger? Its long, slender, ring-marked trunk has begun to lean away from the railing of my balcony, reaching out for the less domestic, more unfamiliar space that lies beyond it.

I was invited by Pascal Bolya, Sabine's fiancé, to attend the opening-day exercises at Lovanium University on Wednesday that marked the beginning of the new academic year. Pascal is a student at this university, built by the Belgians in the 1950s on the immense plateau of Kimwenza, seven miles from Léopoldville. Congolese ironically call this plateau, and the university located on it, the *"colline inspirée"* [inspired hill], referring thereby to the belatedness with which the Belgians founded this institution of higher learning in the Congo; the haughtily remote site that they chose for it—deliberately distancing it from the life of the *Cité* below it; and to the university's Catholic origins. Lovanium, under the aegis of the Catholic University of Louvain, and immediately thereafter the University of Elisabethville under the auspices of the Free University of Brussels and the State University of Liège, were established in the closing years of the colonial era. At the end of the 1959–1960 academic year, when independence came to the Congo, only twenty students had graduated from Lovanium and two from Elisabethville (along with four from universities in Belgium).

In my little Volkswagen, expertly driven by François, I drove to the top of the "inspired hill" to attend the ceremonies. They began with a High Mass, celebrated in the beautiful, modern, fish-shaped church of the university, so full of light and air that it seems to float. The five o'clock afternoon sun came through its ruby red windows as Monseigneur Luc Gillon, the rector and builder of the university, sang the Gregorian refrains of the mass in his small voice and elegantly pronounced Latin. He and the priests assisting him wore vestments that matched the ruby red of the church's windows. The pews of honor were filled with faculty members dressed in the grey academic gowns and berets of the university, and with distinguished political guests invited for the occasion— ministers of the central government, foreign ambassadors, and the like. The mass had hardly begun when there was a great stirring in the congregation, and down the center aisle, no more than a few feet from where I was sitting, strode Moïse Tshombe, prime minister of the Democratic Republic of the Congo, accompanied by an army officer in full dress uniform. This was my first close glimpse of him: a rather short, stubbily-built man, with a round, broad face, dressed in a conservatively cut dark blue suit, who looked intelligent, self-confident, and debonair. An overly ambitious photographer mounted the altar to get a good shot of Tshombe and was chased away by one of the priests assisting Gillon with the celebration of the mass.

At 6 p.m. we all filed out of the church and wended our way to the amphitheater to hear opening-day talks delivered by the rector and vice-rector of Lovanium, and also by the American rector of the new (Protestant) Free University of the Congo located in Stanleyville. The events of the rebellion have made it impossible for the Free University to function in Stanleyville this year, so with ecumenical generosity Lovanium University has invited its adminis- tration, faculty, and students to conduct their classes on this campus.

Tshombe's big, black, shiny automobile was parked in front of the church, flying a miniature Congolese flag. The crowd parted to make room for him as, flanked by Lovanium's rector and vice- rector, he smilingly led the procession to the auditorium. For all its solemnity there was something unreal about this parade of persons dressed in academic and clerical garb, elevated high above the throbbing life of the city of Léopoldville barely visible below us, marching under the sweltering African heat of the setting sun.

Last spring Lovanium University students staged a strike. Their grievances were numerous, extensive, and passionately expressed.

The university had no *"idée-force,"* they protested—no strong, organizing and orienting set of ideas and principles that defined it and gave it a distinctive identity. It was neither truly Catholic nor truly liberal and ecumenical in its religious outlook, they claimed. It was neither African nor Congolese. The university was undemocratically run by a few men of the administration, the striking students contended, who consulted no one, least of all them, and who did not adequately explain or communicate their policy decisions. Faculty relations with them, students complained, were formal, impersonal, cold, or virtually nonexistent. What was more, too many of the faculty were in the Congo for opportunistic reasons, the students alleged: because they could earn higher salaries in Africa than they could in Europe; and in order to build a reputation here that would qualify them for a university position in Belgium or another European country, where they really wanted to work and live. The students also complained bitterly about the unpalatable food served to them in the university cafeteria, and about the lack of an attractive place on campus where they could meet informally.

It is clear that Lovanium University is passing through a crisis of transition, and of failure to make a transition. Perhaps this is inevitable only four years after independence. Ideally it should be an African-Congolese university; but what is a university that is *truly* African and *truly* Congolese? This was the major theme around which the rector of the new Protestant university in Stanleyville structured the talk he delivered in the Lovanium amphitheater on this opening day, in his flat American voice and Midwest-accented French. Frankly, he said, he did not yet know the answer to the question he had posed. It would have to be creatively lived out and gradually crystallized by students, faculty, and administration, searching together. His speech was warmly applauded by the Lovanium students in the audience. They responded to the more conventional remarks of their own rector and vice-rector with tepid applause and with mischievous side comments and laughter. Judging from these reactions, I would predict this will be a turbulent academic year at Lovanium.

It was nine o'clock in the evening by the time we descended from the plateau of Kimwenza to the city below it. François and I ate an improvised supper of sandwiches and orange pop in the car, parked in front of a row of brightly colored houses and small shops lining a dirt street, accompanied by the lively dance music that was playing at the nearby Vis-à-Vis Café, one of the most popular in the *Cité*.

It was good to come down to earth again.

November 8, 1964

This week I received my first letter from Sabine, who reached Lisala safely and is taking up her life again in an area that is only beginning to recover from its invasion and occupation by the rebels. "All is calm and sad," she writes:

> It appears that many people are beginning to return, and many soldiers of the Congolese army have gone to Bumba. At the house I found only Mama and my older brother. Papa had crossed the river to escape the rebels the very day that the army finally succeeded in retaking Lisala. It is because of my photograph that Papa was beaten each day by the rebels; they said my photograph greatly resembled the wife of General Mobutu. The last day the rebels came to take Papa to their camp; they had begun to judge him at the door of our plot [of land]. But happily the gunshots of the approaching army began two kilometers away, and the rebels fled, leaving Papa. Another day Mama went to see my sisters whom she had hidden in another village. The same night thieves came and broke into our house. Yesterday we received a letter from my sisters saying they had arrived safely in the village but that one of them is sick. My older brother will try to cross the river next Monday to see them, and to bring them back here.

LAST NIGHT I invited Adéline Bolamba and Marie-Christine Bangala to go with me to a "*Soirée-Gala*"—a charity affair held at the Zoo restaurant for the benefit of small children. In honor of the occasion Marie-Christine made identical European-style dresses with matching head kerchiefs for herself and me, out of *pagne* material. (It is not uncommon here for close women friends to dress alike for a special outing, as a sign of their intimacy.)

"The Zoo" is a fashionable open-air dining and meeting place, located in a park, that takes its name from the fact that it is adjacent to the city zoo. It looked beautiful last night, with its towering palm trees festooned in colored lights. A sprinkling of Europeans attended the gala, but most of the guests were Congolese men and women in splendid array. The men wore well-cut dark suits, elegant shoes, gleaming white or striped shirts, and modishly narrow ties. The women were dressed in gorgeously colored silk or satin *pagnes*, tall turbans, and long earrings that set off their glistening skin, and their feet were clad in fancy evening slippers. The feature of the *soirée* was the "O.K. Jazz" orchestra, one of the best-known ensembles of Léopoldville. Under the illumined palms, people sat at tables, drinking beer, Coca-Cola, or orange soda, talking, laughing, listening to the orchestra, and rising singly, in couples, or in groups to dance to it. Most of the dancing was the Congolese version of the rumba, or the *cha-cha*. When a waltz, a foxtrot, or a tango was played, only the Europeans got up to dance; when it was a rumba or *cha-cha*, the whole floor was filled with Congolese—dancing couples and small groups of men or women dancing together. It was a beautiful sight—the festively garbed women and men, moving to the beat of the music, with an unbroken, undulating flow of hips, gliding of feet, and artful head gestures.

In the course of the evening three Congolese men whom I knew well came over to the table to greet us. In addition, several strangers approached our table to ask one or another of us to dance. We refused these invitations, as decent, unaccompanied Congolese women are supposed to do. I was struck by the fact that even when the men whom I knew were chatting with us, Adéline and Marie-Christine lowered their heads and their eyes, and their faces assumed identical expressions of inscrutability, as if they had put on stylized masks. When I asked Marie-Christine about this later, she told me this was obligatory, proper behavior. If a woman looks a man straight in the face when they meet and talk in public, she explained, it is assumed they have a clandestine, illicit relationship. If a woman looks too directly at her own fiancé or husband, she is not demonstrating proper respect for him. Eyes and head must be somewhat lowered, too, when you speak to your parents, older siblings, maternal uncle, teacher, priest, pastor, or anyone of greater age or higher status, to whom respect and deference are due.

At midnight I drove Adéline back to her parents-in-law's house in the *Cité*, where she and her two children are temporarily living while they are waiting to join Albert in Italy. Adéline had no sooner passed through the door of her in-laws' house than my Volkswagen was surrounded by five glowering Congolese men: an older man, wrapped in a blanket, and four younger men. The man in the blanket turned out to be Albert's father (Adéline's father-in-law), who was enraged because he thought that Adéline had spent the evening with François, my chauffeur. In the midnight darkness, and somewhat under the influence of the many beers he had consumed with his four companions, Albert's father had seen François in the driver's seat of the Volkswagen but had not noticed that I was seated in the back of the car. By what authority had he spent the evening with Adéline? Albert's father angrily asked François, shaking his fist menacingly in the air and looking into the car. As he did he suddenly noticed me, recognized me as a friend of Adéline and Albert—the American professor who was at the airport to say goodbye to his son when he left for Italy—and realized that Adéline, his daughter-in-law, had spent the evening in my company. Yes, I reassured him, that was so, because I thought it would be a pleasant distraction for her during this difficult time when Albert was so far away. Everything was immediately clarified and set right by that explanation. With many apologies, a great shaking of hands, and a flurry of thank-yous and good-nights, Papa and his four companions went back to their respective houses and beds, and François drove Marie-Christine and me back to our *pension* on Avenue Tombeur de Tabora.

Marie-Christine was as relieved as François by the way I had forestalled a fistfight with Albert's father, who had mistakenly thought he was called upon to defend his son's honor and his daughter-in-law's reputation. What Marie-Christine told me was something I did not know: As an unmarried Congolese girl, going out with a married Congolese woman who was not accompanied by her husband, she was Adéline's principal chaperone. Thus if anything untoward had occurred during our evening together that involved Adéline, Marie-Christine would have been held morally accountable for it.

November 13, 1964

Marie-Christine is trying to teach me some Lingala. So far my vocabulary is extremely limited. I can say, "*Mboti. Okende malamu?*" ["Hello. How are you?"], and also, "*Mama ya yo aboti bana boni?*" ["How many children has your mother given birth to?"], a question commonly asked here, rather than, "How many brothers and sisters do you have?" as it would be phrased in English. After that I run out of conversation.

At least my Lingala lessons are teaching me some things about this culture. For example, the word for friend—*ndeko*—is the same as the word for sister or brother. Apparently family and kinship in Congolese society define, structure, and regulate all other relationships.

At yesterday evening's Lingala lesson, Marie-Christine asked me the following question: "How many people are there in the world?" Not realizing that she had a riddle in mind, I answered pedantically. There are billions of people in the world, I said, but I don't know exactly how many. I'll have to look up the exact world population statistic in the office tomorrow. "*Zéro!*" Marie-Christine replied, laughing, meaning that I had failed the test. "There are only two people in the world—*mobali* and *mwasi*—Man and Woman. That is the correct answer."

November 21, 1964

The rains are heavier and more frequent now. They are strong enough to tear up roads as well as whatever is newly planted, while at the same time they fill the world of Léopoldville with luxuriant foliage and brilliant blossoms.

Yesterday morning my office was the site of an historic scene. François Nkayi, my chauffeur, paid me a visit, accompanied by his young wife and their month-old baby daughter. The purpose of their visit was not only to show me the baby but also to enact a ceremony. François's wife opened the drawstring bag made of antelope skin that she was carrying, and lifted out of it a small, live, clucking hen with a leash around its neck made of cotton *pagne* material. The hen was a gift to me to symbolize the fact that the baby has been given my name!

Back at the *pension* Marie-Christine is the only remaining Congolese boarder in the house. So we are all eating together in one dining room these days, with the result that I am living a culturally schizophrenic life—half-Congolese and half-European/colonialist. At the breakfast, lunch, and supper table, the white schoolteachers, social workers, nurses, and directresses of youth groups staying with us comment on "how slow" the Congolese are. They have no sense of humor, these women say. They do not understand love in general and marriage in particular. They cannot think or work in an organized or orderly fashion. And they season all their food with *pili-pili*—"even pineapple and mangos!"

I flee to my office in the evening to work, as much to escape this chorus as to try to make headway with our research and writing.

November 28, 1964

This has been the week of Opération Dragon Rouge [Red Dragon] in Stanleyville, and we are now living out its tragic aftermath.

During the past two months the rebels in the Eastern Province have been losing terrain and suffering defeat, largely as a consequence of the central government's deployment of mercenaries as ground troops, and the bombings and strafings of rebel areas that have been carried out with the help of planes, bombs, and civilian pilots that United States aid has made possible. In the last weeks of October, as mercenary and Congolese army columns advanced on the city of Stanleyville, rebel leaders, especially Christophe Gbenye (president of the Mouvement National Congolais-Lumumba, the Conseil National de Libération-Gbenye, and of the rebel-proclaimed République Populaire du Congo), declared all Belgians, Americans, and other white foreigners in Stanleyville, and in Paulis (380 kilometers from Stanleyville) to be prisoners of war. Via speeches, political communiqués, letters, telephoned and telegraphed dispatches, and articles in the rebel newspaper *Le Martyr*, Gbenye made increasingly menacing statements to local, national, and international audiences about the fate of the hostages. He adamantly refused all appeals to release them, and threatened to physically punish and kill these prisoners unless the bombing and mercenary actions against the rebel forces ceased.

In this atmosphere the decision was made by Belgium and the United States to launch a rescue operation. At dawn on Tuesday, November 24, Belgian paracommandos, transported by United States air force planes (C-130s), were parachuted into Stanleyville. On November 27 two companies of Belgian paracommandos carried out a similar operation in Paulis. In both places there was bitter ground fighting. Although more than two thousand persons of some eighteen different nationalities were successfully evacuated, in the panic that ensued at least a hundred whites were killed by the rebels, and countless Congolese on both sides fell in battle or were executed.

Marie-Christine is beside herself with worry and grief. She has not had word from her family who live on the left bank of the Congo River in Stanleyville where, it is said, ferocious fighting and horrible massacres took place.

Here in Léopoldville, life has continued almost normally. At dawn on the morning of the parachute drop in Stanleyville, all the residents of our *pension* slept soundly while a torrential rain that had begun the night before fell outside our windows. Not until several hours later did the news of Stanleyville reach us over our transistor radios, and then by word of mouth, chiefly through Protestant and Catholic missionary grapevines. During that day and the next few that followed, we heard many more planes overhead than is usual for Léopoldville, where we are accustomed to the daily roar of a jet passenger plane arriving from Europe in early morning, and the reverberations of another plane leaving for Europe at about eleven every night, with relatively few, largely noiseless local flights in between.

Opération Dragon Rouge turned the N'djili/Léopoldville airport into a combined aircraft deck, frontline battle station, and emergency medicine unit. The giant C-130s that flew paratroopers, evacuated hostages, and transported food, medicines, and relief personnel, are now parked like beached whales all over the field.

December 7, 1964

I am working quietly away in this period of Advent. There is no change of season, no garnishing of stores, no pressure of advertisements, no sound of Christmas music over the radio, no appearance of specially cultivated pine trees to signal the fact that Christmas is approaching. On Christmas Eve, though, and again on Christmas morning, I am told, all the churches of the city are filled to overflowing, with non-Christian as well as Christian worshipers singing gloriously at the top of their lungs. Then, when the church services are over, there is a day of revelry. Cars are decorated with tropical leaves and flowers, and people don fanciful headgear they have fashioned out of metallic paper. These are a blend between the imagined crowns of the Three Magi and the New Year's Eve party hats that Europeans brought to this country.

If all goes well, on Christmas morning at 6 a.m. I will board an Air Congo plane and fly to Lisala to attend the wedding of Sabine and Pascal.

Fighting continues on the Left Bank in Stanleyville and in the interior of the Eastern Province. A process of "cleaning the country of rebels" is taking place that in many ways is more violent and destructive than the rebellion itself.

Yesterday, in peaceful Léopoldville, François's baby daughter was baptized. The baby was named after me in a rather special way. Her full name is Lucy *Voks* Nkayi. "Voks" is a phonetic, Congolese version of "Fox!" François wanted me to be the baby's godmother and was as disappointed and depressed as I have ever seen him when his local parish priest told him that this would not be possible because I am not a Catholic or even a Christian. He still does not understand this. I proposed Marie-Christine as an alternative god-mother for Lucy, and that is what was finally arranged. This new choice of godmother obliged François to purchase another hen—the traditional Congolese gift to the spiritual parent of the child. A hen costs five hundred Congolese francs, which is a lot of money for François. So I suggested that he take the hen that he and his wife gave me and present it to Marie-Christine on this occasion. No, this was not possible, François declared. A gift that has been offered to and accepted by a particular person cannot be transferred to another. And so, at our *pension*, there are now *two* chickens in the family—Marie-Christine's and mine.

BY CHRISTMASTIME Marie-Christine was able to return to Stanley-ville to rejoin her family. To my disappointment, in the end I did not attend Sabine and Pascal's wedding. As so often happens in the Congo, the Lisala-bound flight on which I had a reservation was arbitrarily canceled. Pascal was also detained in Léopoldville. After boarding the plane on which he was originally scheduled to fly to Lisala, he and a number of other passengers were asked to debark by officials who said they did not have the necessary "*laissez-passer*" documents to travel to the interior of the country, where the rebellion was still not totally quelled. As a consequence, Sabine and Pascal's wedding day was changed. Their marriage finally took place at the beginning of January 1965. When Pascal left for Lisala he took the white bridal veil and long, white kid gloves with him that, miraculously, I had been able to purchase for Sabine in a Léopoldville shop.

After the wedding Sabine and Pascal returned to Léopoldville where he resumed his university studies. Sabine was invited to join the staff of the Centre de Recherches Sociologiques. In May 1965 Sabine and I spent a week in Lisala together as part of the center's ongoing study of the rebellion.

A Journey to Lisala
with Sabine

BEFORE OUR departure from Léopoldville to Lisala, Sabine gave me a briefing: her conception of the basic facts I needed to know to prepare me for our visit to her community and region, and for the minisociological research we planned to do while we were there. Here is what she told me.

LISALA WAS part of the province of Moyen-Congo (Middle Congo), formerly the Equator Province, Sabine explained. The major tribe in the area of Lisala, and the one with the greatest political influence throughout the province, was the Ngombe tribe, to which she herself belonged. The Mbuja tribe was the second most important one in the region. After independence, and especially from the end of 1963, the Mbuja people had become resentful of what they called the "Ngombeization" of the local government, and they even said they wanted to see the Mbuja regions of the province (the Bumba territory) separated from the rest of the Moyen-Congo. Ngombe/Mbuja tribal tension had greatly increased.

Lisala was primarily an agricultural region. Its main crops were cassava, peanuts, corn, rice, rubber, cocoa, coffee, and palm nuts and oil. There was a big palm oil refinery in the area, the Société des Cultures Bangala, still owned by the Belgians. Most of the people grew crops for a living. Others worked for the palm oil company, chiefly as *coupeurs de fruit*, cutting the palm nuts off the trees. There were also many schoolteachers in Lisala and employees of the various government offices located there. In addition, numerous people did construction work as carpenters, masons, roadmenders, and the like. A few were local merchants with shops or bars, but the most important merchants in town were Portuguese rather than Congolese.

Economic life in Lisala had been "very hard since independence." Many people had not been paid by the government for months; others had gone for as long as a year without receiving their salaries. The whole situation was due to the fact that "the ministers" and other members of the central and local governments were "corrupt," Sabine said. "They eat everything." Even though the palm oil company did not pay its workers well, many preferred working for this private industry because at least they received their wages regularly. The commodities available for sale in the stores and markets were very expensive, and because of the general economic conditions only a few had the money to buy them.

During 1964, even before the rebels arrived in Lisala on August 30, there was much political disturbance. The troubles were connected with the most important political leader of Lisala and the Moyen-Congo, Jean Bolikango—"*Tata Jean*"—Sabine explained, "who is almost too good." He was a Ngombe, born in Léopoldville of parents who came from Lisala, and was originally a teacher in the Catholic mission school system. As a founder and president of the PUNA party (Parti de l'Unité Nationale), Bolikango had been trying to unite the Ngombe and Mbuja of the Moyen-Congo under the idea of "Bangalahood"—appealing to them to recognize their common membership in the larger Bangala ethnic group. "Independence is not easy," Bolikango insisted, so collaboration with "*good* Europeans" was sensible and advantageous.

Many persons did not agree with his supertribalism or his notions about independence. These differences of opinion, and the rise of RADECO (Rassemblement des Démocrates Congolais), a new political party that tried unsuccessfully to get Bolikango and PUNA to become part of their association, caused serious disorders at the PUNA party congress in Lisala in January 1964. According to Sabine, the central government sent two hundred soldiers to Lisala to put down the disturbance. They behaved "like dogs," she said, going from house to house looking for people who had participated in the congress; arresting many persons, Bolikango among them; "firing their guns everywhere," and killing twelve people, including the burgomaster of Lisala.

There were two primary schools for boys and two for girls run by the Catholic mission in Lisala, Sabine informed me, one Protestant mission primary school, and one public (*officielle*) primary school. The Catholic secondary schools included a *collège* for boys, a teacher training school, and a *collège* that offered technical and agricultural training. There was also a minor seminary in the area. There were no Protestant secondary schools. Those who graduated from the Protestant primary school and went on with their studies usually attended the one public secondary school (*Athénée*) in Lisala.

Young people were eager to have an education, Sabine affirmed. They saw it as a means to achieve a better life than their parents. Neither agriculture nor a trade interested them. They dreamed of living in a city, and when their school days were over becoming "*grandes personnes*" (big men). A large number of young persons had already left Lisala and moved permanently to the city. They returned home only to visit their families or for special occasions like births, weddings, and deaths.

Families in Lisala gave more encouragement and help to boys, than to girls, for going on with their education. "For a girl," said Sabine, "it is hard." Most families felt it was "a waste" to give too much education to a girl when her destiny was to marry and bear children. Parents still directed and controlled the choice of a husband for their daughter. Many women were having painful problems in their marriage—like the wives of the male primary-school teachers in Lisala ("as you will see during our visit," Sabine said). Increasingly, women wanted to speak out about these problems, to stop being forced to remain "behind men," to obtain more education, and to contribute to the building of the country in ways that were not confined to raising a family.

The largest, most important mission in Lisala was the Catholic mission, staffed by Scheutist priests and religious sisters who were Belgian and Flemish. Many people in the area were baptized and practicing Catholics. But there was a lot of negative feeling, Sabine said, about the "colonialist" attitudes and behavior in the communities of fathers and sisters who lived and worked there—especially about how relatively "rich" they were compared with the local population, and how prejudiced some of them were against the Congolese.

There was a major Protestant mission in the area too, in Upoto. "After the Catholics come the Protestants," is the way Sabine put it.

ON SUNDAY, May 9, at dawn, Sabine and I boarded an Air Congo DC-4 for our flight to Lisala. Our fellow passengers included a number of Congolese families; a group of Congolese religious sisters from Buta, accompanied by a Congolese and a European priest on their way to the mission of Umangi; some Portuguese merchants; and the Belgian director of the palm oil company in Binga, 130 kilometers outside Lisala, along with the wives and children of some of the company's executives. This "big boss" of the palm oil company, Sabine told me, had led a cadre of mercenaries into Lisala as part of the operation to retake it from the rebels.

For three hours our plane followed the undulations of the great Congo River while the forests along its edges became thicker and thicker.

Sabine had left Léopoldville with her suitcases so filled with provisions and gifts for the family that we were two thousand Congolese francs overweight! She had packed, among other items, tins of corned beef, packages of margarine, containers of cooking oil, loaves of bread, candies, a *pagne* for her mother, a shirt for her father, and baby clothes for the newborn twins of her older brother. Later I learned that some of the provisions she had brought with her were purchased in order to insure that I would eat well during my stay in Lisala and have certain foods to which I was accustomed. For example, bread was scarce in Lisala, and the loaves that Sabine carried with her were intended primarily for me. She also had a whole pocketbook of letters written by persons from Lisala currently living in Léopoldville, who had asked her to deliver them to their families.

In the airplane Sabine wrote down the names of the members of her family whom I was about to meet. This was how she presented them:

The Koli Family

Papa:	Cyrille K.
Mama:	Elisabeth A.
Older Sister:	Valentine E.
Her Husband:	Raoul M.
Their Children:	1. Jean Pierre M.
	2. Antoine Gérard M.
	3. Etienne M.
	4. Suzanne M.
Older Brother:	Aimé M.
His Wife:	Bernadette M.

Their Children:	1. Joseph Paul
	2. Jacques Charles
	3. Thérèse
	4. Flavien
	5. & 6. The Twins

Sabine M.
Marcelline A.
Elisée B.
Scolastique M.
Evrard B.

Sabine assured me that I would not only be warmly received by her whole family but by "everyone in Lisala"—as her friend and also as an American. The people of Lisala, she explained, felt they had been "saved from the rebels by the Americans," especially by the big planes that they flew into Stanleyville when the rescue operation took place there, and by the white mercenaries (who they mistakenly thought were Americans too) involved in recapturing Lisala.

At the Lisala airport, waiting for us when we arrived, were Sabine's brother-in-law Raoul, her eldest sister Valentine's husband, a primary-school teacher (*moniteur*) who welcomed us on behalf of the family; *Mademoiselle* Isabelle De Backer, a Belgian *assistante sociale* who worked closely with women's groups in the community and who had lived with us for a short time in the *pension* in Léopoldville when she was a refugee from the rebel occupation of Lisala; and the local Catholic bishop, Monsignor Luc Ngandu, who had come to meet us as well as the sisters of Buta.

A great surprise awaited us. Sabine and I would live together in *grand frère* (oldest brother) Aimé's house, Raoul told us. Aimé and his family had been forced to evacuate it during the rebellion and had not yet moved back in. Because of the recent birth of the twins, Aimé, his wife Bernadette, and their children were currently living with Mama and Papa. This enabled Bernadette to have the period of rest to regain her health and strength that was customarily prescribed for a woman who had brought twins into the world. It was also a way of enforcing what I knew was the traditional sexual abstinence between husband and wife that was required after the birth of a child. Sabine later told me that when the time came, Aimé would have to have his mother's permission to live in his own house again with his wife and children.

The whole Koli family had gotten together and prepared Aimé's house for Sabine and me. We would live there alone, guarded by Papa, who would not only act as our watchman but would prepare all our meals for us.

Isabelle De Backer drove us to the house in her little Volkswagen. *Grand frère* Aimé's home was located in the area of Lisala known as the *Nouvelle Cité*, where many primary-school teachers lived. He was a teacher too, and also director of a Catholic primary school for boys. His next-door neighbors were his brother-in-law Raoul, who taught in the school he directed, Raoul's wife, *grande soeur* (oldest sister) Valentine, and their four children. (Sabine's family, I began to realize, was a veritable genealogical tree of teachers. Valentine was also a primary-school teacher before her marriage; and Sabine's younger sisters, Marcelline and Elisée, both taught in a Catholic primary school for girls, as Sabine had previously.)

Aimé and his children (other than the newborn twins), Valentine and her children, and Sabine's three younger sisters, Marcelline, Elisée, and Scolastique, were waiting in front of the house to greet us. The six little boys were dressed up—in shorts, shirts, and caps, and they were all wearing ties from Lourdes that Sabine had bought for them on a pilgrimage to the shrine. Aimé, a tall, handsome, light-skinned man, made me think of a worried-looking Harry Belafonte. Among the girls, the great beauty of the family was definitely Marcelline, with her gorgeous smile and figure, her exquisite taffy-colored complexion, and her bewitching, fun-loving personality.

The door of Aimé's red-brick house was decorated with an archway of palm leaves and bougainvillea blossoms, and a cardboard sign on which the words "*Soyez les bienvenues*" (Welcome to you) had been crayoned inside a hand-drawn banner. The house was lovely. Although much had been stolen from the house by the rebels, who broke many of its windows, removed its screens, and beat on its doors, the family had done an excellent job of repairing the damage. They had also hidden some of their most prized possessions that were now reinstated in the house—notably a big brown radio and a pendulum clock that tolled every quarter-hour, bought by Aimé on a trip he made to Europe. The house consisted of four rooms: a large combined living room and dining room, two bedrooms, and a study/office. A striking African border design was painted at the top of the walls of the living room, on which large, colored pictures of a sunset, of the Atomium in Brussels, and of balloons floating above the Eiffel Tower in Paris also hung. There were many religious objects in the house too: a sentimental picture of Jesus with lambs, a crucifix, a statue of the madonna, wax roses, and a number of religious medals. The house had neither inside plumbing nor electricity. Each morning at sunrise during our stay, *grande soeur* Valentine walked six kilometers back and forth to fetch water for us; and every evening when the sun set, we lit gas lamps. There was an outhouse in the garden made of mud and sticks and palm leaves, and chamber pots under our beds. In an outdoor hut woven of palm fronds, before going to bed each night I bathed under the moon in a tin tub filled with water carried by Bernadette and heated for me by Papa Cyrille.

We were all expected to greet Mama Elisabeth and Papa Cyrille at their house, where other members of the family and friends were in the process of "dancing for the twins." This is a ceremony performed repeatedly for several weeks after the birth of twins, each time visitors come to see them. Twin births, I gathered, were considered to be magically and religiously significant as well as biologically rare—a double blessing that was also fraught with supernatural danger—which was why they called for special rituals. At their brick house—smaller and more modest than Aimé's, and within walking distance of his—Papa and Mama welcomed me. Papa was a dark-skinned man with a leathery, lined face and a strongly muscled body, who on this first meeting, and throughout my stay in Lisala, was always dressed in shorts and an open-necked shirt, with oversized shoes on his sockless feet. He was a forceful and colorful man with a vehement way of speaking and a flair for dramatic gestures. His characteristically ferocious expression (which did not seem to intimidate his wife, children, or grandchildren) was frequently dispelled by huge smiles and hearty bursts of laughter. Like her daughter Sabine, Mama was a small-boned woman of delicate build, with the lean strength of a dancer. But in her ragged *pagne*, with long braids wrapped around her head, a faraway expression on her face, and her arrestingly soft voice, there was something otherworldly about her. We joined the other members of the family in the garden—the twins' mother, Bernadette, and *grande soeur* among them. Arrayed in palm leaves and flower garlands, with white spots painted on their cheeks and their foreheads, they were part of a slow-moving circle of persons, dancing and singing to the beat of tam-tams. Sabine, Isabelle, and I were anointed with white face paint and given places of honor in straw armchairs under the leafy roof of an improvised shelter. For a while we watched the group turn around the garden, clapping our hands in synchrony with the drums. Then Bernadette and Mama brought the twins to Sabine and Isabelle. Each of them took one of the babies in her arms and joined the singing/dancing circle.

At midday Mama, Sabine, her younger sisters, and I returned to Aimé's house where Papa served the dinner he had prepared with the pride of a Congolese *pater familias* who, before his recent retirement, had worked for thirty years as the Scheut mission's cook. The main course was chicken, the traditional Congolese dish for a feast, with a choice of rice or potatoes, accompanied by large glasses of Papa's most choice, homemade, highly fermented palm wine of welcome. The wine was so strong that it felled me. To the great delight and amusement of the family, it forced me to take to my bed in mid-afternoon, where for several hours I fell into the deepest, most stuporous sleep of my life. By the time I awoke the house was filled with a bevy of *monitrices* who had come to visit Sabine.

In the evening, after a light supper, we had what Sabine called a *causerie* with her parents. Mainly it consisted of a conversation with Papa as spokesperson for the family. Sabine acted as interpreter, translating from Lingala to French, as Papa interviewed me about who I was. The questions centered on my family, my nationality, my religion, and my relation to the Congo. Where were you born? Papa asked. Are your parents still alive? What are their names? Do you have any brothers and sisters? When and why did you first come to the Congo? How did you think about the Congo before you came here? Sabine had told Papa I was Jewish—a fact that clearly impressed him because, in his view, that made me a direct descendant of the people of the Old Testament and, as such, someone distantly but authentically related to the holy family. In a more contemporaneous way, being an American enhanced me in Papa's eyes as well, because it was "the Americans," he said, who had "rescued the Congo from the rebels."

Whereas everything American was "good" in his eyes, Papa expressed great wariness about whatever was Flemish—especially what he called "too Flemish." On this first evening in Lisala, and each morning thereafter when I left the house to do my daily stint of participant observation and interviewing, Papa gave me the same warning: "Don't forget they are 'Flamands'!" he cautioned. It was primarily the fathers and sisters of the Catholic mission to whom he attached the label "Flemish." He used it not only to refer to the particular Belgian linguistic group to which they belonged but to some of their attitudes toward Congolese and ways of treating them that he considered colonialist. There was a certain irony in the fact that Papa Cyrille and other Congolese employed the term *Flamands* in the derisive way they had heard many of their French-speaking Belgian colonizers apply it to Flemish compatriots.

But the vigilance that Papa counseled me to maintain when I talked to the priests and the sisters, and to any other Europeans whom I met in Lisala, had another source as well. I was the first white person, he told me, ever to stay with a Congolese family. As a consequence I would not only be scrutinized by the Europeans, but they would be very curious to learn all they could from me about what I was hearing, seeing, and experiencing in a Congolese home. "We are not rich people," said Papa Cyrille, "but we want to give you everything of the best."

It was patently clear, from other things he said, that Papa's reservations about the fathers and sisters did not undermine his fervent Catholicism; the ardor and strictness with which he and Mama Elisabeth had raised their family according to good Christian as well as African/Congolese/Ngombe principles; or the thirty-year-long devotion and pride with which he had served as the Scheut mission's cook.

In the course of this first evening's conversation with Papa, another important focus of his strongly held beliefs emerged: Jean Bolikango, "*Tata Jean*," the PUNA, Lisala, Ngombe, Moyen-Congo leader who, Papa declared, was the one politician who could save the Congo. Mama Elisabeth, Aimé, and Sabine listened to Papa's passionate statements about Bolikango with a mixture of respect and familial amusement.

This *causerie* in the living room, under the glow of the Coleman lamps we had lit when the sun went down, was as enjoyable as it was serious and interesting. It was filled with reminiscences and laughter, including spirited observations on how I had reacted to Papa's palm wine, that were already becoming a family legend. Each time Aimé's cherished European clock chimed the hour, the whole family burst into song along with it, while penetrating the liquid heat and the brick walls and glass windows of the house we could hear the steady beat of *cha-cha* music coming from Lisala's two nearby bars.

The master bedroom of the house had been allocated exclusively to me. That first night, inside the mosquito netting the family had hung around my bed, fortified by the bottle of water, the thermos of coffee, and the plate of cookies that Sabine had placed on the cloth-covered night table beside me, I drifted into deep, heart-of-Africa slumber. Sabine and Papa told me the next day that during the night they heard me singing in my sleep. That meant, Papa told me, that in my dreams I had had a very happy meeting with my ancestors.

I awoke with the first rays of morning light and the crowing of the cocks. *Grande soeur* had already stopped at the house with the supply of water for the day. Sabine and I breakfasted on some of the tinned meat and bread she had brought with her from Léopoldville and stored in the big brown cupboard in the dining area. At 8 a.m. *petite soeur* returned from the market where she had done early-morning shopping for food. Since Lisala houses do not have refrigerators, and most food spoils quickly in the tropical heat, going to the market is a daily affair.

At 8:30, by prearrangement, Isabelle De Backer arrived at the house to drive me to the Catholic mission for my appointment to interview Father Edouard Boutsen, the vice-provincial of the Scheut fathers in this region, where he had lived and worked since 1953. As Isabelle and I drove over the dirt avenues and roads of Lisala, I had my first panoramic view of the town—a small administrative center located on the banks of the Congo River, deep in the rural interior of the country, where most of the people still lived off subsistence agriculture. Huge palms and masses of brilliantly colored flowers grew everywhere, interspersed with unkempt tall grass. Although the roads were not well kept, in both the old and the new *cités* of the town there were an impressive number of solidly built houses in good condition. Along the dusty, red clay paths and roads of Lisala, masses of people moved on foot, in steady procession. Not only had all but a few cars, jeeps, and trucks in the community been stolen, rendered inoperative, or destroyed by the rebels, but most of the bicycles as well. Even this early in the morning the heat was already intense, and particularly along the river's edge there were swarms of mosquitoes in the air.

Perched over the town, like a misplaced medieval castle, was the red-brick Scheut mission with its towering cathedral.

I SPENT the entire morning with Father Boutsen, a tall, slender, bespectacled, middle-aged man who was dressed in a white cassock, under which he wore khaki cotton trousers and an open-necked sports shirt. Father Edouard (as he was known to everyone) was both well informed and perceptive about the social, economic, and political situation. He was also insightfully candid about the activities of the Catholic mission in the area and their impact on the population.

The first missionaries in the region, Father Edouard told me, were Protestant rather than Catholic. The British Baptist Missionary Society arrived there as early as 1890 and created the mission in Upoto that existed to that day. It was one of a string of missions stretching along the Congo River from Matadi to Stanleyville that had been founded by George Grenfell, the renowned English Baptist missionary and Congo explorer. The Belgian Scheut fathers arrived in Lisala almost twenty years later and established their mission there in 1910. They began their work using the classic Catholic missionary approach of baptizing as many people as possible. So energetically and persistently did they pursue this policy that by 1963, according to Father Edouard's estimate, as many as 19,000 persons living in Lisala were baptized Catholics, of a total population of about 25,000.

Although the Catholics of Lisala and environs were inclined to be *pratiquants*—relatively faithful about attending mass and participating in the Church's sacraments—he said, they tended to be more "passive" than Protestants in expressing their Christianity in their daily lives. The fact that the very large Catholic mission was such an "overwhelming block," he felt, contributed to this passivity. It gave the population the sense that all sorts of resources, material and nonmaterial, were already available at the mission, and that "the Good Lord would take care of the rest." There was still another unfortunate side effect of this "big mission" style in Father Edouard's view: it made the mission appear to be a locus of concentrated wealth. For example, having all the mission's vehicles (cars, jeeps, trucks, and so forth) garaged in one place and well maintained by the fathers and religious brothers created the impression that the facilities and monies of the Catholic missionaries not only greatly surpassed those of the average Lisala family but also what members of the local government, profiting from their offices, possessed. This conviction had been a dominating theme in the way the rebels had dealt with the fathers and sisters during their occupation of Lisala, Father Edouard added. If they had had to start over, and it were up to him, he stated vehemently, he would never build a mission like this one again.

In recent years, since the 1950s, he continued, the Scheut mission had been making an effort to work more in depth, particularly in matters concerning marriage, the family, and the education of children in the home as well as at school. Whatever progress may have occurred, Father Edouard admitted, very little advance had been made in increasing the respect, fidelity, or solicitude with which Congolese men treated women, either inside or outside marriage. Furthermore, as some of the practices of the rebels and the reactions of the Lisala population had made plainer than ever, even very devout Catholics, whose relationship to Christianity seemed to pervade their lives, still relied on traditional African magic to ensure good fortune in their daily round—especially in their most important undertakings—and to ward off misfortune.

But Father Edouard's greatest concern, and his own missionary activities, centered on the many young men, sixteen to twenty-five years of age, in Lisala and the surrounding villages, who had completed their primary-school education and were now unemployed. To him they were a disillusioned group, in conflict with the older generation and for the most part strongly disinclined to undertake the agricultural pursuits open to them. Yet they were vital to the area's and the nation's economy. Father Edouard showed me some of the results of the interviews he had conducted with three hundred young men in three different rural centers. Sixty-five percent of the respondents ranked agricultural work lower than any other, contending that persons who tilled the soil had very little self-esteem, that they were viewed by others as "the last" (*basenzi*), "at the bottom" of the society. Responses to questions about relations with village elders and family members were overwhelmingly negative. The young men looked down on the members of the older generation who could not read or write as "backward." "They do not want to listen to us," the youths complained and, what was more, they declared, "we will not obey them." The tensions that existed in their own families, they said, were also due to the fact that their parents and members of their clan were "disappointed and angry with us, because we have wasted their money." Their families had invested money in their studies, the young men explained. They had paid fees for tuition, room and board, the price of a good suit, a bicycle, and so forth, and expected that this money, "increased a hundredfold," would be returned to them when "their children" would have "fine positions" and belong to "the class of the privileged."

In response to these problems, Father Edouard, in collaboration with some of his colleagues, was trying to organize a center that they hoped would "raise the value" of manual work in general and of agricultural work in particular, and in the long run "recreate" and elevate village life. This was to be accomplished by training young Congolese men who already had at least a primary-school education to raise crops and livestock and construct houses and other needed buildings using new, more efficient methods of work. What Father Edouard had in mind was not strictly occupational and technical training but an educational and socialization process that would touch the young men's lives more broadly and deeply, so that they would become the vanguard of a "rural elite" who could serve as role models for others of their age group and background.

In the future, Father Edouard said, a great deal would depend on the qualities of the Congolese director chosen to head the center. In addition to his abilities as an educator, he would have to be a mature and versatile man, tenacious yet flexible, with a "solid dose" of social and civic devotion, a talent for organization, and a great deal of common sense. The prime candidate whom he was recommending, I learned, was none other than Aimé Mosabu, the "director of an important primary school," and Sabine's eldest brother.

BEFORE I returned home for my noontime meal, I interviewed Father Edouard about his experiences during the rebels' invasion and occupation of Lisala.

The rebellion in Lisala, according to Father Edouard, was an "imported" happening. It involved the invasion of the town by young men who were mainly what he called "Swahili peoples" from Stanleyville and other communities in the Eastern Province. They arrived in Lisala via Bumba, where they had been able to count on a certain amount of local sympathy; but they knew in advance that Lisala was a "fief of Bolikango" and, as such, uniformly hostile to them. The rebels entered Lisala emitting loud cries of "*Mai Mulele!*" ("Water of Mulele")—calling upon water purified by sorcerers and the name of Pierre Mulele, the leader of the initial rebellion in the Kwilu province, to empower and protect them. The town reverberated with the sounds of the guns they shot in the air. Most of Lisala's inhabitants had already disappeared into the surrounding forest and villages; the members of the government had fled; and the soldiers of the National Congolese Army had run away too, shedding their uniforms, helmets, and guns as they departed. The rebels were barechested and swathed in leaves, wore hats on their heads fashioned of wildcat skins and festooned with other charms, and had incisions in their foreheads. They were accompanied by a sorcerer, a "delegate" of the most powerful, supersorcerer in the Eastern Province, Mama Onema. The rituals she performed, along with the rebels' "water cry" of "Mai Mulele," their mode of dress, and the various taboos to which they were obliged to adhere, were all part of the traditional war magic that was supposed to confer invulnerability on them as well as guarantee their ultimate victory.

Upon their arrival at the mission the rebels shot at the doors, menacingly commanded everyone to come out, and promptly took every vehicle the fathers had not hidden. The priests were escorted to the rebels' camp by a twenty-year old partisan leader flourishing a gun. At the camp they were forced to sit on the ground and were verbally assailed by a group of frenzied rebels, dangerously high on the hemp they had been smoking, who hurled a series of angry insults against them and furiously denounced Bolikango and Mobutu.

Throughout their stay in Lisala the rebels made many visits each day to the mission: to question the fathers, to requisition and take things, to get their cars, jeeps, and trucks repaired, to look for shortwave radios ("*phonies*") that they feared could be used to contact the enemy, and occasionally to make accusations and threats. By and large, Father Edouard said, at least in their relation to the mission, they lived up to their war magic–prescribed norms and taboos relatively well. "We are not thieves," they repeated again and again. In many cases they even gave the missionaries receipts for the gas and vehicles they took, on which it was stated that the articles in question had been offered to them willingly and that the rebels would eventually return them.

It was Father Edouard's estimate that about half the rebels were more or less indifferent to the Catholic missionaries, and among the other half there was a small group in favor of the mission and a still smaller group against. Only occasionally did they encounter a "fanatic"—like the rebel who told them he had participated in the massacre of the fathers at Kongolo, and was anticipating doing the same in Lisala.

Toward the end of their occupation of Lisala, just before they were attacked by mercenaries, the rebels attempted to normalize things by appointing a local citizen president of Lisala. He was a decent and honest man, said Father Edouard, a member of the Lokele tribe (the Congo River trading people who had become ethnically and politically dominant in Stanleyville), and affiliated with the Mouvement National Congolais (MNC) party. The new president and the major dispatched rebels throughout Lisala and to surrounding villages to call the people together for a mass meeting. Father Edouard was obliged to set up the loudspeaker for the gathering and was installed in what amounted to an armchair of honor in front of the audience, from which he was expected to monitor the sound equipment. The speech that President Kasongo delivered to the assemblage went something like this:

> The rebels did not come to molest you but rather to save you. They are not against you, and they are not thieves. Why are so many people remaining in the forest? Tell them to come back and that all will go well for them. We are only against the military, the police, the politicians, and the radicals of PUNA. We are not against the fathers either. . . . Nor are we against foreigners or merchants. But we *are* against unemployed persons. Everyone here must find work to do or else go back to the village. . . . I have never seen such bad roads as those in Lisala. But now that will come to an end. Everyone will be responsible for putting a certain stretch of road around their house in order. Three months from now, too, each person will have a big field, planted with rice and other crops. If not they will be punished. Prices here are also too high. That is another thing we shall remedy. From now on the cost of things will become more normal. . . .

The mission continued to be guarded by rebel sentinels. Then, on the night of September 11, the guards on duty suddenly began to shout, "*Sangu, Sangu*, the Americans are here!" A small contingent

of mercenaries, no more than fourteen in number—Southern Rho-
desians, rather than Americans—had arrived in Lisala. The rebels,
who had been living in a comfortable, rather "bourgeois" fashion
during their several weeks in Lisala, stripped off their shirts, draped
themselves in leaves, took up their guns and machetes, and crying
"Mai Mulele!" went into battle. By morning the mercenaries had
killed about a hundred of them.

Panic ensued. The mercenaries had used up most of their
ammunition in battle and temporarily left Lisala to get new supplies. The rebels rounded up the fathers and marched them to the
count of "one, two, one, two," pronounced in Flemish as well as in
French by rebels who had been members of the Force Publique
under the Belgian colonial regime. The rebels were both terrified
and furious. Their powers of invulnerability were no longer working
with the whites, they said.

"We are finished with you," they told the fathers menacingly.
"We are going to kill you now." But they pulled the religious
brother/mechanic out of the group of missionaries they had condemned because they needed him to repair their vehicles. They
continued to behave toward the fathers in dangerously contradictory and unpredictable ways. They forbade the priests to pray
"because you are praying against us"; and they took the fathers'
religious medals and rosaries away from them. At times they would
exclaim, "You others, you whites, you priests—you have special
powers sent to you by God that are stronger than ours." At other
times the rebels bragged about the superior strength of their own
special powers.

By this time Lisala was virtually deserted. Even most of the
rebels had left. They were going to Bumba, they had said, to see
their "Mama" and have their powers of invulnerability restored,
after which they would return. The tension of waiting became too
great for the sisters and fathers, who decided to take their chances
on trying to reach the relatively nearby community of Benge. They
set out on foot, and en route met a group of mercenaries who were
heading toward Lisala. Upon reaching Lisala the mercenaries occupied the empty Catholic mission. The rebels did not realize this,
and when they began returning from Bumba early the next morning
and approached the mission, many of them were shot and killed by
the mercenaries who were bivouacked there.

By this time contingents of the National Congolese Army and

of Katangese gendarmes had appeared on the scene. In effect the Lisala phase of the Congo Rebellion had come to an end.

ON THE same day I had this interview with Father Edouard, Sabine and I spent most of the afternoon at home receiving a stream of visitors. The most poignant of them was Laurent A., a neighbor who was a policeman. After living and working for many years in Léopoldville he had been assigned to Lisala in 1963 as part of the current provincial government's policy of calling members of the Bangala tribes back to their home region. Laurent A. was feeling nostalgic about the life he had been forced to leave behind in Léopoldville. In a melancholy frame of mind, he was waiting it out in Lisala, hoping the next local government would change the policy and he would be reassigned to the capital city. If not, he told us, and if things in Lisala did not get better soon, he would leave the police and return to Léopoldville on his own, where he had built a house on a small plot of land in the *Cité*. Meanwhile, Sabine confided in me after he left us, "he drinks too much."

Between visitors Sabine told me about the conversations she had had with the group of *monitrices* who had come by yesterday— young women like herself who were primary-school teachers. They were experiencing many problems, she said. To begin with, all schoolteachers, male as as well as female, were very irregularly paid by the central government. They went for months without receiving any salary at all. There were very few other ways in which women could honorably earn money to tide them over these long periods without pay, Sabine explained, unless they were willing to work in the fields or set up a small market stand. These were alternatives the teachers considered below their intelligence and status. Still, they were used to dressing well and accustomed to other amenities they could no longer afford. They were also bored by the lack of any entertainment in Lisala other than the drinking and dancing in the town's two bars, which proper women were not supposed to frequent on their own. As a consequence, a number of the unmarried *monitrices* had gotten involved with men. In Sabine's words, "they gave themselves to men" in exchange for the money these men lent or paid them. Several of the *monitrices* had become pregnant.

In the evening, after supper, we had another intensive family discussion that covered a range of topics. Papa Cyrille grumbled

about the never-ending kinship obligations to the hordes of relatives constantly arriving in the area, who expected extensive
hospitality (food, lodging, gifts, money, and so forth), and who
continually interfered in intimate family matters—passing judgment, for example, on the sorts of young men who were interested
in Marcelline, Sabine's quite beautiful, still unmarried, *monitrice*
younger sister.

This in turn led Papa to complain to Sabine and Aimé that
Marcelline was not as generous and considerate as she ought to be.
She certainly was not following Sabine's good example, he said.
Instead she was trying to live at home in Lisala the way she had in
Léopoldville during her two years there. She did not help with the
housework, he lamented. She had only gone to fetch water twice
since returning from Léopoldville. She was overly preoccupied with
her clothes, her hair, and her appearance. Nor did Papa approve of
the young man who had announced to the family that he would
like to marry Marcelline. Although her suitor was a *moniteur* (a
primary-school teacher) who knew Flemish and English as well as
French, and who would be going to the University of Elisabethville
the next year to study for a degree in education, Papa found him
insufficiently respectful of his elders, too immodest, and too inclined to try to impress others by throwing his money around.

Talk then turned to the way that many of the *moniteurs* of
Lisala were treating their wives. They had banded together, it
would seem, and mutually agreed severely to restrict the amount of
money they gave to their wives—in some cases limiting the funds
to such small amounts that the women had scarcely enough to
purchase basic food and clothing for the children and themselves.
More than questions of economy were involved in this concerted
action of the *moniteurs*, who continued to spend plenty of money
on their own amusement and on drinking with friends. This was
clearly visible in their stylish dress and their lavish group drinking
at Lisala's two bars. Sabine and Aimé agreed that these teachers
were collectively trying to assert their male dominance and control
over their own wives and, beyond that, over whatever new "eman-
cipated" ideas women more generally were beginning to express in
this postindependence period.

THE NEXT morning when I awoke at 6 a.m., a mirror, writing paper,
and envelopes had been added to the bottle of water, the thermos

of coffee, and the cookies that already stood on the table next to
my bed. (Sabine's work!) It was another hot, sunny, dry, and
mosquito-filled day. After a bath in the garden house, and breakfast, various members of the family came by to greet us as they did
each day before Sabine and I began our round of sociological
interviews. On this particular morning, while Sabine made a visit
to Father Edouard, I called on Monsignor Luc Ngandu, the Congolese bishop of the diocese, who had been at the airport on the day
of our arrival in Lisala.

By and large, the bishop's overview of Lisala's history and its
current state of affairs coincided with Sabine's and Father Edouard's
accounts. He was distressed by all the pillaging that had taken place
at the mission in Umangi. Stealing and destruction at that mission
had been so great, the monsignor said, that it still was not possible
to reopen the secondary school attached to it. At least four other
Catholic missions had also been plundered by villagers. The people
had even stolen some of the missions' religious objects, such as the
chalices used for Communion at mass. Monsignor Ngandu was
struggling to comprehend why this had happened. As he understood it, the ransacking of the missions by inhabitants of nearby
communities had a great deal to do with the economic miseries,
political conflicts, and social difficulties suffered by the rural population since the "first independence." In the midst of all this suffering
and confusion, he said, the mission seemed to them to be a place
of enormous wealth and power. He found it striking, though unsur-
prising, that not a single incident of this sort had occurred in Lisala.

IN THE afternoon, following our lunch of sausage, grilled canned
meat, potatoes, pudding, and mangoes prepared by Papa Cyrille as
usual, and a short siesta, Sabine and I went together to make a
courtesy call on the mother superior of the convent of Scheutist
sisters. It was a visit Sabine had not been looking forward to. "Ma
Mère," as Sabine addressed her, was an elderly, full-waisted woman
garbed in the three-quarter-length, simple white cotton dress and
plain white headpiece of her congregation. She wore black stock-
ings, rather than the more usual white ones, on her stocky legs.
Her manner was at once imperious and ingratiating. She welcomed
me with effusive cordiality and then, after expressing great pleasure
at seeing Sabine again, in rapid succession she addressed the
following remarks to her:

Your sister Elisée [a new *monitrice*] is really too young to teach. She needs an assistant to help her.

I have always thought that Marcelline was a good girl, but now I am not so sure. She does not want to enter the convent as I had hoped she would. What is she doing now? Is she working with young people [*la jeunesse*] in any way?

And you? Now that you are married and living in Léopoldville, what are *you* doing for *la jeunesse*? And how is your household going?

All the mother superior's judgmental comments were delivered in honeyed tones. Sabine listened with what appeared to be polite docility. Only at one point did she speak, when *Ma Mère* suggested that Marcelline's decision to remain a lay person rather than become a nun indicated that she was not a "good girl." "Does that mean I am not a good girl either, because I married and did not enter the convent?" Sabine asked. "I don't understand you, *Ma Mère*," she stated quietly, and then lapsed back into attentive silence. The mother superior continued her moralistic monologuing as if oblivious to Sabine's intervention.

In the note that Sabine later recorded about this meeting in the journal she was keeping, she wrote in Lingala, "Nothing special." For, as she commented to me that evening, she was "used to the way the sisters and the fathers think and act." Nevertheless, Sabine had already decided not to attend the festivities that were scheduled to be held at the mission the next day in honor of the mother superior's twenty-fifth year in religious life.

SABINE AND I made one other visit that afternoon, to the home of Pierre Cherubala, director of the Ministry of the Interior in the provincial government of the Moyen-Congo. Both Sabine and Monsignor Ngandu were eager to have me meet Mr. Cherubala because, in Sabine's words, he was a "good and just man"; a highly intelligent and reflective person who was also deeply religious; a civil servant/administrator of exceptional ability and integrity; and someone who had sharp and true insights into the relationship between the rebellion and the grave economic, political, and social problems facing the entire rural inland of the Congo since independence.

Speaking beautiful French, Pierre Cherubala welcomed us to his home. A slender, fine-boned man with relatively light skin and a mustache, he was wearing immaculately pressed trousers, a white shirt, and a broad silk tie, and he exuded the pleasant fragrance of a good *eau de cologne*. His spacious, well-kept house, located on a large plot of land, still showed many signs of the damage the rebels had done to it. Cherubala's name had been on the "enemy list" of the rebels who came from Stanleyville, he told us, and as soon as they arrived in Lisala they had asked villagers to point the way to his house. He and his family managed to flee into the forest before the rebels reached their door and proceeded to strip the house of as much as they could carry away: a sewing machine, a typewriter, a bicycle, trunks, sofas, armchairs, cushions, bed linens, all his family's clothes and every pair of his children's shoes. He had been able to replace some of what the rebels had stolen, it would seem, because the living room in which our conversation took place was furnished with armchairs, a couch, and a coffee table. Cherubala turned on two electric fans so that we would be as cool as possible, and glasses of beer were served to us by a Congolese man who appeared to be a servant.

Cherubala pointed with pride to the enormous photograph of his wife and children that hung on a wall of the room next to an equally large picture of Jesus of the Sacred Heart. Madame Cherubala, Sabine had told me, was a woman with virtually no formal education who, like her husband, was "a good person." They had eight children—five boys and three girls.

After several days of hiding from the rebels in the forest, Cherubala said, he had surreptitiously brought all the children back to Lisala, where they lived with one of his cousins until the rebellion ended. He knew that as an agent of the administration he was a rebel target, and that the villagers would be reluctant to hide or protect him and his family, partly because they were afraid to do so under the circumstances, and partly because many of them believed that "intellectuals," "politicians," and "authorities" had benefited from independence at their expense. He had also heard that the rebels did not harm children (which turned out to be true), and so he felt that his sons and daughters would be safer in Lisala than in flight with him and his wife. After entrusting the children to the cousin, Mr. and Mrs. Cherubala moved swiftly on foot from one hostile village to another. Eventually they found a canoe and paddled for days on the Congo River until they reached a boat bound for Léopoldville, on which they became passengers. The entire Cherubala family emerged from the rebellion unscathed and were reunited in Lisala. But at present only Cherubala and his eldest son, a student at the local Catholic *collège*, were living in this big house. He had sent his wife and seven other children back to Léopoldville to stay with relatives, he said, because he felt that for the time being, conditions there were better for them and more secure.

Sabine asked Cherubala to provide me with some basic facts about his educational and professional background. He had attended primary and secondary schools run by the Christian Brothers in Bumba, he informed me, and then, in 1959, underwent special training to become a territorial agent. In 1960, a few months after independence, he became a district commissioner in the Lisala area and served in this capacity until the beginning of 1963, when districts were eliminated in the Congo and provinces were formed in their stead. At this point he was named director of internal affairs of the province of the Moyen-Congo.

Encouraged by Sabine, Cherubala proceeded to describe and analyze "the conditions" in the postindependence Congo that, in his opinion, had brought about the rebellion. For all of its disadvantages and abuses, Cherubala stated, the Belgian colonial administration had been highly organized and efficient. It had not merely managed things from afar—from the distant capital cities of Brussels and Léopoldville—but also directly and locally, through an ingeniously designed rational network of structures and offices that extended into the most remote rural areas of the country. Salaries were paid regularly to all categories of workers in every region. Villagers received cash for the abundant crops they raised, including the sizable share of their produce that was transported to larger centers and cities over what, in colonial times, were traversable roads and waterways. Under these conditions, Cherubala said, both urban and rural workers had performed well.

But since independence this was no longer the case, he contended. The quality and output of work had deteriorated everywhere, and in the interior of the country the villages had reverted to subsistence agriculture.

Many factors had contributed to what Cherubala considered this deplorable situation. To begin with, he said, there was the lingering influence of "the dreams of independence": the population's utopian expectations about the wealth and the freedom from commonplace work they would enjoy once they were delivered from colonialism. Such expectations were particularly marked among Congolese youth, Cherubala said, especially those who were receiving a secondary education or more. So great was their disdain for working the land and for manual labor, and so strong their aspirations for positions of prestige, power, and wealth, that many young men now preferred to be unemployed rather than engage in "ordinary" work. These attitudes were reinforced, Cherubala felt, by the increasing failure of parents to take charge of their children's "moral formation" and supervise their behavior. "It is certainly no longer as it was in the time of our ancestors!" he exclaimed.

The fact of the matter was, Cherubala continued, since independence there was such disorganization, corruption, and anarchy in the country that salaries were no longer being paid regularly to the vast numbers of persons whose incomes came from government sources. The roads in the interior had become impassable; trucks and other means of transport were poorly maintained; and it was no longer possible to move a steady flow of produce and needed commodities between the villages and the cities. To a considerable degree, Cherubala suggested, the lack of a "vigorous working spirit" in the Congo, and the unwillingness of the inhabitants of the rural inland to raise large crops, were practical and reasonable responses to these conditions. But in his view they were also self-defeating. All this was worsened, too, by the attitudes of many local and national politicians. "I will protect you if you protect me," was the way they operated, Cherubala said, with the result that "Wrongdoers are not punished. Nothing is done to make people work. And the population has become so used to this kind of anarchy that if someone wants to follow the law, or enforce it, it is *he* whom they consider to be 'bad.'"

In addition, Cherubala went on to say, individuals who were incompetent were placed in high positions largely because they belonged to a particular tribe. This kind of "tribal and racist spirit," he claimed, had dominated the provincial government of the Moyen-Congo since the violent confrontation in January 1964 between members of the PUNA and RADECO parties, with its Mbuja-versus-Ngombe tribal implications, which had influenced the formation of the present provincial government.

Cherubala had a set of recommendations to remedy the postindependence situation, which he shared with us at the end of our
visit. Sabine recorded them in her notebook in this way:

—Pay the workers.
—Make them work.
—Work also.
—Respect the administration.
—Evacuate the produce of the villagers [from the interior of the
   country].
—Create associations to educate young persons for their future.

The list of what needed to be done sounded simple, Cherubala
commented, but it would be very difficult to implement. Still, he
was waiting patiently to see how the next provincial government
would be constituted, hoping there would be signs of change for the
better. If there were not, he warned, the next time rebels came to
Lisala the people would join them.

WE SPENT the evening at home once more with the family. This
time, as Sabine put it, most of our conversation concerned "our
fathers and sisters and their ideas." This was largely evoked by my
description of the visits I had made in the course of the day to
Father Edouard Boutsen, Monsignor Luc Ngandu, and the mother
superior. Some of the things I described seemed to open wounds
inside of *grand frère* Aimé that he attributed to encounters with the
Belgian ("Flemish") priests and religious sisters of the Scheut mission over the years. In a voice filled with emotion, he told me
about these experiences.

To begin with, he said, the fathers had tried to discourage him
from marrying his wife Bernadette because he was a *moniteur* and
she had not had much formal education. When Aimé and his wife
were building their house, he continued, certain of the fathers not
only reprimanded him about his presumptuousness in constructing a
fancy brick house, they also made disapproving comments to many
other persons in the region about the self-importance of this act.
And last year, when the *moniteurs* of Lisala who had not been paid
for six months decided to wage a protest strike against the government, the fathers did nothing to support them and everything to
dissuade them. These were only a few examples, Aimé said, of the
ways in which the missionaries treated Congolese like himself—the

teachers in their schools—as if they were arrogant, irresponsible children.

But the most acute source of Aimé's chagrin stemmed from his conviction that some of the Scheutist fathers had prevented him from becoming director of a center to train young Congolese men to assume leadership in the agricultural development of the area. Although Aimé had been actively involved in the planning of the center and had been recommended by Father Edouard to head it, Aimé was convinced that the project had been stalemated by Belgian priests who did not want a Congolese person to assume that position.

I AWOKE the next morning in a pool of perspiration and a cloud of mosquitoes. This was a double feast day. It marked the twenty-fifth year of the mother superior's life as a religious sister. What Sabine's family referred to as a "Flemish Fête" had been arranged in her honor, including a special mass and tributes by the students enrolled in the Catholic primary school for girls. It was also Aimé's saint's day, which we were planning to celebrate that evening with a family outing at one of Lisala's two local bars.

Sabine and I had agreed that she and I would go shopping to purchase some gifts for Aimé; but before we did we made a visit to Mr. Daniel Mbobozo, the minister of social affairs, planning, and community development in the provincial government. This 9 a.m. appointment was my first opportunity to speak with rather than about a local politician.

Mbobozo, a tall, handsome, young-looking man with light skin, was fashionably dressed in pale blue trousers, a white shirt with gold cuff links and a silk tie, and suede shoes. He wore a large, expensive-looking gold wristwatch. The French he spoke was as elegant as his attire. The state of the house in which he received us, however—his own home—contrasted dramatically to his fastidious grooming: it had been battered by the rebels to the point of dilapidation. Every painted surface was scarred. All the windows were broken or boarded up. Grass grew wildly around the house. Most of its furnishings had been removed or destroyed by the rebels, and little had been done to replace them. The room in which we talked contained only a few chairs, a table covered with a dirty embroidered cloth, and a sideboard on which a broken transistor radio stood. Unframed, poster-sized pictures of Moïse

Tshombe and Jean Bolikango were pasted on the mutilated walls.

Over the glasses of cold beer he served us at this early hour of an already scorching day, Minister Mbobozo (whom Sabine consistently called *Excellence*), began by telling me something of his professional and political career. He was born in the Kungu Territory of the Equator Province, he said, and was trained to be a nurse in a school in Coquilhatville, where he specialized in clinical laboratory work. His practice of nursing was short-lived because from the outset he was "always too interested in too many social issues" that extended beyond matters of health and medicine. In Coquilhatville he became involved not only in a campaign to raise the social status and pay scale of nurses under the Belgian colonial system, but also in the social problems of Congolese youth; and he joined a Bangala association called the Federation of Peoples of the North Equator.

In early 1960, under a pseudonym, he began to write for a newspaper founded by a group of young men from the Equator Province, of which he became the editor. His most noteworthy writings were a series of articles on the policies of Cyrille Adoula who by then (1961) had become prime minister of the now independent Congo. Even though Adoula was a member of the Mbuja tribe like himself, Mbobozo wrote harshly about what he believed was Adoula's excessively close identification with the United States and the United Nations, and the distance he kept from the Soviet Union. Although Mbobozo had written these articles under his nom de plume, Adoula knew he was their author. He made a special trip to Coquilhatville to reprimand Mbobozo and threatened to have him arrested if he did not stop writing such things. After this encounter with Adoula, Mbobozo decided to go on with his studies in Belgium, at a school to train social workers.

Toward the end of 1962 Mbobozo returned to Coquilhatville in the Congo, where he reimmersed himself in local politics. He became active in the PUNA party and was appointed assistant secretary general of the assembly in Coquilhatville. When a new provincial government took office, he was named its minister of social affairs, planning, and community development.

Like everyone else in Lisala, Daniel Mbobozo had many anecdotes to tell about his experiences with the rebel invasion. What distinguished his relationship to these events was that he was acting as interim governor of the province and minister of the interior when the rebels entered Lisala. He had been temporarily appointed to these two key posts by the elected governor, who had gone to Léopoldville in search of the wages the central government had failed to pay the work force in his province for more than ten months.

But it was not Mbobozo's account of the rebellion—of the responsibilities he carried during that period and the dangers he incurred—that I found so telling. Rather it was the comments he made toward the end of our visit about the current social situation in Lisala, and how he dealt with the response his remarks elicited from Sabine. "The people of Lisala do not like to work," he declared, in a speechmaking tone of voice. "They do not cultivate rice and bananas as they could and should. They still raise cassava, but much less than they used to. Many people have left the villages and come to live here. They need work, and when they don't find it they expect the provincial government and PUNA to come to their assistance by giving them money. But we do not have the funds to do this. What we must do is get the people to work the fields and provide them with the tools they need to do this. It is from Lisala, the center of the provincial government and of PUNA, that these efforts should be organized and directed."

At this point, with great politeness and seeming innocence, Sabine asked Mbobozo a piercing double question. *"Excellence,"* she inquired, "what do you think the people expect from the men in political office? And what do these men in office believe their responsibilities are to the people?"

Mbobozo paused momentarily, then resumed his oration. "The people want social well-being. To achieve that, the authorities must demand a certain amount of sacrifice from the population— inviting, exhorting, requiring people to *want* to work, to *like* working, and to work hard and well." Pointing to the untended foliage that enveloped his house, Mbobozo referred to the unwill-ingness of the inhabitants of Lisala to work at cutting down the tall grass that was growing up everywhere and was a breeding ground for the great infestation of mosquitoes from which the town was suffering. "The people here say they are not paid. But if they worked and produced, a certain percentage of what they produced could be taxed by the central government, and some of that money could go to the provincial government to build houses, schools, and medical facilities which in turn would attract more qualified teachers and physicians to an inland area like this one."

Sabine intervened once again. "But *Excellence*," she asked, "do you think that if the people who are located as many as four hundred or five hundred kilometers from any center begin to produce large crops as you recommend, they will have a way of shipping them out?" Mbobozo was clearly thrown off balance. He had to concede this was a real problem. The provincial government needed money from the central government to repair roads, bridges, and ferries, and to purchase trucks and the like, to make this possible. But since independence the provinces had been "disinherited" by these national authorities.

Just as our meeting with Mbobozo was drawing to a close, a telegram was delivered to him from Léopoldville. "Good news!" he exclaimed, smiling broadly. It was a communiqué from the Ministry of Work of the central government, he triumphantly announced, informing him that a representative from Léopoldville was en route to Lisala with money to pay the policemen and the *chefs coutumiers* (traditional chiefs) of the area.

SABINE HAD borrowed Isabelle De Backer's car for the morning. As we drove away from Daniel Mbobozo's house to the store in town where we intended to buy our gifts for Aimé, Sabine gave me her opinion about Minister Mbobozo's "thoughts vis-à-vis the nation." The people of Lisala, and regions like it, were not lazy, as *"les Messieurs,"* the politicians, implied, she stated firmly. Rather they were discouraged and demoralized. They knew that if they worked they would not be paid, and that if they raised crops, what they grew would not be sold and transported. So a vicious circle was created and continued.

On our way to the store we passed the large pink villa that the first Congolese governor of the province had built for himself, and adjacent to it the home he had constructed for his father; the abandoned former hospital for Europeans, a deserted sanitorium, and a number of empty houses formerly occupied by Belgian administrators; the shabby, physicianless Congolese hospital, where nurses were delivering all the medical care; the military police camp and barracks, now occupied by a contingent of paracommandos; and the clusters of brick houses with straw roofs and of mud huts located in the old *Cité*. At the store Sabine had chosen (whose Portuguese proprietor was married to a Congolese woman), I took

Sabine's advice and brought a long-sleeved white shirt and a folding penknife for Aimé. Merchandise in the store was sparse, at prices that exceeded what most people could afford to pay.

After lunch, in the early afternoon, the whole town was thrown into a state of alert. A dark blue plane with two bombs hanging from its underbelly had been sighted overhead. It circled Lisala a number of times and did not respond to the airport's radioed challenges to its identity and mission. Many hours after it flew off, without depositing its cargo of bombs on Lisala, a telegram finally arrived from Léopoldville, cautioning local authorities that a bomber en route to Aketi, which was still occupied by the rebels, would be passing over this territory.

THE EVENING celebration for Aimé was organized by his younger sisters, Sabine, Marcelline, Elisée, and Scolastique. The four of them and I, along with Christine, another *monitrice* and Marcelline's closest friend, and Louis, a cousin of Sabine's husband, accompanied Aimé to a local bar in the *Nouvelle Cité*. It was a shabby, dusty, open-air establishment that consisted of a big wooden dance floor, surrounded by wooden tables and chairs, and a counter on which rows of nonrefrigerated bottles of beer and soda pop were available for sale. There were neither bartenders nor waiters. Customers carried the bottles back to their tables. We had brought our own drinking glasses from home because the family did not consider those provided by the bar sufficiently clean. Lively recorded dance music played nonstop and at full volume over loudspeakers: African jazz, *cha-cha*, and the newest vogue, modern renditions of traditional BaLuba songs. The floor was filled with superb dancers: persons dancing solo and in all-male or all-female groups, as well as male/female couples.

Although Aimé was our guest of honor, as *grand frère* of the family he was also obliged to chaperone us. Whether the women in our party danced, and if so when and with whom, was under his jurisdiction. He was responsible too for protecting us against rude advances or aggressive behavior by men at the bar. Aimé allowed Marcelline and Christine to dance together, but his two younger sisters Elisée and Scolastique were not permitted to dance at all, not even with each other. Each time that a man approached the table to invite one of the girls to dance, Aimé refused on her behalf.

All the people spending this evening at the bar knew or were known to one another, with the exception of the tableful of Katangese gendarmes seated near us. Dressed in camouflage suits and drinking large quantities of beer, they exuberantly toasted the fact that the bomber which had been sighted over Lisala earlier in the day had not had this town as its target.

Many people stopped by our table to greet us, especially the numerous *moniteurs* who were present. At one point four very well-dressed young men, who were teachers in the primary school that Aimé directed, danced joyously past our table in single file, and we all applauded them. The best dancer in the group, Sabine told me, was the son of a Ngombe sorcerer.

Laurent A., the next-door-neighbor policeman, who was already quite drunk, and a mulatto gentleman, who was associated with the provincial government's Department of Education, both came to the table to ask me to dance. In each case Aimé acted as my spokesperson, in exactly the way he had for his sisters, and politely declined the invitation for me.

It was Aimé who decided when it was time for us to leave the bar. As we rose to depart, Laurent A., the policeman/neighbor, joined our group and trudged out of the bar with us. In a loud, drunken voice he congratulated Sabine on the presence of a white person (me!) in her family's midst. Sabine responded with a rebuke. Up to then, she said to Laurent, nothing "messy" had happened during her friend's visit, and she didn't want it to. So, she said, please don't start anything by making remarks like that; and "stop following us around like a chicken!" Sabine's reprimand was frank but not unkind. It was evident that she felt a maternal kind of sympathy for this poor, broken-down policeman; and he in turn took his scolding well.

THE NEXT day we made an early morning stop at Sabine's parents' house to pay a call on Mama Elisabeth and to participate in the continuing ceremony for the twins. From there we proceeded to Isabelle De Backer's house, where she was holding a meeting of a dozen Congolese women whom I had promised to address. They were all leaders of a network of women's social circles (*foyers sociaux*) that Isabelle helped to direct. In close collaboration with Sabine, I prepared a fifteen-minute talk for this occasion in French, which she translated into Lingala as I spoke. Following Sabine's advice and using her vocabulary rather than mine, I briefly described the sociological research in which our center was engaged, emphasizing the fact that "the way we do our work is the way you see us here. We travel directly to the people, to talk to them and to observe. We use our eyes, and we listen well." One of our main studies at this time, I told the women, was our attempt to understand the Congo Rebellion of 1964–1965, which they had directly experienced. We were especially struck, I said, by how closely connected it was with what the people had hoped and expected independence would bring to the Congo, and with their disappointment and anger over what these first postindependence years had actually been like.

But what Sabine was most intent on having me convey to the women was how crucial their role was in the development of the country. The present and future of the Congo were in the hands of its people, I told them—not just in the hands of the men but also in their hands, because it was they "who gave birth and life." Wherever we traveled in the Congo, I continued, we had learned much about the great problems these women faced in their daily lives: in their marriages, with money, with the education of their children, with what relatives on both sides of their families asked of them. We knew, too, that they often felt the work they did as wives and mothers had little to do with the big economic and political happenings in the Congo. But Mama Sabine and I were convinced, I said, that what the women thought and did was as important to the country as what the politicians thought and did. They might not hold political office or fly everywhere in jet planes like the politicians, but they had the right to vote now, and to choose good leaders. And what they did in their families every day was a powerful force, too. They were forming the next generation of this country's citizens and leaders—teachers, doctors, agronomists, politicians—through their care, advice, and example.

These comments triggered an animated discussion. The women expressed pride in the fact that they and the population of Lisala more generally had not succumbed to the rebels. Several of the women declared that if it had been possible, they would have traveled to Léopoldville in March to join in the demonstration for peace by hundreds of women from all over the Congo. There were two aspects of life in America about which they asked me many questions: Were the politicians in America as corrupt as they were in the Congo? And what were American marriages like—above all, how did American husbands treat their wives? Although they did not say so directly, it was clear from the way they phrased their questions and the tone of their voices that they believed America to be a land where there were many "good leaders," where men treated women with greater respect and kindness than in the Congo, and where marriages were less fraught with problems and pain than their own.

At the end of the morning together, the women thanked me for coming to talk with them by singing a traditional song, accompanied by Sabine, who beat out the rhythm on an African drum.

BY 8:30 A.M. the next morning Sabine and I were already engrossed in an interview with Mr. Patrice Engulu, technical adviser to the vice-governor of the Moyen-Congo and a candidate for the governorship of the province. Engulu—a smiling, bespectacled man in his late thirties who was simply dressed in neatly pressed trousers and a tieless white shirt—was well known to Sabine and her family. Before Sabine had met her husband Pascal, Patrice Engulu had asked her parents' permission to marry her. Mama Elisabeth and Papa Cyrille were in favor of such a marriage, but Sabine did not consent. She liked and admired Engulu, but he was almost fifteen years older than she, and he had spent a number of years in the seminary preparing himself for the (Scheut) priesthood before deciding to live his life as a layman. Sabine was convinced that a woman his own age who had seriously considered becoming a religious sister and had been in a convent for a while would be a better partner for him. Engulu did marry such a woman, and it was a good marriage, Sabine told me.

It was apparent that Sabine considered Engulu's perspective on what he referred to as "all the big problems of the province," "the impasse to which their nonsolution has led," and their causal relation to the Congo Rebellion to be the most thoughtful and accurate we had heard. She did not challenge his discussion of these matters by asking him the highly penetrating, unmasking kinds of questions she had addressed to our other informants.

Along with his personal attributes, Engulu's educational background and experience as a civil servant qualified him to speak with insight about the time of troubles through which not only the Moyen-Congo but the entire country was passing. He was one of the first Congolese to graduate from the Institut Social (founded by the Belgian Christian Workers' Movement) in Léopoldville with the degree of *assistant social*. His studies were interrupted several times by the political and administrative responsibilities he was asked to assume during the first years of the Congo's independence. The most important of these was presidency of the Commission for the Reform of Social Legislation in the Congo, whose major task was to create an integrated and equitable social security system for the new nation.

Since 1962 Engulu's chief function had been that of technical adviser, assigned by the central government to work in this capacity for the presidency of his home province. He used his professional training to conduct studies of the major social problems the province faced, and to present his findings on the problems, their causes, and possible solutions to the members of the provincial government. But Engulu did not have permission to work with the population or influential persons within it on any of the problems he had identified and studied. His role as technical adviser had been rendered ineffective by the "inertia of the governmental machine," he said.

In Engulu's opinion, the failure of the provincial and central governments of the Congo to respond dynamically and effectively to the serious problems of independence had caused the rebellion. At the root of the distressing and continually deteriorating conditions in the Congo, he believed, was "the flight of capital" from the country since independence. Many Belgian and other foreign investors had transferred large amounts of capital to other countries, he said. Thus certain firms were closed, companies were cut back, unemployment increased, public services were reduced due to lack of funds, and, as a consequence of all this, mounting "waves of discontent" ran through the population. What Engulu characterized as the disorganized, stalemated, and morally compromised government had been unable to take the situation in hand. There was, he claimed, "a quasi-total breakdown of the public sector," caused mostly by particularism, self-interest, and profiteering. In provincial governments all over the country, politicians had increased the number of ministers, ministerial cabinets, and local bureaus of various kinds without regard for the national budget. "Many of these so-called public services had become family enterprises with positions available only to relatives or intimate friends." What was more, Engulu declared, these "privileged of the regime" had turned state funds into private accounts from which, on all levels of the national as well as the provincial government, they were constantly diverting monies for their own use and enrichment, and to benefit their kin. "Is it any wonder," Engulu exclaimed, "that there are not sufficient funds to foster the recovery of the country? Millions are going into private pockets or are being spent on futile things without any profit for tomorrow." With quiet passion he spoke of the consequences for the youth of the country. When it came to education, he said, "there is no money for the regular payment of teachers, from which continual strikes have resulted, with the disastrous result of truncated instruction for the youth of the Congo. There are no funds to create new schools, no funds to build institutions to protect unemployed youth, or to reeducate delinquent youth, and no funds to set up special schools to retrieve less gifted students." These things were "at the heart of the rebellion," he declared: "a growing number of unemployed, on the one hand, and on the other, of idle young people. Under these conditions, it took no more than a match to set the country afire."

Although Engulu was both indignant and disheartened about the state of the country and of his province, he was not without hope. That was why, he told us, he had decided to become a candidate for governor of the Moyen-Congo. If elected, he said, he intended to tackle the problems with the assistance of a small, competent, and efficient cabinet who would work closely together in conceptualizing and developing programs. They would then turn the work of implementing these programs over to qualified administrators rather than to politicians. This was the way it should be done, he said with unpretentious assurance and just a touch of didacticism: "Administration and politics are not the same thing."

Before we left, Engulu told us what had happened to him during the rebels' occupation of Lisala. Given the current situation of the government, he found it distressing, but not strange, that his life had been endangered by soldiers of the National Congolese Army rather than by the rebels. He was arrested by a group of soldiers who insisted he was a rebel and who decided he must be a rebel leader when they found some foreign coins in his trouser pockets left over from trips he had made abroad. He was imprisoned with six other Congolese men who were also mistakenly identified as rebels. They were stripped of all their clothes as well as their possessions, and continually harassed by soldiers who stood guard outside the windows of their prison, threatening to kill them with the knives they brandished. Only with the help of a soldier who recognized him and gave him advice about how to flee did Engulu manage to escape. With the aid of villagers and a canoe they gave him, he found his way back to Lisala and his family. There the rebels had taken or destroyed everything he owned. He had no home, no clothing, no food, no money, no books; so he and his family had to begin life all over again.

Even if the central government succeeded in putting down the current rebellion in all regions of the country, Patrice Engulu predicted, it would not be finished. As long as the big social problems of the Congo were not solved, he concluded, and there were *messieurs* who benefited from these problems at the expense of the population, there would be other rebellions.

IN THE late afternoon of the same day of our long conversation with Patrice Engulu, Sabine and I made a visit to the Protestant (Baptist) mission in Upoto. As he had promised, Pastor Samuel Kyobe came in a "vehicle" to "collect" us—a big Land Rover truck that he drove himself. He was accompanied by a young British missionary who had been evacuated from Stanleyville in time to escape the rebel massacre there. En route to the house to pick us up, the two men stopped at the Scheut mission to consult the religious brother-mechanic about whether the several other vehicles at the Upoto mission, which had been damaged by the rebels, could be repaired, and if so, at what cost.

Before I wrote the letter to Pastor Kyobe that led him to invite us to Upoto, I had conferred with Sabine and Aimé about it. Both of them had encouraged me to make this contact. Aimé and Sabine explained to me that before independence the relations between young Catholics and Protestants in the region were marked by distrust and enmity that sometimes erupted into open conflict. Since independence, they both felt, things had improved, though contact between persons from the two groups were infrequent. Sabine expressed her willingness to accompany me to the Protestant mission, and Aimé told her he thought it especially important for her to do so in order to help me communicate with the pastor's wife, who spoke very little French or English. Drawing on their mutual observations and experiences at the Protestant mission,

Sabine and Aimé predicted we would be served tea—"but no alcoholic drink!"—and many small cakes during my visit there. "Their way—tea and too many cakes—is European and very Protestant," said Sabine. Her vivid and mischievous description proved to be so accurate that when we arrived at the mission and were served tea and cakes on the verandah, I had to make an effort to keep a straight face.

My first view of the Upoto mission was romantically stirring. Its long, low buildings of weathered brick, worn by time, the seasons, and the inroads of the rebels, overlooked the majestic Congo River and its many palm-fringed islands. It embodied the image of a nineteenth-century mission that I had carried to Africa with me. Later in the evening, under the full moon that had risen above them, the mission and the river became shimmering incarnations of a dream.

In his appearance and manner, Samuel Kyobe, an open and warm man in his late forties, could easily have blended into a meeting of African-American Baptist ministers. He was a graduate of the teacher training school and Protestant seminary in Kimpese, in the Lower Congo; he had made several prolonged visits to England to study and preach; and he had also traveled in South America, particularly to Brazil, where he had spent more than a month. He spoke excellent English and French as well as Ngombe, Lingala, and KiKongo. Pastor Kyobe showed great respect and affection for his wife, a large, stockily built woman of his own age, with a broad, kindly face and straightened, nonbraided hair, who wore a voluminous, flowered house dress. The Kyobes' eldest son, a senior at Wayne State University in Detroit, would soon be returning to the Congo to teach; a daughter was studying in Belgium; and a younger son, who still lived with his parents in Upoto, attended school in Lisala.

The pastor and his wife had a parental relationship with the small British Baptist community they headed, which was comprised of three English missionary couples and one unmarried English woman. The living conditions at the mission were austere to the point of shabbiness, but it was apparent that whatever domestic amenities the missionaries possessed had been brought out to welcome and make us comfortable. After signing a guest book dating from 1890, we were served tea on the verandah, off a table covered with a white linen cloth and set with china and silver

flatware. Later Pastor and Mrs. Kyobe and Sabine and I had dinner
at the home of the woman missionary, where we were joined at
coffeetime by the three couples. Once again, in the bare room
where we dined, the table was elegantly set. The pastor said grace
in Lingala, thanking God for our visit, before we ate a meal of
soup, chicken with tomatoes, cooked bananas, and corn, with both
fruit salad and homemade ice cream for dessert.

One of the missionary wives was a painfully awkward and shy
woman who seemed to be overcome by our visit; but the other
members of the community were lively, intelligent, articulate
people who enjoyed a good conversation. One of the male missionaries (astutely described to me later by Sabine as someone who
looked rather like the European executives of the local palm oil
company) seemed to be an intellectual, with more education than
his colleagues and more upper-class British diction.

Through our discussions with our hosts, during tea, dinner, and
the interludes between them, we learned something of the history
of this venerable British Baptist mission and about its teaching,
social service projects, and health and medical care activities.
There were about four thousand Protestants who "belonged" to the
mission, Pastor Kyobe informed us. The majority were villagers, but
there were also merchants, shopkeepers, and employees in administrative offices in Lisala who were members of the Protestant fold.
Why, I asked him, were there so many more Catholics than
Protestants in this region of the Congo? Three historic facts
accounted for the discrepancy, he replied: the Catholic church
made it relatively easy to become a member; it baptized infants;
and, as important as these religious factors, the Catholic missions
ran an array of primary and secondary schools that surpassed what
the Protestant missions provided.

In the early evening, over after-dinner coffee, stories about
what had taken place at the Upoto mission during the rebellion
began to emerge. Pastor Kyobe was preaching a sermon in the
mission church on the Sunday when the first band of rebels invaded
Lisala. Upon their arrival the rebels had fired their guns so wildly
and continually that the sound traveled all the way to Upoto. This
gave the pastor and his parishioners time to flee before the rebels
reached their community. Pastor Kyobe joined his wife, who had
left the mission a few days earlier to take refuge on one of the small
islands in the Congo River. Two days later, however, with his

younger son and four other people who insisted on accompanying him, he returned to the mission to see what was happening there. While he and his son were inspecting the rooms of their family house, two rebels in a jeep drove into the mission. They fired on the four persons who had come with the pastor, killing one of them, a young male nurse, on the spot. The pastor would have liked to walk out of the house and speak directly to the rebels with the hope of calming them down and reasoning with them, but they were in such a state of agitation, he said, that he realized this was impossible. The rebels entered the house, shouting in Lingala to him and his son to come out. One of the rebels found the two of them in the big wardrobe where they had hidden. In the end the pastor and his son engaged in a protracted fistfight with two rebels outside the house. They managed to fell the rebels and then fled back to the island in the river where they had taken refuge. His narrow escape did not deter Pastor Kyobe from returning periodically to check on the state of the mission. Over time, he and his colleagues told us, the mission was successively pillaged by the rebels, the soldiers of the National Congolese Army, the mercenaries, the Katangese gendarmes, and local villagers. But the church was left untouched, and nothing in it was stolen or desecrated.

At about 9 p.m. we all joined hands as Pastor Kyobe said a prayer of thanks for our visit and expressed the hope we would soon meet again. Then, through the moon-drenched tropical night, he drove Sabine and me home to Lisala, over the bumpy road by which we had come, in the one vehicle at the Upoto Baptist mission that was still functioning.

SATURDAY, MAY 15, was an exceptionally busy day. It began even earlier than usual when a child appeared at the front door of our house. She had been sent by Papa Cyrille to ask me if I ate pork; he had heard that Jewish people were forbidden to do so. The reason for the query was that the next day, in honor of our last full day in Lisala, Papa was planning to kill the big male pig who was enclosed in a sty behind Aimé's house, and to make a roast pork dinner for us.

I was deeply moved by this gesture, not only because of Papa's respect for my religious background but also because I knew how much this pig meant to him. He identified with it in an almost human way, because he and the pig had survived the rebellion together. When the rebels first arrived at Aimé's house, Papa Cyrille was in the backyard feeding the pig. The rebels brandished their weapons and threatened Papa, and then they ordered him to go into the house and bring them water to drink. One of the members of the rebel band, who had gone to school with Aimé and knew Papa, managed to signal to him that he should not turn around or try to enter the house, because if he did so the rebels might shoot him in the back. This same rebel told his companions that he would stay behind and "take care of this case." When they had gone, the rebel scolded Papa: "Are you crazy [*toke*]," he exclaimed, "risking your life to take care of a pig? Even if you are an old man, they will kill you!" He persuaded Papa to leave the house and the pig and Lisala. Several weeks later, after the rebels had been defeated and it was safe to return home, Papa was reunited with his pig, who was unscathed.

I quickly sent word back to Papa Cyrille via the little messenger that he should not sacrifice the pig on my behalf, adding that I would talk to him about it when I saw him. Later, when I told him that it was not religious scruples that had prompted my response but rather my appreciation of his sentiments about the pig, he gruffly thanked me.

SABINE AND I spent the afternoon at home where we were caught up in events. Sabine, Marcelline, and one of Marcelline's *monitrice* friends sat on the living room floor braiding each other's hair, engaged in talking and laughing. Another *monitrice* dropped by to see Sabine, bringing her month-old baby son with her. Mama Elisabeth's sister was the next visitor to arrive. Meanwhile, next door at the home of Sabine's *grande soeur*, Valentine, and her husband Raoul, a group of *moniteurs* had gathered to celebrate Raoul's and also Aimé's tenth anniversary as teachers.

But the high point of the afternoon was certainly what Sabine recorded in her field diary as: "Talk with Papa and his friend Pierre about the problems of the Congo." Pierre M., one of Papa Cyrille's oldest friends, came to the house to see him and to bring me, as an honored guest of the Koli family, the gift of a pineapple and several avocados. This elderly, dignified gentleman, dressed in a worn but immaculate white shirt, khaki trousers, and white sneakers, had been unemployed since independence. In the colonial era he had worked as a domestic servant (a "*boy*") and also as a house painter.

He was not only a frequent and welcome visitor in the Koli family households but was also Papa Cyrille's favorite political interlocutor. Both these elderly men shared the premise that only if Jean Bolikango became "chief" of the Congo could the country be "saved."

On this Saturday afternoon, with Sabine, Marcelline, the two *monitrices*, Mama Elisabeth's sister, and myself as their audience, Papa Cyrille and Pierre M. carried on one of their typical political conversations. It went like this, in alternating monologues:

> The misfortunes of this country began when all the whites left the Congo. They left the country because they were chased by cheaters and communists like Patrice Lumumba. Jean Bolikango always said that we should encourage the whites who were well-disposed to help the country and work with Congolese to stay; and he was right. We were promised that Bolikango would be the leader of the country when independence came. And what happened? Instead we got leaders like Lumumba; like KasaVubu, who is "too soft" and too exclusively interested in the welfare of his fellow BaKongo; and Tshombe, who is a Katanga man.

> Why have we suffered so much here in the Equator region of the country since independence? We have had bad provincial leaders. Our first governor, for example, received money from Bolikango to provide work for the ordinary people of Lisala. The people were put to work doing necessary things like repairing the roads, but they were not paid. In the meantime, the governor and other politicians in his entourage played hide-and-seek with the money. They spent it on themselves and on contributions to political parties like the MNC and the RADECO. We also lost the good physician whom we had working here for a while, because the heads of the provincial government did not do anything to provide a decent house for him or to make sure that he had the medical supplies he needed to do his work.

> What the rebels say is bad in Congolese society is right. If their goal had been to make things better by getting most of the present political leaders out of office, we would be completely in agreement with them. But the way the rebels have gone about achieving their goals, through killing, injuring, destroying, and stealing, is evil.

The first wave of missionaries who came to the Congo were good and pure, but the second wave entered more into politics. At the big missions they employed many Congolese and made them work very hard for insufficient wages. In this regard the missionaries are partly responsible for the fact that certain groups in the Congolese population have developed the mentality and habits of thieves. Their wages were not sufficient for their survival.

God made things not so that people should be rich but so they should receive and have enough to live decently. Why, then, should some people be so rich and others so poor? And yet this is no reason to steal. I have been unemployed since independence, but rather than steal I did all sorts of small work, like cutting and selling wood, so that I could earn a little here and a little there. That way I not only earned my keep, but bit by bit I have been able to put a few francs aside to buy a *pagne* or kerchief for my wife, or a shirt for myself.

At the end of Papa Cyrille and Pierre M.'s political "debate," they asked me to undertake the mission, upon my return home to the United States, of persuading "the Americans" to send agencies, experts, and physicians to help the Congo with their problems. They both vehemently affirmed once again that they looked forward to the day when finally Bolikango would become chief of the whole country.

ON SUNDAY, May 16, our last day in Lisala, Isabelle De Backer and I attended the 7:45 a.m. High Mass, celebrated by Monsignor Ngandu in the mission cathedral. When I returned home I did not dare tell Sabine that after the mass, while I was waiting for Isabelle to fetch her car, the several Belgian sisters who greeted me and engaged me in conversation expressed great curiosity about what it was like to be living with a Congolese family, and real concern about whether I was getting enough to eat.

Most of the day was taken up by a stream of visitors who came to say goodbye to Sabine and her American guest, and to bring letters and packages that they asked Sabine to hand-deliver to members of their family living in Léopoldville.

At the end of the afternoon, close to sunset time, we received a final visitor. It was Paul Mombilo, a renowned magico-religious specialist. He had been encouraged by Aimé to come to see me and tell me about his very special experiences during the rebellion.

He was a very old Ngombe man, toothless, with piercing eyes, who was clad in dirty khaki trousers, a dirty denim shirt, a dusty brown skull cap, and blackened sneakers. In the waning light of the afternoon he told me this story:

One night, at midnight, three rebels arrived in his village to see him. They were young men from the vicinity of Stanleyville. The whole village was asleep. At first the rebels asked him for some hemp to smoke. Then they started to talk about the rebellion. They were very tired of this warfare, they said. Too many of them were being wounded and dying in battle, and many more would be wounded and die. Why was this happening in Lisala? they asked. Why was the population there so hostile to them? The rebels also said they were tired of all the taboos they had to observe— the taboos against washing, against touching, against being with women.

The rebels told Mombilo they intended to kill the sorcerer who had come to Lisala with them, in order to bring the war to an end. They gave Mombilo their sorcerer's mask and her cane, instructing him to keep them safe and to walk everywhere with the cane. This would also help to bring the war to an end, they said. After they had killed their sorcerer, they continued, they wanted Mombilo to cut off her ears and affix these ears to his own chest. Finally they gave him a bullet and asked him to bury it alongside the military camp.

The three rebels then disappeared into the night, and Mombilo never saw them again. But he did carry out all their instructions, he said.

Mombilo had brought the objects entrusted to him by the rebels to show us. From a big piece of wrapping paper he removed the sorcerer's mask and her cane. The raffia mask, elaborately decorated with blue, orange, and white beads, was fashioned with slits for eyes and a nose-shaped protuberance. The cane was a long, brown wooden stick on whose surface many small incisions had been made, in which white powders ("medicines") with magical powers had been inserted.

Quietly, while Mombilo was telling his tale, various members of the family had been arriving at the house, including some of Valentine and Raoul's and Aimé and Bernadette's children. They had formed a transfixed circle around the old sorcerer. Then, just as the sun was plunging from the sky, as it does at sunset time in equatorial Africa, Mombilo put the mask on his face. Rotating his head slowly, the dark pupils of his eyes glimmering through the slits in the mask, he turned his gaze upon each of us. As he did so, a strange, terrifying aura spread through that shadowed and silent room.

"MOTS DES PARENTS" (parents' words) is the final entry that appeared in Sabine's account of our visit to Lisala. On Monday morning, May 17, 1965, after Sabine and I had finished packing our suitcases, just before we left for the airport to return to Léopoldville, Papa Cyrille and Mama Elisabeth gave us their parting words of advice and their farewell benediction.

AT THE time I began to relive my days inside the *pension* on Avenue Tombeur de Tabora in Léopoldville, and my trip to Lisala, through writing about them for this book, I had had no word from Sabine for almost five years. The last letter I had received from her was postmarked "Kansas City, Missouri," mailed from there by a young Zaïrean traveler to whom she had entrusted it. Sabine's letter contained a short Christmas and New Year's message and ended with her hope that God would continue to protect me "so that we can see each other again someday." It was signed, "Your sister Sabine."

Sabine had suffered greatly in her marriage to Pascal. He had left her to live with other women. She had made a life for herself and her daughter Gabrielle, "independently of any man," working as a resident counselor for women students at the University of Kinshasa (formerly Lovanium), where Pascal had been a member of the law faculty.

The more I wrote about Sabine and what we had shared, the more I was saddened by the fact that all my attempts to reach her since that last communication had failed. I did not know where she was or how she was, or whether she was even still alive.

Then, in January 1990, I received an unexpected visit in Philadelphia from Father B., a demographer in Zaïre, whom I knew from my Congo days. He told me that he would do his best to find Sabine for me when he returned to Zaïre, and to deliver a letter to her. He was true to his word. Four months later I received a four-page letter from Sabine, written in Kinshasa. "*Oh! ma soeur Renée*" ("Oh! my sister Renée"), it began:

I just received this very evening your letter of January 14 of this year. I don't know how to explain to you my joy in reading your writing.

My sister, I have never forgotten you in spite of the many trials I have gone through in my life. I wrote a letter to you last year, and the same letter was returned to me two or three months later. I sent it to the address that you had left with me. That caused me a great shock and gave me many sad ideas. . . . I tried again to obtain news about you from many Jesuit fathers, but no one knew anything. And so I waited before trying a second time [to write to you]. . . .

My sister, Renée, today I am going to begin by answering some of your questions, and each time I will speak to you a little bit more about my life.

I am still working at the university. . . . It is not the university that we knew. Everything has broken down. Nowadays young people obstruct a lot, especially the young people at our university. I am responsible for running a residence for girls, in a position with the rank of *chef de bureau* [office head].

As for my health, when I am at ease in my mind, I am well. From time to time gastritis and amoebas attack me. At the moment I feel fairly well. My eyes are getting weaker, and I must change my glasses again. But in general, *ça va.*

At the university I earn 40,000 zaïres a year [about 1,000 American dollars] and live with nine children of my two sisters who are dead—the sisters who came after Marcelline, Elisée, and Scolastique. They died suddenly, one after another, in the same year. The children's fathers abandoned them after the death of their mothers. With my salary, in the face of this family composition, it is not easy. From time to time I give courses in the Lingala language to missionaries, and the little that I earn that way helps me to settle the debts for the children's school fees. I am living in a house on the campus for professors here, that was assigned to Pascal. It was Gabrielle who did much to arrange it. It is a big house which uses up a large part of my salary to maintain.

I have to try hard to live and be happy, because life is a battle, particularly with respect to all those things I counted on doing. My stars were turned upside down and caused the opposite of what I was expecting to happen. Renée, life is a curtain in front of a picture.

Gabrielle has gone through a situation more difficult than mine. She was torn away from me [by Pascal] in 1982 and sent to Belgium to undergo treatment for her skin trouble. She suffered greatly from eczema. Afterward her father neglected her. Nobody took charge of her education as should have been done. She often was left all alone in the hospitals of Europe. She had a baby and was in a more sorry state than before. I had no means with which to help her recover or bring her back. People still see her in Brussels, but she doesn't write to me any more. I don't know why. Her child lives with a family in Belgium. At the end of last year this family was brought before a Brussels court by Pascal, but he lost the case because Gabrielle has given guardian rights to this family until she is in a position to take care of the child herself.

This situation cost me a great deal. My weight dropped to 35 kilograms [77 pounds], as compared with the 54 kilograms [118 pounds] that I weigh at this time. Now the Lord has done much in my heart. I entrusted everything to Him, and I have peace. I know that God will do for Gabrielle what I have not been able to do.

I am here in Kinshasa with Marcelline, but she lives in another district (Masina) that is near the airport. She has a little house and lives there with one of the children of our deceased sisters. She is still a teacher.

Aimé is the director of a school 500 kilometers from Lisala. He continues to take good care of his house and to be resourceful. But although he has the same rank as I do—*chef de bureau*—he earns only 35,000 zaïres a year, compared with my 40,000 zaïres. Life in the interior of the country is a little less expensive, of course, and they can grow things to eat. But what beats everything is the deplorable state of the social life—medical care, etc.

Voilà, Renée, some of the news of my life and of the family. Little by little I will give you more details.

Here, as in the whole world, the international crisis and AIDS rage. Our country has undergone a change into the Third Republic since the 24th of last month, and we are counting practically on that change.

The memory of our stay together remains unforgettable. Every month I go by the house where we met for the first time when I was fleeing the rebellion.

Voilà, my sister, it is two o'clock in the morning. I will stop for today and I will try to write often.

Je t'embrasse tres fort.

Your sister,
SABINE

TWO MONTHS after receiving this letter from Sabine, in July 1990, I spent several weeks in Belgium again, mainly in Brussels. The capital city was full of Zaïreans on summer visits, strolling in the streets and shopping in the stores. I scanned the face of each young Zaïrean woman whom I passed. Two of the chambermaids working on the floor of the hotel where I stayed were from Zaïre—one from the BaKongo, the other from the Kivu region. It was only after I had talked with them as they made up my room that I realized I was looking for Gabrielle—hoping I would meet her by chance and somehow persuade her to reestablish contact with Sabine. I did not find her.

EPILOGUE

Homage to King Baudouin I, upon his death, at the gates of the Royal Palace, Brussels (photo: Le Soir)

What Moeder Clara Sees

I AM eighty-four years old now," Moeder Clara told me matter-of-factly, adding with just a touch of pride that at her last medical checkup the doctor had said, "There is not one organ of my body that is sick or functioning abnormally."

This was the prelude to the day we spent talking in July 1989 in the small apartment in the center of the city of Kortrijk where she had lived for a few years. Moeder Clara had agreed to allow me to interview her in detail about what had changed, and what had not, in her family, village, and region since she and Vader Cyriel first welcomed me to their house on Izegemsestraat in Watermolen in 1962.

When I arrived at her home in mid-morning it was clear that she had been preparing for the visit. The dining room table was already set with her best beige linen cloth for our noonday meal together, and the handwritten memorandum she had made listing the major points she intended to discuss with me had been placed on the table where a centerpiece would ordinarily go.

It was remarkable how little Moeder Clara had aged over the course of the twenty-seven years I had known her. Her figure was trim and her skin smooth and unwrinkled. Her eyes were alert and responsive behind glasses no thicker than they used to be. Her hair—brightened a bit now by a pale blonde rinse—was carefully permanented and worn in the same local beauty parlor nonstyle as in the past. Her voice was as clear and her speech as voluble as ever, and she laughed the identical high-pitched laugh that Jacko the parrot used to imitate when he was alive. Her powers of perception and her lively intelligence had not dimmed, and her wisdom and scope of interest had expanded rather than contracted with the passage of time. A slight stiffness in her otherwise nimble gait and a moderate puffiness around her ankles were the only visible signs that she was no longer in her sixties.

She was enjoying her apartment and the life she had created

within and around it, she said, with convincing zest. She and
Vader Cyriel had lived in a small Kortrijk apartment when they
were first married, in an era when it was no more conventional for
a young, working-class village couple to do so than it was now for a
woman in her eighties like herself. The parallels between her youth
and her old age pleased and amused her.

The apartment was just around the corner from the Grote
Markt, the city's central market place and square, with its late
Gothic and Renaissance Town Hall, its clock-chiming belfry, its
Golden Spurs monument, and the crowds of eating and drinking
spectators who watched the comings and goings in the square from
its rim of busy cafés.

In the front of Moeder Clara's apartment, facing the shop-lined,
banner-festooned street below, was a long, narrow "sitting room"
that she had made into a combined living and dining room. It was
dominated by a large oak dining table with six chairs, and a
Dutch-style brass chandelier suspended over it. Under the windows
overlooking the street scene that she found continually engaging,
Moeder Clara had placed a big comfortable armchair, a hassock,
and an end table on which she piled the newspapers, magazines,
and books she was currently reading. (She was the only person in
the entire Van Marcke family who systematically tried to keep up
with national and international as well as local news; and since
moving to her apartment, where she had easier access to a public
library, she had become a regular borrower and reader of good
Flemish novels.) From the armchair she could not only see the
street but also the screen of the color television set on the opposite
wall. High above the television set, in a gilt and velvet frame, was
a smiling picture of her eldest son, Willy, the Jesuit priest, dressed
in a dark blue, pin-striped suit. Directly below it, on top of the TV,
was a framed color snapshot of her red-brick house on Izegemsestraat, now owned and inhabited exclusively by her daughter
Germaine and Germaine's second husband, Marnix Vanneste. The
only other photographs in this room flanked the breakfront: one,
near the door, was of Willy again, this time garbed in his Roman
collar; the other, hanging over Moeder Clara's armchair, was of her
deceased husband, Vader Cyriel. In her bedroom, at the back of
the apartment, framed wedding pictures of her daughter Mariette
and her sons Karel and Marcel, with their respective spouses, were
grouped in a cluster on the wall adjacent to her bed.

Although she said and genuinely meant that she had no regrets about leaving the house on Izegemsestraat, her decision to move out of it was as painful for her as the events that brought it to pass. Germaine and Marnix had been responsible for her departure.

Germaine, along with her two daughters Lydie and Anne-Marie, had lived with her mother and father for almost seventeen years following the breakdown of her first marriage to a mentally ill husband. When Germaine remarried in 1971, she and her new husband Marnix moved to his house in the nearby West Flemish village of Gullegem. Under the inheritance arrangements that Moeder Clara had made for each of her children, she had accorded Germaine preemptive rights to buy her house. When she and Marnix told her they would like to live in the house while gradually purchasing it, Moeder Clara had made that incrementally possible on financial terms that were very advantageous to them, on condition that she could continue to reside there. Once they began sharing the house with her, Marnix and Germaine mistreated Moeder Clara, restricting her food, activities, and expenses in ways that bordered on abuse. She became an unwelcome boarder in what had previously been her home.

It was not until Moeder Clara decided to move out of the house and look for an apartment in Kortrijk that she told her other children about what she had silently endured. They and their spouses rallied around her, vocally chastising Marnix and Germaine in a family meeting, and finding the apartment for their mother.

Moeder Clara had managed to achieve a modus vivendi with Germaine and Marnix. She described to me how Germaine and Marnix rapidly established a regular schedule of biweekly visits to see her in her apartment—Germaine coming by herself every Wednesday, the two of them arriving together each Friday—"as if nothing had happened." "What gall!" Moeder Clara exclaimed, adding that "it is more and more difficult nowadays to have grown-up children." But, she continued, in order not to put undue strain on "the stable marriage that Germaine and Marnix have had for eighteen years now," and for the sake of overall family unity and peace, she believed that the wisest course of action was to "keep quiet." Nevertheless, she had resolved not to visit the house on Izegemsestraat unless she was formally invited. Before adopting this position, Moeder Clara discussed its justification with the parish priest, who unequivocally supported her stance.

Moeder Clara's relocation and the traumatic circumstances under which it took place neither drained her lifeforce nor diminished her moral authority. She was the dynamic and sagacious matriarch of a still-growing family (that now included thirteen grandchildren and fourteen great-grandchildren)—its vital center, active integrator, and chief mainstay.

BEFORE TRACING out the evolution her family had undergone, Moeder Clara thought it was important to discuss certain developments that had been occurring in Watermolen and the environing West Flemish communities in which she and her husband, the families from which they came, their children, and their grandchildren as well, had lived all their lives.

The population of Watermolen, Moeder Clara announced—the hamlet where she and Vader Cyriel settled early in their marriage, where they raised their children, and where she lived for fifty-eight years before her move to Kortrijk—had grown to 3,500 inhabitants, nearly triple the size it was when she and Vader Cyriel came there in 1928. The number of Watermolen residents had taken a spurt upward in the last years of the 1980s, she said, due in part to a notable improvement in the local economy since the alarming unemployment of the late 1970s and early 1980s. Young people responded by choosing to stay there rather than moving away to seek employment and job advances elsewhere.

Jobs were now available for young workers in some of the region's major companies—for example, at Bekaert, the steel wire and steel cord maker, and manufacturer of mattress springs and mattresses, where Marcel (Van Marcke) had been employed for many years as a metal worker and foreman, and at Barco, the company that produced TV sets, radios, computers, and other electronic equipment, where Mariette, Germaine, and Germaine's two daughters had all worked. New foreign capital had been invested in these and other West Flanders–based businesses, Moeder Clara told me. For instance, Bekaert had sold a 20 percent stake in its computing software group to the Dutch unit of IBM, and money had been coming into local firms from Japanese and American as well as European sources. Many of the stores were disappearing, with the exception of enterprises like Karel's butcher shop, which survived and flourished because it carried the finest cuts of meat that money could buy, for which there was a high demand in Flemish families of all income levels.

There were still other signs that this section of the country was prospering, Moeder Clara continued. More sidewalks, paved roads, and stretches of highway were being constructed. One lovely villa after another was going up, many of them beautifully landscaped with trees and flowers. And in Kortrijk, where the traditional textile industry, particularly its carpet manufacturing sector, had seen a major upswing, both tourism and commerce were flourishing. The hotel across the street from the railroad station had been renovated and acquired a three-star rating; the Hotel Damier in the Grote Markt had been restored to its former glory; a new luxury hotel had been built; and a number of small, modern apartment buildings were being erected.

Compared with other regions of Belgium, Moeder Clara said, Kortrijk and its environs had become so prosperous that it was sometimes called "the Texas of Flanders." The rate of unemployment was the lowest in the country, and there was a great deal of personal wealth as well as capital in the area. She attributed this to the continuing presence and influence of middle-sized family firms in the region that had modernized their means of production and internationalized their business, but had not allowed the control of their enterprises to pass out of local family hands.

The most important festival in Watermolen that spring, Moeder Clara told me, was connected with the economic evolution that the local area had undergone, some of its social concomitants, and what was expected to be a continuing increase in the number of young families living there. On May 20–21, 1989, the 135th anniversary of Watermolen's Catholic parish primary school—Vrije Basisschool Sint-Godelieve—and the inauguration of the newly constructed, larger building in which it would be located from then on, were celebrated. The two-day program included a "Film Festival"; a "Hollywood Show" in which children of the school "guest starred" as Mickey Mouse, Charlie Chaplin, Tom and Jerry, and the Family von Trapp, among others; a lecture demonstration of "DisneyWorld cooking"; an exhibition of paintings and ceramics; the consecration of the premises and the Christian crosses of the new school building by the bishop of Brugge; and an open-house reception for guests in the new locale.

The entire teaching staff was now comprised of lay persons. A recent photograph in the anniversary booklet (*Kroniek*) published for the occasion showed only six elderly teacher-sisters remaining in the convent next to the school. Nevertheless, in the afterword to the *Kroniek* written by the school's headmaster, the sisters were thanked for their century-long contribution, particularly for the "very special, indelible stamp they imprinted on the Catholic education of the Sint-Godelieve parish and school." Moeder Clara was glad this tribute had been paid to the sisters, she said, because all her children had been taught by them when they were students in Sint-Godelieve's elementary school. In fact, for many years, she continued, the entire parish had celebrated a special annual mass to thank the sisters for their good work in running the school and educating their youngsters, until the "dictatorial" priest who was then the local pastor brought it to an end in 1939.

Moeder Clara expressed greater approval of the way the current parish priest saw and did things than of Father Decock's "olden times" style. The present pastor, she said, was the son of a farmer; he "listens and hears what people say"; and he was intelligent and open-minded; yet he was not disrespectful of tradition. His biggest project at the moment was building a new parish church. The existing one had been too gravely damaged that year by a fire of unknown origin simply to repair it; and there was general agreement that, given the actual and anticipated growth in the local population, and the substantial number of persons who were practicing Catholics, constructing a larger church was warranted.

Moeder Clara pointed out that there were not only more younger persons in the area now, but more older persons too. This "greying" of the population, she said, was taking place all over Belgium and Europe. The coexistence of young and old had created problems for both age groups. Most serious of all, in her opinion, were the difficulties that families were experiencing in caring for aging parents. One of the major factors contributing to this, she said, was that in most families the wives as well as the husbands held full-time jobs, so there was no one at home during the day to assume responsibility for the continuous presence and care that many elderly individuals needed. In addition, a sufficiently large "gap" existed between the younger and older generations to reduce the probability that married adult children and their aging parents could live together harmoniously under the same roof. With some reluctance she conceded that a certain "egoism" on the part of

young people was also involved—their preoccupation with themselves and their exclusive concern with "their own" families, which
they defined as their spouse and their children. Quite a few persons
in their seventies and eighties with whom Moeder Clara was
acquainted had gone to live in retirement communities or homes
for the aged. These were so much in demand that they all had long
waiting lists, despite their high cost.

Moeder Clara was grateful for the way she was living at her
advanced age: in her own independent apartment, with a pension
that covered her rent and daily expenses, and enjoying frequent
regular visits from all her children and some of her grandchildren.
She could count on her daughter Mariette to help with the weekly
heavy cleaning and any chores that required assistance. She still
cooked for herself, but in addition Bernadette had arranged for her
to receive some meals at home. She participated in the numerous
gatherings and festivities of the extended family and not infrequently
was at the center of them. Her children and her grandchildren
maintained the tradition of coming to her apartment on New Year's
Day to present their good wishes to her. In return, each of the
grandchildren received a gift from her: "I have always done it and
am determined to keep doing it. This way the family stays together." She spent quite a bit of time, too, at Marcel and Bernadette's country house in the Kwaremont, less than an hour away
from Kortrijk but located in deep, rolling West Flemish farmland,
surrounded by distant hills, grazing cows and horses, and even a
white windmill. She was also welcome to visit Karel and Sylvie
when they vacationed in their house in Spain, and she had done
that several times. But she no longer signed up for the bus trips to
other European countries that used to be part of her annual
itinerary.

Each time she attended mass, she said a certain set of prayers,
expressing her gratitude for her life situation. She prayed for all
those in the family and the village who had died. She offered a
special prayer for Willy's health, asking that the chronic disease
with which he was coping not worsen. She prayed for the pope, his
health, and, she added with a chuckle, for his "lucidity" as well—
obliquely referring to some of the very conservative theological
positions he had taken with which she was not happy. Finally, she
prayed for all those who were alone and forgotten in the world,
wherever they might be.

WITHIN THE framework of these observations and reflections on the evolution of Watermolen, Kortrijk, and her existence within them, Moeder Clara traced out for me the major developments that had occurred in the family lives of each of her four married children— all of whom resided in West Flemish villages or towns close to the hamlet where they were born and raised.

Karel was now sixty-one years old, recently retired, and "very rich," said Moeder Clara, laughing heartily. He and his wife Sylvie worked very hard for thirty-six years in his butcher shop, earning enough to build their own house in Marke, acquire a house in Spain, accumulate a substantial bank account, and develop a portfolio of diversified investments. Moeder Clara was pleased to see them enjoying the first real leisure they had ever known. What was more, Karel had begun to "realize what it is to be older," Moeder Clara commented, and "that is why he is becoming more family oriented." He also felt that because he worked so incessantly and was so preoccupied with earning money, he did not spend enough time with his children or give them enough attention. He and Sylvie visited Moeder Clara twice a week, something they rarely did in the past.

Three of their four children were happily married, and had built houses of their own. Karel and Sylvie's eldest daughter, Marie-Hélène, and their son Dirk each had three children; thus far their younger son Albert had only one child. Albert was a machinist who worked for the railroad. His wife, Margo, a nurse, was employed part-time. Dirk worked in a government employment agency. In partnership with her brother, Dirk's wife, Cécile, carried on her parents' trade, moving from one market to another in the area of Kortrijk with a textile stand. Marie-Hélène's husband, Guy, had an engrossing career in the international division of the Brussels/Lambert Bank. She was doing some part-time language teaching now that their children were older. With as much anxiety as expectancy, she was awaiting the five-year overseas assignment scheduled for Guy, who was moving up in the bank.

Hedwig, the youngest of Karel and Sylvie's children, had not fared so well. After a turbulent marriage and divorce, she and her two children had lived for a while on government-provided unemployment insurance. When she and her husband separated, neither of them had had a cent to their name, even though as a mechanic and gas station attendant he had earned a good salary. Most of the money had been dissipated by the husband who, as Moeder Clara put it, "did not want to give up his young life" after marriage and had stayed out virtually all night, every night. With little more than a primary school education, Hedwig had difficulty getting a job. She was finally hired as an aide in a home for elderly persons. Since her divorce she had had what Moeder Clara euphemistically called "two affairs" before she met the young man with whom she was now living. He, at least, seemed to be kind.

Moeder Clara said firmly that she was not letting Hedwig's domestic situation and divorce upset her the way her daughter Germaine's separation from her first husband did years ago. Some of the patterns in Hedwig's way of life, she added, had become increasingly common in West Flanders since the beginning of the 1970s. These days, before they married, many young adults, still living at home with their parents, were allowed to keep all their earnings. Their mothers and fathers did not ask them to contribute anything to their room and board, nor did they offer to do so. Rather than building up their savings for the future, they used a great deal of their money to buy expensive clothes, cars, and motorbikes, to frequent cafés, and to join disco clubs where they went dancing three or four times a week. Furthermore, many of these young people were "living like husband and wife" with a partner to whom they were not married.

Nor were middle-aged persons immune to this kind of behavior, Moeder Clara said. When Mariette and Germaine worked at the Barco plant, for example, they were both struck by the emphasis that many of their fellow employees placed on having large wardrobes of stylish clothes. Women who came to work wearing the same dress two days in a row were likely to become the objects of vicious jokes. Some of the married couples in their age group competed with one another over how their homes were furnished and where they went on vacations. A good deal of flirting took place between couples, too, not all of which was innocuous. And along with the young men and women who married and divorced a year or two later if things did not go as they had imagined or planned, there were now a considerable number of couples who were breaking up after having been married for twenty years or more.

In Moeder Clara's view these developments resulted from increased prosperity bringing "too much luxury"; from a conception of "the emancipation of women" quite different from the kind she believed she represented; from a breakdown in parental authority; and from the erosion of a religiously based moral sense of right and wrong, and good and evil. In her day, she said, when people married, they assumed it was permanent. They did not have money. They had to work hard to support their family. They knew what they should and had to do, and they did it. She realized how simple this sounded, particularly in contrast to the complicated stresses and conflicts that many now faced.

Moeder Clara went on to tell me that both of her daughter Germaine's girls, Lydie and Anne-Marie, had jobs in the same electronics firm. Lydie was married to a railroad worker, Anne-Marie to a security guard, and they each had two small children.

As for her daughter Mariette, now that she was in her late fifties, Moeder Clara said, and had taken early retirement from her work at Barco on a "bridge pension," she was more relaxed and content than she had been as a younger woman. Mariette's house in Kuurne was not only the most immaculate in the whole Van Marcke family but also the most beautifully and richly furnished—with its fine oak tables, chairs, breakfront, sideboard, and armoires; copper-trimmed oak doors, hardwood floors, and wall-to-wall carpeting; hand-blocked wallpaper and custom-made drapes; brass chandeliers; marble fireplace and chiming mantel clock; Chinese vases, and paintings and sculptures by local Flemish artists; modern kitchen and bathrooms; healthful and expensive Comfortflex mattresses on every bed; and meticulously arranged cupboards, filled with the best household and personal linens.

Mariette's husband, Jan, had also taken early retirement from his job at one of the big carpet-weaving firms in the area. He was proud of the big flower and vegetable garden he had created in the back of the house. He had paved the garden with red-brick walks, enclosed it in whitewashed walls, built a terrace overlooking it— and had even put wall-to-wall carpeting in the toolshed.

Jan and Mariette's eldest son, Pascal, was an assistant to the director of a local branch of the Brussels/Lambert Bank. He was married to a home economics teacher, had built his own house, and had two children. But he and his wife had broken off their relations with Mariette, Jan, and the entire Van Marcke family. In Moeder Clara's opinion this was primarily due to the "greedy, materialistic" values of Pascal's wife and her parents. They had been very dissatisfied with the funds that Mariette, Jan, and Pascal had contributed to the marriage, and had outspokenly criticized Mariette and Jan for how much they had spent, in comparison, on the building and furnishing of their own home and on the education of their sons.

Herman, Mariette and Jan's younger son, had continued his grandfather Cyriel Van Marcke's occupational tradition by training as a printer in a school in Ghent run by the Broeders van Liefde (religious Brothers of Charity). He worked for Lannoo, a prominent Flemish printing firm, where he had steadily risen to the top of his craft, especially in the printing of fine art books. He was still unmarried and looking for a wife who shared his hard-working, unostentatious, family values.

At the end of this detailed review of her family, Moeder Clara spoke finally of her youngest child, fifty-year-old Marcel, his wife Bernadette, and their three daughters and son. As a family unit they had the most frequent contact with Moeder Clara and the warmest relationship with her. Marcel had always been quietly attentive to his mother; Bernadette was more like a daughter than a daughter-in-law; and their children saw a great deal of their *Grootmoeder* Clara, who felt close to them and the way they were living their lives.

Bernadette and Marcel were both still employed, Moeder Clara told me—she as a social assistant responsible for home visits to the elderly, he as a worker/foreman at the Bekaert plant. But in 1991 Marcel would be obliged by the company to take a bridge pension. Although he would be only fifty-two at that time, and felt this was "rather early" to stop working, he had little choice in the matter. Because of the advanced technology that management was introducing into the production process, Bekaert would need fewer workers of his type in the 1990s. Partly for this reason the company was investing six billion Belgian francs, spread over five years, to put almost twelve hundred employees on well-paid bridge pensions. Marcel's working career was scheduled to end in April 1991. When that occurred, said Moeder Clara, five children, two sons-in-law, and two daughters-in-law in her family would all be retired.

Bernadette and Marcel still resided in the small house in Watermolen where Moeder Clara and Vader Cyriel had lived before moving to a bigger house in Izegemsestraat. But upon

Marcel's retirement, he and Bernadette would make their vacation house in the Kwaremont their year-round home. They had gradually been modernizing its electrical supply and plumbing and refurnishing it. Marcel and Bernadette would celebrate their twenty-fifth wedding anniversary there on July 8, Moeder Clara said, with a big family party to which they had invited fifty persons. All the members of the extended family were contributing to a surprise gift for them: top-quality copper hinges and knobs for eight of the doors in the Kwaremont house.

Marcel and Bernadette's two eldest daughters, Greet and Ann, were married to young men from the Kwaremont area, and both couples had settled in the vicinity. Greet, an intensive-care nurse, was expecting her first child. Her husband worked as a truck driver and manual laborer in the construction firm owned by Bernadette's brother-in-law. Ann taught sewing in a secondary school; and her husband, an electrician, was employed by an electronics firm that made prostheses for handicapped people.

Léo, Marcel and Bernadette's only son and youngest child, had just completed his military service, was working as an electrician, and had recently become engaged to a nurse.

But it was her granddaughter Lydwine, Marcel and Bernadette's third-born child, with whom Moeder Clara felt most identified, because she was intelligent, knew her own mind, had the maturity and determination to act accordingly, and at the same time was unselfishly concerned about the welfare of others. Lydwine had just graduated from a social-work school in Kortrijk and was engaged to a baker. She planned to wait at least two years before marrying him, because she felt it would be helpful to their life together if she was a little older, had worked for a while, and had been able to save money for their household.

Moeder Clara admired Lydwine's decision not to marry immediately. She admitted that if she herself had her life to live over, though she would still marry Vader Cyriel, she would not do so again at the age of nineteen. She would marry later and use her years as a single young adult to get more schooling, to study languages (French and English as well as Dutch), and to do more traveling before settling down to family life. When I asked her about the size of the family she would want under present-day circumstances, she unhesitatingly replied that she would choose again to have five children. But, she added, she would want her children to have as good an education as possible, and the cost of university studies had been steadily increasing during the 1980s. She had the impression that as a result there were fewer young people of working-class origins enrolled in Belgian universities than in the 1970s, particularly in expensive faculties like medicine, pharmacy, and law. So if she wanted to give her children every chance for a university education, she said, perhaps having fewer than five children might be more practical.

We had talked from mid-morning to late afternoon with great mutual enjoyment, pausing only to eat our midday dinner together. Finally I came to my last questions. First, in her opinion, did her family still belong to the Belgian working class, or had all the socioeconomic progress that she and her children and grandchildren had made in the course of her lifetime changed their status? And second, could it be said that Watermolen had remained a village in spite of the extensive industrialization and modernization that had occurred since World War II within and around it?

Moeder Clara thought for a moment. It was true, she replied, that her family, like many others in the region, had prospered. In fact, she commented, there was no longer an "underclass" there, as there had been before the war. With the exception of Hedwig, everyone in the family had good jobs, good pay, or good pensions, their own well-furnished houses and cars, abundant food on their tables, and extensive wardrobes. They had more leisure time than in the past, and more contact with the world outside West Flanders through television and travel. Many of the grandchildren had secondary or postsecondary educations; and two of them, Pascal and Guy, had successful careers in one of Belgium's major banks. There was even one Van Marcke family member, Karel, who was a "rich man." And yet, she went on to say, most persons in the family were either employed as skilled workers or craftsmen, jobs that involved manual labor rather than "head work," or they had teaching, nursing, or social service jobs at relatively modest local levels of the country's social welfare bureaucracy. No one in the family other than Willy had had a university education or had moved away from West Flanders where they were born and raised. All the family's social activities took place in the small communities where they lived, primarily in the company of family or with kinlike friends.

They were definitely still a working-class family, Moeder Clara concluded with firmness and a certain amount of pride. But, she added, with an amused expression on her face—remembering that in the era of Belgian colonialism, talented, upwardly mobile Congolese were called "*évolués*" because of the progress they had made—perhaps it was more accurate to say that they now belonged to the "*geevolueerde arbeidersklas*": the "working class that has evolved."

And to her, Watermolen was also still a village. Its population had grown and was more prosperous. It had become more modern, and certain differences now existed between the generations. Yet it continued to be a closely knit, family-centered community, she said, whose inhabitants were mainly "evolved working class" people like the Van Marcke family. Fewer people attended church regularly than in the past, and there were certain aspects of their domestic lives they now considered matters of private conscience rather than the business of the church. But the local parish priest remained a *notable* in the community; and a dynamic group of younger people were taking responsibility for the Christian social activities of the village. They were the new leaders of the Katholieke Werkers Bond and the organizers of events like the celebration of the Vrije Basisschool Sint-Godelieve.

"SO WHAT is my conclusion?" Moeder Clara asked, teasing me and herself by taking on the role of academic interviewer. "It is that the whole family is getting older," she replied to her own question, "and it is also getting younger through the grandchildren and the great-grandchildren. Like the family, the village has changed, but in many ways it is still the village I have always known. And as I have told you before," said Moeder Clara, "life is so interesting—especially the new things that are happening—that I wish I could live to at least one hundred to see how it all turns out."

Belgium Revisited

Everything has changed. . . . Your "Belgian book" will describe situations in a country that will no longer resemble in any way what it was. . . . You had better publish it as soon as possible, while Belgium still exists!

That was the core message I received—*Par Avion / Per Luchtpost* —from a number of Belgian colleagues and friends, just before I returned to Belgium for several weeks in the summer of 1988, primarily to discuss an early draft of this book with them. Belgium, they wrote, with characteristic Belgian irony but deep concern, was undergoing such fundamental and far-reaching change that it was becoming unrecognizable. Whatever values, sentiments, and convictions its citizens once shared were "vanishing"—if, in fact, they had ever existed in the first place. They were being dispelled by the widening differences between Flemish and Walloon cultures as the federalization of the Belgian state advanced, and by their diverging perspectives on the crucial economic, political, and social problems that the country was facing. Belgium *qua* Belgium—its "reality" as a nation and a societal community—was "disappearing" into the past.

Throughout the first years of the 1990s, as I worked on drafts of the book, escalated versions of this message reached me through personal correspondence and the Belgian newspapers and magazines that I read. At the end of 1991 and the beginning of 1992, the possibility of the "breakup" of Belgium and the "separation" of Flanders and Wallony began to be more frequently mentioned, especially in the Flemish press. Some allusions to "separatism" were aggressively stated. But more of them were expressed in rather domestic terms, invoking the image of alternating threats, disputes, and temporary periods of pacification between spouses, "living apart together," with "separate table and bed," in a collapsing Belgian house that was not being properly maintained by its cohabitants and was in danger of being demolished.

I made another short personal trip to Belgium in the summer of 1991 and completed the penultimate draft of the book in early 1993. Belgian friends urged me to return to Belgium one more time to observe and discuss the country's metamorphosis before delivering the manuscript to the publisher. Heeding their advice, I planned such a revisit for the fall of 1993.

Three months before my departure, during the night of July 31, 1993, King Baudouin of the Belgians died unexpectedly at his summer residence in Spain. What ensued during the first days of August, and throughout that entire month, was not confined to the remarkable religious ceremonies and civic rites that took place.* An outpouring of national grief occurred, and of emotional, popular tributes to the high moral values that the king had incarnated as a man and as the symbolic representative of Belgium's collective conscience and identity. "The country still exists!" my Belgian correspondents exclaimed in the numerous letters about the king's death that I received. "It has not fallen off the map. . . . It is a living reality. . . . Since the announcement of King Baudouin's death, the country has turned into Belgium. . . . It has refound itself."

On Sunday, August 1, even before the king's body had arrived in Belgium from Spain, a multitude began to assemble at the Royal Palace in Brussels. Many brought flowers, which they placed in front of the gates or on the lawn of the palace. They carried black, yellow, and red Belgian flags, too—more than anyone had seen displayed, observers remarked, since the day in 1944 when Belgium was liberated from the Nazi occupation. The National Belgian Railway Company issued special "In Homage to King Baudouin" tickets for August 5 and 6, the days the public was admitted to the palace to view the king's body which lay in state, and for August 7, his funeral mass at Saint Michael's Cathedral in Brussels. With these tickets, adults could make a round trip to Brussels from any Belgian station for the reduced fare of one hundred Belgian francs (less than three dollars), and children under twelve who accompa-

---

*My account of the circumstances of King Baudouin's death, his funeral, and how the Belgian public responded to them is drawn from letters and Belgian media coverage of the events—including Flemish- and French-language newspapers and magazines, and videotapes of the entire funeral procession and mass—sent to me by Belgian colleagues and friends. In addition, in November 1993, during my last trip to Belgium, I interviewed a number of people about what they had observed and felt at the time of the king's death.

nied them could travel free. A total of 210,000 tickets were sold, far more than anyone had predicted. The railroad put on 163 extra trains to accommodate the throngs of Belgians, from every region and social milieu of the country, who journeyed to Brussels to pay their last respects to the king as individuals and families.

It was estimated that more than a half-million people came to the palace, bearing what news commentators reported were at least 125,000 bouquets of flowers. While they waited for hours to file past the coffin, they crossed over language barriers, talking feelingly to one another in Flemish and French about the king; and their sense of belonging to a national family that was united in mourning grew.

A funeral mass of "glory and hope" was celebrated on Saturday, August 7. Dressed in white rather than black, surrounded by the members of the royal family, Queen Fabiola led a cortège of national and international dignitaries along the route from the palace to the cathedral, walking behind her husband's flag-draped casket borne on the shoulders of a military honor guard. The procession moved slowly down streets lined with thousands of reverently silent people, while at the request of the Belgian bishops all the bells of the city and of the country rang out. Giant screens had been set up outside the cathedral and in Brussels's Grand-Place so that the great crowd that had gathered could follow the unfolding of the mass on television. Whether they watched it there, or seated in front of television sets in their homes, Belgians were impressed by the "dignity" and "grace," the "serenity" and "courage" with which the queen conducted herself during the mass and throughout the entire day. They were also profoundly moved by the testimonies "for the rights of those humiliated and excluded by society" given at the end of the funeral service by four persons whom the king had known and admired: the social worker who had served as national minister and royal commissioner of immigration; a physician who headed the infectious disease section of a university hospital where he cared for patients with AIDS; a journalist who had published a book (indirectly subsidized by the King Baudouin Foundation) on prostitution as a new form of slavery; and a young woman from Manila in the Philippines, forced into prostitution by Belgian men, who cried inconsolably as her farewell letter to the king was read aloud for her. ("The king came to see us in Antwerp," it declared. "He listened to me. . . . He was shocked. . . . He took our side. He was a true King. I called him my friend. . . . Now that my friend has passed away, who else will help us?")

When the mass ended, the king's coffin, mounted on a small tank, was slowly driven through the winding streets of Brussels toward Notre Dame Church in Laeken, where his body was to be interred in the royal crypt. As it passed, followed by the limousine in which the queen rode, the crowds of spectators on the sidewalks burst into applause. In the Brussels commune of Schaarbeek, with its concentration of immigrant residents, Moroccans, Turks, and Zaïreans clutched photographic portraits of the king and the royal couple, brandished Belgian flags, and held aloft signs of gratitude printed in French and Flemish: *"Merci, Sire. Dank U."*

On Monday, August 9, after Albert II, King Baudouin's brother and successor to the throne, took the constitutional oath of office, the period of national mourning officially ended; but the royal crypt remained open to the public, and it was visited by tens of thousands of men, women, and children during the weeks of August.

WITH THESE powerful, contradictory images of a country that was both losing and rediscovering its sense of coherence, solidarity, and meaning, on the night of October 29, 1993, I flew to Belgium. Early the next morning, when we started our descent toward Brussels, Belgium was invisible from the air—so enveloped in clouds and fog that for a few minute I wryly contemplated the possibility that the country had finally "disappeared," as Belgians were always predicting it might. But as soon as the plane's wheels touched the ground, the contours of a familiar landscape began to emerge from the obscuring fog.

As the taxi drove me toward my hotel through Brussels streets, I was struck by the number of "For Rent" and "For Sale" signs posted on the windows and doors of buildings, houses, and empty store fronts. I was also intrigued by some of the cars we passed with small, metallic emblems of the Belgian flag and the royal crown attached to their rear bumpers, or stickers pasted on their back windows with slogans like, "Don't Touch My Belgium" in French and Flemish, and "We Will Remain United Belgians, In Memory of His Majesty King Baudouin," printed in Flemish, French, and German. I was to see many more of these car decorations in the days to come, especially in Brussels and Liège.

A special summit meeting of the European Community had

been held in Brussels the day before my arrival. It was presided over by Belgium, functioning as the Community's rotating president for a (July through December 1993) six-month term. The major purpose of this one-day meeting was to show that the European Community had the capacity to inaugurate the Maastricht Treaty on European Union despite the long and divisive process of its ratification. As the morning newspapers indicated, the mood surrounding the meeting was somber. The tortuous path to the ratification of Maastricht; the tragic events in former Yugoslavia, especially the war and "ethnic cleansing" in Bosnia, and the inability of Western Europe effectively to intervene in the situation; the severe economic recession gripping Europe and its soaring unemployment rate, expected to reach an average of 11 or 12 percent in the European Community by 1994—had all cast deep shadows over the gathering. Enhancing the pessimism were the labor demonstrations that took place in the streets of Brussels the same day, and the twenty-four-hour strike of public sector workers that had paralyzed the country's rail network. These had been organized by Belgium's socialist labor union (the General Federation of Work of Belgium) to coincide with the European Community meeting and to protest the freeze in wages and cutbacks in social security benefits that the union anticipated would be part of an austerity plan being drafted by the Belgian national government. (Six additional protest strikes were planned for later weeks.) With some bravado, Brussels's major newspaper, *Le Soir*, proclaimed that the Belgian presidency of the European Community would go down in history because at the just-completed summit it had succeeded in resolving the question of the location of various new agencies created by the Community—"a question that had poisoned the life of the Community for years." Chief among these decisions was the agreement to put the European Monetary Institute, the forerunner of a European Community central bank, in Frankfurt, Germany. This accomplishment notwithstanding, and despite affirmations by the leaders of the twelve member nations that the functioning of Europe had been "revived," that they supported the Maastricht timetable for achieving a single European currency, and that they would address the problems of European recession and unemployment together, it was notable that no starting date for a common currency was mentioned, and serious discussion about Europe's ailing economy was deferred until the Community's next meeting in December.

Although Belgium still appeared to be ardently committed to what King Baudouin had referred to in his last address to the country on July 21, 1993, * as its "European task" to "advance the development of a Europe [that is] truly federal," it was clear from the outset of my revisit that pessimism about the imminent attainment of this goal had grown considerably during the past year. The increased discouragement was entwined with an acute sense of economic crisis, European and Belgian, that now pervaded the land. Consternation about Belgium's enormous national debt, which had risen to 135 percent of the gross national product—"the highest debt in the Western world"—and about the spiraling unemployment rate (14.1 percent) was palpable and audible everywhere I went. Even the area of Kortrijk, one of the most prosperous parts of Flanders and the entire country, with the lowest unemployment at the time of my 1988 and 1991 visits, was experiencing economic malaise. My day-long visit with Moeder Clara and her family on November 7, 1993, was edifying in this respect. At age eighty-eight she was as observant as ever, and as enthusiastically interested in local, national, and international developments. She was grateful, she told me, that all her children were receiving comfortable pensions or pre-pensions in their retirement, and that her grandchildren and their spouses were all gainfully employed—earning and saving enough to support themselves and their growing families and to build their own homes. She was nevertheless concerned about the growing number of persons losing their jobs in Kortrijk's supposedly flourishing industries; about the distressing pockets of poverty in certain neighboring communities, particularly among immigrant families; and about what would happen to the national social security system and its allocations under the present economic circumstances. All this economic travail and uncertainty, she reflected, could lead to a significant gain in votes for the Vlaams Blok (the Flemish nationalist party of the extreme right) in the next elections. For Moeder Clara this prospect was more than

---

*July 21 is Belgium's national holiday—the day when it officially celebrates its foundation as a nation-state. Traditionally the king's speech to his compatriots on this day provides an overview of the country's situation, with emphasis on important national values and civic responsibilities.

worrisome because, as she put it bluntly, "They [the Vlaams Blok] are Nazis!"

On a national level, the surest sign that the country considered itself to be facing a grave economic crisis was that the Belgian government had organized a conclave in a château to forge a societal way of dealing with it. When I arrived in Belgium on October 30, the government team had already been meeting for a week in the Val-Duchesse château, working on what it termed its Global Austerity Plan to create employment, safeguard social security, control public debt, and insure international competitiveness of the Belgian economy. Through the scenario of a château conclave, the classic Belgian elements had been set in motion to dramatize the momentousness of the country's economic problems and of the conflicts they evoked, the complexity and precariousness of the deliberations and negotiations involved in tackling them, and the need for elaborate compromises *"a la belge"* between the society's particularistic groups.

Anxiety about where the official transformation of Belgium into a federal state would eventually lead ran as high among the Flemish, Walloon, and Brussels Belgians with whom I conversed during my visit, as their economic concern. On certain issues, particularly the question of federalizing the national social security system, the two sets of worries intersected and reinforced one another. Although the "Saint Michael's agreements," and the 1993 constitutional reforms that followed upon them, supposedly represented the culmination of the twenty-three-year-long evolution of Belgium from a unitary and decentralized state to a federal one, most of the people with whom I spoke were worried that it would not stop there. Many described the federalization of Belgium as a process over which there was now little control; it was driving Flanders, Wallony, and Brussels further and further apart, "mentally" as well as politically and economically, they said, and in the end it might reduce the national government and Belgium itself to no more than an "empty shell." Despite these apprehensions, people expressed pride in the peaceful reform of the Belgian state, according to distinctively Belgian norms of compromise between Flemish and Wallons, in contrast to the violent way in which the nation-state of Yugoslavia had been dismembered.

Nevertheless, the institutionalized mixture of different models of federalism in Flanders and Wallony that resulted from this process of compromise—Belgium's "asymmetrical federalism"—was contributing to continuing proposals that the Flemish and Walloons separate, and also to the generalized fear that this might actually come to pass. Whereas the Flemish government had achieved unification by giving jurisdiction over the Flemish region to the Flemish cultural community (in Belgian parlance, thereby "fusing" their institutions), Walloons had been reluctant to effect such an institutional liaison between the French cultural community and the Walloon region, partly because of the distinction they wished to maintain between the culture of Wallony and that of Brussels, which they regarded as a bilingual Flemish- as well as French-language region, with a "culture of synthesis" that intermingled Brabant, Flemish, Walloon, and foreign elements. The stronger cultural and institutional solidarity of the Flemish, in combination with their greater demographic, economic, and political weight in the country, gave clout to whatever appeals they put forward for the emancipation of Flanders from Wallony.

The most emotionally charged area of Flemish-Walloon tension in November 1993 centered on the persistent demand to federalize social security. This had been enunciated by various Flemish politicians and political parties and by the Flemish press since 1991. Most of the French-speaking Belgians with whom I talked called this development to my attention with dismay. All of them were unequivocally opposed to the idea of splitting Belgian social security into two autonomous systems whose organization and financing would each be independently managed by the Flemish and the Walloon governments. Underlying the Flemish proposal to federalize social security in this way was their recognition that as much as 49 percent of the expenditures of the enormously indebted national government were deployed for social security; they alleged that for years a sizable portion of the Flemish contributions to social security had been transferred to Wallony in order to finance Walloon expenses. In the most polemical presentations of these transfers between regions it was contended that more than one hundred billion Belgian francs "slid" from Flanders to Wallony, or at least a sum of money equivalent to the cost of each Flemish family buying a car for each Walloon family every four years. The more conservative estimates of the transfers fell in the realm of some ten billion francs. At issue, too, were questions of why these transfers occurred, to what extent they were "justified" or resulted from "abuses" of the system, and whether they would continue indefinitely. Among the demographic and socioeconomic conditions that contributed to the disequilibrium in social security expenses, all parties agreed, was the greater number of older persons on pension in Wallony than in Flanders; and a higher average pension, higher unemployment, and higher medical care costs covered by health insurance in Wallony. But interpretations of why these discrepancies existed, and how long they would last, varied greatly.

Deeper than the economic reality and political agitation that surrounded "the transfers" and the possible federalization of social security was the debate about the historical, ethical, and societal significance of the Belgian social security system that these issues provoked. It was the symbolic more than the material meaning of social security, said one of my Belgian discussants, that made the question of its federalization a "national psychodrama." For all Belgians—Flemish and Walloon alike—the social security system was associated with the moral import of World War II, with Belgium's liberation from German occupation, and with the spirit of "social solidarity" that animated postwar efforts to reconstruct a society that would not only prosper economically but would use its resources to promote greater social well-being and social justice. Integral to the "Social Pact" agreed upon by government, employers, and labor right after the war was the foundation of a national social security system. It would "distribute the fruits of common work more justly," and "remove as completely as possible the fears and misery of working men and women." The social democratic model on which this pact was based, compatible with both Christian and socialist values, was viewed as a way to harness the profits of capitalism and put them at the mutual service of all persons and groups in the society. In the eyes of French-speaking Belgians, and many Flemish-speaking ones as well, the notion of federalizing social security fractured the unified and universalistic concept of solidarity on which it was erected. It created a "dualism of solidarities" that invidiously distinguished between those who belonged to one's own particularistic community and those who did not. As one (French) Belgian philosopher vividly put it: "This would be like recommending to the Good Samaritan that he demand an identity card from the person he wishes to aid in order to determine if [that individual] is entitled to a full rate of solidarity or only a reduced rate of *caritas* applicable to members of other *volksgemeenschappen* [peoples or communities]."[*]

The Flemish wing of the country's federated sick funds, its organizations of Flemish employers, and the Flemish members of its labor unions were never enthusiastic about creating separate Flemish and Walloon social security systems. By the time I arrived in Belgium in 1993, the most radical demands for such a split had abated, appeased in part by the national government's promise to try to put an end to unjustified, "nonobjective" social security transfers. But a number of the Walloons and French-speaking *Bruxellois* with whom I talked expressed the fear that the drive to federalize social security might occur again, in a form that could "lacerate" the country.

TO MANY of the persons whom I met during this stay in Belgium I confessed that when I thought of the way Belgians from all social backgrounds responded to King Baudouin's death, I was perplexed by statements about how the strife between Flemish and Walloons threatened the very survival of Belgium as a society. It seemed to me, I said, that in the public's massive tribute to what the king represented, and to the moral qualities he embodied, and through the liturgy of the funeral mass, Belgians had stirringly expressed their shared values and their strong attachment to their country. They testified to the importance they collectively attributed to dignity, courage, honesty, and integrity; to a sense of duty about one's responsibilities and of vocation about one's work; to liberty and loyalty, justice, equity, and solidarity; and to compassionate concern for those who suffer, for the socially deprived, and for the victims of prejudice and discrimination. Belgians also demonstrated the significance they accorded to the family as the locus of personal and societal well-being. This was visible in their journeys to Brussels and to the palace in family groups; and it was audible in the admiration they expressed for the quality of companionship and love that the king and the queen had maintained throughout their more than thirty years of marriage, for the grace with which the royal couple had borne their inability to have children, and for the

---

[*]Philippe Van Parijs, "Solidarité et responsabilité: un conflit insurmountable?" *La Revue Nouvelle*, Vol. 86, No. 11 (November 1993), 58–64.

generosity with which they had turned their personal tragedy into active involvement in promoting the welfare of the country's children. On this occasion Belgians had expressed considerable pride as well in their country and in their conduct as citizens. It brought out the best in us, they said: the sentiments expressed by the population, the discipline of the crowds, the comportment of the public officials were remarkable. The Belgium that was called forth by the king's death, commentators had noted, was the antithesis of the image of a small, pedestrian, materialistic country continually embroiled in its linguistic disputes—an image that Belgians themselves often conjured up and projected to others.

None of the persons with whom I discussed these impressions disputed my observations, but many interpreted them otherwise. *That* Belgium, they said, "united, solidary, and generous," was "a dream"—a dream of what Belgium *could* be, but not what Belgium actually was. The Belgium that ephemerally appeared during the days of national mourning, I was told, belonged to the realm of "symbolic reality." The "instrumental reality" of the country's usual life was very different: fraught with conflict and negative competition between vying groups, each of which defined itself as a minority oppressed by the others. The persons who spoke this way seemed to feel that the innermost reality of their society that rose to the surface in response to the king's death was more illusory than its everyday dissensions and deviations from the ideal.

This was consistent with a complex culture pattern that I had encountered throughout all my years of questing in Belgium: the tendency of Belgians to be highly sensitive to the sphere of their individual and collective existence where emotions and beliefs, values, and symbols reside, while verbally denying their importance in daily life and systematically excluding them from their intellectual and scientific work. *

A number of the persons whom I interviewed considered the manifestations elicited by the king's death to be "spontaneous

---

*I have written more fully about this Belgian culture pattern in "Why Belgium?" *Archives Européennes de Sociologie / European Journal of Sociology,* Vol. 19, No. 2 (1978), 224–226; "Is Religion Important in Belgium?" *Archives Européenes de Sociologie / European Journal of Sociology,* Vol. 23, No. 1 (1982), especially 7 and 30–32; and "Combien de temps une société peut-elle durer avec une identité négative?" *La Revue Nouvelle,* Vol. 92, No. 10 (October 1990), 106–108.

referendums" by the Belgian populace, who were registering a hidden protest against the failure of the country's major political parties (Social-Christian, Socialist, and Liberal) and those in political office to remain responsive to their concerns. The familiar and humane figure of the king, they said, who constantly made personal visits to the people, including the humblest and most neglected among them, contrasted sharply to the country's increasingly impersonal, self-absorbed, and remote politicians. Public exasperation with politicians, their elaborate bureaucracies, endless negotiations, and abstruse decisions, seemed to have grown. I had always found Belgians to be wary about having too much organized political power exercised over them, particularly by the national government. In what a medical scientist I knew referred to as Belgians' "collective subcutaneous memory," they associated such power with the succession of large European countries by which they had been invaded and occupied, and the dangerously aggressive nationalism of big-country conquerors. But it was not primarily these peace- and freedom-loving sentiments that shaped the political mood of the country in November 1993. Rather, something akin to political disaffection seemed to predominate, in the wake of the two decades of federal transformation, the 1993 constitutional reforms, and the economic crisis facing the country. Belgian politicians and statesmen were aware of this public alienation and troubled by it. They made frequent references to the absence of dialogue and the serious incomprehension that had grown up between Belgian citizens and the state; to the need to restore confidence and rebuild a bridge between them; and to the importance of fostering a "new citizenship" and "public-spiritedness" that would actively reinvolve Belgians in the democratic political functioning of the country. Behind these invocations lay considerable anxiety about the "post-democratic" implications of the results of the last (November 1991) national legislative elections, in which the major political parties had lost considerable ground and several Walloon and Flemish parties of the extreme right had gained notable support. The most consequential of these was the Flemish Vlaams Blok party, whose political campaign had called for the progressive independence of Flanders, emphasized the economic and ethnic importance of restricting immigration to Belgium, and called for measures to encourage "non-European" immigrants already present in the country to return to their native lands.

It seemed to me that in November 1993 a sense of greater distance also existed between Belgians and their economic institutions than had been true in the past. Beginning with the decade of the 1960s the Belgian economy had undergone significant change through the greatly expanding presence of foreign business interests in the country. Flanders—particularly the city of Antwerp with its port—was the chief site of the new industries implanted in Belgium. Belgian workers had continued to be among the most skilled and productive in the world, but they were more and more engaged in turning out products for export to other countries, under the aegis of foreign or multinational European and American companies. The Belgian economy became an intermediary one in both these senses. With the raid on Belgium's holding company, the Société Générale de Belgique, staged by Carlo De Benedetti in 1988, and its denouement when the Groupe Suez of France gained majority stockholder control of "the Générale," the Belgian economy entered another stage in its internationalization—its increasing external dependence on French interests financially and with regard to economic decision-making. By 1993 as much as 40 percent of Belgian industrial capital was in French hands. Under these circumstances, for many Belgians their "real" employers and those who ultimately controlled their economic destiny now seemed faceless, far-removed entities.

MY EXPLORATIONS of developments in the Belgian polity and economy turned my thoughts to the house on the Rue Royale, the Errera mansion, where I had been received in the 1960s when it was the *salon* meeting place of a French-speaking Brussels "Establishment." Many of the persons who frequented the house during that period had died, including the man who had presided over it, Jacques Errera. Nothing like the trinary dominance that he and his long-deceased companions, Jean Willems (once director of the National Fund of Scientific Research), and Marcel Dubuisson (former rector of the University of Liège), had exercised over Belgian research and higher education existed any longer; and the economic and political power elite of the country was now preponderantly Flemish. The House of Errera, when I had last seen it in 1987, was an empty, crumbling relic of a bygone era.

I was curious about what the house looked like now, chiefly because in August and September 1992 I had read articles in the

Flemish newspaper *De Standaard* and in the French-language Brussels paper *Le Soir* reporting that the Flemish government had purchased the Hôtel Errera. It was to become the official residence of its minister-president, Luc Van den Brande, by 1994. The articles portrayed the house as a "prestigious mansion," that occupied a "strategic position," overlooking the Palace of Beaux-Arts, alongside the Société Générale, under the windows of the Royal Palace, and within hearing distance of Parliament. *Le Soir* also printed photographs depicting large groups of Flemish persons filing through the downstairs rooms of the house. This was a high point of a regular Flemish tour of Brussels that featured stops at "symbolic temples of political and economic power," the text stated. According to *De Standaard*, extensive renovations would have to be undertaken before Mr. Van den Brande could move into the house.

As I had done in 1978, I took a taxi to 14, rue Royale, the Hôtel Errera, and asked the driver to wait for me while I looked through its rusty, locked gate. The house appeared smaller and more withered than ever. There was no visible sign that serious restorative work on it had begun; but earlier superficial repairs had left it in a curious, bifurcated state. Half the house was whitewashed, half was not. The two stone lions on pilasters that framed its entrance stared blankly into the park across the avenue where a few years earlier the sumptuous Warande Club, reserved for wealthy Flemish members, had been built one hundred meters from the long-standing Cercle Royal Gaulois, a club of French-speaking businessmen associated with large and middle-sized firms. The smiles that the stone lions once wore had disappeared under whitewash. What was one to make of this house in prolonged transition, to which the aura of its past still clung? I wondered as I reentered my taxi and drove away.

AS ALWAYS, the Belgian railroad was my primary mode of transportation, carrying me quickly and punctually, back and forth, between Brussels, Antwerp, Ghent, Kortrijk, Leuven, Liège, and Namur, where I conducted professional interviews and made personal visits. The new food center in Brussels's Central Station was doing a brisk business in groceries as well as takeout sandwiches and beverages; and I watched a uniformed worker clean the floor of the station with a hand-propelled machine rather than with a traditional *torchon*-type mop.

At the foot of the monument in the station's central hall that honored the memory of railway workers who had "died for the Country" in 1914–1918 and 1940–1945, several wreaths had been placed on November 11, 1993—the Armistice Day that marked the seventy-fifth anniversary of the end of World War I. On that day the new King of the Belgians, Albert II, the Royal Military School of Brussels, the Royal Museum of the Army and Military History, the Belgian Association of Youth, and the Association for the Promotion of Public Spiritedness (*civisme*), among others, had paid public tribute to those who fought in this "first world conflict." It was important that Belgian young people remember World War I, they had all affirmed; recall its atrocities; express their gratitude to the Belgian combatants who had liberated the country from enemy occupation; and do everything they could in the future to ensure that such a war would never occur again. In the speech she delivered on this occasion, the president of the Association for the Promotion of Public Spiritedness had also linked the commemoration of the Armistice with declarations about the significance of "living together, in a responsible and solidary way," and about the essentiality of "not closing one's eyes" to what was currently happening in former Yugoslavia and to the besieged population of Sarajevo.

In the station were signs I had never seen before, warning people to beware of pickpockets. They were similar to notices that had appeared in other public places, like post offices and at American Express. New electronic devices to apprehend potential thieves had also been installed in the local bank and post office that I frequented. Everywhere I traveled people told me stories about personal muggings, house burglaries, and store and bank holdups; and they advised me not to carry a handbag. They attributed the disturbing rise in crime and personal insecurity chiefly to the increased consumption of drugs, and users' desperate search for cash to purchase the continual supply they needed. In addition, they said, some of the petty crimes were being committed by unemployed youths.

A few homeless men, carrying their worldly possessions in plastic shopping bags, wandered through Central Station. A greater number of homeless persons were always present in Brussels's North and South Stations—visible reminders to the crowds of Belgians, arriving and departing, that although they had one of the most generous and effective social security systems in Europe, many people in their society lived in a state of poverty and social exclusion. (According to the best estimates available, in 1992, 6 percent of the population was impoverished, and 18 percent was living on the edge of poverty. The incidence and risk of poverty were considerably greater in Wallony than in Flanders. In both these regions the groups most vulnerable to poverty were households in which the head of the family was younger than twenty-five, was of foreign nationality, had no more than a primary-school education, was an unskilled worker, a single parent, or unemployed, ill, or disabled, and also households in which elderly couples were living alone.)*

NUMEROUS AFRICAN passengers were on virtually every train I took to and from Brussels: men and women, often traveling in family groups, with babies and small children, and young adults who appeared to be students. Judging from their speech and physical appearance, most came from Belgium's former colonies in Africa—above all from Zaïre, and from Burundi and Rwanda. Relevant statistics were difficult to obtain, but I was struck by how many more Africans seemed to be present in Belgium than on my two previous visits at the end of the 1980s and the beginning of the 1990s, and by how widely dispersed throughout the country they seemed to be. There were a considerable number of refugees from Zaïre in Belgium, I was told, driven away by President Mobutu Sese Seko's almost thirty years of tyrannical rule and the disastrous conditions to which he had reduced the country. Large sectors of the economy in Zaïre had shut down. Roads, public transportation, telephones and other means of communication, schools, universities, and hospitals no longer functioned normally, if at all. The national currency—the zaïre—had become so worthless that its rate of exchange was ten million zaïres to the dollar, and still rising. Those who were employed received miniscule wages and were faced with long delays in their payment. Meager incomes, unchecked unemployment, soaring food prices, and physical insecurity had

---

*These data were taken from a report on social indicators of the distribution of income, social security, and poverty in Belgium during the period 1985–1992, written by Bea Cantillon, director of the Centrum voor Sociaal Beleid of the University of Antwerp.

made it difficult for Zaïre's cities and towns to feed its inhabitants. In the city, sugar was being sold by the spoonful, bread by the slice, and antibiotics by the capsule. To eat only once in two days was no longer out of the ordinary. Malnutrition was widespread. A massive exodus from Zaïre's urban centers back to the interior of the country was occurring. Subsistence agriculture and barter were being reinstated in the rural areas to which people had migrated to grow the food they needed for daily living. Epidemics of AIDS, sleeping sickness, malaria, measles, tuberculosis, cholera, and dysentery were rampant. Periodic outbreaks of violence, rioting, and looting plagued the country, several times precipitated by Zaïre army soldiers who had not been paid. And since September 1992 ethnic conflict between major tribes in the Shaba, Kasai, and Kivu regions of Zaïre had led to thousands of deaths and casualties, wholesale destruction of property and villages, and the massive displacement of persons who had created improvised enclaves and camps of refugees, several of which had been destroyed by government authorities or gendarmes.

Throughout the month I spent in Belgium, the violence between Hutus and Tutsi that had erupted in Burundi on October 21, when its first democratically elected president, Melchior Ndadaye, a Hutu, was assassinated by Tutsi military officers, escalated into a cycle of interethnic massacres that ravaged the country. Thousands of deaths resulted from the warfare that was waged in village after village, with stones, spears, machetes, clubs, and bows and arrows, as well as guns and grenades. More than 150,000 houses were destroyed. As many as 800,000 persons, 80 percent of whom were women and children, fled into the neighboring countries of Rwanda, Tanzania, and Zaïre. There, huddled in refugee camps, they were suffering from malnutrition and outbreaks of dysentery, malaria, pneumonia, measles, and smallpox.

Belgians' reactions to these catastrophic developments, and to the increased presence of African emigrés in their country, were as complex as their ties with their former colonies. At the end of 1988 King Baudouin had broken off his personal and diplomatic relationship with Mobutu, and Belgium had drastically reduced its aid to Zaïre. This had occurred after soldiers of the Zaïre army had killed a number of students at the University of Lubumbashi who were protesting against the financial, intellectual, and physical conditions under which their education was proceeding. The break also followed a series of vindictive verbal attacks by Mobutu against the historic evils of the Belgian colonial regime in the Congo, the "crimes" of King Léopold II in that era, the postindependence intervention of King Baudouin in Zaïre's commercial affairs, and unspecified "scandals" in the corridors of the Royal Palace that Mobutu's spokesmen had threatened to reveal. When King Baudouin died the population of Zaïre went into mourning for the monarch they had known since he became the fifth king of the Belgians in July 1951. They had affectionately conferred on him the name *Mwana Kitoko* ("handsome child" in Lingala) when, as a twenty-five-year old king, he made his first visit to the Belgian Congo; and they later called him *Bwana Kitoko* ("handsome chief"), or the "honest king." Most Zaïreans understood why Mobutu was not invited to attend King Baudouin's funeral. Instead three prelates of the Catholic church in Zaïre—the cardinal, the bishop who presided over the Episcopal Conference, and the bishop who was president of the High Council of the Republic of Zaïre—were asked to participate in the funeral mass and represent their country.

Belgium had maintained its diplomatic relations with Burundi (which along with Rwanda had been a trust territory administered by Belgium until they were granted independence in 1962). But the Belgian embassy in Bujumbura had chosen not to lodge any Burundi personalities who were in danger. Many, however, were given refuge and assistance in the personal residences of embassy staff, and by Belgians doing overseas service in Burundi. On October 21 the Belgian chapter of Doctors Without Borders, a medical humanitarian and human rights organization, began to send medical teams and materiel to Burundi from Belgium and from their mission in Rwanda. In mid-November, with some reluctance, the Belgian government decided to dispatch a contingent of 350 to 370 paracommandos to Rwanda to help United Nations troops maintain peace between the Hutus and Tutsis of that land, and to render aid to the Burundi refugees who were pouring into the country. The United Nations had requested 800 soldiers, but in light of the 700 Belgian paracommandos who were already involved in the "Restore Hope" UN operation in Somalia, the 650 Belgian soldiers who were participating in military-humanitarian action in east Croatia, and the Belgian transport unit that had been sent to Bosnia, the government had judged this to be excessive.

In Belgium it was apparent that many Africans had been

granted asylum there, and that national and local authorities had made an effort to distribute them throughout the country. During the past two or three years, I was informed, both in Wallony and in Flanders, even in very small communities where they were especially conspicuous, "blacks" had come to live. I heard rumors about an underground movement of Zaïrean refugees who were arriving in Belgium via other European countries. Georgette De Moulin, wife of the Verviers coiffeur, recounted some of the stories she had been told by women in her Présence group about what they regarded as the privileged treatment these Africans were being accorded, and their allegedly exploitive behavior. One of the recurrent stories concerned a Zaïrean man or woman, as the case might be, who purchased expensive clothing in a store, and when asked by the salesperson about the mode of payment, ordered that the bill be sent to the local social assistance agency. Anxiety about unemployment and the burgeoning costs of social security fueled the prejudiced sentiments that underlay such tales.

In Brussels both the police and the local population were disturbed by what they felt was happening in Matonge, a section of the city located in the commune of Ixelles. Its African ambience, stores, restaurants, night clubs, music, and art had attracted and delighted many Belgians and tourists. To an increasing extent, newspapers reported, this area had also become a base of operations for African criminals of all sorts. These included members of the so-called "Zaïrean Connection," who carried out lucrative and sophisticated international white-collar crimes in collaboration with corrupt bureaucrats in Zaïre; and, recently, a new generation of younger African men and their gangs who were engaged in robberies, muggings, carjackings, and in the import, manufacture, and sale of drugs. The Belgian police attributed the greater amount of cocaine that was being smuggled into Brussels from Africa and turned into "crack" crystals to young Zaïreans and Burundians living in Matonge.

At the same time, however, I learned about Belgians who were housing and supporting Zaïrean friends, colleagues, and acquaintances forced by political circumstances to become African exiles. Others to whom I spoke were sharply critical of the Belgian government for being too "Europe-centered" and insufficiently interested in Central Africa—particularly the plight of Belgium's former colonies. One Belgian whom I had known for many years described the "psychological weight of the African cancer" that he and others were feeling: their frustration, sadness, and pain over the tragic events and the deterioration taking place in African countries to which Belgium had once been—and in some ways still was—closely attached.

AT DAWN on November 17, 1993, Prime Minister Jean-Luc Dehaene and his government team emerged from a three-week conclave in the Val-Duchesse château with their global economic austerity plan. That same night the Red Devils, Belgium's national soccer team, played a crucial game against a unified Czechoslovakian team, which was attended by King Albert. The tie score qualified the Devils to compete in the World Cup soccer matches to be held in the United States in 1994. In the November 18 editions of various Belgian newspapers, that victory shared front-page headlines and coverage with news about the "bullish" reaction of financial markets to the Dehaene austerity package, which had sent stocks, bonds, and the Belgian franc soaring. On November 26 Belgium's Christian and Socialist labor unions staged their first concerted, nationwide strike since 1936, protesting aspects of the austerity plan. Its measures, they contended, were too limited and scattered to assure a significant increase in employment; too heavy a burden was placed on workers, especially in social security contributions and benefits; too many considerations were given to employers; and the steps taken to control income tax evasion, and to levy taxes on interest, inherited money, and property, were not strong enough. In response, Prime Minister Dehaene immediately launched a round of meetings with representatives of the unions and of the employers' associations. Their purpose was to amend the plan, through a process of negotiation and Belgian compromise, without dismantling its structure, nullifying its primary goals, or creating new foci of conflict and perceived inequities.

When I departed from Belgium on December 1, that process was still going on. Winter had come to Europe earlier than usual, and it had snowed the day before my plane left for the United States. We took off in the mist created by a warm air current and melting snow. Belgium vanished from view as soon as the plane began its ascent. The Belgian newspaper that the flight attendant offered me contained a long article about a television program scheduled to be shown later in the week. The program was entitled, "Does Belgium Exist?"

"WHAT ARE your conclusions?" I hear Belgian voices asking. After thirty-four years of traversing the country, capped by my 1993 revisit, I can affirm that Belgium does indeed exist. It is often absorbed in its collective self-doubts about its historical authenticity, national reality, and cultural coherence. And it has undergone significant economic, political, and social change during the three decades I have known it. But Belgium has not vanished from the European map or been decimated by internal violence. Nor has it divided into two separate nation-states. ("Not *yet*, that is," a chorus of Belgian voices intones in my ear.) Although the evolution of Belgium from a unitary toward a federal state has taken place gradually, the country is still wrestling with this structural transformation and with the complicated, bitterly disputed compromises it has entailed. Belgium's "asymmetrical" federalism is *sui generis* and very Belgian—belying Belgians' insistence that they have neither a distinctive nor a common culture.

Belgians' ritualized disacknowledgment of shared sentiments, a pattern I first observed during my early years in Belgium, has been reinforced by time. It contributed to their astonishment over the societal emotion that was evoked by King Baudouin's death, to the difficulty they had in understanding the outpouring of feeling, and to their propensity to associate it with a mythical Belgium rather than with the "real world" attributes of their country. In my view, not only the collective sorrow expressed over the death of the king, but also less solemn manifestations, like Belgians' public rejoicing over the Red Devils' international soccer victory, their (self-mocking) custom of calling their resolutions of national conflicts "pacts," and their practice of naming those agreements after the châteaux where they were negotiated and the saints' day on which they were concluded, are all indicators of a common culture. So is Belgians' characteristic denial of the existence of a shared culture, along with the flavor of their ironically witty, self-derisive comments about themselves and their society—what jurist Marc Uyttendaele has termed their "very national sport of auto-flagellation."

I was not as struck in November 1993 by the changes that had taken place in Belgium's culture and social structure as I was by the atmosphere of uncertainty, anxiety, and melancholy that had descended on the country like one of its perennial fogs. Disquietude about the end point of the new federalism, future relations between Flanders and Wallony, control of the economic recession, management of mounting unemployment, mastery of the runaway national debt, protection of the social security system, resolution of an immigration policy, and assurance of public safety were pervasive. Loss of confidence in Belgium's established, institutionalized ways of dealing with these problems was also palpable. These concerns were augmented by Belgians' disappointment over the European Community's difficulties in achieving unity, and by their dismay about economic suffering, xenophobic nationalism, ethnic violence, and neofascistic developments in Eastern Europe with the end of the cold war and the demise of the Soviet empire. A sense of moral impotency hung over the land too: a feeling of helplessness, and something like shame over the failure of Belgium and the other Western democracies to stop the war and atrocities in Bosnia and deal more effectively with the natural and manmade disasters in Africa.

In the final years of the 1990s, the little country at the crossroads of Europe known as Belgium was grappling in its own way with nothing less than the end-of-the-century troubles, malaise, and anomie that beset the whole European continent.

Index

Katholieke Universiteit te Leuven, 110, 112, 130–137, 237
Kaunda, Kenneth, 213, 215, 219–221
Kermesses in Flanders, 126, 162
Kinshasa, Zaïre, 225–247 passim
Kinshasa, University of, 290
Koli family, 251–293 passim
Kortrijk, Flanders, 147–163, 297–310; Begijnhof, 149; Grote Markt, 149, 298; Guldensporenslag, 149, 298; jobs in, 300–301, 316
Kredietbank, 115, 117
Kuyper, Armand De, 115, 117, 130–137 passim
Kyobe, Samuel, 282–285

Laicity movement, 16
Lambert, Madame, 201
Leboucq, Georges, 98
Lefèvre, Théo, 97, 103
Léopold II (king), 33, 328; stamp, 142–143
Léopoldville (Kinshasa), 225–247 passim
Lettres de la Russie, 61
Leuven University. See Katholieke Universiteit te Leuven.
Libaers, Herman, 220
Liège University, 8, 87–107; transfer to Sart Tilman, 91, 105
Liliane (princess), 93
Limbourg, Flanders, 14
Lingala language, 231, 242, 277
Linguistic problems in Belgium, 6, 19–20, 97, 98, 318; language laws, 13–14
Lisala, 229, 231, 232, 248–293; magic in, 259, 261; corruption in, 249, 270–271; crops of, 248; economic life, 248–249; education in, 249–250; family tensions in, 259; re-

bellion in, 248–293 passim; religion in, 250, 256–260, 282–285; schoolteachers in, 264–265, 286; social situation in, 274–275; tribes of, 248; unemployment in, 259
Louvain Catholic University. See Université Catholique de Louvain.
Lovanium University, 237; student strike, 238–239; transition period, 239
Lubumbashi University, 327
Lumumba, Patrice, 12, 287

Maastricht, treaty of, 24, 315
Mademoiselle Jaire, 187
Magritte, René, 61, 167; paintings of, 167, 205
Maison de la Rue d'Egmont, 32–44
Mama Onema, 261
Marie-Thérèse (empress), 46
Martens, Adhémar. See Ghelderode, Michel de.
Martens, Germaine, 199
Martens, Wilfried, 20, 23
Mbobozo, Daniel, 272–275
Mbuja tribe, 248
Medical research in Belgium, 3–10, 32–44, 45–67, 68–86, 87–107
"Medical Scientists in a Château," 7–8, 89
Memling, Hans, works of, 127–128
Memling Hotel, 228
Memling Museum, 127
Mercier, Cardinal Désireé-Joseph, 54, 55
Ministry of Public Health, 124
Miroir de l'Histoire, 54
Mobutu Sese Seko, 326
Molitor, André, 6, 10, 29, 216
Mombilo, Paul, 288–290
Mosabu, Aimé, 232–233, 260,

A NOTE ON THE AUTHOR

Renée C. Fox is Annenberg Professor of the Social Sciences at the University of Pennsylvania. Born in New York City, she studied at Smith College and Harvard University, and later taught sociology at Barnard College and at Harvard University before her appointment at Pennsylvania. The recipient of numerous honorary degrees, prizes, and awards, especially for her studies in the sociology of medicine, she is the author of *Experiment Perilous, The Emerging Physician* (with Willy De Craemer), *Essays in Medical Sociology,* and *The Sociology of Medicine,* and of *The Courage to Fail* and *Spare Parts* (both with Judith P. Swazey). She lives in Philadelphia.